Webster's Spelling

Of The English Language
New Revised Edition

Includes a section of
often misspelled
words

NICHOLS

Publishing Group

Imprint of Allied Publishing Group, Inc
Copyright © 2003 V. Nichols
Printed in the U.S.A.

Spelling Rules

Most **PLURAL NOUNS** form the plural by adding an s, as in *face faces, noun nouns* -- but there are exceptions.
If a word ends in a **CONSONANT AND Y**, change the y to i and add es, as in *berry berries, fly flies*. If it ends in a **VOWEL AND Y**, just add s, as in *toy toys, monkey, monkeys*.
If a noun ends in CH, SH, SS, S, X or Z, add es, as in *bunch bunches, wish wishes, pass passes, box boxes*.

Most **POSSESSIVE SINGULAR NOUNS** are formed by adding an 's, as in *child's, school's, Lee's, Tommy's*.
POSSESSIVE PLURAL NOUNS NOT ENDING IN S are formed by adding 's, as in *children children's*.
POSSESSIVE PLURAL NOUNS ENDING IN S add only an apostrophe, as in *Davis Davis', cats cats', senators senators'*.
PLURAL COMPOUND NOUNS use the plural of the final word, as in *playground playgrounds, rosebush rosebushes, bookshelf bookshelves*.

ADVERBS are generally formed by adding ly to an adjective, a participle, or a noun, as in *neat neatly, careful carefully, critical critically, bold boldly*.
If an adjective ends in le, just change the e to a y, as in *able ably, simple simply, busy busily*.

CONTRACTIONS use the ' to shorten a word or word group, as in *is not isn't, it is it's, did not, didn't*.

When a **SUFFIX** is added to a word, if the word ends with the letter that begins the suffix, keep both consonants, as in *mean meanness, real really*.
If the suffix begins with a **CONSONANT** and the word ends in a **SILENT e**, keep the e, as in *care careful*.
Drop the e if the suffix begins with a **VOWEL**, as in *complete completion, excite, exciting*.

A

aard-vark
a-back
ab-a-cus
 ab-a-cus-es
 ab-a-ci
a-baft
 abaft-ment
 abaft-ed
ab-a-lo-ne
a-ban-don
 aban-doned
 aban-don-er
 aban-don-ment
a-base
 a-based
 a-bas-ing
 a-base-ment
a-bash
 a-bash-ment
a-bate
 a-bat-ed
 a-bat-ing
 a-bat-a-ble
 a-bate-ment
aba-tis
ab-at-oir
ab-ba-cy
 ab-ba-tial
ab-bess
ab-bey
 ab-beys
ab-bot
ab-bre-vi-a-tion
 ab-bre-vi-ate
 ab-bre-vi-at-ed
 ab-bre-vi-at-ing
 ab-bre-vi-a-tor
ab-di-cate
 ab-di-cat-ed
 ab-di-cat-ing
 ab-di-ca-tion

ab-do-men
 ab-dom-i-nal
 ab-dom-i-nal-ly
ab-duce
ab-duct
 ab-duc-tion
 ab-duc-tor
 ab-duct-ing
a-beam
a-bed
ab-er-rance
 ab-er-ran-cy
ab-er-rant
 ab-er-rant-ly
ab-er-ra-tion
 ab-er-ra-tion-al
a-bet
 a-bet-ted
 a-bet-ting
 a-bet-ment
 a-bet-tor
 a-bet-ter
a-bey-ance
ab-hor
 ab-horred
 ab-hor-ring
 ab-hor-rence
 ab-hor-rer
ab-hor-rence
ab-hor-rent
 ab-hor-rent-ly
a-bide
 a-bid-er
 a-bid-ed
 a-bid-ing
 a-bid-ance
a-bid-ing
 a-bid-ing-ly
a-bil-i-ty
 a-bil-i-ties
ab-ject
 ab-ject-ly
 ab-ject-ness

ab-jec-tion
ab-jure
 ab-jured
 ab-jur-ing
 ab-ju-ra-tion
 ab-jur-er
ab-late
 ab-lat-ed
 ab-lat-ing
 ab-la-tion
 ab-la-tive
ab-laut
a-blaze
a-ble
 a-bler
 a-blest
 a-bly
a-ble-bod-ied
a-bloom
ab-lu-tion
 ab-lu-tion-ar-y
ab-ne-gate
 ab-ne-gat-ed
 ab-ne-gat-ing
 ab-ne-ga-tor
 ab-ne-ga-tion
ab-nor-mal
 ab-nor-mal-ly
 ab-nor-mal-i-ty
 ab-nor-mal-i-ties
a-board
a-bode
a-boil
a-bol-ish
 a-bol-ish-a-ble
 a-bol-ish-er
 a-bol-ish-ment
a-b-oma-sum
 a-b-oma-sal
a-bom-i-na-ble
 a-bom-i-na-bly
a-bom-i-nate
 a-bom-i-nat-ed

a-bom-i-na-tion
a-bom-i-na-tor
ab-o-rig-i-ne
ab-o-rig-i-nal
ab-o-rig-i-nal-ly
a-born-ing
a-bort
a-bort-er
a-bor-ti-fa-cient
a-bor-tion
a-bor-tion-ist
a-bor-tive
a-bor-tive-ness
a-bor-tive-ly
a-bout-face
a-bove-board
ab-ra-ca-dab-ra
abrad-ant
a-brade
a-brad-ed
a-brad-er
a-bra-sion
a-bra-sive
a-bra-sive-ly
ab-re-act
a-breast
a-bridge
a-bridged
a-bridg-ing
a-bridg-ment
a-bridge-ment
a-broach
a-broad
ab-ro-gate
ab-ro-gat-ed
ab-ro-gat-ing
ab-ro-ga-tion
ab-rupt
abrupt-ness
abrupt-ly
ab-scess
ab-scessed
ab-scis-sa

ab-scis-sas
ab-scis-sae
ab-scis-sion
ab-scond
ab-scond-er
ab-sence
ab-sent
ab-sent-ly
ab-sen-tee
ab-sen-tee-ism
ab-sent-mind-ed
ab-sent-mind-ed-ly
ab-sinthe
ab-so-lute
ab-so-lute-ly
ab-so-lu-tion
ab-so-lut-ism
ab-so-lut-ist
ab-solve
ab-solved
ab-solv-ing
ab-sorb
ab-sorb-er
ab-sorb-a-bil-i-ty
ab-sorb-a-ble
ab-sorb-tive
ab-stain
ab-stain-er
ab-sten-tion
ab-sti-nence
ab-sti-nent
ab-ste-mi-ous
ab-ste-mi-ous-ly
ab-stract
ab-stract-ly
ab-strac-tion
ab-strac-tive
ab-stract-ed
ab-stract-ed-ly
ab-strac-tion-ism
ab-strac-tion-ist
ab-struse
ab-struse-ly

ab-surd
ab-surd-i-ty
ab-surd-ly
a-bub-ble
a-build-ing
a-bud-dance
a-bun-dant
a-bun-dant-ly
a-buse
a-bused
a-bus-ing
a-bus-er
a-bu-sive
a-bu-sive-ly
a-but
a-but-ter
a-but-ted
a-but-ting
a-but-ment
a-but-tals
a-but-ting
a-buzz
a-bye
a-bysm
a-bys-mal
a-bys-mal-ly
a-byss
a-bys-sal
a-ca-cia
ac-a-deme
ac-a-dem-ic
ac-a-dem-i-cal-ly
ac-a-dem-i-cal
acad-e-mi-cian
a-cad-e-my
a-cad-e-mies
a-can-thus
a-can-thus-es
a-can-thi
a cap-pel-la
ac-cede
ac-ced-ed
ac-ced-ing

ac-ce-le-ran-do
ac-cel-er-ate
  ac-cel-er-at-ed
  ac-cel-er-at-ing
  ac-cel-er-a-tive
  ac-cel-er-at-ing-ly
ac-cel-er-a-tion
ac-cel-er-a-tor
ac-cel-er-om-e-ter
ac-cent
  ac-cent-less
ac-cen-tu-al
  ac-cen-tu-al-ly
ac-cen-tu-ate
  ac-cen-tu-at-ed
  ac-cen-tu-at-ing
  ac-cen-tu-a-tion
ac-cept
  ac-cept-ing-ly
  ac-cept-ance
  ac-cept-er
  ac-cept-or
ac-cept-a-ble
  ac-cept-a-bil-i-ty
  ac-cept-a-bly
  ac-cept-a-ble-ness
ac-cept-ed
  ac-cept-ed-ly
ac-cess
ac-ces-si-ble
  ac-ces-si-bil-i-ty
  ac-ces-si-bly
ac-ces-sion
  ac-ces-sion-al
ac-ces-so-ry
  ac-ces-so-ri-ly
ac-ci-dent
  ac-ci-dent-ly
  ac-ci-den-tal
  ac-ci-den-tal-ly
ac-ci-dent--prone
ac-cip-i-ter
  ac-cip-i-trine

ac-claim
  ac-claim-er
ac-cla-ma-tion
ac-clam-a-to-ry
ac-cli-mate
  ac-cli-mat-ed
  ac-cli-mat-ing
  ac-cli-ma-tion
ac-cli-ma-tize
  ac-cli-ma-tized
  ac-cli-ma-tiz-er
  ac-cli-ma-tiz-ing
ac-cliv-i-ty
  ac-cliv-i-ties
ac-co-lade
ac-com-mo-date
  ac-com-mo-dat-ed
  ac-com-mo-dat-ing
  ac-com-mo-da-tive
  ac-com-mo-dat-er
  ac-com-mo-da-tion
ac-com-pa-ni-ment
ac-com-pa-nist
ac-com-pa-ny
  ac-com-pa-nied
  ac-com-pa-ny-ing
  ac-com-pa-nies
ac-com-plice
ac-com-plish
  ac-com-plish-a-ble
  ac-com-plish-ment
  ac-com-plish-er
  ac-com-plished
ac-cord
  ac-cord-ance
  ac-cord-ing
  ac-cord-ing-ly
  ac-cor-dant
  ac-cor-dant-ly
ac-cor-di-on
  ac-cor-di-on-ist
ac-cost
ac-couche-ment

ac-cou-cheur
ac-count
  ac-count-a-ble
  ac-count-a-bil-i-ty
  ac-count-a-bly
ac-count-an-cy
ac-count-ant
  ac-count-ant-ship
ac-count-ing
ac-cou-tre-ment
ac-cred-it
  ac-cred-i-table
  ac-cred-i-ta-tion
ac-crete
  ac-creting
  ac-creted
ac-cre-tion
  ac-cre-tive
  ac-cre-tion-ary
ac-cru-al
ac-crue
  ac-crued
  ac-cru-ing
  ac-cru-a-ble
  ac-crue-ment
ac-cul-tur-ate
  ac-cul-tur-ating
  ac-cul-tur-ated
ac-cul-tur-a-tion
  ac-cul-tur-a-tion-al
  ac-cul-tur-a-tive
ac-cum-u-late
  ac-cum-u-lat-ed
  ac-cum-u-lat-ing
ac-cum-u-la-tion
ac-cu-mu-la-tive
  ac-cu-mu-la-tive-ly
ac-cum-u-la-tor
ac-cu-ra-cy
  ac-cu-ra-cies
ac-cu-rate
  ac-cu-rate-ly
  ac-cu-rate-ness

ac-curs-ed
ac-curst
ac-curs-ed-ly
ac-cus-al
ac-cu-sa-tion
ac-cu-sa-tive
ac-cuse
ac-cus-er
ac-cus-ed
ac-cus-ing
ac-cu-sa-tion
ac-cu-sa-to-ry
ac-cus-tom
ac-cus-tom-a-tion
ac-cus-tomed
ac-cus-tomed-ness
ace-dia
a-cel-da-ma
a-cel-lu-lar
a-ce-quia
a-cerb
a-cer-bi-ty
ac-er-o-la
ac-er-vate
ac-er-vate-ly
ac-er-va-tion
ac-e-tab-u-lar-ia
ac-e-tab-u-lum
ac-e-tab-u-lar
ac-et-al-de-hyde
ac-et-amide
ac-et-amin-o-phen
ac-et-an-i-lide
ac-e-tate
a-ce-tic
a-cet-i-fy
a-cet-i-fied
a-cet-i-fy-ing
a-ce-ti-fi-ca-tion
a-ce-ti-fi-er
ace-e-tone
ac-e-ton-ic
ace-tous

a-cet-y-late
a-cet-y-lat-ing
a-cet-y-lat-ed
a-cet-y-la-tion
a-cet-y-la-tive
a-ce-tyl-cho-line
a-ce-tyl-cho-lin-ic
a-cet-y-lene
a-cet-y-le-nic
ache
ached
ach-ing
a-chene
a-chieve
a-chiev-ed
a-chiev-ing
a-chiev-a-ble
a-chiev-er
a-chieve-ment
a-chla-myd-e-ous
a-chlor-hy-dric
a-chon-drite
a-chon-drit-ic
ach-ro-mat-ic
ach-ro-ma-tic-i-ty
ach-ro-ma-tize
a-cic-u-la
a-cic-u-late
a-cic-u-lar
ac-id
ac-id-ness
ac-id-ly
ac-id-ic
a-cid-i-fy
a-cid-i-fied
a-cid-i-fy-ing
a-cid-i-fi-ca-tion
a-cid-i-fi-er
a-cid-i-ty
ac-i-do-phile
ac-i-do-phil-ic
ac-i-do-sis
ac-i-dot-ic

a-cid-u-late
a-cid-u-lat-ed
a-cid-u-lat-ing
a-cid-u-la-tion
a-cid-u-lent
a-cid-u-lous
ac-i-nar
ac-i-nus
ac-i-nous
ac-knowl-edge
ac-knowl-edged
ac-knowl-edg-ing
ac-me
ac-ne
ac-ned
ac-o-lyte
ac-o-nite
a-corn
a-cous-tic
a-cous-ti-cal
a-cous-ti-cal-ly
a-cous-tics
ac-quaint
ac-quaint-ance
ac-quaint-ance-ship
ac-qui-esce
ac-qui-esc-ed
ac-qui-esc-ing
ac-qui-es-cence
ac-qui-es-cent
ac-qui-es-cent-ly
ac-quire
ac-quired
ac-quir-ing
ac-quir-er
ac-quit
ac-quit-ted
ac-quit-ting
ac-quit-tal
a-cre
a-cre-age
ac-rid
acrid-i-ty

ac-ri-mo-ni-ous
ac-ri-mo-ni-ous-ly
ac-ri-mo-ny
ac-ro-bat
ac-ro-bat-ic
ac-ro-nym
ac-ro-pho-bi-a
a-crop-o-lis
a-cros-tic
a-cros-ti-cal-ly
a-cryl-ic
ac-ry-lo-ni-trile
act-ing
ac-tin-i-a
ac-tin-i-an
ac-tin-ic
ac-tin-i-cal-ly
ac-tin-ism
ac-tin-i-um
ac-ti-nom-e-ter
ac-ti-nom-e-try
ac-ti-no-mor-phic
ac-ti-no-mor-phy
ac-ti-no-my-ces
ac-ti-no-my-ce-tal
ac-ti-no-my-co-sis
ac-ti-no-my-cot-ic
ac-ti-non
ac-ti-no-zo-an
ac-tion
ac-tion-a-ble
ac-tion-a-bly
ac-ti-vate
ac-ti-vat-ed
ac-ti-vat-ing
ac-ti-va-tion
ac-ti-va-tor
ac-tive
ac-tive-ly
ac-tiv-ism
ac-tiv-ist
ac-tiv-i-ty
ac-tiv-i-ties

ac-tor
ac-tress
ac-tu-al
ac-tu-al-ly
ac-tu-al-i-ty
ac-tu-al-i-ties
ac-tu-al-ize
ac-tu-al-ized
ac-tu-al-iz-ing
ac-tu-al-i-za-tion
ac-tu-ar-y
ac-tu-ar-ies
ac-tu-ar-i-al
ac-tu-ate
ac-tu-at-ed
ac-tu-at-ing
ac-tu-a-tion
ac-tu-a-tor
a-cu-i-ty
a-cu-i-ties
a-cu-men
a-cu-mi-nate
ac-u-punc-ture
a-cute
a-cute-ly
a-cut-er
a-cy-clic
ac-yl
ad-age
a-da-gio
ad-a-mant
ad-a-mant-ly
ad-a-man-tine
a-dapt
a-dapt-er
a-dapt-ed-ness
a-dapt-a-ble
a-dapt-a-bil-i-ty
ad-ap-ta-tion
ad-ap-ta-tion-al
ad-ap-ta-tion-al-ly
a-dap-tive
a-dap-tive-ly

a-d-ap-tiv-i-ty
add
add-a-ble
add-i-ble
ad-dax
ad-dax-es
ad-dend
ad-den-dum
ad-den-da
ad-der
ad-dict
ad-dic-tion
ad-dict-ed
ad-dic-tive
ad-di-tion
ad-di-tion-al
ad-di-tion-al-ly
ad-di-tive
ad-di-tive-ly
ad-di-tiv-i-ty
ad-dle
ad-dress
ad-dress-er
ad-dress-ee
ad-dress-a-ble
ad-duce
ad-duc-ing
ad-duced
ad-duc-er
ad-duct
ad-duc-tion
ad-duc-tive
a-de-lan-ta-do
a-demp-tion
ad-e-nine
ad-e-ni-tis
ad-e-noid
ad-e-noi-dal
ad-e-no-ma
aden-o-sine
a-dept
a-dept-ly
ad-e-qua-cy

ad-e-quate
ad-e-quate-ly
ad-here
ad-hered
ad-her-ing
ad-her-ence
ad-her-ent
ad-her-ent-ly
ad-he-sion
ad-he-sion-al
ad-he-sive
ad-he-sive-ly
ad-he-sive-ness
ad hoc
ad ho-mi-nem
ad-i-a-bat-ic
a-dieu
ad in-fi-ni-tum
a-di-os
ad-i-pose
ad-i-pos-i-ty
ad-ja-cen-cy
ad-ja-cen-cies
ad-ja-cent
ad-ja-cent-ly
ad-jec-tive
ad-jec-ti-val
ad-join
ad-join-ing
ad-journ
ad-journ-ment
ad-judge
ad-judged
ad-judg-ing
ad-ju-di-cate
ad-ju-di-cat-ed
ad-ju-di-cat-ing
ad-ju-di-ca-tion
ad-ju-di-ca-tor
ad-junct
ad-junc-tive
ad-jure
ad-jured

ad-jur-ing
ad-ju-ra-tion
ad-ju-ra-to-ry
ad-jur-er
ad-just
ad-just-a-ble
ad-just-er
ad-jus-tor
ad-just-ment
ad-ju-tan-cy
ad-ju-tant
ad lib
ad libbed
ad lib-bing
ad-man
ad-men
ad-min-is-ter
ad-min-is-ter-ing
ad-min-is-tered
ad-min-is-trate
ad-min-is-trat-ing
ad-min-is-trated
ad-min-is-tra-tion
ad-min-is-tra-tive
ad-min-is-tra-tor
ad-mi-ral
ad-mi-ral-ty
ad-mire
ad-mired
ad-mir-ing
ad-mi-ra-tion
ad-mi-rer
ad-mis-si-ble
ad-mis-si-bil-i-ty
ad-mis-sion
ad-mis-sive
ad-mit
ad-mit-ted
ad-mit-ting
ad-mit-ted-ly
ad-mit-tance
ad-mix
ad-mix-ture

ad-mon-ish
ad-mon-ish-er
ad-mo-ni-tion
ad-mon-i-to-ry
ad-mon-ish-ing-ly
ad-mon-ish-ment
a-do
a-do-be
ad-o-les-cence
ad-o-les-cent
ad-o-les-cent-ly
a-dopt
a-dopt-a-ble
a-dop-tion
a-dop-tive
a-dore
a-dored
a-dor-ing
a-dor-a-ble
a-do-ra-tion
a-dorn
a-dorn-ment
a-doze
a-dre-nal
ad-re-nal-ly
a-dren-a-line
a-drift
a-droit
a-droit-ly
ad-sorb
ad-sor-bent
ad-sorp-tion
ad-u-late
ad-u-lat-ed
ad-u-lat-ing
ad-u-la-tor
ad-u-la-to-ry
a-dult
a-dult-hood
a-dul-ter-ate
a-dul-ter-at-ed
a-dul-ter-at-ing
a-dul-ter-ant

a-dul-ter-a-tion
a-dul-ter-y
  a-dul-ter-ies
a-dul-ter-er
  a-dul-ter-ous
ad-um-brate
  ad-um-brat-ed
  ad-um-brat-ing
ad va-lo-rem
ad-vance
  ad-vanced
  ad-vanc-ing
  ad-vance-ment
ad-van-tage
  ad-van-taged
  ad-van-tag-ing
ad-van-ta-geous
  ad-van-ta-geous-ly
ad-vent
ad-ven-ti-tious
ad-ven-tive
ad-ven-ture
  ad-ven-tured
  ad-ven-tur-ing
  ad-ven-tur-er
ad-ven-ture-some
ad-verb
  ad-ver-bi-al
ad-ver-sar-y
  ad-ver-sar-ies
ad-verse
  ad-verse-ly
  ad-verse-ness
ad-ver-si-ty
  ad-ver-si-ties
ad-vert
  ad-vert-ence
  ad-vert-ent
ad-ver-tise
  ad-ver-tised
  ad-ver-tis-ing
  ad-ver-tis-er
ad-ver-tise-ment

ad-vice
ad-vise
  ad-vised
  ad-vis-ing
  ad-vis-a-bil-i-ty
  ad-vi-sor
ad-vis-ed-ly
ad-vise-ment
ad-vi-so-ry
ad-vo-ca-cy
  ad-vo-ca-cies
  ad-vo-cate
  ad-vo-cat-ed
  ad-vo-cat-ing
  ad-vo-ca-tion
ae-gis
ae-on
aer-ate
  aer-at-ed
  aer-at-ing
  aer-a-tion
  aer-a-tor
aer-en-chy-ma
aer-i-al
  aer-i-al-ly
  aer-i-al-ist
aer-ie
aer-i-fy
  aer-i-fi-ca-tion
aer-obe
aero-me-chan-ics
aero-naut-ics
  aero-nau-ti-cal
  aero-nau-tic
aero-pause
aer-o-plane
aer-o-sol
  aero-sol-ize
  aero-sol-iza-tion
  aero-sol-iz-ing
  aero-sol-ized
aer-o-space
aero-sphere

aero-stat
aero-stat-ics
aes-thete
aes-thet-ic
  aes-thet-i-cal-ly
  aes-thet-i-cal
afar
afeard
af-fa-ble
  af-fa-bil-i-ty
  af-fa-bly
af-fair
af-fect
  af-fect-ing
  af-fect-ing-ly
af-fec-tive
af-fec-ta-tion
af-fect-ed
  af-fect-ed-ly
  af-fect-ed-ness
af-fec-tion
  af-fec-tion-ate
  af-fec-tion-ate-ly
af-fer-ent
  af-fer-ent-ly
af-fi-ance
  af-fi-anced
  af-fi-anc-ing
af-fi-da-vit
af-fil-i-ate
  af-fil-i-at-ed
  af-fil-i-at-ing
af-fin-i-ty
  af-fin-i-ties
af-firm
  af-firm-a-ble
  af-firm-a-bly
  af-fir-ma-tion
  af-firm-a-tive
af-fix
  af-fix-a-ble
  af-fix-ment
  af-fix-a-tion

af-fla-tus
af-flict
  af-flic-tion
af-flu-ence
  af-flu-ent
  af-flu-ent-ly
af-fray
af-fri-cate
  af-fric-a-tive
  af-fri-ca-tion
af-front
af-ghan
afield
afire
aflame
af-la-tox-in
afloat
aflut-ter
afoot
afore
afore-men-tioned
afore-said
afore-thought
a for-ti-o-ri
afoul
afraid
afreet
afresh
af-ter
af-ter-ef-fect
af-ter-glow
af-ter--hours
af-ter-life
af-ter-most
af-ter-noon
af-ter-taste
af-ter-thought
af-ter-time
af-ter-ward
  af-ter-wards
again
against
agape

aga-pe-ic
agar
ag-ate
ag-ate-ware
aga-ve
agaze
age
  aged
  ag-ing
  age-ing
  aged
  age-less
  age-long
agen-cy
  agen-cies
agen-da
  agen-da-less
agent
  agen-tial
ag-glom-er-ate
  ag-glom-er-at-ed
  ag-glom-er-at-ing
  ag-glom-er-a-tion
  ag-glom-er-a-tive
ag-glu-ti-nate
  ag-glu-ti-nat-ed
  ag-glu-tin-at-ing
  ag-glu-ti-na-tion
  ag-glu-ti-na-tive
ag-gran-dize
  ag-gran-dized
  ag-gran-diz-ing
  ag-gran-dize-ment
  ag-gran-diz-er
ag-gra-vate
  ag-gra-vat-ed
  ag-gra-vat-ing
  ag-gra-va-tion
ag-gre-gate
  ag-gre-gat-ed
  ag-gre-gat-ing
  ag-gre-ga-tion
  ag-gre-ga-tive

ag-gress
  ag-gress-ive
  ag-gress-ive-ly
  ag-gress-ive-ness
  ag-gres-sor
  ag-gres-sion
ag-grieve
  ag-grieved
  ag-griev-ing
aghast
ag-ile
  ag-ile-ly
  agil-i-ty
agin-ner
agio
ag-i-tate
  ag-i-tat-ed
  ag-i-tat-ing
  ag-i-tat-ed-ly
  ag-i-ta-tion
  ag-i-ta-tor
  ag-i-ta-tion-al
agleam
aglow
agly-con
ag-nail
ag-nate
  ag-na-tion
  ag-nat-i-cal-ly
  ag-nat-ic
ag-nize
  ag-niz-ing
  ag-nized
ag-no-men
  ag-nom-i-na
ag-nos-tic
  ag-nos-ti-cism
agog
ag-o-nal
agon-ic
ag-o-nist
ag-o-nis-tic
  ag-o-nis-ti-cal-ly

ag-o-nis-ti-cal
ag-o-nize
ag-o-nized
ag-o-niz-ing
ag-o-niz-ing-ly
ag-o-ny
ag-o-nies
ag-o-ra-pho-bia
ag-o-ra-pho-bic
ag-o-ra-pho-bi-ac
agrar-i-an
agrar-i-an-ism
agree
agreed
agree-ing
agree-a-bil-i-ty
agree-a-ble
agree-a-ble-ness
agree-a-bly
agree-ment
ag-ri-busi-ness
ag-ri-cul-ture
ag-ri-cul-tur-al
ag-ri-cul-tur-ist
agron-o-my
ag-ro-nom-ic
ag-ro-nom-i-cal
agron-o-mist
ag-ro-nom-i-cal-ly
aground
ague
agu-ish-ly
agu-ish
aha
ahead
ahem
ahoy
aide-de-camp
ai-grette
ai-guille
ai-guil-lette
ai-ki-do
ail

ail-ing
ail-ment
ai-lan-thus
ai-ler-on
aim-less
air-less
air-less-ness
air-borne
air-brush
air-con-di-tion
air-con-di-tioned
air con-di-tion-er
air con-di-tion-ing
air-craft
air-field
air-mail
air-man
air-men
air-plane
air-port
air pres-sure
air-sick-ness
air-space
air-wave
airy
air-i-er
air-i-est
air-i-ness
air-i-ly
aisle
ajar
akim-bo
akin
al-a-bas-ter
al-a-bas-trine
a la carte
alack
alac-ri-ty
alac-ri-tous
alarm
alarm-ing
alarm-ing-ly
alarm-ist

alarm-ism
alas
alate
alat-ed
al-ba-core
al-ba-cores
al-ba-tross
al-ba-tross-es
al-be-do
al-be-it
al-bi-no
al-bi-nos
al-bi-nism
al-bum
al-bu-men
al-bu-min
al-bu-mi-nous
al-che-my
al-che-mist
al-che-mize
al-che-miz-ing
al-che-mized
al-co-hol
al-co-hol-ic
al-co-hol-ism
al-co-hol-i-cal-ly
al-cove
al-de-hyde
al-de-hy-dic
al-der
al-der-man
al-der-man-ic
ale-a-to-ry
alee
alert
alert-ness
alert-ly
ale-wife
ale-wives
al-ex-an-drine
al-ex-an-drite
alex-ia
al-fal-fa

al-fil-a-ria
al-for-ja
al-fres-co
al-ga
al-gae
al-gal
al-goid
al-ge-bra
al-ge-bra-ic
al-ge-bra-ic-al
al-ge-bra-ic-al-ly
al-ge-bra-ist
al-go-rithm
al-go-rith-mic
ali-as
ali-as-es
al-i-bi
al-i-bi-ing
al-i-bied
alien
alien-a-ble
alien-a-bil-i-ty
alien-ate
alien-at-ed
alien-at-ing
alien-ator
alien-ist
alien-ism
ali-form
alight
alight-ed
alit
alight-ing
alight-ment
align
align-ment
alike
al-i-ment
al-i-men-tal
al-i-men-tal-ly
al-i-men-ta-tion
al-i-men-ta-ry
al-i-men-ta-ry ca-

nal
al-i-mo-ny
al-i-mo-nies
aline-ment
al-i-quant
al-i-quot
alive
alive-ness
al-ka-li
al-ka-lies
al-ka-lis
al-ka-line
al-ka-lin-i-ty
al-ka-lize
al-ka-lized
al-ka-liz-ing
al-ka-li-za-tion
al-ka-loid
al-ka-loi-dal
all-Amer-i-can
all-a-round
al-lay
al-layed
al-lay-ing
al-lay-er
al-le-ga-tion
al-lege
al-leged
al-leg-ing
al-lege-a-ble
al-leg-ed-ly
al-le-giance
al-le-go-ry
al-le-go-ries
al-le-gor-ic
al-le-gor-i-cal
al-le-gor-i-cal-ly
al-le-gor-ist
al-le-gret-to
al-le-gro
al-le-gros
al-ler-gen
al-ler-gen-ic

al-ler-gy
al-ler-gies
al-ler-gic
al-ler-gist
al-le-vi-ate
al-le-vi-at-ed
al-le-vi-at-ing
al-le-vi-a-tion
al-le-vi-a-tor
al-le-vi-a-tive
al-le-vi-a-to-ry
al-ley
al-leys
al-li-ance
al-lied
al-li-ga-tor
all--in-clu-sive
all--in-cul-sive-ness
al-lit-er-ate
al-lit-er-at-ed
al-lit-er-at-ing
al-lit-er-a-tive
al-lit-er-a-tive-ly
al-lit-er-a-tive-ness
al-lit-er-a-tion
al-lo-ca-ble
al-lo-cate
al-lo-cat-ed
al-lo-cat-ing
al-lo-ca-tion
al-lo-cu-tion
al-log-a-mous
al-log-a-my
al-lo-ge-ne-ic
al-lo-graph
al-lo-graph-ic
al-lom-er-ism
al-lom-er-ous
al-lo-path
al-lop-a-thy
al-lo-path-ic
al-lo-path-i-cal-ly
al-lop-a-thist

al-lo-phone
al-lo-phon-ic
al-lo-pu-ri-nol
al-lo-ste-ric
al-lo-ste-ri-cal-ly
al-lot
al-lot-ted
al-lot-ting
al-lot-ment
al-lot-ta-ble
al-lot-ter
al-lo-trope
al-lo-trop-ic
al-lo-trop-cal-ly
al-lot-ro-py
al-lot-ro-pism
al-lo-trope
al-lo-trop-ic
al-lo-trop-i-cal-ly
al-low
al-low-a-ble
al-low-a-bly
al-low-ed-ly
al-low-ance
al-low-anced
al-low-anc-ing
al-loy
all--pow-er-ful
all--pur-pose
all right
all-spice
al-lude
al-lud-ed
al-lud-ing
al-lure
al-lured
al-lur-ing
al-lure-ment
al-lur-er
al-lur-ing-ly
al-lu-sion
al-lu-sive
al-lu-sive-ly

al-lu-sive-ness
al-lu-via
al-lu-vi-al
al-lu-vi-um
al-lu-viums
al-ly
al-lies
al-lied
al-ly-ing
al-ma mat-er
al-ma-nac
al-man-dine
al-man-dite
al-mighty
al-mighti-ness
al-mond
al-mo-ner
al-most
alms-giv-er
alms-giv-ing
alms-house
al-ni-co
al-oe
aloft
alo-ha
alone
alone-ness
along
along-shore
along-side
aloof
aloof-ly
aloof-ness
al-o-pe-cia
al-paca
al-pen-glow
al-pen-stock
al-pes-trine
al-pha
al-pha-bet
al-pha-bet-ic
al-pha-bet-i-cal
al-pha-bet-i-cal-ly

al-pha-bet-i-za-tion
al-pha-bet-ize
al-pha-bet-ized
al-pha-bet-iz-ing
al-ready
al-so
al-tar
al-ter
al-ter-a-bil-i-ty
al-ter-a-ble
al-ter-ant
al-ter-a-tion
al-ter-a-tive
al-ter-cate
al-ter-cat-ing
al-ter-cat-ed
al-ter-ca-tion
al-ter e-go
al-ter-nate
al-ter-nat-ed
al-ter-nat-ing
al-ter-nate-ly
al-ter-na-tion
al-ter-na-tive
al-ter-na-tive-ly
al-ter-na-tive-ness
al-ter-na-tor
al-though
al-tim-e-ter
al-tim-e-try
al-ti-pla-no
al-ti-tude
al-to
al-to-cu-mu-lus
al-to-gether
al-to-re-lie-vo
al-to-stra-tus
al-tru-ism
al-tru-is-tic
al-tru-is-ti-cal-ly
al-tru-ist
al-lu-mi-na
alu-mi-nate

alu-mi-nif-er-ous
al-u-min-i-um
alu-mi-nous
alu-mi-num
alum-na
  alum-nae
alum-nus
  alum-ni
al-ve-o-lar
  al-ve-o-lus
  al-ve-o-li
al-ways
alys-sum
amain
amal-gam
  amal-gam-a-ble
  amal-gam-ate
  amal-gam-at-ed
  amal-gam-at-ing
  amal-gam-a-tion
aman-u-en-ses
  aman-u-en-ses
am-a-ryl-lis
amass
  amass-ment
  amass-er
am-a-teur
  am-a-teur-ism
  am-a-teur-ish
  am-a-teur-ish-ly
  am-a-teur-ish-ness
am-a-tive
  am-a-tive-ness
  am-a-tive-ly
am-a-to-ry
am-au-ro-sis
amaze
  amazed
  amaz-ing
  amaz-ed-ly
  amaz-ed-ness
  amaze-ment
  amaz-ing-ly

am-bas-sa-do-ri-al
am-ber
  amber-gris
am-ber-jack
am-bi-dex-trous
  am-bi-dex-trous-ly
  am-bi-dex-ter-i-ty
am-bi-ance
  am-bi-ence
am-bi-ent
am-big-u-ous
  am-big-u-ous-ly
  am-big-u-ous-ness
am-bi-gu-i-ty
am-bit
am-bi-tion
  am-bi-tion-less
am-bi-tious
  am-bi-tious-ly
  am-bi-tious-ness
am-biv-a-lence
  am-biv-a-lent
  am-biv-a-lent-ly
am-bi-ver-sion
  am-bi-ver-sive
am-bi-vert
am-ble
  am-bled
  am-bling
  am-bler
am-blyg-o-nite
am-bly-opia
am-bo-cep-tor
am-bro-sia
  am-bro-sial-ly
  am-bro-sial
  am-bro-type
ambs-ace
am-bu-la-crum
am-bu-lance
am-bu-la-to-ry
am-bu-lant
am-bu-late

am-bu-lat-ed
am-bu-lat-ing
am-bu-la-tion
am-bus-cade
  am-bus-cad-ed
  am-bus-cad-ing
  am-bus-cad-er
am-bush
  am-bush-ment
  am-bush-er
ameba
amel-io-rate
  amel-io-rat-ed
  amel-io-rat-ing
  amel-io-ra-ble
  amel-io-ra-tion
  amel-ior-a-tive
  amel-io-ra-tor
amen
ame-na-ble
  ame-na-bil-i-ty
  ame-na-ble-ness
  ame-na-bly
amend
  amend-a-ble
  amend-er
  amend-ment
  amends
amend-i-ty
  amend-i-ties
amerce
  amerced
  amerc-ing
  amerce-a-ble
  amerce-ment
  amerce-er
Amer-i-ca
Amer-i-can
Amer-i-ca-na
Amer-i-can-ism
am-e-thyst
  am-e-thys-tine
am-e-tro-pia

ami-a-ble
ami-a-bil-i-ty
ami-a-bly
ami-a-ble-ness
ami-ca-ble
am-i-ca-bil-i-ty
am-i-ca-bly
am-i-ca-ble-ness
am-ice
amid
amidst
am-ide
amid-ic
amid-ships
ami-go
amine
amino acid
ami-no-ac-id-uria
ami-no-py-rine
amir
amiss
am-i-to-sis
am-i-tot-ic
am-i-tot-i-cal-ly
am-i-ty
am-me-ter
am-mi-no
am-mon-nia
am-mon-ic
am-mo-ni-ac
am-mo-ni-um
am-mu-ni-tion
am-ne-sia
am-ne-sic
am-nes-tic
am-nes-ty
am-ni-on
am-ni-ons
am-ni-on-ic
am-nia
am-ni-ot-ic
a-moe-ba
a-moe-bae

a-moe-bas
a-moe-bic
a-moe-ban
á-moe-boid
a-mok
a-mong
a-mongst
a-mon-til-la-do
a-mor-al
a-mo-ral-i-ty
a-mor-al-ism
a-mor-al-ly
amo-ret-to
am-or-ist
am-o-rous
am-o-rous-ly
am-o-rous-ness
a-mor-phism
a-mor-phous
a-mor-phous-ness
a-mor-phous-ly
am-or-tize
am-or-tized
am-or-tiz-ing
am-or-ti-za-tion
am-or-tiz-able
a-mount
a-mour
am-per-age
am-pere
am-per-sand
am-phet-a-mine
ám-phib-ia
am-phib-i-an
am-phib-i-ous
am-phib-i-ous-ly
am-phib-i-ous-ness
am-phi-the-a-ter
am-phi-the-at-ric
am-pho-ra
am-phe-rae
am-phe-ras
am-ple

am-pler
am-plest
am-ple-ness
am-ply
am-pli-fy
am-pli-fied
am-pli-fy-ing
am-pli-fi-ca-tion
am-pli-fi-er
am-pli-tude
am-pul
am-pu-tate
am-pu-tat-ed
am-pu-tat-ing
am-pu-ta-tion
am-pu-tee
a-muck
am-u-let
a-muse
a-mused
a-mus-ing
a-muse-ment
a-mus-ed
am-yl-ase
a-nach-ro-nism
a-nach-ro-nis-tik
a-nach-ro-nous
an-a-con-da
an-aer-obe
an-aes-the-sia
an-aes-thet-ic
an-a-gram
an-a-gram-mat-ic
an-a-gram-mat-i-cal
ana-gram-ma-tized
--gram-ma-tiz-ing
a-nal
an-a-lects
an-al-ge-sic
an-al-ge-sics
an-a-log
an-a-log-i-cal

an-a-log-i-cal-ly
a-nal-o-gize
a-nal-o-gized
a-nal-o-giz-ing
a-nal-o-gy
a-nal-o-gies
a-nal-o-gous
a-nal-y-sis
a-nal-y-ses
an-a-lyst
an-a-lyt-ic
an-a-lyt-ics
an-a-lyze
an-a-lyzed
an-a-lyz-ing
an-a-lyz-a-ble
an-a-ly-za-tion
an-a-lyz-er
an-a-pest
an-a-pes-tic
an-ar-chism
an-ar-chis-tic
an-ar-chy
an-ar-chic
an-ar-chi-cal
a-nath-e-ma
a-nath-e-mas
a-nath-e-ma-tize
a-nath-e-ma-tized
a-nath-e-ma-tiz-ing
a-nat-o-mize
a-nat-o-mized
a-nat-o-mizing
a-nat-o-mi-za-tion
a-nat-o-my
a-nat-o-mies
a-nat-om-i-cal
a-nat-om-i-cal-ly
a-nat-o-mist
an-ces-tor
an-ces-tral
an-ces-tress
an-ces-try

an-chor
an-chor-age
an-cho-ress
an-cho-rite
an-cho-vy
an-cient
an-cient-ly
an-cient-ness
an-cil-lary
an-dan-te
and-i-ron
an-dro-gen
an-drog-y-nous
an-drog-y-ny
an-dros-ter-one
an-ec-dote
an-ec-dot-age
an-ec-do-tal
an-ec-dot-ist
a-ne-mia
a-ne-mic
an-e-mom-e-ter
an-e-mom-e-try
a-nem-o-ne
an-er-oid
an-es-the-sia
an-es-thet-ic
an-es-the-tize
an-es-the-tized
an-es-the-tiz-ing
an-eu-rysm
an-eu-rism
an-eu-rys-mal
a-new
an-ga-ry
an-gel
an-gel-ic
an-gel-i-cal
an-gel-i-cal-ly
an-gel-i-ca
an-ger
an-gi-na
an-gi-na pec-to-ris

an-gi-o-sperm
an-gi-o-sper-mous
an-gle
an-gler
an-gle-worm
an-gling
an-go-ra
an-gos-tu-ra bark
an-gry
an-gri-ly
an-gri-ness
ang-strom u-nit
an-guish
an-gu-lar
an-gu-lar-i-ty
an-gu-lar-ly
an-hy-dride
an-hy-drous
an-i-line
an-i-mad-vert
an-i-mad-ver-sion
an-i-mal
an-i-mal-cule
an-i-mal-cu-lar
an-i-mal-ism
an-i-mal-i-ty
an-i-mal-ize
an-i-mal-ized
an-i-mal-iz-ing
an-i-mate
an-i-mat-ed
an-i-mat-ing
an-i-ma-tion
a-ni-ma-to
an-i-mism
an-i-mis-tic
an-i-mos-i-ty
an-i-mus
an-i-on
an-ise
an-i-seed
an-i-sette
an-kle

an-kle-bone
an-klet
an-ky-lose
  an-ky-losed
  an-ky-los-ing
  an-ky-lo-sis
  an-ky-lot-ic
an-nal-ist
  an-nal-is-tic
an-nals
an-neal
an-ne-lid
  an-nel-i-dan
an-nex
  an-nex-a-tion
  an-nex-a-tion-ist
an-ni-hi-late
  an-ni-hi-lat-ed
  an-ni-hi-lat-ing
  an-ni-hi-la-tion
  an-ni-hi-la-tor
an-ni-ver-sa-ry
  an-ni-ver-sa-ries
an-no Dom-i-ni
an-no-tate
  an-no-tat-ed
  an-no-tat-ing
  an-no-ta-tion
  an-no-ta-tor
an-nounce
  an-nounced
  an-nounc-ing
  an-nounce-ment
  an-nounc-er
an-noy
  an-noy-ance
  an-noy-er
an-nu-al
an-nu-i-ty
an-nu-i-tant
an-nul
  an-nulled
  an-nul-ling

an-nul-ment
an-nu-lar
  an-nu-lar-i-ty
  an-nu-lar-ly
an-nu-late
an-nu-let
an-nu-lus
  an-nu-lus-es
an-nun-ci-a-tion
an-nun-ci-ate
  an-nun-ci-at-ed
  an-nun-ci-at-ing
  an-nun-ci-a-tor
an-ode
  an-od-ic
an-o-dyne
a-noint
  a-noint-er
  a-noint-ment
a-nom-a-ly
  a-nom-a-lism
  a-nom-a-lous
  a-nom-a-lous-ly
an-o-mie
  an-o-my
an-o-nym
  a-non-y-mous
  an-o-nym-i-ty
  a-non-y-mous-ly
a-noph-e-les
an-oth-er
an-ox-ia
an-ser-ine
an-swer
  an-swer-a-ble
ant-ac-id
an-tag-o-nist
  an-tag-o-nism
  an-tag-o-nis-tic
  an-tag-o-nize
  an-tag-o-nized
  an-tag-o-niz-ing
ant-arc-tic

an-te
  an-ted
  an-te-ing
ant-eat-er
an-te--bel-lum
an-te-ced-ence
  an-te-ced-ent
  an-te-cede
  an-te-ced-ed
  an-te-ced-ing
an-te-cham-ber
an-te-choir
an-te-date
  an-te-dat-ed
  an-te-dat-ing
an-te-di-lu-vi-an
an-te-lope
  an-te-lopes
an-te me-rid-i-em
an-ten-na
  an-ten-nae
  an-ten-nas
an-te-pe-nult
  an-te-pe-nul-ti-mate
an-te-ri-or
an-te-room
an-them
an-ther
an-ther-id-i-um
an-thol-o-gy
  an-thol-o-gies
  an-thol-o-gist
  an-thol-o-gize
  an-thol-o-giz-ing
an-tho-zo-an
an-thra-cene
  an-thra-cite
  an-thra-cit-ic
an-thrax
  an-thra-ces
an-thro-po-cen-tric
an-thro-po-gen-e-sis
an-thro-poid

an-thro-pol-o-gy
  an-thro-po-log-ic
  an-thro-po-log-i-cal
  an-thro-pol-o-gist
an-thr-pom-e-try
  an-thro-po-met-ric
an-ti-air-craft
an-ti-bi-o-sis
an-ti-bi-ot-ic
  an-ti-bod-y
  an-ti-bod-ies
an-tic
an-ti-christ
an-tic-i-pate
  an-tic-i-pat-ed
  an-tic-i-pat-ing
  an-tic-i-pa-tion
  an-tic-i-pa-tive
  an-tic-i-pa-to-ry
an-ti-cler-i-cal
  an-ti-cler-i-cal-ism
an-ti-cli-max
  an-ti-cli-mac-tic
an-ti-cli-nal
  an-ti-cline
an-ti-cy-clone
an-ti-dote
  an-ti-dot-al
an-ti-fed-er-al
  an-ti-fed-er-al-ist
  an-ti-fed-er-al-ism
an-ti-freeze
an-ti-gen
an-ti-he-ro
an-ti-his-ta-mine
an-ti-log-a-rithm
an-ti-ma-cas-sar
an-ti-mis-sile
an-ti-mo-ny
an-ti-pas-to
an-tip-a-thy
an-ti-phon
  an-tiph-o-nal

an-ti-pode
  an-ti-quar-i-an
  an-ti-quar-y
  an-ti-quar-ies
an-ti-quate
  an-ti-quat-ed
  an-ti-quat-ing
  an-ti-quat-ed
an-tique
  an-tiqed
  an-tiq-uing
  an-tique-ly
an-tiq-ui-ty
  an-tiq-ui-ties
an-ti-Sem-i-tism
an-ti-sep-sis
an-ti-sep-tic
an-ti-se-rum
an-ti-slav-er-y
an-ti-so-cial
an-tith-e-sis
  an-tith-e-ses
an-ti-thet-i-cal
an-ti-tox-in
  an-ti-tox-in
an-ti-trust
ant-ler
  ant-ler-ed
an-to-nym
an-trum
an-tra
a-nus
an-vil
anx-i-e-ty
  anx-i-e-ties
anx-ious
an-y
an-y-bod-y
  an-y-bod-ies
an-y-how
an-y-more
an-y-one
an-y-place

an-y-thing
an-y-way
an-y-where
an-y-wise
a-or-ta
  a-or-tas
  a-or-tae
  a-or-tal
  a-or-tic
a-pace
a-pache
a-part
a-part-heid
a-part-ment
ap-a-thy
  ap-a-thet-ic
  ap-a-thet-i-cal-ly
ape
a-per-ri-tif
ap-er-ture
a-pex
  a-pex-es
  a-pi-ces
  ap-i-cal
a-pha-sia
a-phe-li-on
  a-phe-lia
a-phid
a-phis
  a-phi-des
aph-o-rism
  aph-o-rist
aph-ro-dis-i-ac
a-pi-an
a-pi-ar-i-an
a-pi-a-rist
a-pi-ary
  a-pi-ar-ies
a-pi-cul-ture
  a-pi-cul-tur-al
  a-pi-cul-tur-ist
a-piece
ap-ish

ap-ish-ly
ap-ish-ness
a-plomb
a-poc-a-lypse
a-poc-a-lyp-tic
a-poc-o-pe
a-poc-ry-phal
ap-o-gee
a-po-lit-i-cal
a-pol-o-get-ics
a-pol-o-gist
a-pol-o-gize
a-pol-o-gized
a-pol-o-giz-ing
a-pol-o-gy
a-pol-o-gies
ap-o-plec-tic
ap-o-plex-y
a-port
a-pos-ta-sy
a-pos-ta-sies
a-pos-tate
a-pos-ta-tize
a-pos-ta-tized
a-pos-to-tiz-ing
a pos-te-ri-o-ri
a-pos-tle
a-pos-tle-ship
a-pos-to-late
ap-os-tol-ic
ap-os-tol-i-cal
a-pos-tro-phe
a-poth-e-cary
a-poth-e-car-ies
ap-o-thegm
ap-o-phthegm
ap-o-theg-mat-ic
a-poth-e-o-sis
a-poth-e-o-ses
a-poth-e-o-size
a-poth-e-o-sized
ap-pall
ap-palled

ap-pal-ling
ap-pa-rat-us
ap-pa-rat-us-es
ap-par-el
ap-par-ent
ap-pa-ri-tion
ap-pa-ri-tion-al
ap-peal
ap-peal-a-ble
ap-peal-er
ap-pear
ap-pear-ance
ap-pease
ap-peased
ap-peasing
ap-pease-ment
ap-peas-a-ble
ap-peas-er
ap-pel-lant
ap-pel-late
ap-pel-la-tion
ap-pel-la-tive
ap-pend
ap-pen-dage
ap-pend-ant
ap-pen-dec-to-my
ap-pen-di-ci-tis
ap-pen-dix
ap-pen-dix-es
ap-pen-di-ces
ap-per-cep-tion
ap-per-cep-tive
ap-per-tain
ap-pe-tite
ap-pe-tiz-er
ap-pe-tiz-ing
ap-plaud
ap-plause
ap-ple
ap-ple-jack
ap-pli-ance
ap-pli-ca-ble
ap-pli-ca-bil-i-ty

ap-pli-ca-ble-ness
ap-pli-cant
ap-pli-ca-tion
ap-pli-ca-tive
ap-pli-ca-to-ry
ap-pli-ca-tor
ap-plied
ap-ply
ap-ply-ing
ap-point
ap-point-a-ble
ap-point-ee
ap-point-er
ap-point-ment
ap-por-tion
ap-por-tion-ment
ap-pose
ap-posed
ap-pos-ing
ap-po-site
ap-po-si-tion
ap-po-si-tion-al
ap-pos-i-tive
ap-praise
ap-prais-al
ap-praised
ap-praiser
ap-prais-ing
ap-pre-ci-a-ble
ap-pre-ci-a-bly
ap-pre-ci-ate
ap-pre-ci-at-ed
ap-pre-ci-at-ing
ap-pre-ci-a-tion
ap-pre-ci-a-tive
ap-pre-hend
ap-pre-hen-si-ble
ap-pre-hen-sion
ap-pre-hen-sive
ap-pren-tice
ap-pren-tic-ed
ap-pren-tic-ing
ap-pren-tice-ship

ap-prise
ap-prised
ap-pris-ing
ap-prize
ap-proach
ap-proach-a-bil-i-ty
ap-proach-a-ble
ap-pro-ba-tion
ap-pro-ba-tive
ap-pro-ba-to-ry
ap-pro-pri-ate
ap-pro-pri-at-ed
ap-pro-pri-at-ing
ap-pro-pri-ate-ly
ap-pro-pri-a-tor
ap-pro-pri-a-tion
ap-pro-pri-a-tive
ap-prox-i-mate
ap-prox-i-mate-ly
ap-prox-i-ma-tion
ap-pur-te-nance
ap-pur-te-nant
ap-ri-cot
a-pri-o-ri
a-pron
ap-ro-pos
apt
apt-ly
apt-ness
ap-ter-ous
ap-ti-tude
aq-ua
aq-uas
aq-uae
a-qua-cul-ture
aq-ua-ma-rine
aq-ua-naut
aq-ua-plane
aquar-ia
aquar-i-um
aquar-i-ums
a-quat-ic
aq-ua-tint

aq-ue-duct
a-que-ous
aq-ui-line
ar-a-besque
ar-a-ble
a-rach-nid
a-rach-ni-dan
ar-ba-lest
ar-ba-lest-er
ar-ba-list
ar-bi-ter
ar-bi-tral
ar-bit-ra-ment
ar-bi-trar-y
ar-bi-trar-i-ly
ar-bi-trate
ar-bi-trat-ed
ar-bi-trat-ing
ar-bi-tra-ble
ar-bi-tra-tor
ar-bi-tra-tion
ar-bor
ar-bo-re-al
ar-bo-res-cent
ar-bo-re-ta
ar-bo-re-tum
ar-bo-re-tums
ar-bor-vi-tae
ar-bu-tus
arc
arced
arc-ing
ar-cade
arch
arch-ly
ar-cha-ic
ar-cha-ism
ar-cha-ist
ar-cha-is-tic
arch-du-cal
arch-duke
arch-en-e-my

arch-en-e-mies
arch-er
ar-cher-y
arch-e-type
ar-che-typ-al
ar-che-typ-i-cal
arch-fiend
ar-chi-e-pis-co-pal
ar-chi-e-pis-co-pate
ar-chi-pel-a-goes
ar-chi-pel-a-gos
ar-chi-tect
ar-chi-tec-ton-ic
ar-chi-tec-ture
ar-chi-trave
ar-chive
ar-chi-val
ar-chi-vist
ar-chon
arch-priest
arch-way
arc-tic
ar-dent
ar-dent-ly
ar-dor
ar-du-ous
ar-du-ous-ly
ar-e-a
ar-e-al
ar-e-a-way
a-re-na
a-re-o-la
a-re-o-lae
a-re-o-las
ar-gent
ar-gen-tine
ar-gil
ar-gon
ar-go-sy
ar-go-sies
ar-got
ar-got-ic
ar-gue

ar-gued
ar-gu-ing
ar-gu-a-ble
ar-gu-er
ar-gu-ment
ar-gu-men-ta-tion
ar-gu-men-ta-tive
ar-gyle
ar-gyll
a-ri-a
ar-id
a-rid-i-ty
a-right
a-rise
a-rose
a-ris-en
a-ris-ing
ar-is-toc-ra-cy
ar-is-toc-ra-cies
aris-to-crat
aris-to-crat-ic
a-rith-me-tic
a-rith-met-i-cal
a-rith-me-ti-cian
ar-ma-da
ar-ma-dil-lo
ar-ma-ment
ar-ma-ture
ar-mi-stice
ar-moire
ar-mor
ar-mor-er
ar-mor-y
ar-mor-ies
arm-pit
ar-my
ar-mies
ar-ni-ca
a-ro-ma
ar-o-mat-ic
ar-o-mat-i-cal
a-round
a-rouse

a-roused
a-rous-ing
ar-peg-gi-o
ar-peg-gi-os
ar-raign
ar-raign-ment
ar-range
ar-ranged
ar-rang-er
ar-rang-ing
ar-range-ment
ar-rant
ar-rant-ly
ar-ras
ar-ray
ar-rear
ar-rest
ar-rest-er
ar-rest-or
ar-ri-val
ar-rive
ar-rived
ar-riv-ing
ar-ro-gant
ar-ro-gat-ed
ar-ro-gat-ing
ar-ro-ga-tion
ar-row
ar-row-head
ar-row-root
ar-roy-o
ar-roy-os
ar-se-nal
ar-se-nate
ar-se-nic
ar-son
ar-son-ist
ar-te-ri-al
ar-te-ri-o-scle-ro-sis
ar-ter-y
ar-ter-ies
ar-te-sian well
art-ful

art-ful-ly
ar-thri-tis
ar-thrit-ic
ar-thro-pod
ar-throp-o-dal
ar-throp-o-dous
ar-ti-choke
ar-ti-cle
ar-tic-u-lar
ar-tic-u-late
ar-tic-u-lat-ed
ar-tic-u-lat-ing
ar-tic-u-late-ly
ar-tic-u-lar-tor
ar-tic-u-la-tion
ar-te-fact
ar-ti-fact
ar-ti-fice
ar-tif-i-cer
ar-ti-fi-cial
ar-ti-fi-ci-al-i-ty
ar-ti-fi-cial-ly
ar-til-ler-y
ar-til-ler-ist
ar-ti-san
art-ist
ar-tiste
ar-tis-tic
ar-tis-ti-cal-ly
art-ist-ry
art-y
as-bes-tos
as-bes-tus
as-cend
as-cend-ance
as-cend-ence
as-cend-an-cy
as-cend-en-cy
as-cend-ant
as-cend-ent
as-cen-sion
as-cent
as-cer-tain

as-cer-tain-a-ble
as-cer-tain-ment
as-cet-ic
as-cet-is-al
as-cet-i-cism
as-cot
as-cribe
as-cribed
as-crib-ing
as-crib-a-ble
a-sep-sis
a-sep-tic
a-sex-u-al
a-sex-u-al-i-ty
a-sex-u-al-ly
a-shamed
a-sham-ed-ly
ash-en
ash-lar
ash-ler
a-shore
ash-y
a-side
as-i-nine
a-skance
a-skew
a-slant
a-slope
a-so-cial
as-par-a-gus
as-pect
as-pen
as-per-i-ty
as-perse
as-persed
as-pers-ing
as-per-sion
as-phalt
as-phal-tic
as-pho-del
as-phyx-ia
as-phyx-i-ate
as-phyx-i-at-ed

as-phyx-i-a-tion
as-pic
as-pi-dis-tra
as-pir-ant
as-pi-rate
as-pi-rat-ed
as-pi-rat-ing
as-pi-ra-tion
as-pi-ra-tor
as-pire
as-pired
as-pir-ing
as-pir-er
as-pi-rin
as-sail
as-sail-a-ble
as-sail-ant
as-sas-sin
as-sas-si-nate
as-sas-si-nat-ed
as-sas-si-na-tion
as-sault
as-say
as-say-er
as-sem-blage
as-sem-ble
as-sem-bled
as-sem-bling
as-sem-bler
as-sem-bly
as-sem-blies
as-sem-bly-man
as-sem-bly-men
as-sent
as-sent-er
as-sert
as-sert-er
as-ser-tion
as-ser-tive
as-ser-tive-ly
as-sess
as-sess-a-ble
as-sess-ment

as-sess-or
as-set
as-si-du-i-ty
as-sid-u-ous
as-sid-u-ous-ly
as-sid-u-ous-ness
as-sign
as-sign-a-bil-i-ty
as-sign-a-ble
as-sign-a-bly
as-sig-na-tion
as-sign-ee
as-sign-ment
as-sist
as-sist-ance
as-sis-tant
as-size
as-so-ci-ate
as-so-ci-at-ed
as-so-ci-at-ing
as-so-ci-a-tion
as-so-nance
as-sort
as-sor-ted
as-sort-ment
as-sume
as-sumed
as-sum-ing
as-sump-tion
as-sur-ance
as-sure
as-sured
as-sur-ing
as-sur-er
as-sur-ed-ly
as-ter
as-ter-isk
a-stern
as-ter-oid
as-ter-oi-dal
asth-ma
asth-mat-ic
a-stig-ma-tism

as-tig-mat-ic
a-stir
as-ton-ish
  as-ton-ish-ing
  as-ton-ish-ment
as-tound
  as-tound-ing
a-strad-dle
as-tra-khan
as-tral
a-stray
a-stride
as-trin-gent
  as-trin-gen-cy
as-tro-dome
as-tro-labe
as-trol-o-gy
  as-trol-o-ger
  as-tro-log-ic
  as-tro-log-i-cal
as-tro-naut
  as-tro-nau-tics
  as-tro-nau-ti-cal
as-tro-nom-ic
  as-tro-nom-i-cal-ly
as-tron-o-my
  as-tron-o-mer
as-tro-phys-ics
  as-tro-phys-i-cist
as-tute
  as-tute-ly
a-sun-der
a-sy-lum
a-sym-me-try
  asym-met-ric
  asym-met-ri-cal
  asym-met-ri-cal-ly
at-a-vism
  at-a-vist
  at-a-vis-tic
a-tax-ia
  a-tax-ic
at-el-ier

a-thirst
ath-lete
  ath-let-ic
  ath-let-ics
a-thwart
a-tilt
at-las
  at-las-es
at-mos-phere
at-oll
at-om
ato-nal-i-ty
  ato-nal
a-tone
  a-toned
a-top
a-tri-um
a-tro-cious
  a-tro-cious-ly
a-troc-i-ty
  a-troc-i-ties
at-ro-phy
  at-ro-phies
  at-ro-phied
at-ro-pine
at-tach
  at-tach-a-ble
  at-tach-ment
at-tack
at-tain
  at-tain-a-ble
  at-tain-a-bil-i-ty
  at-tain-ment
at-tain-der
at-taint
at-tar
at-tempt
  at-tempt-a-ble
at-tend
  at-tend-ance
  at-tend-ant
at-ten-tion
at-ten-tive

at-ten-u-ate
  at-ten-u-at-ed
  at-ten-u-at-ing
  at-ten-u-a-tion
at-test
  at-tes-ta-tion
at-tic
at-tire
  at-tired
  at-tir-ing
at-ti-tude
at-ti-tu-di-nize
  at-ti-tu-di-nized
at-tor-ney
at-tract
  at-trac-tive
  at-tract-or
  at-trac-tion
at-tri-bute
  at-tri-but-ed
  at-tri-but-ing
  at-tri-bu-tion
  at-trib-u-tive
at-tri-tion
at-tune
  at-tuned
  at-tun-ing
a-typ-i-cal
  a-typ-ic
  a-typ-i-cal-ly
au-burn
au cou-rant
auc-tion
  auc-tion-eer
au-da-cious
  au-dac-i-ty
au-di-ble
  au-di-bly
au-di-ence
au-di-o
au-di-o-vis-u-al
au-dit
au-di-tion

au-dit-or
au-di-to-ri-um
au-di-to-ry
au-ger
aug-ment
 aug-ment-a-ble
 aug-men-ta-tion
 aug-ment-a-tive
au-grat-in
au-gur
 au-gu-ry
 au-gu-ries
au-gust
 au-gust-ly
auk
aunt
au-ra
 au-ras
 au-rae
au-ral
 au-ral-ly
au-re-ate
au-re-ole
au-re-voir
au-ri-cle
au-rif-er-ous
au-ro-ra
au-ro-ra bor-e-al-is
aus-cul-tate
 aus-cul-tat-ed
 aus-cul-tat-ing
 aus-cul-ta-tion
aus-tere
 aus-ter-i-ty
 aus-ter-i-ties
aus-tral
au-then-tic
 au-then-ti-cat-ed
 au-then-ti-cat-ing
 au-then-ti-ca-tion
au-thor
au-thor-i-tar-i-an
 au-thor-i-ta-tive

au-thor-i-ty
 au-thor-i-ties
au-thor-ize
 au-thor-ized
 au-thor-iz-ing
 au-thor-i-za-tion
au-thor-ship
au-to
au-to-bi-og-ra-phy
 au-to-bi-og-ra-phies
 au-to-bi-og-ra-pher
au-toc-ra-cy
 au-toc-ra-cies
au-to-crat
 au-to-crat-ic
 au-to-crat-i-cal
au-toc-ra-cy
 au-toc-ra-cies
au-to-graph
au-to-mat
au-to-mat-ic
au-to-ma-tion
au-to-mate
 au-to-mat-ed
 au-to-mat-ing
au-tom-a-tism
au-tom-a-ton
 au-tom-a-tons
 au-tom-a-ta
au-to-mo-bile
au-to-mo-tive
au-to-nom-ic
 au-to-nom-i-cal-ly
au-ton-o-mous
 au-ton-o-mous-ly
au-ton-o-my
 au-ton-o-mies
 au-ton-o-mist
au-top-sy
au-to-sug-ges-tion
au-tumn
 au-tum-nal
aux-il-ia-ry

 aux-il-ia-ries
a-vail
 a-vail-a-bil-i-ty
 a-vail-ably
av-a-lanche
 av-a-lanched
 av-a-lanch-ing
a-vant-garde
av-a-rice
 av-a-ri-cious
 av-a-ri-cious-ly
a-vast
av-a-tar
a-ve
a-venge
 a-venged
 a-veng-ing
 a-veng-er
av-e-nue
a-ver
 a-verred
 a-ver-ment
av-er-age
 av-er-aged
 av-er-ag-ing
a-verse
 a-verse-ly
a-ver-sion
a-vi-a-tion
a-vi-a-tor
av-id
a-void
a-vow
a-wait
a-wake
a-wak-en
awe
awe-some
awe-struck
aw-ful
 aw-ful-ly
 aw-ful-ness
awhile

awk-ward
awk-ward-ly
awn
awned
awn-ing
awry
ax
ax-es
ax-i-al
ax-i-al-ly
ax-i-om
ax-i-o-mat-ic
ax-i-o-mat-i-cal
ax-is
ax-es
ax-le
azal-ea
az-i-muth
az-i-muth-al
az-ure

B

bab-bitt
bab-ble
bab-bled
bab-bling
bab-bler
ba-bel
ba-boon
ba-bush-ka
ba-by
ba-bies
ba-bied
ba-by-ing
bac-ca-lau-re-ate
bac-ca-rat
bac-cha-nal
bac-cha-na-li-an
bac-chant
bac-chant-te
bach-e-lor
bach-e-lor-hood

bac-il-lar-y
bac-cil-lus
bac-cil-li
back-bite
back-bit
back-bit-ten
back-bit-er
back-board
back-fire
back-fired
back-fir-ing
back-gam-mon
back-ground
back-hand
back-hand-ed
back-ing
back-lash
back-log
back-slide
back-slid
back-slid-den
back-slid-ing
back-slid-er
back-spin
back-stop
back-stroke
back-talk
back-up
back-ward
back-wards
back-wash
back-water
back-woods
back-woods-man
ba-con
bac-ter-ia
bac-ter-i-um
bac-te-ri-al
bac-te-ri-al-ly
bac-te-ri-cide
bac-te-ri-ci-dal
bac-te-ri-ol-o-gy
bac-te-ri-ol-o-gist

bac-te-ri-o-log-i-cal
bac-te-ri-o-phage
bad
bade
badge
badged
badg-ing
badg-er
bad-i-nage
bad-land
bad-lands
bad-ly
bad-min-ton
bad-tem-pered
baf-fle
baf-fled
baf-fling
baf-fler
bag
bagged
bag-ging
ba-gasse
bag-a-telle
ba-gel
bag-gage
bag-gy
bag-gi-er
bag-gi-est
bag-man
bagn-io
bag-pipe
bag-pi-per
bah
bail
bail-iff
bail-i-wick
bails-man
bails-men
bairn
bait
bake
baked
bak-ing

bak-er
bak-er-y
bak-er-ies
bak-ing pow-der
bak-ing so-da
bak-sheesh
bak-shish
bal-a-lai-ka
bal-ance
bal-anced
bal-anc-ing
bal-anc-er
bal-brig-gan
bal-co-ny
bal-co-nies
bald
bald-ness
bal-der-dash
bald-head
bal-dric
bale
baled
bal-ing
ba-leen
bale-ful
bale-ful-ly
balk
balk-er
bal-kan-ize
bal-kan-ized
bal-kan-iz-ing
bal-kan-i-za-tion
balk-y
balk-i-er
balk-i-est
bal-lad
bal-lade
bal-lad-eer
bal-lad-ry
bal-last
ball-bear-ing
bal-le-ri-na
bal-let

bal-lis-tic
bal-lis-tics
bal-lis-ti-cian
bal-loon
bal-lot
bal-lot-ed
bal-lot-ing
ball-room
bal-ly-hoo
balm
balm-y
balm-ier
balm-i-est
balm-i-ly
ba-lo-ney
bal-sa
bal-sam
bal-us-ter
bal-us-trade
bam-bi-no
bam-bi-nos
bam-boo
ban
banned
ban-ning
ba-nal
ba-nal-i-ty
ban-nan-a
band-age
band-aged
band-ag-ing
ban-dana
ban-dan-na
ban-deau
ban-deaux
ban-de-role
ban-dit
ban-dits
ban-dit-ti
ban-dit-ry
band-mas-ter
band-o-leer
ban-do-lier

bands-man
bands-men
band-stand
band-wa-gon
ban-dy
ban-died
ban-dy-ing
ban-dy--leg-ged
bane-ful
ban-ful-ness
ban-gla-desh
ban-gle
ban-ish
ban-ish-ment
ban-i-ster
ban-jo
bank
bank-er
bank-ing
bank-note
bank-rupt
bank-rupt-cy
bank-rupt-cies
ban-ner
banns
ban-quet
ban-quet-ter
ban-quette
ban-tam
ban-tam-weight
ban-ter
ban-ter-er
ban-ter-ing-ly
ban-yan
ban-zal
ba-o-bab
bap-tism
bap-tis-mal
bap-tist
bap-tist-ery
bap-tis-ter-ies
bap-tize
bap-tized

bap-tiz-er
bap-tiz-ing
bar
 barred
 bar-ring
bar-bar-ic
bar-ba-rism
bar-bar-i-ty
 bar-bar-i-ties
bar-ba-rize
 bar-ba-rized
 bar-ba-riz-ing
bar-ba-rous
bar-be-cue
 bar-be-cued
 bar-be-cu-ing
bar-ber
bar-ber-ry
 bar-ber-ries
bar-ber-shop
bar-bi-tal
bar-bi-tu-rate
 bar-bi-tur-ic
bar-busse
bar-ca-role
bard
bare
 bar-er
 bar-est
bare-back
bare-faced
bare-foot
bare-hand-ed
bare-ly
bar-gain
 bar-gain-er
barge
 barg-ed
 barg-ing
bar-i-tone
bar-i-um
bar-keep-er
bar-ken-tine

bark-er
bar-ley
bar-maid
bar-man
 bar-men
bar-mitz-vah
barm-y
bar-na-cle
barn-storm
 barn-storm-er
 barn-storm-ing
barn-yard
bar-o-graph
ba-rom-et-er
 bar-o-met-ric
 bar-o-met-ric-al
bar-on
 ba-ro-ni-al
bar-on-age
bar-on-ess
bar-on-et
 bar-on-et-age
 bar-on-et-cy
bar-o-ny
 bar-o-nies
ba-roque
barque
bar-quen-tine
bar-rack
bar-ra-cu-da
 bar-ra-cu-das
bar-rage
 bar-raged
 bar-rag-ing
bar-ra-try
 bar-ra-tries
 bar-ra-tor
 bar-ra-trous
bar-rel
 bar-reled
 bar-relled
 bar-rel-ling
bar-ren

bar-ren-ly
bar-ren-ness
bar-rette
bar-ri-cade
 bar-ri-cad-ed
 bar-ri-cad-ing
bar-ri-er
bar-ring
bar-ri-o
 bar-ri-os
bar-ris-ter
bar-room
bar-row
bar-ten-der
bar-ter
 bar-ter-er
ba-sal
ba-salt
base-ment
bash-ful
 bash-ful-ly
ba-sic
 ba-si-cal-ly
ba-sil
ba-sil-i-cia
bas-i-lisk
ba-sin
ba-sis
bas-ket
bas-ket-ball
bas-ket-ry
bas-re-lief
bas-si-net
bas-tard
baste
 bast-ed
 bast-ing
bas-tille
bas-ti-on
 bas-ti-oned
bat
 bat-ted
 bat-ting

bat-ter
batch
bate
  bat-ed
  bat-ing
bathe
  bathed
  bath-ing
  bath-er
bath-i-nette
ba-thos
bath-y-scaphe
bath-y-sphere
ba-tik
ba-tiste
bat-on
bat-ten
bat-ter
bat-tery
bat-tle
  bat-tled
  bat-tling
bat-tle dore
bat-tle-field
bat-tle-ment
bat-ty
  bat-ti-er
  bat-ti-est
bau-ble
bawd-y
  bawd-i-er
  bawd-i-est
bay-o-net
  bay-o-net-ted
  bay-o-net-ing
bay-ou
ba-zaar
ba-zoo-ka
beach
bea-con
bead
  bead-ed
  bead-like

bead-y
  bead-i-er
  bead-i-est
beak
  beaked
beak-er
beam
  beam-ed
bear
  bear-ing
  bear-a-ble
  bear-a-bly
  bear-er
beard
  beard-ed
  beard-less
bear-skin
beast
  beast-li-ness
  beast-ly
  beast-li-er
  beast-li-est
beat
  beat-en
  beat-ing
  beat-er
be-a-tif-ic
be-at-i-fy
  be-at-i-fied
  be-at-i-fi-ca-tion
be-at-i-tude
beat-nik
beau
  beaus
  beaux
beau geste
beau-te-ous
  beau-te-ous-ly
beau-ti-cian
beau-ti-fy
  beau-ti-fied
  beau-ti-fy-ing
  beau-ti-fi-ca-tion

  beau-ti-fi-er
  beau-ti-ful
beau-ty
beaux-arts
bea-ver
be-calm
beck-on
be-cloud
be-come
  be-com-ing
  be-com-ing-ly
bed
  bed-ded
  bed-ding
be-daub
be-daz-zle
  be-daz-zled
  be-daz-zling
  be-daz-zle-ment
bed-bug
bed-clothes
be-deck
be-dev-il
  be-dev-iled
  be-dev-il-ing
  be-dev-il-ment
be-dew
bed-fast
bed-fel-low
be-dim
  be-dimmed
  be-dim-ming
bed-lam
bed-pan
be-drag-gle
  be-drag-gled
  be-drag-gling
bed-rid-den
bed-rock
bed-room
bed-sore
bed-spread
bed-spring

bed-time
bee-bread
beech
beef
beef-eat-er
beef-steak
beef-y
  beef-i-er
  beef-i-est
bee-hive
bee-line
beer-y
  beer-i-er
  beer-i-est
beest-ings
bees-wax
bee-tle
  bee-tled
  bee-tling
bee-tle-browed
be-fall
  be-fall-en
  be-fall-ing
be-fit
  be-fit-ted
  be-fit-ting
be-fog
  be-fogged
  be-fog-ging
be-fore
be-fore-hand
be-foul
be-friend
be-fud-dle
  be-fud-dled
  be-fud-dling
beg
  beg-ged
  beg-ging
be-get
  be-get-ten
  be-got
  be-got-ten

beg-gar
  beg-gar-dom
  beg-gar-hood
  beg-gar-ly
be-gin
  be-gan
  be-gun
  be-gin-ning
  be-gin-ner
be-go-ni-a
be-grime
  be-grimed
  be-grim-ing
be-grudge
  be-grudged
  be-grudg-ing
  be-grudg-ing-ly
be-guile
  be-guiled
  be-guil-ing
  be-guil-er
be-half
be-have
  be-haved
  be-hav-ing
be-hav-ior
  be-hav-ior-ism
  be-hav-ior-ist
  be-hav-ior-is-tic
be-head
be-he-moth
be-hest
be-hind
be-hind-hand
be-hold
  be-hold-ing
  be-hold-er
  be-hold-en
be-hoove
  be-hooved
  be-hoov-ing
beige
be-ing

be-la-bor
be-lat-ed
  be-lat-ed-ly
  be-lat-ed-ness
be-lay
  be-lay-ed
  be-lay-ing
belch
bel-dam
be-lea-quer
bel-fry
  bel-fries
be-lie
  be-lied
  be-ly-ing
be-lief
be-lieve
  be-lieved
  be-liev-ing
  be-liev-a-ble
  be-liev-er
be-lit-tle
  be-lit-tled
  be-lit-tling
bel-la-don-na
bell-boy
bell bouy
belle
belles let-tres
bell-hop
bel-li-cose
  bel-li-cos-i-ty
bel-lig-er-ence
  bel-lig-er-en-cy
  bel-li-ger-ent
  bel-lig-er-ent-ly
bel-low
  bel-lows
bell-weth-er
bel-ly
  bel-lies
  bel-lied
  bel-ly-ing

bel-ly-ache
 bel-ly-ach-ing
bel-ly-but-ton
be-long
 be-long-ings
be-loved
be-low
belt
 belt-ed
belt-way
be-lu-ga
be-mire
 be-mired
 be-mir-ing
be-moan
be-muse
 be-mused
 be-mus-ing
bench
bend
 bend-ing
 bend-er
be-neath
ben-e-dict
ben-e-dic-tion
ben-e-fac-tion
ben-e-fac-tor
 ben-e-fac-tress
ben-e-fice
 ben-e-ficed
 ben-e-fic-ing
be-nef-i-cence
be-nef-i-cent
be-ne-fi-cial
 ben-e-fi-cial-ly
 ben-e-fi-ci-ar-ies
ben-e-fit
 ben-e-fit-ed
 ben-e-fit-ing
be-nev-o-lence
 be-nev-o-lent
 be-nev-o-lent-ly
be-night-ed

be-nign
 be-nig-ni-ty
 be-nig-ni-ties
 be-nign-ly
be-nig-nant
 be-nig-nan-cies
 be-nig-nan-cy
ben-i-son
ben-ny
 ben-nies
be-numb
bent
ben-zene
ben-zine
ben-zo-ate
ben-zo-in
ben-zol
be-queath
be-quest
be-rate
 be-rat-ed
 be-rat-ing
be-reave
 be-reaved
 be-reav-ing
be-reft
be-ret
ber-ga-mot
ber-i-ber-i
berke-li-um
ber-ry
 ber-ries
 ber-ried
 ber-ry-ing
ber-serk
berth
ber-tha
ber-yl
be-ryl-li-um
be-seech
 be-seeched
 be-seech-ing
 be-seech-ing-ly

be-set
 be-set-ting
be-shrew
be-side
 be-sides
be-siege
 be-sieged
 be-sieg-ing
 be-sieg-er
be-smear
be-smirch
bes-om
be-sot
 be-sot-ted
 be-sot-ting
be-spat-ter
be-speak
 be-speak-ing
best
bes-tial
 bes-tial-ly
 bes-ti-al-i-ty
 bes-ti-al-i-ties
be-stir
 be-stirred
 be-stir-ring
be-stow
 be-stow-al
be-strew
be-stride
 be-strid-den
 be-strid-ing
bet
 bet-ted
 bet-ting
be-ta
be-take
 be-tak-en
 be-tak-ing
be-ta rays
be-ta-tron
be-tel
beth-el

be-tide
 be-tid-ed
 be-tid-ing
be-to-ken
be-tray
 be-tray-al
 be-tray-er
be-troth
 be-troth-al
 be-troth-ed
bet-ter
bet-ter-ment
bet-tor
be-tween
be-twixt
bev-el
 bev-eled
 bev-el-ing
bev-er-age
bev-y
 bev-ies
be-wail
be-ware
be-wil-der
 be-wil-der-ing-ly
 be-wil-der-ment
be-witch
 be-witch-er
 be-witch-ery
 be-witch-ing
 be-witch-ing-ly
 be-witch-ment
be-yond
be-zique
bi-an-nu-al
bi-as
 bi-ased
 bi-as-ing
bi-ax-i-al
 bi-ax-i-al-ly
bi-be-lot
Bi-ble
 Bib-li-cal

Bib-li-cal-ly
bib-li-og-ra-phy
 bib-li-og-ra-phies
 bib-li-o-graphic
bib-li-o-ma-ni-a
 bib-li-o-ma-ni-ac
bib-li-o-phile
bib-u-lous
bi-cam-er-al
bi-car-bo-nate
bi-ce-te-nary
 bi-cen-te-nar-ies
bi-cen-ten-ni-al
bi-ceps
bi-chlo-ride
bick-er
bi-con-cave
bi-con-vex
bi-cus-pid
 bi-cus-pi-dal
 bi-cus-pi-date
bi-cy-cle
 bi-cy-cled
 bi-cy-cling
 bi-cy-cler
 bi-cy-clist
bid
 bid-den
 bid-da-ble
 bid-der
bid-dy
 bid-dies
bide
 bid-ed
 bid-ing
bi-en-ni-al
 bi-en-ni-al-ly
bier
bi-fid
bi-fo-cal
 bi-fo-cals
bi-fur-cate
 bi-fur-cat-ed

bi-fur-cat-ing
bi-fur-ca-tion
big
 big-ger
 big-gest
big-a-my
 big-a-mies
 big-a-mist
 big-a-mous
big-heart-ed
big-horn
bight
big-no-ni-a
big-ot
 big-ot-ed
 big-ot-ed-ly
 big-ot-ry
 big-ot-ries
bi-jou
 bi-joux
bi-ju-gous
bi-ki-ni
bi-lat-er-al
 bi-lat-er-al-ly
bil-ber-ry
 bil-ber-ries
bilge
bil-i-ary
bi-lin-gual
bil-ious
bilk
bill
 bil-led
 bil-ling
bil-la-bong
bill-board
bill-let
bil-let-doux
bill-fold
bill-hook
bil-liards
bil-lings-gate
bil-lion

bil-lion-are
bil-lionth
bil-low
bil-low-y
bil-low-ier
bil-low-i-est
bil-ly goat
bi-met-al-lism
bi-met-al-list
bi-me-tal-lic
bi-month-ly
bi-month-lies
bi-na-ry
bi-nate
bin-au-ral
bind
bind-ing
bind-er
bind-ery
bind-er-ies
binge
bin-go
bin-na-cle
bi-noc-u-lar
bi-no-mi-al
bio-chem-is-try
bio-chem-i-cal
bio-chem-ist
bi-o-cide
bi-o-e-col-o-gy
bi-o-en-gi-neer-ing
bi-o-gen-e-sis
bi-o-ge-net-ic
bi-og-ra-phy
bi-og-ra-pher
bi-o-graph-ic
bi-o-graph-i-cal
bi-o-graph-i-cal-ly
bi-ol-o-gy
bi-o-log-i-cal
bi-ol-o-gist
bi-o-met-rics
bi-o-nom-ics

bi-o-phys-ics
bi-o-phys-i-cal
bi-o-phys-i-cist
bi-op-sy
bi-op-sies
bi-o-sphere
bi-o-tin
bi-par-ti-san
bi-par-tite
bi-par-ti-tion
bi-ped
bi-ped-al
bi-plane
bi-po-lar
bi-po-lar-i-ty
birch
birch-en
bird-bath
bird-brain
bird-brained
bird-call
bird-ie
bird-lime
bird-man
bird's-eye
bi-ret-ta
birth-day
birth-mark
birth-place
birth-right
birth-stone
bis-cuit
bi-sect
bi-sec-tion
bi-sec-tor
bi-sex-u-al
bish-op
bish-op-ric
bis-muth
bi-son
bisque
bis-ter
bis-tered

bis-tro
bis-tros
bi-sul-fide
bitch
bite
bit-ten
bit-ing
bit-ing-ly
bit-stock
bit-ter
bit-ter-ish
bit-ter-ly
bit-ter-ness
bit-tern
bit-ter-root
bit-ters
bit-ter-sweet
bi-tu-men
bi-tu-mi-nous coal
bi-va-lent
bi-va-lence
bi-valve
bi-val-vu-lar
biv-ou-ac
biv-ou-acked
biv-ou-ack-ing
bi-week-ly
bi-week-lies
bi-year-ly
bi-zarre
bi-zarre-ly
bi-zarre-ness
blab
blab-bed
blab-bing
blab-ber
blab-ber-mouth
black-ball
black-ber-ry
black-ber-ries
black-bird
black-board
black-en

black-guard
black-head
black-ing
black-jack
black-list
black-mail
black-out
black-smith
black-snake
black-top
blad-der
blade
  blad-ed
blame
  blamed
  blam-ing
  blam-a-ble
  blame-a-ble
  blame-ful
  blame-less
  blame-less-ly
  blame-less-ness
blame-wor-thy
blanch
  blanc-er
  blanch-ing
blanc-mange
bland
  bland-ly
  bland-ness
blan-dish
  blan-dish-er
  blan-dish-ment
blank
  blank-ly
  blank-ness
blan-ket
blare
  blared
  blar-ing
blar-ney
blas-pheme
  blas-phemed

blas-phem-ing
blas-phem-er
blas-phem-ies
blas-phe-my
blast-ed
bas-tu-la
blat
  blat-ted
  blat-ting
bla-tant
  bla-tan-cy
  bla-tant-ly
blath-er
blaze
  blazed
  blaz-ing
bla-zer
bleach
bleach-er
bleak
  bleak-ly
  bleak-ness
blear
  bleary
  blear-i-ness
bleed
  bleed-ing
  bleed-er
blem-ish
blench
blend
  blend-ed
  blend-ing
  blend-er
bless
  bless-ed
  bles-sing
  bless-ed-ness
blind
  blind-ing
  blind-ing-ly
  blind-ly
  blind-ness

blind-fold
blind-man's bluff
blink-er
bliss
  bliss-ful
  bliss-ful-ly
  bliss-ful-ness
blis-ter
  blis-ter-y
blithe
  blithe-ly
blithe-some
  blithe-some-ly
blitz-krieg
bliz-zard
block
  block-er
block-ade
  block-ad-ed
  block-ad-ing
  block-ad-er
block-bus-ter
block-head
block-house
block-ish
  block-ish-ly
blocky
blond
blood-curd-ling
blood bank
blood-ed
blood-hound
blood-less
  blood-less-ly
  blood-less-ness
blood-let-ting
blood pres-sure
blood re-la-tion
blood-shed
blood-shot
blood-stone
blood-suck-er
blood-thirst-y

blood-thirst-i-ly
bloody
blood-i-er
blood-i-est
blood-ied
blood-y-ing
blood-i-ly
blood-i-ness
bloom-ers
bloom-ing
bloom-ing-ly
bloop-er
blos-som
blot
blot-ted
blot-ting
blotch
blotchy
blot-ter
blow
blown
blow-ing
blow-er
blow-fly
blow-flies
blow-gun
blow-hole
blow-out
blow-pipe
blow-torch
blow-up
blow-y
blowz-y
blub-ber
blub-bery
blu-cher
bludg-eon
blue
blu-er
blu-est
blue-ness
blue-bell
blue-ber-ry

blue-ber-ries
blue-bird
blue-blood-ed
blue-bon-net
blue-coat
blue-col-lar
blue-fish
blue-grass
blue-jac-ket
blue-nose
blue-pen-cil
blue-print
blu-et
blu-ing
blun-der
blun-der-er
blun-der-ing-ly
blun-der-buss
blunt
blunt-ly
blunt-ness
blur
blur-red
blur-ring
blur-ry
blush
blushed
blush-ing
blush-ing-ly
blus-ter
blus-ter-er
blus-ter-ing-ly
blus-ter-ous
blus-ter-y
bo-a
board-er
board-walk
boast
boas-ter
boast-ful
boast-ful-ness
boast-ing-ly
boat-house

boat-man
boat-swain
bob
bob-bed
bob-bing
bob-bin
bob-ble
bob-bled
bob-bling
bob-by-pin
bob-cat
bob-o-link
bob-sled
bob-tail
bob-white
bock
bode
bod-ed
bod-ing
bod-ice
bod-i-ly
bod-kin
bod-y
bod-ied
bod-y-ing
bod-y-guard
bog
bog-gy
bog-ging
bo-gey
bog-gle
bog-gled
bog-gling
bog-gler
bo-gus
bo-gy
boil-er
bois-ter-ous
bois-ter-ous-ly
bo-la
bo-las
bold
bold-ly

bold-ness
bold-face
bo-le-ro
bol-lix
boli-worm
boll weevil
bo-lo
bo-lo-gna
bo-lo-ney
bol-ster
  bol-ster-er
bolt
  bolt-ed
  bolt-er
bom-bard
  bom-bard-ment
bom-bar-dier
bom-bast
  bom-bas-tic
  bom-bas-ti-cal-ly
bomb-er
bomb-proof
bomb-shell
bomb-sight
bo-na fide
bo-nan-za
bon-bon
bond-age
bond-ed
bond-man
  bond-men
  bonds-men
bone
  boned
  bon-ing
bone-head
bon-er
bon-fire
bon-go
  bon-gos
  bon-gies
bon-ho-mie
bo-ni-to

bon-net
bon-ny
bon-sai
bo-nus
  bo-nus-es
bon voy-age
bon-y
  bon-i-er
  bon-i-est
boo
  booed
  boo-ing
boo-by
  boo-bies
boo-by trap
boo-dle
boo-hoo
  boo-hooed
  boo-hoo-ing
book
  book-bind-er
book-case
book-end
book-ie
book-ish
book-keep-ing
  book-keep-er
book-let
book-mak-er
book-mark
book-mo-bile
book-plate
book-sell-er
  book-sell-ing
book-stall
book-worm
boo-me-rang
boon docks
boon-dog-gle
boor
  boor-ish
boost
  boost-er

boot-black
boot-ee
boot-jack
boot-leg
  boot-legged
  boot-leg-ging
  boot-leg-ger
boot-less
  boot-less-ly
boot-lick
  boot-lick-er
boo-ty
  boo-ties
booze
  booz-er
  booz-y
  booz-i-er
  booz-i-est
bo-rax
bor-der
  bor-der-ed
  bor-der-ing
bor-der-land
bor-der-line
bore
  bored
  bor-ing
  bor-er
bo-re-al
bore-dom
bo-ric
bo-ron
bor-ough
bor-row
  bor-row-er
borsch
bosh
bosk-y
bos-om
boss-ism
boss-y
  boss-i-er
  boss-i-est

bo-sun
bot-a-ny
  bo-tan-i-cal
  bot-a-nist
  bot-a-nize
botch
  botchy
  botch-i-er
  botch-i-est
both-er
  both-er-some
bot-tle
  bot-tled
  bot-tling
  bot-tle-ful
  bot-tler
bot-tle-neck
bot-tom
  bot-tom-less
bot-u-lism
bou-doir
bouf-fant
bough
bought
bouil-lon
boul-der
boul-e-vard
bounce
  bounced
  bounc-ing
bound
bound-a-ry
  bound-a-ries
bound-er
bound-less
  bound-less-ness
boun-te-ous
  boun-te-ous-ness
boun-ti-ful
boun-ty
  boun-ties
bou-quet
bour-bon

bour-geois
bour-geoi-sie
bou-tique
bou-ton-niere
bo-vine
bow-el
bow-ery
bow-ie
bow-ing
bowl
bow-leg
  bow-leg-ged
bowl-er
bow-line
bow-ling
bow-man
  bow-men
bow-string
box
  box-ful
  box-fuls
box-car
box-er
box-ing
box of-fice
boy
  boy-hood
  boy-ish
  boy-ish-ly
boy-cott
boy-friend
boy-sen-ber-ry
  boy-sen-ber-ries
brace
  bra-ced
  brac-ing
brace-let
brac-er
bra-ces
brack-en
brack-et
brack-ish
  brack-ish-ness

bract
brae
brag
  brag-ged
  brag-ging
brag-gart
braid
  braid-er
  braid-ing
braille
brain-child
brain-less
brain-pow-er
brain-storm
  brain-storm-ing
brain-wash-ing
brain-y
  brain-i-er
  brain-i-est
braise
  braised
  brais-ing
bram-ble
  bram-bly
branch
  branch-ed
brand
  brand-er
brand-ish
brand-new
bran-dy
  bran-dies
  bran-died
  bran-dy-ing
bra-sier
bras-se-rie
  bras-se-ries
bras-siere
brassy
  brass-i-er
  brass-i-est
brat
  brat-tish

brat-ty
bra-va-do
brave
  braved
  brav-ing
  brav-ery
bra-vo
  bra-vos
bra-vu-ra
brawl
  braw-ler
brawn
  brawny
  brawn-i-er
bra-zen
bra-zier
breach
bread
  bread-ed
breadth-ways
break
  break-ing
  break-a-ble
break-age
brak-er
breath
breathe
  breathed
  breath-ing
breath-er
breath-ing
breath-tak-ing
  breath-tak-ing-ly
breathy
  breath-i-er
  breath-i-est
breech-es
breech-load-er
bred
breed
  breed-ing
breeze
  breezy

breez-i-er
breez-i-est
breth-ren
bre-vet
  bre-vet-ted
  bre-vet-ting
bre-vi-a-ry
  bre-vi-a-ries
brev-i-ty
bri-ar
  bri-ary
bribe
  bribed
  brib-ing
  brib-a-ble
  brib-er-ies
birb-ery
bric-a-brac
brick-lay-er
  brick-lay-ing
brick-work
bride
  brid-al
bride-groom
brides-maid
bridge
bri-dle
  bri-dled
  bri-dling
brief
  brief-ly
  brief-ing
bri-er
bri-gade
bri-a-dier
brig-an-tine
bright
  bright-ly
  bright-en
bril-liance
  bril-lian-cy
  bril-liant
brim

brimmed
brim-ming
brim-stone
brine
briny
bring
  bring-ing
brink
bri-oche
bri-quet
  bri-quette
brisk
  brisk-ly
bris-ket
bris-tle
  bris-tled
britch-es
brit-tle
broach
  broached
  broach-ing
broad-cast
  broad-cast-ed
  broad-cast-ing
broad-cloth
broad-mind-ed
broad-side
bro-cade
  bro-cad-ed
  bro-cad-ing
broc-co-li
bro-chure
broil-er
bro-ken
bro-ker
bro-ker-age
bro-mide
bro-mine
bron-chi
  bron-chi-al
  bron-chi-tis
  bron-chue
bron-co

bron-cos
bron-to-saur
bronze
bronz-ed
bronz-ing
brooch
brood
brood-ing
brook
broom-stick
broth-el
broth-er
broth-ers-in-law
broth-er-ly
brow-beat
brow-beat-en
brow-beat-ing
brown
brown-ie
browse
browsed
brows-ing
bru-in
bruise
bruis-ed
bruis-er
bruis-ing
brunch
bru-net
brusque
bru-tal
bru-tal-i-ty
bru-tal-ize
bru-tal-ized
bru-tal-iz-ing
bru-tal-i-za-tion
brut-ish
bub-ble
bub-bled
bub-bling
bub-bler
bu-bon-ic plague

buc-ca-neer
buck-board
buck-et
buck-et-ed
buck-et-ing
buck-eye
buck-le
buck-tooth
buck-teeth
buck-toothed
buck-wheat
bu-col-ic
bud
bud-ded
bud-ding
bud-dy
budge
budg-et
buff-er
buf-fet
buf-fet-ed
buf-fet-ing
bug-a-boo
bug-gy
bug-gi-er
bug-gi-est
bu-gle
bu-gled
bu-gling
bu-gler
build
build-er
build-ing
built--in
built-up
bulb
bul-ba-ceous
bul-bar
bul-bous
bulge
bulged
bulg-ing
bulgy

bulk-head
bulk-y
bulk-i-er
bulk-i-est
bulk-i-ly
bul-let
bul-le-tin
bul-let-proof
bull-fight
bull-fight-er
bull-fight-ing
bull-finch
bul-lion
bull-pen
bull's-eye
bul-ly
bul-lies
bul-lied
bul-ly-ing
bul-rush
bul-wark
bum
bum-mer
bum-mest
bum-ble-bee
bump-er
bump-kin
bump-tious
bump-y
bump-i-er
bump-i-est
bunch
bunchy
bun-co
bun-combe
bun-dle
bun-dled
bun-dling
bun-ga-low
bun-gle
bun-gled
bun-gling
bun-gler

bun-ion
bunk-er
bunk-house
bun-ko
bun-kum
bun-ny
  bun-nies
bun-ting
bu-oy
buoy-an-cy
  buoy-ant
  buoy-ant-ly
bur-ble
bur-den
bur-den-some
bur-dock
bu-rette
burg-er
bur-gess
bur-glar
  bur-glar-ize
  bur-glar-ized
  bur-glar-iz-ing
  bur-gla-ries
  bur-gla-ry
bur-gle
  bur-gled
  bur-gling
bur-i-al
bur-lap
bur-lesque
  bur-lesqued
  bur-les-quing
  bur-les-quer
bur-ly
  bur-li-er
  bur-li-est
burn
  burn-ed
  burnt
  burn-ing
  burn-a-ble
burn-er

bur-nish
  bur-nish-er
bur-noose
burn-sides
burp
burr
  burred
  bur-ring
bur-ro
  bur-ros
bur-row
  bur-row-er
bur-sa
  bur-sae
  bur-sal
bur-sar
  bur-sa-ri-al
  bur-sa-ry
  bur-sa-ries
bur-si-tis
burst
  burst-ing
  burst-er
bur-y
  bur-ied
  bur-y-ing
bus-boy
bus-by
  bus-bies
bushed
bu-shi-do
bush-ing
bush-man
  bush-men
bush-mas-ter
bush-whack
  bush-whack-er
  bush-whack-ing
bush-y
  bush-i-er
  bush-i-est
bus-i-ly
busi-ness

busi-ness-like
busi-ness-man
  busi-ness-men
  busi-ness-wom-an
bus-kin
  bus-kined
bus-tard
bus-tle
  bus-tled
  bus-tling
  bus-tler
bus-y
  bus-i-er
  bus-i-est
  bus-ied
  bus-y-ing
bu-ta-di-ene
bu-tane
butch-er
butch-ery
  butch-er-ies
but-ler
butte
but-ton
but-tress
bu-ty-ric
bux-om
buy
  bought
  buy-ing
buz-zard
by-gong
by-law
byte

C

cab
ca-bal
  ca-balled
  ca-ball-ing
cab-a-la
  cab-a-lis-tic

cab-a-lis-ti-cal
ca-bal-le-ro
ca-ban-a
ca-bane
cab-a-ret
cab-bage
cab-by
cab-in
cab-i-net
cab-i-net-maker
cab-i-net-work
ca-ble
  ca-bled
  ca-bling
ca-ble-gram
ca-ble-laid
ca-ble-way
cab-o-chon
ca-boo-dle
ca-boose
cab-o-tage
ca-bret-ta
ca-bril-la
cab-ri-ole
cab-ri-o-let
cab-stand
ca-ca-o
cach-a-lot
cache
  cached
  cach-ing
cache-pot
ca-chet
ca-chou
ca-chu-cha
ca-cique
cack-le
  cackler
cac-o-e-thes
ca-coph-o-ny
  ca-coph-o-nies
  ca-coph-o-ous
  ca-coph-o-ous-ly

cac-ta-ceuos
cac-toid
cac-tus
  cac-tus-es
cac-ti
ca-cu-mi-nal
cad
  cad-dish
ca-das-tre
ca-dav-er
  ca-dav-er-ic
  ca-dav-er-ous
cad-die
  cad-died
cad-dis
cad-dis fly
cad-dish
cad-dis-wor
cad-dy
  cad-dies
cade
ca-delle
ca-dence
ca-den-za
ca-det
cadge
  cadger
  cadged
  cadg-ing
cad-mi-um
ca-dre
ca-du-ce-us
  ca-du-cei
ca-du-ci-ty
cea-su-ra
  cae-su-rae
ca-fe
caf-e-te-ria
caf-feine
caf-tan
cage
  caged
  cag-er

ca-gey
ca-hier
ca-hoot
cai-man
cairn
cais-son
cai-tiff
caj-e-put
ca-jole
cake
  caked
cal-a-bash
cal-a-ba-zil-l
cal-a-boose
ca-la-di-um
cal-a-man-de
cal-a-mine
cal-a-mint
ca-lam-i-ty
  ca-lam-i-ties
  ca-lam-i-tous
  ca-lam-i-tous-ly
cal-a-mon-din
cal-a-mus
cal-an-do
cal-ca-ne-us
cal-car
cal-car-e-ous
cal-ce-i-form
cal-cic
cal-ci-fy
  cal-ci-fied
  cal-ci-fy-ing
  cal-ci-fi-ca-tion
cal-ci-mine
cal-cine
  cal-cin-a-tion
cal-cite
cal-ci-um
cal-cu-la-ble
  cal-cu-la-bil-i-ty
cal-cu-late
  cal-cu-lat-ed

cal-cu-lat-ing
cal-cu-la-tion
cal-cu-la-tor
cal-cu-lus
cal-cu-lus-es
cal-de-ra
cal-dron
cal-e-fac-to-ry
cal-en-dar
cal-en-der
ca-len-dri-cal
cal-ends
ca-len-du-la
cal-en-ture
ca-les-cence
caft
cafe-skin
cal-i-ber
cal-i-brate
cal-i-brat-ed
cal-i-brat-ing
cal-i-bra-tion
cal-i-co
cal-i-coes
ca-lic-u-lus
Cal-i-for-nia
cal-i-for-nite
cal-i-pash
cal-i-per
ca-liph
cal-iph-ate
cal-is-then-ics
calk
call
cal-la
call-a-ble
call-board
call-boy
cal-lig-ra-pher
cal-lig-ra-phy
call-ing
cal-li-o-pe
cal-lose

cal-los-i-ty
cal-lous
cal-loused
cal-lous-ly
cal-lous-ness
cal-low
cal-lus
cal-lus-es
calm
cal-ma-tive
cal-o-mel
ca-lor-ic
cal-o-rie
cal-o-ries
cal-o-rif-ic
cal-o-rim-e-te
ca-lotte
cal-trops
cal-u-met
ca-lum-ni-ate
cal-um-ny
cal-va-dos
Cal-va-ry
calve
calved
calx
ca-lyp-so
ca-lyp-sos
ca-lyp-tra
ca-lyx
ca-lyx-es
cal-y-ces
cam
ca-ma-ra-de-r
ca-ma-ra-de-rie
cam-a-ril-la
cam-ber
cam-bist
cam-bi-um
cam-bric
came
cam-el
ca-mel-lia

ca-mel-o-pard
cam-e-o
cam-era
cam-er-al
cam-i-on
ca-mise
cam-i-sole
cam-let
cam-o-mile
cam-ou-flage
cam-ou-flaged
cam-ou-flag-ing
camp
cam-paign
cam-pa-ni-le
cam-pa-ni-les
cam-pan-u-late
camp-er
cam-pes-tral
camp-fire
camp-ground
cam-phor
cam-phor-ic
cam-pim-e-ter
camp-site
cam-pus
cam-pus-es
camp-y
cam-shaft
can
canned
can-ning
Can-a-da
Canadian
ca-nal
ca-naled
ca-nal-ing
can-a-lic-u-lus
ca-nal-ize
ca-nard
ca-nar-y
ca-nas-ta
can-can

can-cel
  can-celed
  can-cel-ing
  can-cel-la-tion
can-cer
  can-cer-ous
can-cri-zans
can-de-la-bra
can-de-la-brum
can-did
can-di-da-cy
  can-di-da-cies
  can-di-date
can-died
can-dle
can-dle-ber-ry
can-dle-light
can-dle-pin
can-dle-pow-er
can-dor
can-dy
  can-dies
  can-dy-ing
candy-tuft
cane
cane-brake
ca-nel-la
can-er
ca-nine
can-is-ter
can-ker
  can-ker-ous
can-na
can-na-bin
can-na-bis
canned
can-ner
can-nery
  can-ner-ies
can-ni-bal
  can-ni-bal-ize
  can-ni-bal-ism
  can-ni-ba-lis-tic

can-ni-kin
can-non
can-non-ade
can-non-ball
can-non-eer
can-nu-la
can-ny
  can-nier
can-not
ca-noe
can-on
ca-non-i-cal
can-on-ize
  can-on-ized
  can-on-i-za-tion
can-o-py
cant
can't
can-ta-bi-le
can-ta-loup
  can-ta-loupe
  can-ta-lope
can-tan-ker-ous
can-ta-ta
can-ta-trice
can-teen
can-ter
can-thar-is
can-thus
can-ti-cle
can-ti-lev-er
can-to
  can-tos
can-ton
can-ton-ment
can-tor
can-tus
can-vas
can-vass
can-yon
cap
ca-pa-bil-i-ty
  cap-pa-bil-i-ties

ca-pa-ble
  ca-pa-bly
ca-pa-cious
ca-pac-i-tance
ca-pac-i-tate
  ca-pac-i-tat-ed
  ca-pac-i-tat-ing
ca-pac-i-tive
ca-pac-i-tor
ca-pac-i-ty
  ca-pac-i-ties
ca-par-i-son
cape
cap-e-lin
ca-per
cap-er-cail-li
cape-skin
ca-pi-as
cap-il-lar-i-ty
cap-il-lar-y
  cap-il-lar-ies
cap-i-tal
cap-i-tal-ism
cap-i-tal-ist
  capitalistic
cap-i-ta-tion
cap-i-tol
ca-pit-u-late
  ca-pit-u-lat-ed
  ca-pit-u-lat-ing
  ca-pit-u-la-tor
ca-pit-u-lum
ca-pon
ca-pote
capric acid
ca-price
  ca-pri-cious
  ca-pri-cious-ly
ca-pri-cious
Capricorn
cap-ri-fi-ca-t
cap-ri-fig
cap-ri-ole

cap-ri-oled
cap-ri-ol-ing
cap-si-cum
cap-size
cap-stan
cap-stone
cap-su-late
cap-su-lated
capsulation
cap-sule
cap-su-lar
cap-tain
cap-tain-cy
captainship
cap-tion
cap-tious
cap-tious-ness
cap-ti-vate
captivation
captivator
cap-tive
cap-tiv-i-ty
cap-tiv-i-ties
cap-tor
cap-ture
cap-tured
cap-tur-ing
cap-tur-er
ca-puche
cap-y-ba-ra
car
ca-ra-ca-ra
car-ack
car-a-cole
car-a-coled
car-a-col-ing
car-a-cul
ca-rafe
car-a-mel
car-a-mel-ize
ca-ran-gid
car-a-pace
car-at

car-a-van
car-a-van-sa-ry
car-a-van-sa-ries
car-a-vel
car-a-way
car-ba-mate
car-ba-zole
car-bide
car-bi-nol
car-bo-hy-drate
car-bo-late
car-bo-lat-ed
car-bol-ic
car-bon
carbonization
carbonize
cabonous
car-bo-na-ceous
car-bo-na-do
car-bo-nate
car-bo-na-tion
carbon copy
carbon dating
carbon dioxide
carbon disulfide
carbonic acid
carbonium ion
car-bon-ize
car-bon-ized
car-bon-iz-ing
car-bon-i-za-tion
car-bon mon-ox-ide
carbon paper
carbon process
car-boy
car-bun-cle
car-bu-ret
car-bu-re-tor
car-cass
car-cin-o-gen
car-cin-o-gen-ic
car-ci-no-ma
car-ci-no-mas

car-ci-no-ma-ta
car-ci-no-ma-to-sis
card
car-da-mom
car-di-ac
cardiac massage
car-di-gan
car-di-nal
car-di-o-gram
car-di-o-graph
car-di-o-graphy
car-di-oid
car-di-ol-o-gy
cardiologist
car-di-o-vas-cu-lar
car-di-tis
car-doon
care
ca-reen
ca-reer
ca-reer-ism
care-free
care-ful
care-ful-ly
care-less
care-less-ly
care-less-ness
ca-ress
ca-ress-ing-ly
car-et
care-tak-er
care-worn
car-fare
car-go
car-gos
car-hop
Caribbean Sea
car-i-bou
car-i-ca-ture
car-i-ca-tured
car-i-ca-tur-ing
car-i-ca-tur-ist
car-ies

car-il-lon
car-il-lonned
car-i-lon-ning
car-i-o-ca
car-min-a-tive
car-mine
car-nage
car-nal
car-nal-i-ty
car-nal-ly
car-nall-ite
car-nas-si-al
car-na-tion
car-nel-ian
car-ni-val
car-ni-vore
car-niv-o-rous
car-niv-o-rous-ly
car-ob
car-ol
car-om
car-o-tene
ca-rot-id
ca-rot-i-noid
ca-rous-al
ca-rouse
ca-roused
ca-rous-ing
ca-rous-er
car-ou-sel
carp
car-pel
car-pen-ter
car-pen-try
car-pet
car-pet-ing
car-pol-o-gy
car-port
car-pus
car-riage
car-ri-er
car-ri-ole
car-rot

car-roty
car-rousel
car-ry
car-ried
car-ry-ing
car-ry-all
cart
cart-age
carte-blanche
car-tel
car-ti-lage
car-ti-lag-i-nous
car-to-gram
car-tog-ra-phy
car-tog-ra-pher
car-to-graph-ic
car-ton
car-toon
car-toon-ist
car-tridge
car-tu-lar-y
cart-wheel
car-va-crol
carve
car-y-at-id
car-vel
car-y-at-id
car-y-at-ids
car-y-at-i-des
car-y-op-sis
ca-sa-ba
cas-cade
cas-cad-ed
cas-cad-ing
cas-ca-ril-la
case
ca-se-a-tion
ca-sein
case-mate
case-mat-ed
case-ment
case-ment-ed
case-work

case-work-er
cash
cash-ew
cash-ier
cash-mere
cas-ing
ca-si-no
cask
cas-ket
cas-que
cas-sa-va
cas-se-role
cas-sette
cas-sit-er-ite
cas-si-no
cas-sock
cas-socked
cas-so-wary
cas-so-war-ies
cast
cast-ing
cas-ta-net
cast-a-way
caste
cas-tel-lat-ed
cast-er
cas-ti-gate
cas-ti-gat-ed
cas-ti-gat-ion
cas-ti-gat-or
cast-ing
cast i-ron
cas-tle
cast-off
cas-tor
cas-trate
cas-trat-ed
cas-trat-er
cas-tra-tion
cas-u-al
cas-u-al-ty
cas-u-al-ties
cas-u-ist

cas-u-ist-ic
cas-u-ist-ry
cas-u-ist-ries
cat
ca-tab-o-lism
cat-a-chre-sis
cat-a-clysm
cat-a-cly-mal
cat-a-comb
ca-tad-ro-mous
cat-a-falque
cat-a-lep-sy
cat-a-lep-tic
cat-a-log
cat-a-loged
cat-a-log-ing
cat-a-log-er
ca-tal-pa
ca-tal-y-sis
ca-tal-y-ses
cat-a-lyt-ic
cat-a-lyst
cat-a-lyze
cat-a-lyzed
cat-a-lyz-ing
cat-a-ma-ran
cat-am-ne-sis
cat-a-mount
cat-a-pla-sia
cat-a-plex-y
cat-a-pult
cat-a-ract
ca-tarrh
ca-tas-ta-sis
ca-tas-tro-phe
cat-as-troph-ic
cat-a-to-ni-a
ca-taw-ba
cat-bird
cat-call
catch
caught
catch-ing

catch-all
catch-er
catch-up
cat-e-chism
cat-e-chis-mal
cat-e-chize
cat-e-chu
cat-e-chu-men
cat-e-gor-i-cal
cat-e-gor-i-cal-ly
cat-e-go-ry
cat-a-go-ries
cat-e-gor-ize
cat-e-gor-ized
cat-e-gor-iz-ing
cat-e-nate
ca-ter
ca-ter-er
cat-er-pil-lar
ca-ter-waul
cat-fish
cat-fish-es
cat-gut
cat-head
ca-thar-sis
ca-thar-ses
ca-thar-tic
ca-the-dral
cath-e- ter-ize
cath-e-ter
ca-thex-is
cath-ode
ca-thol-i-con
cat-i-on
cat-nap
cat-napped
cat-nap-ping
cat-nip
cat's-paw
cat-sup
cat-tail
cat-ta-lo
cat-tle

cat-tle-man
cat-tleya
cat-ty
cat-tier
cat-ti-est
cat-ti-ly
cat-ti-ness
cat-ty-cor-ner
Cau-ca-sian
cau-cus
cau-cus-es
cau-cused
cau-cus-ing
cau-dal
cau-date
cau-dat-ed
cau-dex
cau-dle
caught
caul-dron
cau-li-flow-er
caulk
caulk-er
caus-al
caus-al-ly
cau-sal-i-ty
cau-sal-i-ties
cau-sa-tion
cause
cau-se-rie
cause-way
caus-tic
caus-ti-cal-ly
cau-ter-ize
cau-ter-ized
cau-ter-iz-ing
cau-ter-i-za-tion
cau-ter-y
cau-ter-ies
cau-tion
cau-tion-ary
cau-tious
cav-al-cade

cav-a-lier
  cav-a-lier-ly
cav-al-ry
ca-vate
cav-a-ti-na
cave
ca-ve-at
cave-man
cav-ern
  cav-ern-ous
cav-ier
cav-il
  cav-iled
  cav-il-ing
cav-i-ty
  cav-i-ties
ca-vort
cay
cay-enne
cay-man
  cay-mans
cay-use
cease
cease-fire
cease-less
ce-cum
ce-dar
cede
  ced-ed
  ced-ing
ce-dil-la
cei-ba
ceil-ing
ceil-om-e-ter
cel-a-don
cel-an-dine
cel-a-brant
cel-e-brate
  cel-e-brat-ed
  cel-e-brat-ing
  cel-e-bra-tion
  cel-e-bra-tor
ce-leb-ri-ty

ce-leb-ri-ties
ce-ler-i-ty
cel-er-y
ce-les-ta
ce-les-tial
ce-li-ac
cel-i-ba-cy
  cel-i-bate
cell
cel-lar
cel-lar-ette
cell-block
cel-lo
  cel-los
  cel-list
cel-lo-phane
cel-lu-lar
cel-lu-lase
cel-lule
cel-lu-lite
cel-lu-lose
ce-ment
ce-men-ta-tion
ce-men-tum
cem-e-ter-y
ce-no-bite
ce-nog-a-my
cen-o-taph
cen-ser
cen-sor
  cen-so-ri-al
  cen-sor-ship
cen-so-ri-ous
  cen-so-ri-ous-ly
  cen-so-ri-ous-ness
cen-sure
  cen-sured
  cen-sur-ing
  cen-sur-er
cen-sus
  cen-sus-es
  cen-sused
  cen-sus-ing

cent
cen-tare
cen-taur
cen-te-nar-i-an
cen-te-na-ry
  cen-te-nar-ies
cen-ten-ni-al
cen-ter
cen-ti-are
cen-ti-grade
cen-ti-gram
cen-tile
cen-ti-li-ter
cen-ti-me-ter
cen-ti-pede
cen-to
cen-tral
  cen-tral-ize
  cen-tral-ized
  cen-tral-iz-ing
cen-trif-u-gal
cen-tri-fuge
cen-trip-e-tal
cen-tro-bar-ic
cen-tro-sphere
cen-tu-ri-an
cen-tu-ry
  cen-tu-ries
ceph-a-lal-gia
ce-phal-ic
ceph-a-li-za-tion
ceph-a-lo-pod
ceph-a-lo-tho-rax
ce-ram-ic
  ce-ram-ics
cer-a-mist
ce-rar-gy-rite
ce-rate
cer-car-i-a
cere
ce-re-al
cer-e-bel-lum
cer-e-bral

cer-e-brate
cer-e-brum
cer-e-mo-ni-al
  cer-e-mo-no-al-ism
cer-e-mo-ny
  cer-e-mo-nies
ce-rise
ce-rite
cer-met
ce-ro
ce-ro-plas-tic
cer-tain
cer-tain-ty
  cer-tain-ties
cer-tif-i-cate
  cer-tif-i-ca-tion
cer-ti-fy
  cer-ti-fied
  cer-ti-fy-ing
cer-ti-o-ra-ri
cer-ti-tude
ce-ru-le-an
ce-ruse
cer-ve-lat
cer-vi-cal
cer-vi-ci-tis
cer-vix
  cer-vix-es
  cer-vi-ces
ce-sar-ean
ce-si-um
ces-sa-tion
ces-sion
cess-pool
ces-tode
ce-ta-cean
  ce-ta-ceous
ces-tus
ce-ta-cean
ce-tane
chafe
  chafed
  chaf-ing

chaf-er
chaff
  chaf-fer
  chaff-er-er
chaf-finch
chafing dish
cha-grin
  cha-grined
  cha-grin-ing
chain
chain letter
chain reaction
chain saw
chain-smoke
chair
chair lift
chair-man
  chair-men
chair-person
chaise
chaise longue
chal-ced-o-ny
chal-cocite
chal-et
chal-ice
chalk
chalk-board
chalk-stone
chalk up
challah
chal-lenge
  chal-lenged
  chal-leng-ing
challis
chalone
chalumeau
cha-lyb-e-ate
cham-ber
cham-ber-lain
cham-ber-maid
cham-bray
cha-me-le-on
cham-fer

cham-ois
champ
cham-pagne
cham-per-ty
cham-pi-gnon
cham-pi-on
  cham-pi-on-ship
chance
chance-ful
chan-cel-lor
chance-med-ley
chan-cer-y
chan-cre
chan-croid
chanc-y
  chanc-i-er
  chanc-i-est
chan-de-lier
chan-dler
change
  changed
  chang-ing
  chang-a-ble
chan-nel
chant
chan-te-relle
chan-teuse
chan-ti-cleer
cha-os
cha-ot-ic
chap
cha-pa-re-jos
chap-ar-ral
cha-peau
  cha-peaux
chap-el
chap-e-ron
chap-er-one
chap-fall-en
chap-i-ter
chap-lain
chap-let
chaps

chap-ter
cha-que-ta
char
  charred
  char-ring
char-a-cin
char-ac-ter
char-ac-ter-is-tic
char-ac-ter-ize
  char-ac-ter-ized
  char-ac-ter-iz-ing
  char-ac-ter-i-za-tion
  char-ac-ter-iz-er
cha-rade
char-coal
chard
charge
  charged
  charg-ing
  charg-er
char-i-ot
  char-i-ot-eer
cha-ris-ma
char-i-ta-ble
  char-i-ta-ble-ness
  char-i-ta-bly
char-i-ty
  char-i-ties
cha-riv-a-ri
char-kha
char-la-tan
  char-la-tan-ism
char-ley horse
char-lock
char-lotte
charm
  charm-ing
char-meuse
char-nel
char-qui
chart
char-ta-ceous
char-ter

char-tist
char-treuse
char-wom-an
chary
  char-i-er
  char-i-est
chase
  chased
  chas-ing
  chas-er
chasm
chas-sis
chaste
  chaste-ly
chas-ten
chas-tise
  chas-tised
  chas-tis-ing
  chas-tis-ment
  chas-tis-er
  chas-ti-ty
chas-u-ble
chat
  chat-ted
  chat-ting
cha-teau
  cha-teaux
chat-e-laine
cha-toy-ant
chat-tel
chat-ter
chat-ter-box
chat-ty
  chat-ti-er
  chat-ti-est
  chat-ti-ly
  chat-ti-ness
chauf-feur
chaus-sure
chau-vin-ist
  chau-vin-ism
  chau-vin-is-tic
chaw

cheap
  cheap-ly
  cheap-ness
  cheap-en
cheap-skate
cheat
check
check-er-board
check-list
check-mate
  check-mat-ed
  check-mat-ing
check-out
check-point
check-room
check-up
ched-dar
cheek
cheek-bone
cheek-y
  cheek-i-er
  cheek-i-est
  cheek-i-ness
cheer
cheer-ful
  cheer-ful-ly
  cheer-ful-ness
cheer-lead-er
cheer-less
  cheer-less-ly
  cheer-less-ness
chee-y
  cheer-i-er
  cheer-i-est
  cheer-i-ly
  cheer-i-ness
cheese
cheese-burg-er
cheese-cake
cheese-cloth
chees-y
  chees-i-er
  chees-i-est

chees-i-ness
chee-tah
chef
che-la
che-lo-ni-an
chem-i-cal
  chem-i-cal-ly
che-mise
chem-ist
chem-is-try
chem-o-ther-a-py
che-mot-ro-pism
chem-ur-gy
che-nille
cher-ish
che-root
cher-ry
  cher-ries
cher-so-nese
chert
cher-ub
  cher-ubs
  cher-u-bim
  che-ru-bic
cher-vil
chess
chess-man
  chess-men
chest
chest-nut
chest-y
  chest-i-er
  chest-i-est
chev-ron
chew
  chew-er
che-wink
chi-an-ti
chi-a-ro-scu-ro
chi-ca-lo-te
chi-cane
chi-can-ery
  cha-can-er-ies

chi-chi
chick
chick-a-dee
chic-ken
chic-ken-heart-ed
chic-le
chic-o-ry
  chic-o-ries
chide
  chid-ed
chief
  chief-ly
chief-tain
chif-fon
chif-fo-nier
chig-ger
chi-gnon
chig-oe
chil-blain
child
chil-dren
child-bear-ing
child-birth
child-hood
child-ish
  child-ish-ly
  child-like
chili
  chil-ies
chill
  chill-ing-ly
chill-y
  chill-i-er
  chill-i-est
  chill-i-ness
chime
chi-me-ra
chi-mer-ic
  chi-mer-i-cal
  chi-mer-i-cal-ly
  chi-mer-i-cal-ness
chim-ney
chim-pan-zee

chin
chinned
chin-ning
chi-na
chine
Chi-nese
chi-no
chi-nos
chi-noi-se-rie
chin-qua-pin
chintz-y
  chintz-i-er
  chintz-i-est
chip
chipped
chip-ping
chip-munk
chip-per
chi-rog-ra-pher
chi-rog-ra-phy
chi-rop-o-dist
chi-ro-prac-tic
chi-ro-prac-tor
chirp
chirr
chis-el
  chis-eled
  chis-el-ing
  chis-el-er
chit-chat
chi-tin
chi-ton
chit-ter-ling
chiv-al-ry
  chiv-al-ries
  chiv-al-ric
  chiv-al-rous
  chiv-al-rous-ly
  chiv-al-rous-ness
chive
chlo-ral
chlo-ral-ose
chlo-rate

chlo-ride
chlo-rin-ate
chlo-rine
chlo-rite
chlo-ro-ben-zene
chlo-ro-form
clo-ro-phyll
chlo-ro-pic-rin
chlo-ro-sis
chock
chock-full
choc-o-late
  choc-o-laty
choice
  choice-ly
  choice-ness
choir
choir-boy
choke
  choked
  chok-ing
  chok-er
chol-e-cys-tec-to-my
chol-er
chol-era
chol-er-ic
cho-les-te-rol
cho-line
chol-la
choose
  chose
  cho-sen
  choos-ing
choos-y
  choos-i-er
  choos-i-est
chop
  chopped
  chop-ping
chop-per
  chop-pi-ness
chop-py
  chop-pi-er

chop-i-est
chop-sticks
chop su-ey
cho-ral
  cho-ral-ly
cho-rale
chord
  chord-al
chore
cho-rea
cho-re-og-ra-phy
  cho-re-og-ra-pher
  cho-re-o-graph-ic
cho-ric
chor-is-ter
cho-rog-ra-phy
chor-tle
  chor-tled
  chor-tling
cho-rus
  cho-rus-es
  cho-rused
  cho-rus-ing
chose
cho-sen
chow-der
chow mein
chrism
Christ
chris-ten
  chris-ten-ing
Chris-tian
Chis-ti-an-i-ty
  Chris-ti-an-i-ties
Christ-mas
chro-mate
chro-mat-ic
  chro-mat-i-cal-ly
chro-mat-ics
chro-ma-tin
chro-mic
chro-mi-um
chro-mo

chro-mus
chro-mo-some
chro-mo-sphere
chron-ic
  chron-i-cal-ly
chron-i-cle
  chron-i-cled
  chron-i-cling
  chron-i-cler
chron-o-log-i-cal
  chron-o-log-i-cal-ly
chro-nol-o-gy
  chro-nol-o-gies
  chro-nol-o-gist
chro-nom-e-ter
  chron-o-met-ric
chrys-a-lis
  chry-sa-lis-es
  chry-sal-i-des
chry-san-the-mum
chrys-o-lite
chub-by
  chub-bi-er
  chub-bi-est
  chub-bi-ness
chuck-full
chuck-le
  chuck-led
  chuck-ling
chuk-ker
chum-my
  chum-mi-er
  chum-mi-est
chunk
  chunky
  chunk-i-er
  chunk-i-est
church
  church-li-ness
  church-ly
church-go-er
church-man
  church-men

church-war-den
church-yard
churl-ish
 churl-ish-ly
 churl-ish-ness
churn-er
chut-ney
chutz-pah
ci-bo-ri-um
 ci-bo-ria
ci-ca-da
 ci-ca-das
 ci-ca-dea
cic-a-trix
 cic-a-tri-ces
 cic-a-trize
 cic-a-trized
 cic-a-triz-ing
cic-e-ro-ne
ci-der
ci-gar
cig-a-rette
cil-ia
 cil-i-ar-y
cil-i-ate
cin-cho-na
cinc-ture
cin-der
cin-e-ma
 cin-e-mas
 cin-e-mat-ic
cin-e-ma-to-graph
 cin-e-ma-tog-ra-phy
cin-e-rar-i-um
cin-na-bar
cin-na-mon
cinque-foil
ci-on
ci-pher
cir-ca
cir-ca-di-an
cir-cle
 cir-cled

cir-cling
cir-clet
cir-cuit
 cir-cu-i-tous
 cir-cu-i-tous-ly
 cir-cu-i-tous-ness
cir-cu-lar
 cir-cu-lar-ize
 cir-cu-lar-ized
 cir-cu-lar-iz-ing
 cir-cu-lar-i-za-tion
cir-cu-la-tion
 cir-cu-late
 cir-cu-lat-ed
 cir-cu-lat-ing
 cir-cu-la-tive
 cir-cu-la-tor
 cir-cu-la-to-ry
cir-cum-am-bi-ent
cir-cum-cise
 cir-cum-cised
 cir-cum-cis-ing
 cir-cum-cis-er
 cir-cum-ci-sion
cir-cum-fer-ence
 cir-cum-fer-en-tial
cir-cum-flex
cir-cum-flu-ent
cir-cum-fuse
 cir-cum-fus-ing
 cir-cum-fu-sion
cir-cum-lo-cu-tion
 cir-cum-lo-cu-to-ry
cir-cum-nav-i-gate
cir-cum-scribe
 cir-cum-scribed
 cir-cum-scrib-ing
 cir-cum-scrib-er
 cir-cum-scrip-tion
 cir-cum-scrip-tive
cir-cum-spect
cir-cum-stance
 cir-cum-stan-tial

cir-cum-vent
 cir-cum-ven-tion
 cir-cum-ven-tive
cir-cus
 cir-cus-es
cir-rho-sis
 cir-rhot-ic
cir-rus
cis-tern
cit-a-del
cite
 cit-ed
 cit-ing
ci-ta-tion
cith-a-ra
cit-i-zen
 cit-i-zen-ship
cit-i-zen-ry
 cit-i-zen-ries
cit-rate
cit-ric
cit-ron
cit-ron-el-la
cit-rus
cit-tern
city
 cit-ies
ci-ty-state
civ-et
civ-ic
 civ-ics
civ-il
ci-vil-ian
ci-vil-i-ty
 ci-vil-i-ties
civ-i-li-za-tion
civ-i-lize
 civ-i-lized
 civ-i-liz-ing
clab-ber
claim
 claim-a-ble
 claim-ant

claim-er
clair-voy-ance
clair-voy-ant
clam
clammed
clam-ming
clam-bake
clam-bar
clam-my
clam-mi-er
clam-mi-est
clam-mi-ly
clam-mi-ness
clam-or
clam-or-ous
clan
clan-nish
clan-des-tine
clang-or
clang-or-ous
clans-man
clans-men
clap
clapped
clap-ping
clap-board
clap-per
clap-trap
claque
clar-et
clar-i-fy
clar-i-fied
clar-i-fy-ing
clar-i-fi-ca-tion
clar-i-net
clar-i-net-ist
clar-i-on
clar-i-ty
class-a-ble
clas-sic
clas-si-cal
clas-si-cal-ly
clas-si-cism

clas-si-cist
clas-si-fy
clas-si-fied
clas-si-fy-ing
clas-si-fi-er
clas-si-fi-ca-tion
class-mate
class-room
class-y
class-i-er
class-i-est
clat-ter
clause
claus-i-cle
claus-tro-pho-bia
clav-i-chord
clav-i-cle
cla-vier
clay
clay-ey
clay-more
clean-cut
clean-er
clean-ly
clean-li-er
clean-li-est
clean-li-ness
cleanse
cleansed
cleans-ing
cleans-er
clean-up
clear
clear-ly
clear-ness
clear-ance
clear-cut
clear-ing
clear-sight-ed
cleav-age
cleave
cleaved
cleav-ing

cleav-er
clef
cleft
clem-en-cy
clem-ent
clere-sto-ry
clere-sto-riees
cler-gy
cler-gies
cler-gy-man
cler-gy-men
cler-ic
cler-i-cal
cler-i-cal-ism
cler-i-cal-ist
clev-er
clev-er-ly
clev-er-ness
clev-is
clev-is-es
clew
cli-ent
cli-en-tele
cliff-hang-er
cli-mac-ter-ic
cli-mate
cli-mat-ic
cli-mat-i-cal
climb
climb-a-ble
climb-er
clinch-er
cling
cling-ing
cling-ing-ly
cling-er
clin-ic
clin-i-cal
clin-i-cal-ly
clink-er
clip
clipped
clip-ping

clip-per
clique
  cliqu-ey
  cliqu-ish
clit-o-ris
clo-a-ca
  clo-a-cae
  clo-a-cal
clob-ber
clock-wise
clock-work
clod
  clod-dish
  clod-dy
clog
  clog-ged
  clog-ging
clois-ter
  clois-tral
close
  closed
  clos-ing
  clos-est
  close-ly
  close-ness
close-fist-ed
close-mouthed
clos-et
  clos-et-ed
  clos-et-ing
close-up
clo-sure
clot
  clot-ted
  clot-ting
clothe
  clothed
  cloth-ing
clothes-horse
clothes-line
clothes-pin
cloth-ier
cloth-ing

clo-ture
cloud-burst
cloud-y
  cloud-i-er
  cloud-i-est
  cloud-i-ly
  cloud-i-ness
clo-ven
clo-ver
clo-ver-leaf
clown
  clown-ish
cloy
  cloy-ing-ly
club
  clubbed
  club-bing
club-foot
club-house
clump
  clumpy
clum-sy
  clum-si-er
  clum-si-est
  clum-si-ly
  clum-si-ness
clus-ter
coach-man
  coach-men
co-ag-u-late
  co-ag-u-lat-ed
  co-ag-u-lat-ing
  co-ag-u-la-tion
co-a-lesce
  co-a-lesced
  co-a-les-cing
  co-a-les-cence
  co-a-les-cent
co-a-li-tion
coarse
  coars-er
  coars-est
  coars-en

  coarse-ly
coast-er
coast-line
coat-ing
co-au-thor
coax
  coax-ing-ly
co-balt
cob-ble
  cob-bled
  cob-bling
cob-bler
cob-ble-stone
co-bra
cob-web
  cob-webbed
  cob-web-by
co-ca
co-caine
coc-cyx
  coc-cy-ges
  coc-cyg-e-al
coch-le-a
cock-ade
cock-a-too
cock-crow
cock-er span-iel
cock-eyed
cock-fight
cock-le
cock-le-bur
cock-le-shell
cock-ney
  cock-neys
cock-pit
cock-roach
cocks-comb
cock-sure
cock-tail
cocky
  cock-i-er
  cock-i-est
  cock-i-ness

co-coa
co-co-nut
co-coon
cod
  cod-fish
cod-dle
  cod-dled
  cod-dling
code
  cod-ed
  cod-ing
co-deine
codg-er
cod-i-cil
cod-i-fy
  cod-i-fied
  cod-i-fy-ing
  cod-i-fi-ca-tion
cod-liv-er oil
co-ed
co-ed-u-ca-tion
coe-len-ter-ate
co-e-qual
co-erce
  co-erced
  co-er-cing
  co-er-ci-ble
  co-er-cion
  co-er-cive
co-ex-ist
  co-ex-ist-ence
  co-ex-ist-ent
cof-fee
cof-fee-house
cof-fee-pot
cof-fer
cof-fin
co-gent
  co-gen-cy
  co-gent-ly
cog-i-tate
  cog-i-tat-ed
  cog-i-tat-ing

cog-i-ta-ble
cog-i-ta-tive
cog-nac
cog-nate
cog-ni-tion
  cog-ni-tive
cog-ni-zance
  cog-ni-zant
cog-wheel
co-hab-it
  co-hab-i-ta-tion
co-here
  co-hered
  co-her-ing
co-her-ent
  co-her-ence
  co-her-en-cy
  co-her-ent-ly
co-he-sion
co-he-sive
  co-hes-sive-ly
  co-hes-sive-ness
co-hort
coif-feur
coif-fure
  coif-fured
  coif-fur-ing
coin-age
co-in-cide
  co-in-cid-ed
  co-in-cid-ing
co-in-ci-dence
co-in-ci-den-tal
  co-in-ci-den-tal-ly
co-i-tion
co-i-tus
  co-i-tal
coke
  coked
  cok-ing
co-la
col-an-der
cold-blood-ed

cole-slaw
col-ic
  col-icky
col-i-se-um
co-li-tis
col-lab-o-rate
  col-lab-o-rat-ed
  col-lab-o-rat-ing
  col-lab-o-ra-tion
  col-lab-o-ra-tor
col-lage
col-lapse
  col-lapsed
  col-laps-ing
  col-laps-si-ble
col-lar
col-lar-bone
col-late
  col-lat-ed
  col-lat-ing
  col-la-tion
  col-la-tor
col-lat-er-al
col-league
col-lect
  col-lect-i-ble
  col-lec-tor
  col-lect-ed
  col-lec-tion
col-lec-tive
  col-lec-tive-ly
  col-lect-tiv-i-ty
  col-lec-tiv-ism
  col-lect-tiv-ize
  col-lec-tiv-iz-ing
  col-lec-tiv-i-za-tion
col-lege
  col-le-gi-al
col-le-gian
col-le-giate
col-lide
  col-lid-ed
  col-lid-ing

col-li-sion
col-li-mate
 col-li-mat-ed
 col-li-mat-ing
 col-li-ma-tion
col-lo-cate
 col-lo-cat-ed
 col-lo-cat-ing
 col-lo-ca-tion
col-loid
col-lo-qui-al
 col-lo-qui-al-ly
 col-lo-qui-al-ism
col-lo-quy
 col-lo-quies
col-lu-sion
 col-lu-sive
co-logne
co-lon
colo-nel
co-lo-ni-al
 co-lo-ni-al-ism
 co-lo-ni-al-ist
col-o-nist
col-o-nade
col-o-ny
 col-o-nies
 col-o-nize
 col-o-nized
 col-o-niz-ing
 col-o-niz-er
 col-o-ni-za-tion
col-or
 col-or-er
 col-or-less
col-or-a-tion
col-or-blind
 col-or-blind-ness
col-or-cast
col-ored
col-or-fast
col-or-ful
col-or-ing

co-los-sal
co-los-sus
 co-los-si
colt-ish
col-um-bine
col-umn
 co-lum-nar
 co-lumned
col-um-nist
co-ma
 co-mas
 co-ma-tose
com-bat
 com-bat-ed
 com-bat-ing
com-bat-ant
com-ba-tive
comb-er
com-bi-na-tion
 com-bi-na-tion-al
 com-bi-na-tive
com-bine
 com-bined
 com-bin-ing
 com-bin-a-ble
 com-bin-er
com-bo
 com-bos
com-bust-ti-ble
 com-bus-ti-bil-i-ty
con-bus-tion
 com-bus-tive
come
 com-ing
come-back
co-me-di-an
 co-me-di-enne
come-down
com-e-dy
 com-e-dies
come-ly
 come-li-ness
come-on

com-er
com-et
come-up-pance
com-fort
 com-fort-a-ble
 com-fort-a-bly
com-fort-er
com-fy
 com-fi-er
 com-fi-est
com-ic
 com-i-cal
com-ing
com-i-ty
 com-i-ties
com-ma
 com-mas
com-mand
com-man-dant
com-man-deer
com-mand-er
 com-mand-er-ship
com-mand-ment
com-man-do
 com-man-dos
com-mem-o-rate
 com-mem-o-rat-ed
 com-mem-o-rat-ing
 com-mem-o-ra-ble
 com-mem-o-ra-tion
 com-mem-o-ra-tive
com-mence
 com-menced
 com-menc-ing
com-mence-ment
com-mend
 com-mend-a-ble
 com-mend-a-bly
com-men-da-tion
 com-mend-a-to-ry
com-men-su-rate
 com-men-su-rate-ly
 com-men-su-ra-tion

com-ment
com-men-tary
  com-men-tar-ies
  com-men-ta-tor
com-merce
com-mer-cial
  com-mer-cial-ism
  com-mer-cial-ize
  com-mer-cial-ized
  com-mer-cial-iz-ing
com-mie
com-mis-er-ate
  com-mis-er-at-ed
  com-mis-er-at-ing
  com-mis-er-a-tion
  com-mis-er-a-tive
com-mis-sar
com-mis-sar-y
  com-mis-sar-ies
com-mis-sion
  com-mis-sioned
com-mis-sion-er
com-mit
  com-mit-ted
  com-mit-ting
  com-mit-ment
com-mit-tee
  com-mit-tee-man
  -wo-man
com-mode
com-mo-di-ous
com-mod-i-ty
  com-mod-i-ties
com-mo-dore
com-mon
com-mon-al-ty
  com-mon-al-ties
com-mon-place
com-mons
com-mon-wealth
com-mo-tion
com-mu-nal
  com-mu-nal-i-ty

com-mune
com-muned
com-mun-ing
com-mu-ni-cant
com-mu-ni-cate
  com-mu-ni-cat-ed
  com-mu-ni-cat-ing
  com-mu-ni-ca-ble
  com-mu-ni-ca-tive
  com-mu-ni-ca-tion
com-mun-ion
  com-mun-ism
  com-mun-ist
com-mu-ni-ty
  com-mu-ni-ties
com-mu-nize
  com-mu-nized
  com-mu-niz-ing
com-mu-ta-tion
com-mu-ta-tor
com-mute
  com-mut-ed
  com-mut-ing
  com-mut-a-ble
com-mut-er
com-pact
com-pan-ion
  com-pan-ion-a-ble
  com-pan-ion-ship
com-pa-ny
  com-pa-nies
com-pa-ra-ble
  com-par-a-bil-i-ty
com-par-a-tive
com-pare
  com-pared
  com-par-ing
com-par-i-son
com-part-ment
  com-part-men-tal
  com-part-ment-ed
com-pass
com-pas-sion

com-pas-sion-ate
com-pat-ible
  com-pat-i-bly
  com-pat-i-bil-i-ty
com-pa-tri-ot
com-peer
com-pel
  com-pelled
  com-pel-ling
com-pem-di-ous
  com-pen-di-um
com-pen-sate
  com-pen-sat-ed
  com-pen-sat-ing
  com-pen-sa-tive
  com-pen-sa-tor
  com-pen-sa-to-ry
com-pen-sa-tion
com-pete
  com-pet-ed
  com-pet-ing
com-pet-i-tor
com-pe-tence
  com-pe-ten-cy
com-pe-tent
com-pe-ti-tion
com-pet-i-tive
com-pile
  com-piled
  com-pil-ing
  com-pi-la-tion
com-pla-cence
  com-pla-cen-cy
  com-pla-cent
com-plain
com-plain-ant
com-plaint
com-plai-sance
  com-plai-sant
com-plect-ed
com-ple-ment
  com-ple-men-tal
  com-ple-men-ta-ry

com-plete
  com-plet-ed
  com-plet-ing
  com-plet-a-ble
com-ple-tion
com-plex
com-plex-ion
  com-plex-ioned
com-plex-i-ty
  com-plex-i-ties
com-pli-ance
  com-pli-an-cy
  com-pli-ant
com-pli-cate
  com-pli-cat-ed
  com-pli-cat-ing
  com-pli-ca-tion
com-plic-i-ty
  com-plic-i-ties
com-pli-ment
com-ply
  com-plied
  com-ply-ing
com-po-nent
com-port
com-port-ment
com-pose
  com-posed
  com-pos-ing
com-pos-er
com-pos-ite
com-po-si-tion
com-post
com-po-sure
com-pote
com-pound
com-pre-hend
  com-pre-hend-i-ble
com-pre-hen-si-ble
  com-pre-hen-si-bly
com-pre-hen-sion
com-pre-hen-sive
com-press

com-presed
com-press-i-ble
com-press-i-bil-i-ty
com-pres-sion
com-pres-sor
com-prise
  com-prised
  com-pris-ing
com-pro-mise
  com-pro-mised
  com-pro-mis-ing
comp-trol-ler
com-pul-sion
com-pul-sive
com-pul-so-ry
com-punc-tion
com-pute
  com-put-ed
  com-put-ing
  com-pu-ta-tion
com-pu-ter
com-put-er-ize
  com-put-er-ized
  com-put-er-iz-ing
  com-put-er-i-za-tion
com-rade
  com-rade-ship
com-sat
con
  conned
  con-ning
con-cave
con-ceal
  con-ceal-a-ble
  con-ceal-ment
con-cede
  con-ced-ed
  con-ced-ing
con-ceit
  con-ceit-ed
con-ceive
  con-ceived
  con-ceiv-ing

con-ceiv-a-ble
con-ceiv-a-bly
con-cen-trate
  con-cen-tra-ted
  con-cen-trat-ing
  con-cen-tra-tive
  con-cen-tra-tion
con-cen-tric
  con-cen-tri-cal
  con-cen-tric-i-ty
con-cept
  con-cep-tu-al
con-cep-tion
  con-cep-tive
con-cep-tu-al-ize
  con-cep-tu-al-ized
  con-cep-tu-al-iz-ing
con-cern
  con-cerned
  con-cern-ing
con-cert
con-cert-ed
con-cer-ti-na
con-cert-mas-ter
con-cer-to
con-ces-sion
con-ces-sion-aire
conch
  conchs
con-cil-i-ate
  con-cil-i-at-ed
  con-cil-i-at-ing
  con-cil-i-a-tion
  con-cil-i-a-to-ry
con-cise
  con-cise-ness
  con-cise-ly
con-clave
con-clude
  con-clud-ed
  con-clud-ing
con-clu-sion
con-clu-sive

con-coct
con-coc-tion
con-com-i-tant
con-com-i-tance
con-cord
con-cord-ance
con-cord-ant
con-course
con-crete
con-cret-ed
con-cret-ing
con-cre-tion
con-cre-tive
con-cu-bine
con-cur
con-curred
con-cur-ring
con-cur-rence
con-cur-rent
con-cus-sion
con-cus-sive
con-demn
con-dem-na-ble
con-dem-na-tion
con-dem-na-to-ry
con-dense
con-densed
con-dens-ing
con-den-sa-ble
con-den-sa-tion
con-dens-er
con-de-scend
con-de-scend-ing
con-de-scen-sion
con-di-ment
con-di-tion
con-di-tion-al
con-di-tion-er
con-di-tion-ed
con-dole
con-doled
con-dol-ing
con-do-la-to-ry

con-do-ler
con-do-lence
con-dom
con-do-min-i-um
con-done
con-doned
con-don-ing
con-do-na-tion
con-dor
con-duce
con-duced
con-duc-ing
con-duct
con-duct-i-bil-i-ty
con-duct-i-ble
con-duct-ance
con-duc-tion
con-fer-ence
con-fer-en-tial
con-fess
con-fess-ed-ly
con-fes-sion
con-fes-sion-al
con-fes-sor
con-fet-ti
con-fi-dant
con-fi-dante
con-fide
con-fid-ed
con-fid-ing
con-fi-dence
con-fi-dent
con-fi-den-tial
con-fig-u-ra-tion
con-fig-u-ra-tion-al
con-fine
con-fined
con-fin-ing
con-fine-ment
con-firm
con-firm-a-ble
con-fir-ma-tion
con-fir-ma-tive

con-fir-ma-to-ry
con-fir-med
con-firm-ed-ly
con-firm-ed-ness
con-fis-cate
con-fis-cat-ed
con-fis-cat-ing
con-fis-ca-tion
con-fis-ca-tor
con-fis-ca-to-ry
con-fla-gra-tion
con-flict
con-flict-ing
con-flic-tive
con-flic-tion
con-flu-ence
con-flu-ent
con-flux
con-form
con-form-ist
con-form-ism
con-form-a-ble
con-form-a-bly
con-form-ance
con-for-ma-tion
con-form-i-ty
con-form-i-ties
con-found
con-found-ed
con-found-ed-ly
con-front
con-fron-ta-tion
con-fuse
confused
con-fus-ing
con-fus-ed-ly
con-fus-ed-ness
con-fu-sion
con-fute
con-futed
con-fut-ing
con-fu-ta-tion
con-ga

con-gas
con-geal
  con-geal-ment
con-gen-ial
  con-ge-ni-al-i-ty
  con-gen-ial-ly
con-gen-i-tal
con-ger
  con-ge-ries
con-gest
  con-ges-tion
  con-ges-tive
con-glom-er-ate
  con-glom-er-at-ing
  con-glom-er-a-tion
con-grat-u-late
  con-grat-u-lat-ed
  con-grat-u-lat-ing
  con-grat-u-la-tor
  con-grat-u-la-to-ry
  con-grat-u-la-tion
con-gre-gate
  con-gre-gat-ed
  con-gre-gat-ing
con-gre-ga-tion
  con-gre-ga-tion-al
con-gress
  con-gres-sion-al
con-gress-man
  con-gress-men
  con-gress-wom-an
  con-gress-wom-en
con-gru-ent
  con-gru-ent-ly
  con-gru-ence
  con-gru-en-cy
  con-gru-en-cies
con-gru-i-ty
  con-gru-i-ties
con-gru-ous
  con-gru-ous-ly
con-ic
  con-i-cal

co-ni-fer
con-jec-ture
  con-jec-tured
  con-jec-tur-ing
  con-jec-tur-al
con-join
con-joint
  con-joint-ly
con-ju-gal
  con-ju-gal-ly
con-ju-gate
  con-ju-gat-ed
  con-ju-gat-ing
  con-ju-ga-tion
  con-ju-ga-tive
con-junc-tion
  con-junc-tive
con-jur-a-tion
con-jure
  con-jured
  con-jur-ing
  con-jur-er
con-nect
con-nec-tor
con-nec-tion
con-nec-tive
con-nip-tion
con-nive
  con-nived
  con-niv-ing
  con-niv-ance
con-nois-seur
con-note
  con-not-ed
  con-not-ing
  con-no-ta-tion
  con-no-ta-tive
con-nu-bi-al
  con-ni-bi-al-ly
con-quer
  con-quer-a-ble
  con-quer-or
con-quest

co-ni-fer
con-quis-ta-dor
  con-quis-ta-dors
  con-quis-ta-dor-es
con-san-quin-e-ous
  con-san-quin-i-ty
con-science
con-sci-en-tious
  con-sci-en-tious-ly
con-scious
  con-scious-ly
  con-scious-ness
con-script
  con-scrip-tion
con-se-crate
  con-se-crat-ed
  con-se-crat-ing
  con-se-cra-tive
  con-se-cra-tion
con-sec-u-tive
  con-sec-u-tive-ly
con-sen-sus
con-sent
  con-sent-er
con-se-quence
  con-se-quent
  con-se-quent-ly
con-se-quen-tial
  con-se-quen-tial-ly
con-ser-va-tion
  con-ser-va-tion-al
  con-ser-va-tion-ist
con-serv-a-tive
  con-ser-va-tism
  con-ser-va-tive-ly
con-serv-a-to-ry
  con-serv-a-to-ries
con-serve
  con-served
  con-serv-ing
  con-serv-a-ble
  con-serv-er
con-sid-er
  con-sid-er-a-ble

con-sid-er-a-bly
con-sid-er-ate
con-sid-er-a-tion
con-sid-er-ing
con-sign
con-sign-er
con-sign-or
con-sign-ment
con-sign-ee
con-sist
con-sist-en-cy
con-sist-en-cies
con-sist-ence
con-sist-ent
con-sist-ent-ly
con-sis-to-ry
con-sis-to-ries
con-so-la-tion
con-sol-a-to-ry
con-sole
con-soled
con-sol-ing
con-sol-a-ble
con-sol-i-date
con-sol-i-dat-ed
con-sol-i-dat-ing
con-sol-i-da-tion
con-so-nant
con-so-nance
con-so-nant-ly
con-so-nan-tal
con-sort
con-sor-ti-um
con-sor-tia
con-spic-u-ous
con-spic-u-ous-ly
con-spic-u-ous-ness
con-spire
con-spired
con-spir-ing
con-spir-a-cy
con-spir-a-cies
con-spir-a-tor

con-spir-a-to-ri-al
con-spir-er
con-spir-ing-ly
con-sta-ble
con-sta-ble-ship
con-stab-u-lar-y
con-stab-u-lar-ies
con-stant
con-stan-cy
con-stant-ly
con-stel-la-tion
con-ster-na-tion
con-sti-pate
con-sti-pa-tion
con-stit-u-en-cy
con-stit-u-en-cies
con-stit-u-ent
con-sti-tute
con-sti-tu-tion
con-sti-tu-tion-al
con-sti-tu-tion-al-ly
con-strain
con-strain-a-ble
con-strained
con-straint
con-strict
con-stric-tive
con-stric-tion
con-stric-tor
con-struct
con-struc-tor
con-struc-tion
con-struc-tion-al
con-struc-tive
con-struc-tive-ly
con-struc-tive-ness
con-strue
con-strued
con-stru-ing
con-stru-a-ble
con-stru-er
con-sul
con-su-lar

con-sul-ship
con-su-late
con-sult
con-sul-ta-tion
con-sult-ant
con-sume
con-sumed
con-sum-ing
con-sum-a-ble
con-sum-er
con-sum-mate
con-sum-mat-ed
con-sum-mat-ing
con-sum-mate-ly
con-sum-ma-tion
con-sump-tion
com-sump-tive
con-tact
con-ta-gion
con-ta-gious
con-ta-gious-ness
con-tain
con-tain-a-ble
con-tain-er
con-tain-ment
con-tam-i-nate
con-tam-i-nat-ed
con-tam-i-nat-ing
con-tam-i-nant
con-tam-i-na-tion
con-tam-i-na-tive
con-tam-i-na-tor
con-tem-plate
con-tem-plat-ed
con-tem-plat-ing
con-tem-pla-tion
con-tem-pla-tive
con-tem-po-rar-y
con-tem-po-rar-ies
con-tempt
con-tempt-i-ble
con-tempt-i-bly
con-temp-tu-ous

con-temp-tu-ous-ly
con-tend
con-tend-er
con-tent
con-tent-ment
con-tent-ed
con-tent-ed-ly
con-tent-ed-ness
con-ten-tion
con-ten-tious
con-ten-tious-ly
con-ten-tious-ness
con-ter-mi-ous
con-test
con-test-a-ble
con-test-er
con-test-ant
con-text
con-tig-u-ous
con-ti-gu-i-ty
con-ti-gu-i-ties
con-tig-u-ous-ly
con-tig-u-ous-ness
con-ti-nence
con-ti-nen-cy
con-ti-nent
con-ti-nent-ly
con-ti-nen-tal
con-tin-gent
con-tin-gen-cies
con-tin-gent-ly
con-tin-u-al
con-tin-u-al-ly
con-tin-u-ance
con-tin-ue
con-tin-ued
con-tin-u-ing
con-tin-u-a-tion
con-tin-u-er
con-ti-nu-i-ty
con-ti-nu-i-ties
con-tin-u-ous
con-tin-u-ous-ly

con-tin-u-um
con-tin-ua
con-tort
con-tor-tion
con-tor-tive
con-tor-tion-ist
con-tour
con-tra-band
can-tra-cep-tive
con-tra-cep-tion
con-tract
con-tract-ed
con-tract-i-ble
con-trac-tu-al
con-trac-tion
con-trac-tive
con-trac-tile
con-trac-tor
con-tra-dict
con-tra-dict-a-ble
con-tra-dic-tion
con-tra-dic-to-ry
con-tra-dis-tinc-tion
con-trail
con-tral-to
con-tral-tos
con-tral-ti
con-trap-tion
con-tra-pun-tal
con-tra-ri-wise
con-tra-ry
con-tra-ries
con-tra-ri-ly
con-tra-ri-ness
con-trast
con-trast-a-ble
con-trast-ing-ly
con-tra-vene
con-tra-vened
con-tra-ven-ing
con-tra-ven-er
con-tra-ven-tion
con-trib-ute

con-trib-ut-ed
con-trib-ut-ing
con-trib-ut-a-ble
con-trib-u-tor
con-trib-u-tory
con-tri-bu-tion
con-trite
con-trite-ly
con-trite-ness
con-tri-tion
con-trive
con-triv-ed
con-triv-ing
con-triv-ance
con-trol
con-trolled
con-trol-ling
con-trol-la-ble
con-trol-ler
con-trol-ler-ship
con-tro-ver-sy
con-tro-ver-sies
con-tro-ver-sal
con-tro-ver-sial-ly
con-tro-vert
con-tu-me-ly
con-tu-me-lies
con-tuse
con-tused
con-tus-ing
con-tu-sion
co-nun-drum
cov-va-lesce
con-va-lesced
con-va-les-cing
con-va-les-cence
con-va-les-cent
con-vec-tion
con-vene
con-vened
con-ven-ing
con-ven-er
con-ven-ience

con-ven-ient
con-ven-ient-ly
con-vent
con-ven-tion
con-ven-tion-al
con-ven-tion-al-ism
con-ven-tion-al-ist
con-ven-tion-al-i-ty
con-ven-tion-al-ize
con-ven-tion-al-ized
con-verge
con-verged
con-verg-ing
con-ver-gence
con-ver-gen-cy
con-ver-gent
con-ver-sant
con-ver-sa-tion
con-ver-sa-tion-al
con-verse
con-versed
con-vers-ing
con-verse-ly
con-ver-sion
con-vert
con-vert-er
con-vert-i-ble
con-vert-i-bil-i-ty
con-vert-i-bly
con-vex
con-vex-ly
con-vex-i-ty
con-vey
con-vey-a-ble
con-vey-ance
con-vey-er
con-vey-or
con-vict
con-vic-tion
con-vic-tion-al
con-vince
con-vinced
con-vinc-ing

con-vinc-er
con-vinc-i-ble
con-viv-i-al
con-viv-i-al-i-ty
con-viv-i-al-ly
con-vo-ca-tion
con-vo-ca-tion-al
con-voke
con-voked
con-vok-ing
con-vok-er
con-vo-lute
con-vo-lut-ed
con-vo-lut-ing
con-vo-lute-ly
con-vo-lu-tion
con-voy
con-vulse
con-vulsed
con-vuls-ing
con-vul-sion
con-vul-sive
con-vul-sive-ly
co-ny
coo
cooed
coo-ing
coo-ing-ly
cook-book
cook-er-y
cook-e-ries
cook-out
cool
cool-ish
cool-ly
cool-ness
cool-ant
cool-er
coo-lie
coo-lies
coon-skin
coop-er
coop-er-age

co-op-er-ate
co-op-er-at-ed
co-op-er-at-ing
co-op-er-a-tion
co-op-er-a-tive
co-op-er-a-tive-ly
co-opt
co-op-ta-tion
co-or-di-nate
co-or-di-nat-ed
co-or-di-nat-ing
co-or-di-nate-ly
co-or-di-na-tor
co-or-di-na-tion
coo-tie
cop
copped
cop-ping
cope-stone
co-pi-lot
co-pi-ous
co-pi-ous-ly
co-pi-ous-ness
cop-out
cop-per
cop-per-y
cop-per-head
cop-per-plate
cop-pice
cop-ra
copse
cop-u-la
cop-u-las
cop-u-lae
cop-u-lar
cop-u-late
cop-u-lat-ed
cop-u-lat-ing
cop-u-la-tion
cop-u-la-tive
cop-u-la-tive-ly
copy
cop-ies

cop-ied
cop-y-ing
cop-y-book
cop-y-cat
cop-y-ist
cop-y-right
co-quet
  co-quet-ted
  co-quet-ting
co-quet-ry
  co-quet-ries
co-quette
  co-quet-tish
  co-quet-tish-ly
cor-a-cle
cor-al
cor-bel
cord-age
cor-date
  cor-date-ly
cor-dial
  cor-dial-i-ty
  cor-dial-ness
  cor-dial-ly
cor-dil-le-ra
cord-ite
cor-don
cor-do-van
cor-du-roy
cord-wood
core
  cored
  cor-ing
co-re-la-tion
co-re-spond-ent
co-ri-an-der
cor-ker
cork-screw
corn-cob
cor-nea
  cor-ne-al
cor-ner
cor-ner-stone

cor-net
  cor-net-ist
corn-flow-er
cor-nice
corn-starch
cor-nu-co-pi-a
corn-y
  corn-i-er
  conr-i-est
co-rol-la
cor-ol-lar-y
  cor-ol-lar-ies
co-ro-na
  co-ro-nas
  co-ro-nae
cor-o-nar-y
co-ro-na-tion
cor-o-ner
  cor-o-ner-ship
cor-o-net
  cor-o-net-ed
cor-po-ral
cor-po-rate
  cor-po-rate-ly
  cor-po-ra-tive
cor-po-ra-tion
cor-po-rat-ism
cor-po-re-al
  cor-po-re-al-i-ty
  cor-po-re-al-ness
corps
corpse
corps-man
  corps-men
cor-pu-lent
  cor-pu-lence
  cor-pu-len-cy
cor-pus
cor-pus-cle
  cor-pus-cu-lar
cor-ral
  cor-ralled
  cor-ral-ling

cor-rect
  cor-rect-a-ble
  cor-rect-i-ble
  cor-rect-ness
  cor-rec-tor
cor-rec-tion
  cor-rec-tion-al
cor-rec-tive
cor-re-late
  cor-re-lat-ed
  cor-re-lat-ing
cor-re-la-tion
cor-rel-a-tive
cor-re-spond
  cor-re-spond-ing
  cor-re-spond-ing-ly
cor-re-spond-ence
cor-re-spond-ent
cor-ri-dor
cor-ri-gi-ble
  cor-ri-gi-bil-i-ty
  cor-ri-gi-bly
cor-rob-o-rate
  cor-rob-o-rat-ed
  cor-rob-o-rat-ing
  cor-rob-o-ra-tion
  cor-rob-o-ra-tive
  cor-rob-o-ra-to-ry
cor-rode
  cor-rod-ed
  cor-rod-ing
  cor-rod-i-ble
cor-ro-sion
cor-ro-sive
cor-ru-gate
  cor-ru-gat-ed
  cor-ru-gat-ing
  cor-ru-ga-tion
cor-rupt
  cor-rupt-er
  cor-rup-ti-ble
  cor-rup-ti-bil-i-ty
  cor-rupt-ly

cor-rupt-ness
cor-rup-tion
cor-sage
cor-sair
cor-set
cor-set-ed
cor-tex
cor-ti-ces
cor-ti-cal
cor-ti-sone
co-run-dum
co-sig-na-to-ry
cos-met-ic
cos-mic
cos-mi-cal-ly
cos-mog-o-ny
cos-mog-o-nies
cos-mo-gon-ic
cos-mo-go-nist
cos-mog-o-ny
cos-mog-o-nist
cos-mog-ra-phy
cos-mog-ra-phies
cos-mog-ra-pher
cos-mo-graph-ic
cos-mol-o-gy
cos-mol-o-gies
cos-mo-log-ic
cos-mol-o-gist
cos-mo-naut
cos-mo-pol-i-tan
cos-mop-o-lite
cos-mos
cost-ly
cost-li-er
cost-li-est
cost-li-ness
cost--plus
cos-tume
cos-tumed
cos-tum-ing
cos-tum-er
co-sy

co-si-er
cos-i-est
co-te-rie
co-ter-mi-nous
co-til-lion
cot-tage
cot-ter
cot-ton
cot-ton-y
cot-ton-mouth
cot-ton-seed
cot-ton-tail
cot-ton-wood
couch
coun-cil
coun-cil-or
coun-cil-man
coun-cil-lor-ship
count
count-a-ble
count-down
coun-te-nance
coun-te-nanced
coun-te-nanc-ing
coun-te-nanc-er
count-er
coun-ter-act
coun-ter-ac-tion
coun-ter-ac-tive
coun-ter-at-tack
coun-ter-charge
coun-ter-charged
coun-ter-char-ging
coun-ter-claim
coun-ter-claim-ant
coun-ter-clock-wise
coun-ter-cul-ture
coun-ter-feit
coun-ter-feit-er
coun-ter-mand
coun-ter-meas-ure
coun-ter-of-fen-sive
coun-ter-pane

coun-ter-part
coun-ter-point
coun-ter-poise
coun-ter-poised
coun-ter-pois-ing
coun-ter-sign
coun-ter-sig-na-ture
coun-ter-sink
coun-ter-sank
coun-ter-sunk
coun-ter-spy
coun-ter-spies
coun-ter-weight
coun-tees
count-less
coun-tri-fied
coun-try
coun-tries
coun-try-man
coun-try-men
coun-try-wom-an
coun-try-wom-en
coun-try-side
coun-ty
coun-ties
coup
coups
coup-le
coup-led
coup-ling
coup-ler
cou-pon
cour-age
cou-ra-geous
cour-i-er
course
coursed
cours-ing
cours-er
cour-te-ous
cour-te-ous-ly
cour-te-sy
cour-te-sies

court-house
cour-ti-er
court-ly
  court-li-er
  court-li-est
court-mar-tial
  courts-mar-tial
  court-mar-tialed
court-room
court-ship
cous-in
  cous-in-hood
  cous-in-ly
cou-tu-rier
cov-e-nant
  cov-e-nan-ter
  cov-e-nan-tor
cov-er-age
cov-er-all
cov-er-let
cov-ert
  cov-ert-ly
  cov-ert-ness
cov-er-up
cov-et
  cov-et-a-ble
  cov-et-er
cov-et-ous
  cov-et-ous-ly
cov-ey
cow-ard
  cow-ard-ly
cow-ard-ice
cow-boy
cow-er
  cow-er-ing-ly
cow-hide
cowl
  cowled
cow-lick
cow-man
  cow-men
co-work-er

cow-poke
cow-ry
  cow-rie
  cow-ries
cox-swain
coy
  coy-ly
coy-o-te
coz-en
  coz-en-age
  coz-en-er
crab
  crabbed
  crab-bing
  crab-by
crack-down
crack-er
crack-ing
crack-le
  crack-led
  crack-ling
crack-up
cra-dle
  cra-dled
  cra-dling
crafts-man
  crafts-man-ship
crafty
  craft-i-er
  craft-i-est
  craft-i-ly
  craft-i-ness
crag
  crag-ged
  crag-gy
  crag-gi-ness
cram
  crammed
  cram-ming
  cram-mer
cran-ber-ry
  cran-ber-ries
crane

craned
cran-ing
cra-ni-um
  cra-ni-ums
  cra-nia
  cra-ni-al
  cra-ni-ate
  cra-ni-al-ly
crank-case
crank-shaft
crank-y
  crank-i-er
  crank-i-est
  crank-i-ly
  crank-i-ness
cran-ny
  cran-nies
  cran-nied
crash-land
crass
  crass-ly
  crass-ness
crate
  crat-ed
  crat-ing
cra-ter
  cra-ter-al
  cra-tered
cra-vat
crave
  craved
  crav-ing
  crav-er
  crav-ing-ly
craw-fish
crawl
  crawl-y
  crawl-ing-ly
crawl-er
cray-fish
cray-on
craze
  craz-ing

cra-zy
cra-zi-er
cra-zi-est
cra-zi-ly
cream-er
cream-er-y
cream-er-ies
cre-ate
cre-at-ed
cre-at-ing
cre-a-tion
cre-a-tion-al
cre-a-tive
cre-a-tive-i-ty
cre-a-tor
crea-ture
cre-dence
cre-den-za
cred-i-ble
cred-i-bil-i-ty
cred-i-bly
cred-it
cred-it-a-ble
cred-it-a-bil-i-ty
cred-it-a-bly
cred-i-tor
cre-do
cre-dos
cred-u-lous
creek
creel
cre-ma-to-ry
cre-ma-to-ri-um
cre-o-sote
crepe
creped
crep-ing
cre-pus-cu-lar
cres-cen-do
cres-cent
crest
crest-ed
crest-less

crest-fall-en
cre-tin-ism
cre-tonne
crev-ice
crew-el
crib
cribbed
crib-bing
crib-ber
crib-bage
crick-et
crim-i-nal
crim-i-nal-i-ty
crim-i-nal-ly
crim-i-nol-o-gy
crim-i-nol-o-gist
crimpy
crimp-i-er
crimp-i-est
crim-son
cringe
cringed
cring-ing
crin-kle
crin-kled
crin-kli-est
crip-ple
crip-pled
crip-pling
cri-sis
cri-ses
criss-cross
cri-te-ri-on
cri-te-ria
crit-ic
crit-i-cal
crit-i-cal-ly
crit-i-cal-ness
crit-i-cism
crit-i-cize
crit-i-cized
crit-i-ciz-ing
crit-i-ciz-a-ble

cri-tique
crit-er
croak-y
croak-i-er
croak-i-est
crois-sant
cro-ny
cro-nies
crook-ed
croon-er
crop
cropped
crop-ping
crop-per
cro-quette
cross-bar
cross-bow
cross-bred
cross-breed
cross-breed-ing
cross-coun-try
cross-cut
cross-ex-am-ine
cross-ex-am-ined
cross-ex-am-in-ing
cross-ing
cross-pol-li-na-tion
cross-pol-li-nate
cross-pur-pose
cross-ref-er-ence
cross-stitch
cross-ways
crotch-ety
crotch-et-i-ness
crouch
croup
croupy
crou-pi-er
crou-ton
crow-bar
crow's--foot
crow's--feet
crow's--nest

cru-cial
cru-ci-al-i-ty
cru-cial-ly
cru-ci-ble
cru-ci-fix
cru-ci-fix-ion
cru-ci-form
cru-ci-fy
cru-ci-fied
cru-ci-fy-ing
crude
crud-er
crud-est
crude-ly
crude-ness
cru-di-ty
cru-di-ties
cru-el
cru-el-ly
cru-et
cruise
cruised
cruis-ing
cruis-er
crul-ler
crum-ble
crum-bled
crum-bling
crum-bly
crunchy
crunch-i-er
crunch-i-est
cru-sade
cru-sad-er
crush-er
crush-ing
crush-ing-ly
crus-ta-cean
crust-y
crust-i-er
cry
cried
cry-ing

cry-ba-by
cry-o-gen-ics
cry-o-sur-gery
crypt
crypt-al
crypt-a-nal-y-sis
crypt-ic
cryp-ti-cal
cryp-ti-cal-ly
cryp-to-gram
cryp-to-graph
cryp-tog-ra-phy
cryp-to-graph-ic
cryp-tog-ra-pher
crys-tal
crys-tal-line
crys-tal-lize
crys-tal-lized
crys-tal-liz-ing
crys-tal-liz-er
crys-tal-liz-a-ble
crys-tal-li-za-tion
cub-by
cub-bies
cu-bic
cu-bi-cle
cu-bit
cudg-el
cudg-eled
cudg-el-ing
cui-sine
cul-de-sac
culs-de-sac
cu-li-nary
cul-mi-nant
cul-mi-nate
cul-mi-nat-ed
cul-mi-nat-ing
cul-mi-na-tion
cu-lottes
cul-pa-ble
cul-pa-bil-i-ty
cul-pa-bly

cul-prit
cult
cul-tic
cul-ti-vate
cul-ti-vat-ed
cul-ti-vat-ing
cul-ti-va-tion
cul-ti-va-ble
cul-ti-vat-a-ble
cul-ti-va-tor
cul-tur-al
cul-ture
cul-tured
cul-tur-ing
cul-vert
cum-ber
cum-ber-some
cum-brance
cum lau-de
cum-mer-bound
cum-mu-late
cum-mu-lat-ed
cum-mu-lat-ing
cum-mu-la-tion
cum-mu-la-tive
cu-ne-i-form
cum-ni-lin-gus
cun-ning
cun-ning-ly
cup-board
cup-ful
cup-fuls
cu-pid-i-ty
cu-po-la
cur-a-ble
cur-a-bil-i-ty
cur-a-bly
cu-rate
cur-a-tive
cu-ra-tor
cu-ra-to-ri-al
cu-ra-tor-ship
curb-ing

curb-stone
cur-dle
  cur-dled
  cur-dling
cure
  cured
  cur-ing
cure-all
cur-few
cu-ria
  cu-ri-ae
cu-ri-al
cu-rie
cu-ri-o
  cu-ri-os
cu-ri-os-i-ty
  cu-ri-os-i-ties
cu-ri-ous
cu-ri-um
curl
  curl-er
curl-i-cue
curly
  curl-i-er
  curl-i-est
cur-rant
cur-ren-cy
  cur-ren-cies
cur-rent
cur-ric-u-lum
  cur-ric-u-lums
  cur-ric-u-la
  cur-ri-c-u-lar
cur-rish
cur-ry
  cur-ries
  cur-ri-er
curse
cur-sive
  cur-sive-ly
curt
cur-tail
  cur-tail-ment

cur-tain
curt-sy
  curt-sies
  curt-sied
  curt-sy-ing
cur-va-ceous
cur-va-ture
curve
  cruved
  curv-ing
cur-vi-lin-e-ar
cush-ion
cush-y
  cush-i-er
  cush-i-est
cus-pid
  cus-pi-dal
cus-pi-date
cus-pi-dor
cuss-ed
  cuss-ed-ly
  cuss-ed-ness
cus-tard
cus-to-dian
  cus-to-di-an-ship
cus-to-dy
  cus-to-dies
  cus-to-di-al
cus-tom
cus-tom-ary
  cus-tom-ar-ies
  cus-tom-ar-i-ly
  cus-tom-ar-i-ness
cus-tom-built
cus-tom-er
cus-tom-ize
  cus-tom-ized
  cus-tom-iz-ing
cus-tom-made
cu-ta-ne-ous
cu-ti-cle
cut-lery
cut-let

cut-ting
  cut-ting-ly
cut-tle
cut-up
cy-an-ic
cy-cle
cy-clic
  cy-cli-cal
  cy-cli-cal-ly
cy-clom-e-ter
cy-clone
cy-clo-rama
  cy-clo-ram-ic
cy-clo-tron
cyg-net
cyl-in-der
  cy-lin-dric
  cy-lin-dri-cal
cym-bal
  cym-bal-ist
cyn-ic
  cyn-i-cism
cyn-i-cal
  cyn-i-cal-ly
cy-no-sure
cy-pher
cy-press
cyst
  cys-tic
cys-tic fi-bro-sis
cy-tol-o-gy
  cy-tol-o-gist
czar
  czar-e-vitch
  cza-ri-na

D

dab
  dabbed
  dab-bing
dab-ble
  dab-bled

dab-bing
dab-bler
dac-tyl
dac-tyl-ic
dad-dy--long-legs
daf-fo-dil
daf-fy
daf-fi-er
daf-fi-est
dag-ger
da-guerre-o-type
dahl-ia
dai-ly
dai-lies
dain-ty
dain-ti-er
dain-ti-est
dain-ties
dain-ti-ly
dai-qui-ri
dair-y
dair-ies
dair-y-man
dair-y-men
da-is
dai-sy
dai-sies
dal-ly
dal-lied
dal-ly-ing
dal-li-ance
dam-age
dam-aged
dam-ag-ing
dam-age-a-ble
dam-a-scene
dam-a-scened
dam-a-scen-ing
dam-ask
damn
dam-na-ble
dam-na-ble-ness
dam-na-bly

dam-na-tion
damned
damp-en
damp-er
dam-sel
dam-son
dan-de-li-on
dan-der
dan-dle
dan-dled
dan-dling
dan-druff
dan-dy
dan-dies
dan-di-er
dan-di-est
dan-dy-ism
dan-ger
dan-ger-ous
dan-ger-ous-ly
dan-gle
dan-gled
dan-gling
dan-gler
dank
dank-ly
dank-ness
dan-seuse
dan-seus-es
dap-per
dap-ple
dap-pled
dap-pling
dare
dared
dar-ing
dare-dev-il
dar-ing-ly
dark
dark-ish
dark-ly
dark-en
dark-ling

dark-room
dar-ling
dar-ling-ly
darn-er
dart-er
dash-board
dash-ing
das-tard
das-tard-li-ness
das-tard-ly
da-ta
date
dat-ed
dat-ing
dat-a-ble
dat-er
date-less
date-line
da-tive
da-tum
daub
daub-er
daugh-ter
daugh-ter-ly
daugh-ter--in--law
daugh-ters--in--law
daunt-less
daunt-less-ly
daunt-less-ness
dau-phin
dav-en-port
dav-it
daw-dle
daw-dled
daw-dling
daw-dler
dawn
day-break
day-dream
day-dream-er
day-light
day-time
daze

dazed
daz-ing
daz-ed-ly
daz-zle
daz-zled
dea-con
dea-con-ry
dea-con-ship
dea-con-ess
dead-beat
dead-en
dead-en-er
dead-end
dead-line
dead-lock
dead-ly
dead-li-er
dead-li-est
dead-li-ness
dead-pan
dead-wood
deaf
deaf-ly
deaf-ness
deaf-en
deaf-en-ing-ly
deaf-mute
deal
dealt
deal-ing
deal-er
dean-ship
dear
dear-ly
dearth
death
death-less
death-ly
death-blow
death-trap
death-watch
de-ba-cle
de-bar

de-barred
de-bar-ring
de-bar-ment
de-bark
de-bar-ka-tion
de-base
de-based
de-bas-ing
de-base-ment
de-bas-er
de-bate
de-bat-ed
de-bat-ing
de-bat-a-ble
de-bat-er
de-bauch
de-bauch-er
de-bauch-ment
de-bauch-ery
de-bauch-er-ies
deb-au-chee
de-ben-ture
de-bil-i-tate
de-bil-i-tat-ed
de-bil-i-tat-ing
de-bil-i-ta-tion
de-bil-i-ty
de-bil-i-ties
deb-it
deb-o-nair
de-bris
debt-or
de-bunk
de-bunk-er
de-but
deb-u-tante
de-cade
dec-a-dent
dec-a-dence
dec-a-dent-ly
dec-a-gon
dec-a-gram
dec-a-he-dron

dec-a-he-drons
de-cal
de-camp
de-camp-ment
de-cant
de-cant-er
de-cap-i-tate
de-cap-i-tat-ed
de-cap-i-tat-ing
de-cap-i-ta-tion
dec-a-pod
de-cath-lon
de-cay
de-crease
de-creased
de-ceit
de-ceit-ful
de-ceit-ful-ly
de-ceit-ful-ness
de-ceive
de-ceived
de-ceiv-ing
de-ceiv-er
de-ceiv-ing-ly
de-ceiv-a-ble
de-cel-er-ate
de-cel-er-at-ed
de-cel-er-at-ing
de-cel-er-a-tion
de-cen-cy
de-cen-cies
de-cen-ni-al
de-cen-ni-al-ly
de-cent
de-cent-ly
de-cen-tral-ize
de-cen-tral-ized
de-cen-tral-iz-ing
de-cen-tral-i-za-tion
de-cep-tion
de-cep-tive
de-cep-tive-ly
de-cep-tive-ness

dec-i-bel
de-cide
 de-cid-ed
 de-cid-ing
 de-cid-a-ble
 de-cid-ed-ly
de-cid-u-ous
 de-cid-u-ous-ly
dec-i-mal
dec-i-mate
 dec-i-mat-ed
 dec-i-mat-ing
 dec-i-ma-tion
de-ci-pher
 de-ci-pher-a-ble
de-ci-sion
de-ci-sive
 de-ci-sive-ly
 de-ci-sive-ness
deck-le edge
de-claim
 dec-la-ma-tion
 de-clam-a-tory
de-clas-si-fy
 de-clas-si-fied
 de-clas-si-fy-ing
de-clen-sion
dec-li-na-tion
de-cline
 de-clined
 de-clin-ing
 de-clin-a-ble
de-cliv-i-ty
 de-cliv-i-ties
de-code
 de-cod-ed
 de-cod-ing
 de-cod-er
de-com-pose
 de-com-posed
 de-com-pos-ing
 de-com-po-si-tion
de-com-press

de-com-pres-sion
de-con-tam-i-nate
 de-con-tam-i-nat-ed
 -con-tam-i-nat-ing
 -con-tam-i-na-tion
de-con-trol
 de-con-trolled
 de-con-trol-ling
de-cor
de-co-rate
 dec-o-rat-ed
 dec-o-rat-ing
 dec-o-ra-tion
 dec-o-ra-tive
 dec-o-ra-tive-ly
 dec-o-ra-tor
dec-o-rous
 dec-o-rous-ly
de-co-rum
de-coy
de-crease
 de-creased
 de-creas-ing
 de-creas-ing-ly
de-cree
 de-creed
 de-cree-ing
de-crep-it
 de-crep-i-tude
 de-crep-it-ly
de-cre-scen-do
 de-cre-scen-dos
de-cry
 de-cried
 de-cry-ing
 de-cri-al
ded-i-cate
 ded-i-cat-ed
 ded-i-cat-ing
 ded-i-ca-to-ry
 ded-i-ca-tive
 ded-i-ca-tion
de-duce

de-duc-i-ble
de-duct
 de-duct-i-ble
de-duc-tion
 de-duc-tive
 de-duc-tive-ly
deep
 deep-ly
 deep-ness
deep-en
deep-root-ed
deep-seat-ed
deer-skin
de-es-ca-late
 de-es-ca-lat-ed
 de-es-ca-lat-ing
 de-es-ca-la-tion
de-face
 de-faced
 de-fac-ing
 de-face-ment
 de-fac-er
de fac-to
de-fame
 de-famed
 de-fam-ing
 def-a-ma-tion
 de-fam-a-to-ry
 de-fam-er
de-fault
 de-fault-er
de-feat
de-feat-ism
 de-feat-ist
def-e-cate
 def-e-cat-ed
 def-e-cat-ing
 def-e-ca-tion
de-fect
de-fec-tion
 de-fec-tor
de-fec-tive
 de-fec-tive-ly

de-fec-tive-ness
de-fend
de-fend-er
de-fend-ant
de-fense
de-fense-less
de-fense-less-ly
de-fense-less-ness
de-fen-si-ble
de-fen-si-bil-i-ty
de-fen-si-bly
de-fen-sive
de-fen-sive-ly
de-fer
de-ferred
de-fer-ring
de-fer-ment
def-er-ence
def-er-en-tial
def-er-en-tial-ly
de-fi-ance
de-fi-ant
de-fi-ant-ly
de-fi-cient
de-fi-cien-cy
de-fi-cien-cies
de-fi-cient-ly
def-i-cit
de-file
de-filed
de-fil-ing
de-fine
de-fined
de-fin-ing
de-fin-er
de-fin-a-ble
de-fin-a-bly
def-i-nite
def-i-nite-ly
def-i-nite-ness
def-i-ni-tion
de-fin-i-tive
de-fin-i-tive-ly

de-flate
de-flat-ed
de-flat-ing
de-fla-tion
de-fla-tion-ary
de-flect
de-flec-tion
de-flec-tive
de-flec-tor
de-flow-er
de-fo-li-ate
de-fo-li-at-ed
de-fo-li-at-ing
de-for-est
de-for-est-a-tion
de-form
de-for-ma-tion
de-formed
de-form-i-ty
de-form-i-ties
de-fraud
de-fray
de-fray-al
de-fray-ment
de-fray-a-ble
de-frost
de-frost-er
deft
deft-ly
deft-ness
de-funct
de-fy
de-fied
de-fy-ing
de-fi-er
de-gen-er-ate
de-gen-er-at-ed
de-gen-er-at-ing
de-gen-er-ate-ly
de-gen-er-a-cy
de-gen-er-a-tion
de-gen-er-a-tive
de-grade

de-graded
de-grad-ing
deg-ra-da-tion
de-gree
de-his-cence
de-his-cent
de-hy-drate
de-hy-drat-ed
de-hy-drat-ing
de-hy-dra-tion
de-i-fy
de-i-fied
de-i-fy-ing
de-i-fi-ca-tion
de-i-fi-er
deign
de-ist
de-ism
de-is-tic
de-is-ti-cal
de-i-ty
de-i-ties
de-ject-ed
de-jec-ted-ly
de-jec-tion
de ju-re
de-lay
de-lay-er
de-lec-ta-ble
de-lec-ta-ble-ness
de-lec-ta-bly
de-lec-ta-tion
del-e-gate
del-e-gat-ed
del-e-gat-ing
del-e-ga-tion
de-lete
de-let-ed
de-let-ing
de-le-tion
del-e-te-ri-ous
de-lib-er-ate
de-lib-er-at-ed

de-lib-er-at-ing
de-lib-er-ate-ly
de-lib-er-ate-ness
de-lib-er-a-tion
de-lib-er-a-tive
de-lib-er-a-tor
del-i-ca-cy
del-i-ca-cies
del-i-cate
del-i-cate-ly
del-i-cate-ness
del-i-ca-tes-sen
de-li-cious
de-li-cious-ly
de-li-cious-ness
de-lim-it
de-lim-i-ta-tion
de-lin-e-ate
de-lin-e-at-ed
de-lin-e-at-ing
de-lin-e-a-tion
de-lin-e-a-tor
de-lin-quent
de-lin-quen-cy
de-lin-quen-cies
de-lir-i-um
de-lir-i-ums
de-lir-ia
de-lir-i-ous
de-lir-i-ous-ly
de-liv-er
de-liv-er-a-ble
de-liv-er-er
de-liv-er-ance
de-liv-ery
de-liv-er-ies
de-louse
de-loused
de-lous-ing
del-phin-i-um
del-ta
del-toid
de-lude

de-lud-ed
de-lud-ing
de-lud-er
de-lu-sive
de-lu-so-ry
de-lu-sive-ly
del-uge
del-uged
del-ug-ing
de-lu-sion
de-luxe
delve
delved
delv-ing
dem-a-gogue
dem-a-gogu-ery
dem-a-gog-ic
dem-a-gog-i-cal
de-mand
de-mand-er
de-mar-ca-tion
de-mean
de-mean-or
de-ment-ed
de-men-tia
de-mer-it
dem-i-god
de-mise
de-mised
de-mis-ing
dem-i-tasse
de-mo-bi-lize
de-mo-bi-lized
de-mo-bi-liz-ing
de-mo-bi-li-za-tion
de-moc-ra-cy
de-moc-ra-cies
dem-o-crat
dem-o-crat-ic
dem-o-crat-i-cal-ly
de-moc-ra-tize
de-moc-ra-tized
de-moc-ra-tiz-ing

de-moc-ra-ti-za-tion
de-mog-ra-phy
de-mog-ra-pher
dem-o-graph-ic
de-mol-ish
de-mol-ish-er
dem-o-li-tion
de-mon
de-mon-ic
de-mon-e-tize
de-mon-e-tized
de-mon-e-tiz-ing
de-mon-e-ti-za-tion
de-mo-ni-ac
de-mo-ni-a-cal
de-mon-ol-o-gy
de-mon-ol-o-gist
dem-on-strate
dem-on-strat-ed
dem-on-strat-ing
de-mon-stra-ble
de-mon-stra-bly
de-mon-stra-tion
de-mon-stra-tive
de-mon-stra-tive-ly
dem-on-stra-tor
de-mor-al-ize
de-mor-al-ized
de-mor-al-iz-ing
de-mor-al-i-za-tion
de-mor-al-iz-er
de-mote
de-mot-ed
de-mot-ing
de-mo-tion
de-mur
de-murred
de-mur-ring
de-mur-ral
de-mur-er
de-mur-est
de-mure-ly
de-mure-ness

de-mur-rage
de-nat-u-ral-ize
  de-nat-u-ral-ized
  de-nat-u-ral-iz-ing
  -nat-u-ral-i-za-tion
de-na-ture
  de-na-tured
  de-na-tur-ing
den-drite
den-dro-lite
den-drol-o-gy
den-e-ga-tion
de-ni-al
de-ni-er
den-im
den-i-zen
de-nom-i-nate
  de-nom-i-nat-ed
  de-nom-i-nat-ing
de-nom-i-na-tion
  de-nom-i-na-tion-al
de-nom-i-na-tive
de-nom-i-na-tor
de-note
  de-not-ed
  de-not-ing
  de-no-ta-tion
de-noue-ment
de-nounce
  de-nounced
  de-noun-cing
  de-nounce-ment
  de-nun-ci-a-tion
  de-nun-ci-a-to-ry
dense
  den-ser
  den-sest
  dense-ly
  dense-ness
den-si-ty
  den-si-ties
den-tal
den-tate

den-ti-frice
den-tin
den-tist
den-tist-ry
den-ti-tion
den-ture
de-nude
  de-nud-ed
  de-nud-ing
den-u-da-tion
de-nun-ci-ate
  de-nun-ci-at-ed
  de-nun-ci-at-ing
  de-nun-ci-a-tion
  de-nun-ci-a-to-ry
de-ny
  de-nied
  de-ny-ing
de-o-dor-ant
  de-o-dor-ize
  de-o-dor-ized
  de-o-dor-iz-ing
de-part
  de-part-ed
de-part-ment
  de-part-men-tal
de-par-ture
de-pend
  de-pend-ence
de-pend-a-ble
  de-pend-a-bly
  de-pend-a-bil-i-ty
de-pend-en-cy
  de-pend-en-cies
de-pend-ent
de-pict
  de-pic-tion
de-pil-a-to-ry
  de-pil-a-to-ries
de-plete
  de-plet-ed
  de-plet-ing
  de-ple-tion

de-plor-a-ble
  de-plor-a-bly
de-plore
  de-plored
  de-plor-ing
de-ploy
  de-ploy-ment
de-po-nent
de-pop-u-late
  de-pop-u-lat-ed
  de-pop-u-lat-ing
  de-pop-u-la-tion
de-port
  de-por-ta-tion
de-port-ment
de-pose
  de-posed
  de-pos-ing
  de-pos-a-ble
de-pos-it
  de-pos-i-tor
dep-o-si-tion
de-pos-i-to-ry
de-pot
de-prave
  de-praved
  de-prav-ing
  de-prav-i-ty
dep-re-cate
  dep-re-cat-ed
  dep-re-cat-ing
  dep-re-cat-ing-ly
  dep-re-ca-tion
dep-re-ca-to-ry
de-pre-ci-ate
  de-pre-ci-at-ed
  de-pre-ci-at-ing
  de-pre-ci-a-tion
  de-pre-ci-a-to-ry
  de-pre-ci-a-tor
dep-re-date
  dep-re-dat-ed
  dep-re-dat-ing

dep-re-da-tion
de-press
de-pres-sant
de-pressed
de-pres-sion
de-prive
  de-prived
  de-priv-ing
  dep-ri-va-tion
depth
dep-u-ta-tion
de-pute
  de-put-ed
  de-put-ing
dep-u-tize
  dep-u-tized
  dep-u-tiz-ing
dep-u-ty
  dep-u-ties
  dep-u-ty-ship
de-rail
  de-rail-ment
de-range
  de-ranged
  de-rang-ing
  de-range-ment
der-e-lict
  der-e-lic-tion
de-ride
  de-rid-ed
  de-rid-ing
de-ri-sion
de-ri-sive
  de-ri-sive-ly
  de-ri-so-ry
der-i-va-tion
de-riv-a-tive
de-rive
  de-rived
  de-riv-ing
  de-riv-a-ble
der-ma
  der-mal

der-ma-tol-o-gy
  der-ma-to-log-i-cal
  der-ma-tol-o-gist
der-mis
der-o-gate
  der-o-gat-ed
  der-o-gat-ing
  der-o-ga-tion
de-rog-a-to-ry
  de-rog-a-to-ri-ly
der-rick
der-rin-ger
der-vish
des-cant
de-scend
  de-scend-a-ble
de-scend-ant
de-scent
de-scribe
  de-scribed
  de-scrib-ing
  de-scrib-a-ble
  de-scrib-er
de-scrip-tion
  de-scrip-tive
  de-scrip-tive-ly
  de-scrip-tive-ness
de-scry
  de-scried
  de-scry-ing
des-e-crate
  des-e-crat-ed
  des-e-crat-ing
  des-e-cra-tion
de-seg-re-gate
  de-seg-re-gat-ed
  de-seg-re-gat-ing
  de-seg-re-ga-tion
des-ert
de-sert
  de-sert-er
  de-ser-tion
des-ha-bille

des-ic-cate
  des-ic-cat-ed
  des-ic-cat-ing
  des-ic-ca-tion
  des-ic-ca-tive
de-sid-er-a-tum
de-sign
des-ig-nate
  des-ig-nat-ed
  des-ig-nat-ing
  des-ig-na-tion
  des-ig-na-tive
  des-ig-na-tor
de-sign-ed-ly
de-sign-er
de-sign-ing
de-sire
  de-sired
  de-sir-ing
  de-sir-a-ble
  de-sir-a-bil-i-ty
  de-sir-a-bly
  de-sir-ous
de-sist
des-o-late
  des-o-lat-ed
  des-o-lat-ing
  des-o-late-ly
  des-o-la-tion
de-spair
  de-spair-ing
  de-spair-ing-ly
des-per-a-do
  des-per-a-does
des-per-ate
  des-per-ate-ly
  des-per-ate-ness
  des-per-a-tion
des-pi-ca-ble
  des-pi-ca-bly
de-spise
  de-spised
  de-spis-ing

de-spite
de-spoil
  de-spoil-er
  de-spo-li-a-tion
de-spond
  de-spond-en-cy
  de-spond-ence
  de-spond-ent
  de-spond-ent-ly
des-pot
  des-pot-ic
  des-pot-i-cal-ly
des-pot-ism
des-sert
des-ti-na-tion
des-tine
  des-tined
  des-tin-ing
des-ti-ny
  des-ti-nies
des-ti-tute
  des-ti-tu-tion
de-stroy
de-stroy-er
de-struc-tion
  de-struct-i-ble
  de-struct-i-bil-i-ty
de-struc-tive
  de-struc-tive-ly
  de-struc-tive-ness
des-ue-tude
des-ul-to-ry
  des-ul-to-ri-ly
de-tach
  de-tach-a-ble
de-tached
de-tach-ment
de-tail
  de-tailed
de-tain
  de-tain-ment
  de-tain-er
de-tect

de-tect-a-ble
de-tec-tion
de-tec-tive
de-tec-tor
de-ten-tion
de-ter
  de-terred
  de-ter-ring
de-ter-gent
de-te-ri-o-rate
  de-te-ri-o-rat-ed
  de-te-ri-o-rat-ing
  de-te-ri-o-ra-tion
de-ter-mi-na-ble
de-ter-mi-nant
de-ter-mi-na-tion
  de-ter-mi-na-tive
de-ter-mine
  de-ter-mined
  de-ter-min-ing
  de-ter-min-er
de-ter-mined
  de-ter-mined-ly
de-ter-min-ism
  de-ter-min-ist
de-ter-rent
  de-ter-rence
de-test
  de-test-a-ble
  de-test-a-bly
de-tes-ta-tion
de-throne
  de-throned
  de-thron-ing
  de-throne-ment
de-tour
de-tract
  de-trac-tion
  de-trac-tor
det-ri-ment
  det-ri-men-tal
  det-ri-men-tal-ly

de-tri-tus
deuce
deu-te-ri-um
de-val-u-ate
  de-val-u-at-ed
  de-val-u-at-ing
  de-val-u-a-tion
dev-as-tate
  dev-as-tat-ed
  dev-as-tat-ing
  dev-as-ta-tion
de-vel-op
  de-vel-op-ment
de-vel-op-er
de-vi-ate
  de-vi-at-ed
  de-vi-at-ing
  de-vi-ant
  de-vi-a-tion
de-vice
de-vi-ous
  de-vi-ous-ly
de-vise
  de-vised
  de-vis-ing
  de-vis-a-ble
  de-vis-al
  de-vi-see
  de-vi-sor
de-void
de-volve
  de-volved
  de-volv-ing
  dev-o-lu-tion
de-vote
  de-vot-ing
de-vot-ed
  de-vot-ed-ly
dev-o-tee
de-vo-tion
  de-vo-tion-al
de-vour
  de-vour-er

de-vour-ing-ly
de-vout
de-vout-ly
de-vout-ness
dew-drop
dew-lap
dewy
dew-i-er
dew-i-est
dew-y-eyed
dex-ter-ous
dex-ter-i-ty
dex-ter-ous-ly
dex-trose
di-a-be-tes
di-a-bet-ic
di-a-bol-ic
di-a-bol-i-cal
di-a-bol-i-cal-ly
di-a-crit-ic
di-a-crit-i-cal
di-a-crit-i-cal-ly
di-a-dem
di-ag-nose
di-ag-nosed
di-ag-nos-ing
di-ag-no-sis
di-ag-no-ses
di-ag-nos-tic
di-ag-nos-ti-cian
di-ag-o-nal
di-ag-o-nal-ly
di-a-gram
di-a-gramed
di-a-gram-ing
di-a-gram-mat-ic
di-a-gram-mat-i-cal
di-al
di-aled
di-al-ing
di-a-lect
di-a-lec-tal
di-a-lec-tic

di-a-lec-ti-cal
di-a-lec-ti-cian
di-a-logue
di-am-e-ter
di-a-met-ric
di-a-met-ric-al
di-a-met-ric-al-ly
dia-mond
dia-per
di-aph-a-nous
di-a-phragm
di-ar-rhea
di-a-ry
di-as-to-le
di-as-tol-ic
di-a-ther-mic
di-a-tom
di-a-ton-ic
dib-ble
dib-bled
dib-bling
di-chot-o-my
di-chot-o-mous
di-cho-tom-ic
dic-tate
dic-ta-tion
dic-ta-tor
dic-ta-to-ri-al
dic-ta-to-ri-al-ly
dic-tion-ary
dic-tum
di-dac-tic
di-dac-ti-cally
di-er-e-ses
di-e-tary
di-e-tet-ic
di-e-tet-i-cal
di-e-tet-i-cal-ly
di-e-tet-ics
di-e-ti-tian
dif-fer-ence
dif-fer-enced
dif-fer-en-cing

dif-fer-ent
dif-fer-ent-ly
dif-fer-en-tial
dif-fer-en-tial-ly
dif-fer-en-ti-ate
dif-fer-en-ti-at-ed
dif-fi-cult
dif-fi-cult-ly
dif-fi-dence
dif-fi-dent
dif-fi-dent-ly
dig-ger
dig-gings
dig-it-al
dig-i-tal-is
dig-ni-fied
dig-ni-fy
dig-ni-fy-ing
dig-ni-tary
dig-ni-tar-ies
dig-ni-ty
di-gress
di-gres-sion
di-gres-sive
di-he-dral
di-lap-i-dat-ed
di-lap-i-da-tion
dil-a-ta-tion
di-late
di-lat-ed
di-lat-ing
di-lat-a-ble
di-la-tion
dil-a-to-ry
dil-a-to-ri-ly
di-lem-ma
dil-et-tan-te
dil-et-tan-tes
dil-i-gence
dil-i-gent
dil-i-gent-ly
dil-ly-dal-ly
di-lute

di-lut-ed
di-lut-ing
di-men-sion
di-men-sion-al
di-min-ish
di-min-ish-a-ble
di-min-u-en-do
di-min-u-en-dos
dim-i-nu-tion
di-min-u-tive
di-min-u-tive-ness
dim-ple
dim-pled
dim-pling
din-er
di-nette
din-ghy
din-ghies
din-ner
di-no-saur
di-o-cese
di-oc-e-san
di-o-ram-a
diph-the-ri-a
di-plo-ma
di-plo-ma-cy
di-plo-ma-cies
dip-lo-mat
dip-lo-mat-ic
dip-lo-mat-i-cal-ly
dip-per
dip-so-ma-nia
dip-so-ma-ni-ac
di-rect
di-rect-ness
di-rec-tion
di-rec-tion-al
di-rec-tive
di-rect-ly
di-rec-tor
di-rec-to-ri-al
di-rec-tor-ship
di-rec-to-rate

di-rec-to-ry
di-rec-to-ries
dis-a-buse
dis-a-bused
dis-a-bus-ing
dis-ad-van-tage
dis-ad-van-taged
dis-af-fect
dis-af-fec-tion
dis-af-fect-ed
dis-a-gree
dis-a-gree-ing
dis-a-gree-a-ble
dis-a-gree-ment
dis-al-low
dis-al-low-ance
dis-ap-pear
dis-ap-pear-ance
dis-ap-point
dis-ap-point-ment
dis-ap-pro-ba-tion
dis-ap-prove
dis-ap-prov-al
dis-arm
dis-ar-ma-ment
dis-ar-range
dis-ar-ranged
dis-ar-rang-ing
dis-ar-ray
dis-as-sem-ble
dis-as-ter
dis-as-trous
dis-as-trous-ly
dis-a-vow
dis-a-vow-al
dis-band
dis-band-ment
dis-be-lieve
dis-be-lief
dis-be-liev-er
dis-burse
dis-bursed
dis-burs-ing

dis-burs-er
dis-cern-ing
dis-cern-ment
dis-charge
dis-charged
dis-charg-ing
dis-char-ger
dis-ci-ple
dis-ci-ple-ship
dis-ci-pline
dis-ci-plines
dis-ci-pli-nary
dis-claim-er
dis-close
dis-closed
dis-clos-er
dis-clo-sure
dis-coid
dis-col-or
dis-col-or-a-tion
dis-com-fit
dis-com-fi-ture
dis-com-fort
dis-com-mode
dis-com-mod-ing
dis-com-pose
dis-com-posed
dis-com-pos-ing
dis-con-cert
dis-con-cert-ed
dis-con-nect
dis-con-nec-tion
dis-con-so-late
dis-con-tent
dis-con-tent-ed
dis-con-tin-ue
dis-con-tin-ued
dis-con-tin-u-ing
dis-con-tin-u-ous
dis-cord
dis-cord-ance
dis-cord-ant-ly
dis-count

dis-cour-age
dis-cour-ag-ing
dis-course
dis-coursed
dis-cours-ing
dis-cour-te-ous
dis-cour-te-sy
dis-cov-er
dis-cov-er-a-ble
dis-cov-er-er
dis-cov-er-y
dis-cov-er-ies
dis-cred-it
dis-cred-it-a-bly
dis-creet
dis-crep-an-cy
dis-crep-an-cies
dis-crete
dis-cre-tion
dis-cre-tion-ary
dis-crim-i-nate
dis-crim-i-nate-ly
dis-crim-i-na-to-ry
dis-crim-i-na-tor
dis-cur-sive
dis-cur-sive-ly
dis-cur-sive-ness
dis-cus
dis-cus-es
dis-cuss
dis-cuss-i-ble
dis-cus-sion
dis-dain
dis-dain-ful
dis-dain-ful-ly
dis-ease
dis-eased
dis-em-bark
dis-em-body
dis-em-bod-ied
dis-em-bod-y-ing
dis-em-bow-el
dis-em-bow-eled

dis-em-bow-el-ing
dis-en-chant
dis-en-chant-ment
dis-en-cum-ber
dis-en-fran-chise
dis-en-fran-chised
dis-en-fran-chis-ing
dis-en-gage
dis-en-gaged
dis-en-gag-ing
dis-en-tan-gle
dis-en-tan-gled
dis-en-tan-gling
dis-es-tab-lish
dis-fa-vor
dis-fig-ure
dis-fig-ured
dis-fig-ur-ing
dis-fig-ure-ment
dis-gorge
dis-gorged
dis-gorg-ing
dis-grace
dis-graced
dis-grac-ing
dis-grace-ful
dis-grace-ful-ly
dis-grun-tle
dis-grun-tled
dis-grun-tling
dis-gust
dis-gust-ed
dis-gust-ing
dis-ha-bille
dis-har-mo-ny
dis-har-mo-nies
dis-heart-en
dis-hev-eled
dis-hon-est
dis-hon-est-ly
dis-hon-es-ty
dis-hon-es-ties
dis-hon-or

dis-hon-or-a-ble
dis-hon-or-a-bly
dis-il-lu-sion
dis-in-cline
dis-in-clined
dis-in-fect
dis-in-her-it
dis-in-te-grate
dis-in-ter-es-ted
dis-in-ter-est-ed-ly
dis-junc-tion
dis-loy-al
dis-loy-al-ty
dis-o-be-di-ence
dis-or-der-ly
dis-o-ri-ent
dis-pos-a-ble
dis-qual-i-fy
dis-qui-et
dis-re-spect
dis-re-spect-ful
dis-rup-tive
dis-rupt-er
dis-sat-is-fy
dis-sat-is-fy-ing
dis-sem-blance
dis-sem-i-nate
dis-sem-i-nat-ing
dis-sem-i-na-tor
dis-sent
dis-ser-tate
dis-ser-ta-ting
dis-ser-ta-tion
dis-serv-ice
dis-si-dent
dis-sim-i-lar
dis-sim-i-lar-i-ty
dis-sim-i-late
dis-sim-i-lat-ing
dis-sim-i-la-tive
dis-si-pate
dis-si-pa-tion
dis-so-nance

dis-so-nant
dis-suade
  dis-sua-sion
  dis-sua-sive
dis-tance
dis-taste
  dis-taste-ful-ly
dis-tem-per
dis-til-late
dis-till-ery
dis-tin-guish
dis-tract
  dis-tract-ing
dis-trib-ute
  dis-trib-ut-ed
  dis-tri-bu-tion
  dis-tri-u-tor
dis-u-nite
di-van
di-verge
  di-ver-gence
  di-ver-gent
di-verse
di-ver-sion
div-i-dend
di-vi-sor
di-vulge
  di-vulg-ing
  di-vul-gence
do-a-ble
doc-tor-ate
doc-u-ment
dod-der
dog-ma
dog-mat-ic
  dog-mat-i-cal
dol-drums
dol-or-ous
dol-phin
do-mes-tic
do-mes-ti-cate
do-mes-tic-i-ty
dom-i-cile

dom-i-cil-ing
dom-i-nance
dom-i-nant
dom-i-neer
do-min-ion
dop-ey
  dop-i-est
  dop-i-ness
dor-mant
dor-mer
dor-mi-to-ry
dos-age
dos-si-er
dou-ble-faced
douche
dow-a-ger
dow-el
down-ward-ly
doz-ing
doz-en
drag-on
dra-per-y
drib-ble
  drib-bled
  drib-bling
  drib-bler
drill-ing
dri-ly
driv-el
  driv-eled
  driv-el-ing
driz-zle
  driz-zling
  driz-zly
drom-e-dar-y
droop
  droop-y
  droop-i-er
  droop-i-est
drop-per
dross
drought
  drought-y

drought-i-er
drought-i-est
drowned
drowse
  drowsed
  drows-ing
  drow-si-ness
drudge
drug-gist
dru-id
drum-mer
drunk-ard
drunk-en
  drunk-en-ness
dry-ad
du-al
  du-al-i-ty
du-al-ism
  du-al-ist
  du-al-is-tic
du-bi-ous
  du-bi-e-ty
  du-bi-ous-ly
du-cal
duch-ess
duck-ling
duc-tile
du-el
  du-eled
  du-el-ing
  du-el-ist
duke-dom
dul-cet
dum-found
dunce
dun-ga-ree
dun-geon
dun-nage
du-o-dec-i-mal
du-o-de-num
  du-o-de-na
  du-o-de-nal
du-pli-cate

du-pli-cat-ing
du-pli-ca-tor
du-plic-i-ty
du-ra-ble
du-ra-bil-ity
du-ra-bly
dur-ance
du-ra-tion
du-ti-a-ble
du-ti-ful
du-ti-ful-ly
du-ti-ful-ness
dwarf
dwarf-ish
dwin-dle
dwin-dled
dwin-dling
dye-stuff
dy-ing
dy-nam-ic
dy-nam-i-cal
dy-nam-i-cal-ly
dy-na-mism
dy-na-mite
dy-na-mo
dy-nas-ty
dy-nas-ties
dyne
dys-en-tery
dys-func-tion
dys-pep-sia
dys-pep-tic
dys-pep-ti-cal
dys-tro-phy

E

ea-ger
ea-ger-ly
ea-ger-ness
ea-gle
ea-gle eyed
ea-glet

earl-dom
ear-ly
ear-li-er
ear-li-est
ear-mark
ear-muff
earn
earn-er
ear-nest
ear-nest-ly
earn-ings
ear-ring
earth-en
earth-ly
earth-li-er
earth-li-est
earth-quake
earth-y
ear-wax
ease
eased
eas-ing
ea-sel
ease-ment
eas-i-ly
eas-i-ness
east-er-ly
east-ern
east-ward
eas-y
eas-i-er
eas-i-est
eas-y-go-ing
eat
ebb
eb-on-y
eb-on-ies
e-bul-lience
e-bul-lient
e-bul-li-tion
ec-cen-tric
ec-cen-tri-cal-ly
ec-cen-tric-i-ty

ec-cen-tric-i-ties
ec-cle-si-as-tic
ec-cle-si-as-ti-cal
ec-cle-si-as-ti-cal-ly
ech-e-lon
e-chi-no-derm
ech-o
e-cho-ic
e-clair
ec-lec-tic
ec-lec-ti-cal-ly
ec-lec-ti-cism
e-clipse
e-clipsed
e-clips-ing
e-clip-tic
e-col-o-gy
e-c-o-log-ic
e-c-o-log-i-cal
e-col-o-gist
e-co-nom-ic
e-co-nom-i-cal
e-co-nom-ics
e-con-o-mist
e-con-o-mize
e-con-o-mized
e-con-o-miz-ing
e-con-o-miz-er
e-con-o-my
e-con-o-mies
ec-o-sys-tem
ec-ru
ec-sta-sy
ec-sta-sies
ec-stat-ic
ec-stat-i-cal
ec-to-morph
ec-to-mor-phic
ec-to-plasm
ec-u-men-i-cal
ec-u-men-ic
ec-u-men-i-cal-ly
ec-u-men-ism

ec-ze-ma
e-de-ma
  e-de-ma-ta
e-den-tate
edg-y
ed-i-ble
e-dict
ed-i-fice
ed-i-fy
  ed-i-fied
  ed-i-fy-ing
  ed-i-fi-ca-tion
ed-it
e-di-tion
ed-i-tor
  ed-i-tor-ship
ed-i-to-ri-al
  ed-i-to-ri-al-ly
  ed-i-to-ri-al-ize
  ed-i-to-ri-al-lized
ed-u-cate
  ed-u-cat-ed
  ed-u-cat-ing
  ed-u-ca-ble
ed-u-ca-tor
ed-u-ca-tion
  ed-u-ca-tion-al
e-duce
  e-duced
  e-duc-ing
  e-duc-i-ble
  e-duc-tion
eel
ee-rie
  ee-ri-er
  ee-ri-est
  ee-ri-ly
ef-fect
  ef-fec-tive
  ef-fec-tive-ness
  ef-fec-tive-ly
ef-fec-tu-al
  ef-fec-tu-al-i-ty

ef-fec-tu-ate
  ef-fec-tu-at-ed
  ef-fec-tu-at-ing
ef-fem-i-nate
  ef-fem-i-na-cy
  ef-fem-i-na-cies
  ef-fem-i-nate-ly
ef-fete
ef-fi-ca-cious
ef-fi-ca-cy
  ef-fi-ca-cies
ef-fi-cien-cy
  ef-fi-cien-cies
ef-fi-cient
  ef-fi-cient-ly
ef-fi-gy
  ef-fi-gies
ef-flo-resce
ef-flu-ent
  ef-flu-ence
ef-flu-vi-um
  ef-flu-via
  ef-flu-vi-ums
  ef-flu-vi-al
ef-fron-ter-y
  ef-fron-ter-ies
ef-ful-gent
  ef-ful-gence
ef-fuse
  ef-fused
  ef-fus-ing
ef-fu-sion
ef-fu-sive
  ef-fu-sive-ly
egal-i-tar-i-an
  egal-i-tar-i-an-ism
egg-nog
egg-plant
e-go
  e-gos
e-go-cen-tric
e-go-ism
  e-go-ist

e-go-is-tic
e-go-tism
e-go-tis-tic
e-go-tis-ti-cal
e-gre-gious
  e-gre-gious-ly
e-gress
e-gret
el-der-down
eight
  eighth
eight-ball
eight-fold
eight-y
  eight-ies
  eight-i-eth
ei-ther
e-jac-u-late
  e-jac-u-lat-ed
  e-jac-u-lat-ing
  e-jac-u-la-tion
e-ject
  e-jec-tion
  e-ject-ment
  e-jec-tor
eke
  eked
  ek-ing
e-lab-o-rate
  e-lab-o-rat-ed
  e-lab-o-rat-ing
  e-lab-o-rate-ly
  e-lab-o-ra-tion
e-lapse
  e-lapsed
  e-laps-ing
e-las-tic
  e-las-ti-cal-ly
  e-las-tic-i-ty
e-late
  e-lat-ed
  e-lat-ing
  e-la-tion

el-bow
el-bow-room
el-der
  eld-er-ship
el-der-ly
  eld-er-li-ness
eld-est
e-lect
e-lec-tion
e-lec-tion-eer
e-lec-tive
e-lec-tor
e-lec-tor-ate
e-lec-tric
  e-lec-tri-cal
  e-lec-tri-cal-ly
e-lec-tri-cian
e-lec-tric-i-ty
e-lec-tri-fy
  e-lec-tri-fied
  e-lec-tri-fy-ing
  e-lec-tri-fi-ca-tion
e-lec-tro-cute
  e-lec-tro-cut-ed
  e-lec-tro-cut-ing
  e-lec-tro-cu-tion
e-lec-trode
e-lec-tro-dy-nam-ics
e-lec-trol-y-sis
  e-lec-tro-lyze
  e-lec-tro-lyzed
  e-lec-tro-lyz-ing
e-lec-tro-lyte
  e-lec-tro-lyt-ic
e-lec-tro-mag-net
  e-lec-tro-mag-net-ic
e-lec-tron
e-lec-tron-ic
  e-lec-tron-ics
  e-lec-tron-i-cal-ly
e-lec-tro-plate
  e-lec-tro-plat-ed
  e-lec-tro-plat-ing

e-lec-tro-ther-a-py
e-lec-trum
el-ee-mos-y-nar-y
el-e-gant
  el-e-gance
  el-e-gan-cy
  el-e-gant-ly
el-e-ment
  el-e-men-tal
  el-e-men-tal-ly
el-e-men-ta-ry
  el-e-men-ta-ri-ly
el-e-phant
  el-e-phan-tine
el-e-vate
  el-e-vat-ed
  el-e-vat-ing
el-e-va-tion
el-e-va-tor
e-lev-en
  e-lev-enth
elf
e-lic-it
el-i-gi-ble
  el-i-gi-bil-i-ty
  el-i-gi-bly
e-lim-i-nate
  e-lim-i-nat-ed
  e-lim-i-nat-ing
  e-lim-i-na-tion
  e-lim-i-na-tor
e-lite
  e-lit-ism
  e-lit-ist
e-lix-ir
el-lipse
el-lip-sis
  el-lip-ses
el-lip-ti-cal
  el-lip-tic
  el-lip-ti-cal-ly
el-o-cu-tion
  el-o-cu-tion-ary

el-o-cu-tion-ist
e-lon-gate
  e-lon-gat-ed
  e-lon-gat-ing
  e-lon-ga-tion
e-lope
el-o-quence
el-o-quent
  el-o-quent-ly
else-where
e-lu-ci-date
  e-lu-ci-dat-ed
  e-lu-ci-dat-ing
  e-lu-ci-da-tion
  e-lu-ci-da-tor
e-lude
  e-lud-ed
  e-lud-ing
  e-lu-sion
e-lu-sive
  e-lu-sive-ly
elv-ish
e-ma-ci-ate
  e-ma-ci-at-ed
  e-ma-ci-at-ing
  e-ma-ci-a-tion
em-a-nate
  em-a-nat-ed
  em-a-nat-ing
  em-a-na-tion
e-man-ci-pate
  e-man-ci-pat-ed
  e-man-ci-pat-ing
  e-man-ci-pa-tor
em-balm
  em-balm-er
  em-balm-ment
em-bank-ment
em-bar-go
  em-bar-goes
  em-bar-goed
  em-bar-go-ing
em-bark

em-bar-ka-tion
em-bark-ment
em-bar-rass
em-bar-rass-ing-ly
em-bar-rass-ment
em-bas-sy
em-bas-sies
em-bat-tle
em-bat-tled
em-bat-tling
em-bat-tle-ment
em-bed
em-bed-ded
em-bed-ding
em-bel-lish
em-bel-lish-ment
em-ber
em-bez-zle
em-bez-zled
em-bez-zling
em-bez-zle-ment
em-bez-zler
em-bit-ter
em-bit-ter-ment
em-blem
em-blem-at-ic
em-blem-at-i-cal
em-bod-y
em-bod-ied
em-bod-y-ing
em-bod-i-ment
em-bold-en
em-bo-lism
em-bo-lus
em-bos-om
em-boss
em-boss-ment
em-bou-chure
em-brace
em-braced
em-brac-ing
em-broi-der
em-broi-dery

em-broi-der-ies
em-broil
em-broil-ment
em-bry-o
em-bry-os
em-bry-on-ic
em-bry-ol-o-gy
em-cee
em-ceed
em-cee-ing
e-mend
em-er-ald
e-merge
e-merged
e-merg-ing
e-mer-gence
e-mer-gent
e-mer-gen-cy
e-mer-gen-cies
e-mer-i-tus
e-mer-y
e-met-ic
em-i-grant
em-i-grate
em-i-grat-ed
em-i-grat-ing
em-i-gra-tion
em-i-nence
em-i-nent
em-i-nent-ly
em-i-nent do-main
em-is-sary
em-is-sar-ies
e-mis-sion
e-mis-sive
e-mit
e-mit-ted
e-mit-ting
e-mit-ter
e-mol-lient
e-mol-u-ment
e-mote
e-mot-ed

e-mot-ing
e-mo-tive
emo-tion
emo-tion-al
emo-tion-al-ly
emo-tion-al-ism
em-pan-el
em-pa-thize
em-pa-thized
em-pa-thiz-ing
em-pa-thy
em-pa-thet-ic
em-path-ic
em-per-or
em-pha-sis
em-pha-ses
em-pha-size
em-pha-sized
em-pha-siz-ing
em-phat-ic
em-phat-i-cal-ly
em-phy-se-ma
em-pire
em-pir-i-cal
em-pir-i-cal-ly
em-pir-i-cism
em-pir-i-cist
em-place-ment
em-ploy
em-ploy-a-ble
em-ploy-ee
em-ploy-er
em-ploy-ment
em-po-ri-um
em-po-ri-ums
em-po-ria
em-pow-er
em-press
emp-ty
emp-ti-er
emp-ti-est
emp-tied
emp-ty-ing

emp-ti-ly
emp-ti-ness
emp-ty--hand-ed
emp-ty--head-ed
e-mu
em-u-late
em-u-lat-ed
em-u-lat-ing
em-u-la-tion
e-mul-si-fy
e-mul-si-fied
e-mul-si-fy-ing
e-mul-si-fi-ca-tion
e-mul-si-fi-er
emul-sion
emul-sive
en-a-ble
en-a-bled
en-a-bling
en-act
e-nam-el
e-nam-eled
e-nam-el-ing
e-nam-el-er
e-nam-el-ware
en-am-or
en-am-ored-ness
en-camp
en-camp-ment
en-cap-su-late
en-cap-su-lat-ed
en-cap-su-lat-ing
en-cap-sule
en-case
en-cased
en-cas-ing
en-ceinte
en-ceph-a-li-tis
en-ceph-a-lit-ic
en-ceph-a-lon
en-ceph-a-la
en-chant
en-chant-er

en-chant-ress
en-chant-ing
en-chant-ing-ly
en-chant-ment
en-chi-la-da
en-cir-cle
en-cir-cled
en-cir-cling
en-cir-cle-ment
en-clave
en-close
en-closed
en-clos-ing
en-clo-sure
en-code
en-cod-ed
en-cod-ing
en-co-mi-ast
en-com-pass
en-com-pass-ment
en-core
en-coun-ter
en-cour-age
en-cour-aged
en-cour-ag-ing
en-cour-ag-ing-ly
en-croach
en-croach-er
en-croach-ment
en-crust
en-crus-ta-tion
en-cum-ber
en-cum-brance
en-cy-clo-pe-di-a
en-cy-clo-pe-dic
en-cy-clo-pe-di-cal
en-cyst
en-dan-ger
en-dan-ger-ment
en-dear
en-dear-ment
en-dea-vor
en-dem-ic

en-dem-i-cal
en-dem-i-cal-ly
end-ing
end-less
end-less-ly
end-most
en-do-crine
en-do-cri-nol-o-gy
en-do-crin-o-log-ic
en-do-cri-nol-o-gist
en-dog-e-nous
en-do-sperm
en-dow
en-dow-ment
en-due
en-dued
en-du-ing
en-dur-ance
en-dure
en-dured
en-dur-ing
en-dur-a-ble
en-dur-a-bly
end-ways
en-e-ma
en-e-my
en-e-mies
en-er-get-ic
en-er-get-i-cal
en-er-get-i-cal-ly
en-er-gize
en-er-gized
en-er-giz-ing
en-er-gi-zer
en-er-gy
en-er-gies
en-er-vate
en-er-vat-ed
en-er-vat-ing
en-er-va-tion
en-fee-ble
en-fee-bled
en-fee-bling

en-fee-ble-ment
en-fi-lade
en-fi-lad-ed
en-fi-lad-ing
en-fold
en-fran-chise
en-fran-chised
en-fran-chis-ing
en-fran-chise-ment
en-gage
en-gaged
en-gag-ing
en-gage-ment
en-gen-der
en-gine
en-gi-neer
en-gorge
en-gorged
en-gorg-ing
en-gorge-ment
en-grave
en-graved
en-grav-ing
en-grav-er
en-gross
en-grossed
en-gross-er
en-gross-ing
en-gross-ing-ly
en-gross-ment
en-gulf
en-gulf-ment
en-hance
en-hanced
en-hanc-ing
en-hance-ment
e-nig-ma
en-ig-mat-ic
en-ig-mat-i-cal
en-ig-mat-i-cal-ly
en-join
en-join-er
en-join-ment

en-large
en-larged
en-larg-ing
en-large-a-ble
en-larg-er
en-large-ment
en-light-en
en-light-en-ment
en-list
en-list-ed
en-list-ment
en-liv-en
en-liv-en-er
en-mesh
en-mi-ty
en-mi-ties
en-no-ble
en-no-bled
en-no-bling
en-no-ble-ment
en-no-bler
en-nui
e-nor-mi-ty
e-nor-mi-ties
e-nor-mous
e-nor-mous-ly
e-nor-mous-ness
e-nough
en-plane
en-planed
en-plan-ing
en-rage
en-raged
en-rag-ing
en-rap-ture
en-rap-tured
en-rap-tur-ing
en-rich
en-rich-er
en-rich-ment
en-roll
en-roll-ment
en route

en-sconce
en-sconced
en-sconc-ing
en-sem-ble
en-shrine
en-shrin-ing
en-shroud
en-sign
en-si-lage
en-si-laged
en-si-lag-ing
en-slave
en-slaved
en-slav-ing
en-slave-ment
en-slav-er
en-snare
en-snared
en-snar-ing
en-snare-ment
en-snar-er
en-snar-ing-ly
en-sue
en-sued
en-su-ing
en-su-ing-ly
en-sure
en-sured
en-sur-ing
en-sur-er
en-tail
en-tail-er
en-tail-ment
en-tan-gle
en-tan-gled
en-tan-gling
en-tan-gle-ment
en-tan-gler
en-tente
en-ter
en-ter-a-ble
en-ter-i-tis
en-ter-prise

en-ter-pris-ing
en-ter-pris-ing-ly
en-ter-tain
en-ter-tain-er
en-ter-tain-ing
en-ter-tain-ing-ly
en-ter-tain-ment
en-thrall
en-thralled
en-thrall-ing
en-thrall-ment
en-throne
en-throned
en-thron-ing
en-throne-ment
en-thuse
en-thused
en-thus-ing
en-thu-si-asm
en-thu-si-ast
en-thu-si-as-tic
-en-thu-si-as-ti-cal-ly
en-tice
en-ticed
en-tic-ing
en-tice-ment
en-tic-er
en-tic-ig-ly
en-tire
en-tire-ly
en-tire-ness
en-tire-ty
en-tire-ties
en-ti-tle
en-ti-tled
en-ti-tling
en-ti-tle-ment
en-ti-ty
en-ti-ties
en-to-mol-o-gy
en-to-mol-o-gies
en-to-mo-log-ic
en-to-mo-log-i-cal

en-to-mol-o-gist
en-tou-rage
en-trails
en-train
en-train-er
en-trance
en-trance-way
en-tranced
en-tranc-ing
en-trance-ment
en-tranc-ing-ly
en-trant
en-trap
en-trapped
en-trap-ping
en-trap-ment
en-treat
en-treat-ing-ly
en-treat-ment
en-treat-y
en-tree
en-trench
en-trench-ment
en-tre-pre-neur
en-tre-pre-neur-i-al
en-tre-pre-neur-ship
en-tro-py
en-trust
en-trust-ment
en-try
en-tries
en-twine
en-twined
en-twin-ing
e-nu-mer-ate
e-nu-mer-at-ed
e-nu-mer-at-ing
e-nu-mer-a-tion
e-nu-mer-a-tive
e-nu-mer-a-tor
e-nun-ci-ate
e-nun-ci-at-ed
e-nun-ci-at-ing

e-nun-ci-a-tion
e-nun-ci-a-tive
e-nun-ci-a-tor
en-u-re-sis
en-u-ret-ic
en-vel-op
en-vel-oped
en-vel-op-ing
en-vi-a-ble
en-vi-a-ble-ness
en-vi-a-bly
en-vi-ous
en-vi-ous-ly
en-vi-ous-ness
en-vi-ron
en-vi-ron-ment
en-vi-ron-men-tal
-vi-ron-men-tal-ly
en-vi-rons
en-vis-age
en-vis-aged
en-vis-ag-ing
en-vi-sion
en-voy
en-vy
en-vies
en-vied
en-vy-ing
en-vi-er
en-vy-ing-ly
en-zyme
en-zy-mat-ic
en-zy-mat-i-cal-ly
e-on
ep-au-let
e-phed-rine
e-phem-er-al
e-phem-er-al-ness
e-phem-er-al-ly
ep-ic
ep-i-cal
ep-i-cen-ter
ep-i-cure

epi-cu-re-an
ep-i-dem-ic
ep-i-dem-i-cal-ly
ep-i-der-mis
ep-i-der-mal
ep-i-der-mic
ep-i-glot-tis
ep-i-gram
ep-i-logue
ep-i-log
epis-co-pa-cy
epsi-co-pa-cies
epis-co-pal
epis-co-pa-lian
epis-co-pa-lian-ism
epis-co-pate
ep-i-sode
ep-i-sod-ic
ep-i-sod-i-cal
ep-i-sod-i-cal-ly
e-pis-te-mol-o-gy
e-pis-te-mol-o-gist
e-pis-tle
e-pis-to-lar-y
ep-i-taph
ep-i-taph-ic
ep-i-taph-ist
ep-i-thet
ep-i-thet-ic
ep-i-thet-i-cal
e-pit-o-me
epit-o-mize
epit-o-mized
epit-o-miz-ing
ep-och
ep-och-al
ep-ox-y
ep-ox-y res-in
ep-si-lon
eq-ua-ble
eq-ua-bil-i-ty
eq-ua-ble-ness
eq-ua-bly

e-qual
e-qualed
e-qual-ling
e-qual-ly
e-qual-ness
e-qual-i-tar-i-an
e-qual-i-tar-i-an-ism
e-qual-i-ty
e-qual-i-ties
e-qual-ize
e-qual-ized
e-qual-iz-ing
e-qual-i-za-tion
e-qual-iz-er
e-qua-nim-i-ty
e-quate
e-quat-ed
e-quat-ing
e-qua-tion
e-qua-tion-al
e-qua-tion-al-ly
e-qua-tor
e-qua-to-ri-al
e-qua-to-ri-al-ly
e-ques-tri-an
e-ques-tri-enne
e-qui-dis-tance
e-qui-dis-tant
e-qui-dis-tant-ly
e-qui-lat-er-al
e-qui-li-brate
e-qui-li-brat-ed
e-qui-li-brat-ing
e-qui-li-bra-tion
e-qui-l-bra-tor
e-qui-lib-ri-um
e-qui-lib-ri-ums
e-qui-lib-ria
e-quine
e-qui-noc-tial
e-qui-nox
e-quip
e-quipped

e-quip-ping
e-quip-per
e-quip-ment
e-qui-poise
eq-ui-ta-ble
eq-ui-ta-ble-ness
eq-ui-ta-bly
equi-ty
eq-ui-ties
e-quiv-a-lance
e-quiv-a-len-cy
e-quiv-a-lent
e-quiv-a-lent-ly
e-quiv-o-cal
e-quiv-o-cal-ly
e-quiv-o-cal-ness
e-quiv-o-cate
e-quiv-o-cat-ed
e-quiv-o-cat-ing
e-quiv-o-ca-tor
e-quiv-o-ca-tion
e-ra
e-rad-i-cate
e-rad-i-cat-ed
e-rad-i-cat-ing
e-rad-i-ca-ble
e-rad-i-ca-tion
e-rad-i-ca-tive
e-rad-i-ca-tor
e-rase
e-rased
e-ras-ing
e-ras-a-bil-i-ty
e-ras-a-ble
e-ras-er
e-ras-ure
e-rect
e-rect-a-ble
e-rect-er
e-rec-tive
e-rect-ly
e-rect-ness

e-rec-tile
  e-rec-til-i-ty
e-rec-tion
e-rec-tor
er-go
er-mine
e-rode
  e-rod-ed
  e-rod-ing
e-rog-e-nous
e-ro-sion
e-rot-ic
  e-rot-i-cal-ly
e-rot-i-cism
err
  err-ing-ly
er-rand
er-rant
  er-rant-ly
er-rat-ic
  er-rat-i-cal-ly
er-ra-tum
  er-ra-ta
er-ro-ne-ous
  er-ro-ne-ous-ly
  er-ro-ne-ous-ness
er-ror
  er-ror-less
er-satz
erst-while
er-u-dite
  er-u-dite-ly
  er-u-dite-ness
er-u-di-tion
e-rupt
  e-rup-tion
  e-rup-tive
  e-rup-tive-ly
  e-rup-tive-ness
es-ca-lade
  es-ca-lad-ed
  es-ca-lad-ing
  es-ca-lad-er

es-ca-late
  es-ca-lat-ed
  es-ca-lat-ing
  es-ca-la-tion
es-ca-la-tor
es-cal-lop
es-ca-pade
es-cape
  es-caped
  es-cap-ing
  es-cap-er
es-ca-pee
es-cap-ist
  es-cap-ism
es-carp-ment
es-chew
  es-chew-al
  es-chew-er
es-cort
es-cri-toire
es-crow
es-cutch-eon
  es-cutch-eoned
e-soph-a-gus
es-o-ter-ic
  es-o-ter-i-cal
  es-o-ter-i-cal-ly
es-pal-ier
es-pe-cial
  es-pe-cial-ly
  es-pe-cial-ness
es-pi-o-nage
es-pla-nade
es-pouse
  es-poused
  es-pous-ing
  es-pous-er
es-pous-al
es-pres-so
es-prit
es-prit de corps
es-py
  es-pied

  es-py-ing
es-quire
  es-quired
  es-quir-ing
es-say
  es-say-er
  es-say-ist
es-sence
es-sen-tial
  es-sen-ti-al-i-ty
  es-sen-tial-ly
  es-sen-tial-ness
es-tab-lish
  es-tab-lish-er
  es-tab-lish-ment
es-tate
es-teem
es-thete
  es-thet-ic
es-ti-ma-ble
  es-ti-ma-ble-ness
  es-ti-ma-bly
es-ti-mate
  es-ti-mat-ed
  es-ti-mat-ing
  es-ti-ma-tive
  es-ti-ma-tor
es-ti-ma-tion
es-trange
  es-tranged
  es-trang-ing
  es-trange-ment
  es-tran-ger
es-trus
es-tu-ar-y
  es-tu-ar-ies
  es-tu-ar-i-al
etch
  etch-er
  etch-ing
e-ter-nal
  e-ter-nal-ly
e-ter-ni-ty

e-ter-nize
  e-ter-nized
  e-ter-niz-ing
  e-ter-ni-za-tion
eth-a-nol
e-ther
e-the-re-al
  e-the-re-al-i-ty
  e-the-re-al-ly
  e-the-re-al-ness
e-the-re-al-ize
  e-the-re-al-ized
  e-the-re-al-iz-ing
  e-the-re-al-i-za-tion
eth-ic
  eth-i-cal
  eth-i-cal-ly
  eth-ics
eth-nic
  eth-ni-cal
  eth-ni-cal-ly
eth-nol-o-gy
eth-yl
eti-ol-o-gy
  eti-o-log-ist
  eti-o-log-i-cal
  eti-o-log-i-cal-ly
et-i-quette
e-tude
et-y-mol-o-gy
  et-y-mol-o-gies
  et-y-mo-log-ic
  et-y-mo-log-i-cal
  et-y-mol-o-gist
eu-ca-lyp-tus
  eu-ca-lyp-tus-es
  eu-ca-lyp-ti
eu-gen-ic
eu-lo-gise
  eu-lo-gized
  eu-lo-giz-ing
  eu-lo-gis-tic
  eu-lo-gis-ti-cal-ly

eu-nuch
eu-phe-mism
  eu-phe-mist
  eu-phe-mis-tic
  eu-phe-mis-ti-cal
  eu-phe-mis-ti-cal-ly
eu-phe-mize
  eu-phe-mized
  eu-phe-miz-ing
eu-pho-ni-ous
  eu-pho-ni-ous-ly
eu-re-ka
eu-tha-na-sia
e-vac-u-ate
  e-vac-u-at-ed
  e-vac-u-at-ing
  e-vac-u-a-tion
  e-vac-u-a-tive
  e-vac-u-a-tor
e-vac-u-ee
e-vade
  e-vad-ed
  e-vad-ing
  e-vad-a-ble
  e-vad-er
  e-vad-ing-ly
e-val-u-ate
  e-val-u-at-ed
  e-val-u-at-ing
  e-val-u-a-tion
  e-val-u-a-tor
ev-a-nes-cent
  ev-a-nes-cence
  ev-a-nes-cent-ly
e-van-gel
  evan-gel-i-cal
  evan-gel-ic
  evan-gel-i-cal-ism
  evan-gel-i-cal-ly
  evan-gel-i-cal-ness
evan-ge-lism
  evan-ge-lis-tic
  evan-ge-lis-ti-cal-ly

evan-ge-list
evan-ge-lize
  evan-ge-lized
  evan-ge-liz-ing
  evan-ge-li-za-tion
  evan-ge-liz-er
e-va-sion
e-va-sive
  e-va-sive-ly
  e-va-sive-ness
e-ven
  e-ven-ly
  e-ven-ness
e-ven-hand-ed
eve-ning
e-vent
e-vent-ful
  event-ful-ly
  event-ful-ness
e-ven-tu-al
  e-ven-tu-al-ly
  e-ven-tu-al-i-ty
  e-ven-tu-al-i-ties
e-ven-tu-ate
  e-ven-tu-at-ed
  e-ven-tu-at-ing
ev-er
ev-er-green
ev-er-last-ing
  ev-er-last-ing-ly
  ev-er-last-ing-ness
ev-er-more
e-vert
  e-ver-si-ble
  e-ver-sion
eve-ry
eve-ry-body
eve-ry-day
eve-ry-one
eve-ry-thing
eve-ry-where
e-vict
  e-vic-tion

e-vic-tor
ev-i-dence
ev-i-denced
ev-i-denc-ing
ev-i-dent
ev-i-dent-ly
ev-i-den-tial
ev-i-den-tial-ly
e-vil
e-vince
e-vinced
e-vinc-ing
e-vin-ci-ble
e-vis-cer-ate
e-vis-cer-at-ed
e-vis-cer-at-ing
e-vis-cer-a-tion
e-voke
e-voked
e-vok-ing
ev-o-ca-tion
ev-o-lu-tion
ev-o-lu-tion-al
ev-o-lu-tion-ary
ev-o-lu-tion-ism
ev-ol-lu-tion-ist
e-volve
e-volved
e-volv-ing
e-volv-a-ble
e-volve-ment
e-volv-er
ew-er
ex-ac-er-bate
ex-ac-er-bat-ed
ex-ac-er-bat-ing
ex-ac-er-ba-tion
ex-act
ex-act-a-ble
ex-ac-tor
ex-act-ing
ex-act-ing-ly
ex-act-ing-ness

ex-act-i-tude
ex-act-ly
ex-ag-ger-ate
ex-ag-ger-at-ed
ex-ag-ger-at-ing
ex-ag-ger-a-tion
ex-ag-ger-a-tor
ex-am
ex-am-i-na-tion
ex-am-ine
ex-am-ined
ex-am-in-ing
ex-am-ple
ex-am-pled
ex-am-pling
ex-as-per-ate
ex-as-per-at-ed
ex-as-per-at-ing
ex-as-per-a-tion
ex-ca-vate
ex-ca-vat-ed
ex-ca-vat-ing
ex-ca-va-tion
ex-ca-va-tor
ex-ceed
ex-ceed-ing
ex-ceed-ing-ly
ex-cel
ex-celled
ex-cel-ling
ex-cel-lence
ex-cel-len-cy
ex-cel-len-cies
ex-cel-lent
ex-cel-lent-ly
ex-cel-si-or
ex-cept
ex-cept-ing
ex-cep-tion
ex-cep-tion-a-ble
ex-cep-tion-al
ex-cerpt
ex-cess

ex-ces-sive
ex-ces-sive-ly
ex-change
ex-changed
ex-chang-ing
ex-change-a-bil-i-ty
ex-change-a-ble
ex-chan-ger
ex-cheq-uer
ex-cise
ex-cised
ex-cis-ing
ex-cis-a-ble
ex-ci-sion
ex-cit-a-ble
ex-cit-a-bil-i-ty
ex-cit-a-bly
ex-ci-ta-tion
ex-cite
ex-cit-ed
ex-cit-ing
ex-cit-ed
ex-cit-ed-ly
ex-cit-ed-ness
ex-cite-ment
ex-cit-ing
ex-cit-ing-ly
ex-claim
ex-cla-ma-tion
ex-clam-a-to-ry
ex-clam-a-to-ri-ly
ex-clude
ex-clu-sion
ex-clu-sive
ex-clu-sive-ly
ex-clu-sive-ness
ex-clu-siv-i-ty
ex-com-mu-ni-cate
ex-co-ri-ate
ex-co-ri-at-ed
ex-co-ri-at-ing
ex-co-ri-a-tion
ex-cre-ment

ex-cre-men-tal
ex-cres-cense
ex-cres-cent
ex-cre-ta
ex-cre-tal
ex-crete
ex-cret-ed
ex-cret-ing
ex-cre-tion
ex-cru-ci-ate
ex-cru-ci-at-ed
ex-cru-ci-at-ing
ex-cru-ci-at-ing-ly
ex-cru-ci-a-tion
ex-cur-sive
ex-cur-sive-ly
ex-cur-sive-ness
ex-cus-a-to-ry
ex-cuse
ex-e-cra-ble
ex-e-cra-ble-ness
ex-e-cra-bly
ex-e-cra-tion
ex-e-cute
ex-e-cut-ed
ex-e-cut-ing
ex-e-cut-a-ble
ex-e-cut-er
ex-e-cu-tion
ex-e-cu-tion-er
ex-ec-u-tive
ex-ec-u-tive-ly
ex-ec-u-tor
ex-ec-u-tor-ship
ex-e-ge-sis
ex-em-pli-fy
ex-em-pli-fied
ex-em-pli-fy-ing
ex-em-pli-fi-a-ble
ex-em-pli-fi-ca-tion
ex-empt
ex-emp-tion
ex-er-cise

ex-er-cised
ex-er-cis-ing
ex-er-cis-er
ex-ert
ex-er-tion
ex-fo-li-ate
ex-fo-li-at-ed
ex-fo-li-at-ing
ex-fo-li-a-tion
ex-hal-la-tion
ex-hale
ex-haled
ex-hal-ing
ex-hal-ant
ex-haust
ex-hib-it
ex-hib-it-a-ble
ex-hib-i-tor
ex-hib-i-to-ry
ex-hi-bi-tion
ex-hi-bi-tion-ism
ex-hi-bi-tion-ist
ex-hi-bi-tion-is-tic
ex-hil-a-rate
ex-hort
ex-hor-ta-tive
ex-hor-ta-to-ry
ex-hort-er
ex-hort-ing-ly
ex-hor-ta-tion
ex-hume
ex-humed
ex-hum-ing
ex-i-gen-cy
ex-i-gen-cies
ex-i-gent
ex-i-gent-ly
ex-ile
ex-iled
ex-ist
ex-ist-ence
ex-ist-ent
ex-is-ten-tial

ex-is-ten-tial-ly
ex-it
ex li-bris
ex-o-dus
ex of-fi-ci-o
ex-og-a-my
ex-og-a-mous
ex-og-e-nous
ex-og-e-nous-ly
ex-on-er-ate
ex-or-bi-tant
ex-or-bi-tance
ex-or-bi-tant-ly
ex-o-tic
ex-ot-i-cal-ly
ex-ot-i-cism
ex-pand
ex-pand-er
ex-panse
ex-pan-si-ble
ex-pan-sion
ex-pan-sion-ism
ex-pan-sion-ist
ex-pan-sive
ex-pan-sive-ly
ex-pan-sive-ness
ex-pa-ti-ate
ex-pa-ti-at-ed
ex-pa-ti-at-ing
ex-pa-ti-a-tion
ex-pa-tri-ate
ex-pa-tri-at-ed
ex-pa-tri-at-ing
ex-pa-tri-a-tion
ex-pect
ex-pect-a-ble
ex-pect-a-bly
ex-pect-ing-ly
ex-pect-an-cy
ex-pect-an-cies
ex-pect-ant
ex-pect-ant-ly
ex-pec-ta-tion

ex-pec-to-rate
ex-pec-to-rat-ed
ex-pec-to-rat-ing
ex-pec-to-ra-tion
ex-pe-dite
ex-pe-dit-ed
ex-pe-dit-ing
ex-pe-dit-er
ex-pe-di-tion
ex-pe-di-tious
ex-pe-di-tious-ly
ex-pel
ex-pelled
ex-pel-ling
ex-pend
ex-pend-a-ble
ex-pend-a-bil-i-ty
ex-pend-i-ture
ex-pense
ex-pen-sive
ex-pen-sive-ly
ex-pe-ri-en-tial
ex-pe-ri-en-tial-ly
ex-per-i-ment
ex-per-i-men-ta-tion
ex-per-i-men-tal
ex-per-i-men-tal-ism
ex-per-i-men-tal-ist
ex-per-i-men-tal-ly
ex-pert
ex-pert-ly
ex-pert-ness
ex-per-tise
ex-pi-ra-tion
ex-pir-a-to-ry
ex-pire
ex-pired
ex-pir-ing
ex-plain
ex-plain-a-ble
ex-plain-er
ex-pla-na-tion

ex-plan-a-to-ry
ex-plan-a-to-ri-ly
ex-ple-tive
ex-pli-ca-ble
ex-pli-cate
ex-pli-cat-ed
ex-pli-cat-ing
ex-pli-ca-tion
ex-pli-ca-tive
ex-pli-ca-tor
ex-plic-it
ex-plic-it-ly
ex-plic-it-ness
ex-plode
ex-plod-ed
ex-plod-ing
ex-plod-er
ex-ploit
ex-ploit-a-ble
ex-ploi-ta-tion
ex-ploit-er
ex-ploit-ive
ex-plore
ex-plo-ra-tion
ex-plor-a-to-ry
ex-plor-er
ex-plo-sion
ex-plo-sive
ex-plo-sive-ly
ex-plo-sive-ness
ex-po-nent
ex-po-nen-tial
ex-po-nen-tial-ly
ex-port
ex-port-a-ble
ex-por-ta-tion
ex-port-er
ex-pose
ex-posed
ex-pos-ing
ex-pos-er
ex-po-si-tion
ex-pos-i-tor

ex-pos-i-to-ry
ex post fac-to
ex-pos-tu-late
ex-po-sure
ex-pound
ex-pound-er
ex-press
ex-press-er
ex-press-i-ble
ex-pres-sion
ex-pres-sive
ex-pres-sive-ly
ex-pres-sive-ness
ex-press-ly
ex-press-way
ex-pro-pri-ate
ex-pro-pri-at-ing
ex-pro-pri-a-tor
ex-pro-pri-a-tion
ex-pul-sion
ex-pul-sive
ex-punge
ex-pur-gate
ex-pur-ga-to-ry
ex-pur-ga-to-ri-al
ex-qui-site
ex-qui-site-ly
ex-qui-site-ness
ex-tant
ex-tem-po-rize
ex-tem-po-rized
ex-tem-po-riz-ing
ex-tem-po-ri-za-tion
ex-tem-po-riz-er
ex-tend
ex-tend-i-bil-i-ty
ex-tend-i-ble
ex-tend-ed
ex-tend-ed-ly
ex-tend-ed-ness
ex-tend-er
ex-ten-si-ble
ex-ten-si-bil-i-ty

ex-ten-sion
ex-ten-sion-al
ex-ten-sive
ex-ten-sive-ly
ex-ten-sive-ness
ex-tent
ex-ten-u-ate
ex-te-ri-or
ex-te-ri-or-ly
ex-ter-mi-nate
ex-ter-mi-nat-ed
ex-ter-mi-nat-ing
ex-ter-mi-na-tion
ex-ter-nal
ex-ter-nal-ly
ex-tinct
ex-tinc-tion
ex-tin-guish
ex-tin-guish-a-ble
ex-tin-guish-er
ex-tin-guish-ment
ex-tir-pate
ex-tir-pat-ed
ex-tir-pat-ing
ex-tir-pa-tion
ex-tir-pa-tive
ex-tol
ex-tol-ler
ex-tol-lingly
ex-tol-ment
ex-tort
ex-tor-ter
ex-tor-tive
ex-tor-tion
ex-tra
ex-tract
ex-tract-a-ble
ex-trac-tive
ex-trac-tion
ex-tra-cur-ric-u-lar
ex-tra-dite
ex-tra-ne-ous
ex-tra-ne-ous-ly

ex-tra-ne-ous-ness
ex-traor-di-nary
ex-traor-di-nar-i-ly
ex-trap-o-late
ex-trap-o-lat-ed
ex-trap-o-lat-ing
ex-trap-o-la-tion
ex-tra-sen-so-ry
ex-tra-ter-res-tri-al
ex-tra-ter-ri-to-ri-al
ex-trav-a-gance
ex-trav-a-gan-cy
ex-trav-a-gant
ex-trav-a-gant-ly
ex-trav-a-gan-za
ex-treme
ex-treme-ly
ex-treme-ness
ex-trem-ist
ex-trem-ism
ex-trem-i-ty
ex-trem-i-ties
ex-tri-cate
ex-tri-cat-ed
ex-tri-cat-ing
ex-tri-ca-ble
ex-tri-ca-tion
ex-trin-sic
ex-tro-vert
ex-tro-ver-sion
ex-trude
ex-u-ber-ance
ex-u-ber-ant
ex-u-ber-ant-ly
ex-ude
ex-ud-ed
ex-ud-ing
ex-u-da-tion
ex-ult
ex-ult-ant
ex-ult-ant-ly
ex-ul-at-tion
ex-ult-ing-ly

ex-ur-ban-ite
eye
eyed
eye-ing
eye-ball
eye-glass
eye-glass-es
eye-hole
eye-let
eye-lid
eye-o-pen-er
eye-o-pen-ing
eye-wit-ness
ey-rie
ey-ry
ey-ries

F

fa-ble
fa-bled
fab-ric
fab-ri-cate
fab-ri-cated
fab-ri-cat-ing
fab-ri-ca-tion
fab-u-lous
fab-u-lous-ness
fa-cade
fa-cades
face
faced
fac-ing
face card
face--lift
fac-et
fa-ce-tious
fa-ce-tious-ly
fa-cial
fa-cial-ly
fac-ile
fac-ile-ly
fac-ile-ness

fa-cil-i-tate
fa-cil-i-ty
fac-ing
fac-sim-i-le
fact
fac-tion
  fac-tion-al
  fac-tion-al-ly
fac-ti-tious
  fac-ti-tious-ly
fac-ti-tious-ness
fac-tor
fac-to-ry
  fac-to-ries
fac-to-tum
fac-tu-al
fac-ul-ty
fad
  fad-dish
  fad-dist
fade
  fad-ed
  fad-ing
fa-er-ie
  fa-ery
  fa-er-ies
fag
  fag-ged
  fag-ging
fag-got
fag-ot
Fahr-en-heit
fail-ing
  fail-ing-ly
fail-safe
fail-ure
faint
  faint-ly
  faint-ness
faint-heart-ed
fair
  fir-ness
fair-ground

fair-ly
fair-mind-ed
fair--trade
fair-y
  fair-ies
fair-y-like
fair-y tale
faith
faith-ful
faith-ful-less
fake
  faked
  fak-ing
  fak-er
fal-con
  fal-con-ry
fall
  fall-en
  fall-ing
fal-la-cious
  fal-la-cious-ly
fal-la-cy
fall-guy
fal-li-ble
  fal-li-bly
fail-ing star
fall-out
fal-low
  fal-low-ness
false
  fals-er
  fals-est
false-hood
fal-si-fy
  fal-si-fied
  fal-si-fy-ing
  fal-si-fi-er
fal-si-ty
fal-ter
  fal-ter-er
  fal-ter-ing-ly
fame
  famed

fa-mil-ial
fa-mil-iar
  fa-mil-iar-ly
fa-mil-i-ar-i-ty
fa-mil-iar-ize
  fa-mil-iar-ized
  fa-mil-iar-iz-ing
fam-ily
  fam-i-lies
fam-ine
fam-ish
fam-ished
fa-mous
  fa-mous-ly
fan
  fan-like
  fan-ner
fa-nat-ic
  fa-nat-i-cal
fa-nat-i-cism
fa-nat-i-cize
  fa-nat-i-cized
fan-ci-er
fan-ci-ul
  fan-ci-ful-ly
fan-cy
  fan-cies
  fan-ci-ly
  fan-ci-ness
fan-cy-work
fan-fare
fang
  fanged
fan-light
fan-tas-tic
  fan-tas-ti-cal
fan-ta-sy
  fan-ta-sies
far
  far-ther
  far-thest
far-a-way
farce

farced
farc-ing
far-ci-cal
far-ci-cal-ly
fare
fared
far-ing
fare-well
far-fetched
far-flung
farm
farm-er
farm-hand
farm-house
farm-ing
farm-yard
far-off
far-reach-ing
far-reach-ing-ly
far-see-ing
far-sight-ed
far-sight-ed-ly
far-ther
far-ther-most
far-thest
fas-ci-a
fas-ci-ae
fas-ci-cle
fas-ci-cled
fas-ci-nate
fas-ci-nat-ed
fas-ci-nat-ing
fas-ci-na-tion
fas-cism
fas-cist
fa-scis-tic
fash-ion
fash-ion-ble
fast
fas-ten
fas-ten-er
fas-ten-ing
fas-tid-i-ous

fas-ti-di-ous-ly
fat
fat-ter
fat-test
fa-tal
fa-tal-ly
fa-tal-ism
fa-tal-ist
fa-tal-i-ty
fa-tal-i-ties
fate
fat-ed
fat-ing
fate-ful
fate-ful-ly
fate-ful-ness
fa-ther
fa-ther-hood
fa-ther-ly
fa-ther-in-law
fa-thers-in-law
fa-ther-land
fath-om
fath-om-a-ble
fath-om-less
fa-tique
fa-tiqued
fa-tiq-uing
fat-i-ga-ble
fat-ten
fat-ten-er
fa-tu-i-ty
fa-tui-ties
fat-u-ous
fat-u-ous-ly
fau-cet
fault
fault-find-er
fault-find-ing
fault-less
fault-less-ly
fault-less-ness
fault-y

fault-i-er
fault-i-est
fault-i-ly
fau-na
fau-nas
fau-nae
faux pas
fa-vor
fa-vor-ing-ly
fa-vor-a-ble
fa-vor-ably
fa-vored
fa-vored-ly
fa-vored-ness
fa-vor-ite
fa-vor-it-ism
fawn
faze
fazed
faz-ing
fe-al-ty
fear
fear-ful
fear-ful-ly
fear-less
fear-less-ly
fea-si-ble
fea-si-bil-i-ty
fea-si-bly
feast
feat
feath-er
fea-thered
feath-er-bed-ding
fea-ture
fea-tured
fea-tur-ing
fea-ture-ness
fe-brile
fe-ces
fe-cal
feck-less
fe-cund

fe-cun-di-ty
fe-cun-date
  fe-cun-dat-ed
  fe-cun-da-tion
fed-er-al
fed-er-al-ism
fed-er-li-ist
fed-er-al-ize
  fed-er-al-ized
  fed-er-al-iz-ing
  fed-er-al-i-za-tion
  fed-er-al-ly
fed-er-ate
  fed-er-at-ed
  fed-er-at-ing
fed-er-a-tion
fee
fee-ble
  fee-bler
  fee-blest
  fee-bly
fee-ble-mind-ed
feed-back
feel
  feel-ing
feel-er
feel-ing
  feel-ing-ly
  feel-ing-ness
feign
  feigned
  feign-ed-ly
  feign-er
  feign-ing-ly
feint
feist-y
  feist-i-er
  feist-i-est
fe-lic-i-tate
  fe-lic-i-tat-ed
  fe-lic-i-tat-ing
  fe-lic-i-ta-tion
fe-lic-i-tous

fe-lic-i-tous-ly
fe-lic-i-ty
  fe-lic-i-ties
fe-line
  fe-line-ly
  fe-line-i-ty
fell
fel-la-ti-o
fel-low
fel-low-ship
fe-lon
fel-o-ny
  fel-o-nies
  fe-lo-ni-ous
  fe-lo-ni-ous-ly
fe-male
fem-i-nine
  fem-i-nine-ly
  fem-i-nine-ness
  fem-i-nin-i-ty
fem-i-nism
  fem-i-nist
  fem-i-nis-tic
fem-i-nize
  fem-i-nized
  fem-i-niz-ing
fe-mur
  fe-murs
  fem-o-ra
  fem-o-ral
fen
  fen-ny
  fen-ni-er
  fen-ni-est
fence
  fecned
  fenc-ing
  fenc-er
fen-der
fe-ral
fer-ment
  fer-ment-a-ble
fer-men-ta-tion

fern
fern-er-y
  fern-er-ies
fe-ro-cious
  fe-ro-cious-ly
  fe-ro-ci-ty
fer-ret
  fer-ret-er
fer-ro-con-crete
fer-ro-mag-net-ic
fer-ru-gi-nous
fer-rule
fer-ry
  fer-ries
  fer-ry-boat
  fer-ry-man
fer-tile
  fer-tile-ly
  fer-tile-ness
fer-til-i-ty
fer-ti-li-za-tion
fer-ti-li-za-tion-al
fer-ti-lize
  fer-ti-lized
  fer-ti-liz-ing
  fer-ti-liz-a-ble
fer-ti-liz-er
fer-vent
  fer-ven-cy
fer-vid
  fer-vid-ly
  fer-vid-ness
fer-vor
fes-ter
fes-ti-val
fes-tive
  fes-tive-ly
  fes-tive-ness
fes-tiv-i-ty
fes-toon
  fes-toon-ery
  fes-toon-er-ies
fe-tal

fetch
fetch-er
fetch-ing
  fetch-ing-ly
fete
fet-id
  fet-id-ly
  fet-id-ness
fet-ish
fet-ish-ism
  fet-ish-ist
  fet-ish-is-tic
fet-lock
fet-ter
fet-tle
fe-tus
  fe-tus-es
feud
  feud-ist
feu-dal
feu-dal-ism
feu-dal-ist
  feu-dal-is-tic
feu-dal-i-za-tion
feu-dal-ize
  feu-dal-ized
  feu-dal-iz-ing
fe-ver
fe-ver blis-ter
fe-ver-ish
  fe-ver-ish-ly
  fe-ver-ish-ness
fe-ver-ous
fe-ver-ous-ly
few
few-ness
fez-zes
fi-as-co
  fi-as-cos
  fi-as-coes
fi-at
fib
fi-ber

fi-bered
fi-ber-board
fi-ber-glass
fi-bril
fi-bril-la-tion
fi-broid
fi-brous
fib-u-la
  fib-u-las
  fib-u-lae
fick-le
  fick-le-ness
fic-tion
  fic-tion-al
  fic-tion-al-ly
fic-ti-tious
fid-dle
  fid-dler
  fid-dled
fi-del-i-ty
fidg-et
  fidg-ety
field-er
field-glass
fiend
  fiend-ish
  fiend-ish-ly
  fiend-ish-ness
fierce
  fierce-ly
  fierce-ness
fier-y
  fier-i-er
  fier-i-est
  fier-i-ly
fier-i-ness
fif-teen
fif-teenth
fifth
fif-ti-eth
fif-ty
  fif-ties
fight

fight-er
fig-ment
fig-u-ra-tion
fig-u-ra-tive
  fig-u-ra-tive-ly
  fid-u-ra-tive-ness
fig-ure
  fig-ured
  fig-ur-ing
  fig-ur-er
fig-ure-head
fig-ur-ine
fil-a-ment
  fil-a-men-ta-ry
  fil-a-men-ed
  fil-a-men-tous
filch
file
  filed
  fil-ing
fi-let
fi-let mi-gnon
fil-i-al
  fil-i-al-ly
fil-i-bus-ter
fil-i-gree
  fil-i-greed
  fil-i-gree-ing
  fil-lings
fill-er
fil-let
fill-ing
fil-lip
fil-ly
  fil-lies
film-strip
film-y
  film-i-er
  film-i-est
  film-i-ness
fil-ter
filth
  filth-i-ness

filthy
filth-i-er
filth-i-est
fin
  finned
  fin-ning
  fin-less
  fin-like
fi-na-gled
  fi-na-gling
  fi-na-gler
fi-nal
fi-na-le
fi-nal-ist
fi-nal-i-ty
  fi-nal-i-ties
fi-nal-ize
  fi-nal-ized
  fi-nal-iz-ing
  fi-nal-ly
fi-nance
  fi-nanced
  fi-nanc-ing
  fi-nan-cial
  fi-nan-cial-ly
fin-an-cier
finch
find
  found
  find-ing
find-er
fine
  fin-er
  fin-est
  fine-ly
  fine-ness
fin-er-y
  fin-er-ies
fi-nesse
  fi-nessed
  fi-ness-ing
fin-ger
fin-ger-bowl

fin-ger-ing
fin-ger-nail
fin-ger-print
fin-i-al
fin-i-cal
  fin-i-cal-ly
fin-ick-y
  fin-ick-ing
fin-is
  fin-is-es
fin-ish
  fin-ished
  fin-ish-er
fi-nite
  fi-nite-ly
  fi-nite-ness
fire
  fired
  fir-ing
  fir-er
fire-arm
fire-ball
fire-brand
fire-bug
fire-crack-er
fire-fight-er
fire-fly
  fire-flies
fire-man
fire-place
fire-plug
fire-pow-er
fire-proof
fire-side
fire-trap
fire-wa-ter
fire-wood
fire-works
fir-ing-squad
firm
  firm-ly
  firm-ness
fir-ma-ment

first-born
first-hand
first-ling
first-ly
first-rate
first-string
fis-cal
  fis-cal-ly
fish-er
fish-er-man
  fish-er-men
fish-er-y
  fish-er-ies
fish-hook
fish-ing
fish-wife
  fish-wived
fish-y
  fish-i-er
  fish-i-est
fis-sle
fis-sion
fis-sure
  fis-sured
  fis-sur-ing
fist-ic
fist-i-cuff
fit
  fit-ter
  fit-test
  fit-ted
  fit-ting
  fit-ly
  fit-ness
fit-ful
  fit-ful-ly
  fit-ful-ness
fit-ting
  fit-ting-ly
  fit-ting-ness
five-fold
five-and-ten
fix

fix-a-ble
fixed
fix-ed-ly
fix-er
fix-a-tion
fix-a-tive
fix-ings
fix-i-ty
fix-i-ties
fix-ture
fiz-zle
fiz-zled
fiz-zling
fiz-zy
fiz-zi-er
fiz-zi-est
flab-ber-gast
flab-by
flab-bi-er
flab-bi-est
flab-bi-ly
flab-bi-ness
flac-cid
flag
flagged
flag-ging
flag-el-lant
flag-el-lat-ed
flag-el-lat-ing
flag-el-la-tion
fla-gi-tious
flag-on
flag-pole
flag-rank
fla-grant
fla-grant-ly
flag-ship
flag-stone
flail
flair
flake
flaked
flak-ing

flak-y
flak-i-er
flak-i-est
flak-i-ness
flam-boy-ant
flam-boy-ance
flam-boy-an-cy
flam-boy-ant-ly
flame
flamed
flam-ing
flam-ing-ly
flam-ma-ble
flange
flank
flank-er
flan-nel-ette
flap
flapped
flap-ping
flap-per
flap-jack
flare
flared
flar-ing
flare-up
flash-back
flash-light
flash-i-er
flash-i-est
flash-i-ly
flash-i-ness
flask
flat
flat-ly
flat-ted
flat-ting
flat-ness
flat-car
flat-foot
flat-foot-ed
flat-foot-ed-ly
falt-ten

flat-ten-er
flat-ter
flat-ter-er
flat-ter-ing-ly
flat-ter-y
flat-ter-ies
flat-u-lent
flat-u-lence
flat-u-len-cy
flat-u-lent-ly
flat-ware
flaunt
flaunt-er
flaunt-ing-ly
flanty
flaunt-i-er
flaunt-i-est
flau-tist
fla-vor
fla-vored
fla-vor-less
fla-vor-ing
flaw-less
fla-zen
flax-seed
flay-er
flea-bite
flea-bit-ten
fleck
flec-tion
fledge
fledged
fledg-ing
fledg-ling
flee
fled
flee-ing
fleece
fleeced
fleec-ing
fleec-y
fleec-i-er
fleec-i-est

fleec-i-ness
fleet
  fleet-ly
  fleet-ness
fleet-ing
  fleet-ing-ly
  fleet-ing-ness
flesh-ly
  flesh-li-er
  flesh-li-est
flesh-pots
flesh-y
  flesh-i-ert
  flesh-i-est
flesh-i-ness
flex-i-ble
  flex-i-bil-i-ty
  flex-i-bly
flex-ion
flex-or
flex-ure
fib-ber-ti-gib-bet
flick-er
  flick-er-ing
fli-er
flight
  flight-less
flight-y
  flight-i-er
  flight-i-est
  flight-i-ly
  flight-i-ness
flim-flam
  flim-flammed
  flim-flam-ming
firm-sy
  firm-si-er
  firm-si-est
  firm-si-ly
  firm-si-ness
flinch
  flinch-er
  flinch-ing-ly

fin-ders
fling
  flung
  fling-ing
flint-y
  flint-i-er
  flint-i-est
  flint-i-ness
flip
  flipped
  flip-ping
flip-flop
flip-pant
  flip-pan-cy
  flip-pant-ly
flip-per
flirt-er
flir-ta-tion
  flir-ta-tious
flit
  flit-ted
  flit-ting
  flit-ter
float-a-ble
float-a-tion
float-er
float-ing
floc-cu-lent
  floc-cu-lence
flocked
flood-gate
flood-light
  flood-lit
floor-ing
floor-walk-er
floo-zy
  floo-zies
flop
  flopped
  flop-ping
  flop-per
flop-house
flop-py

flop-pi-er
flop-pi-est
flop-pi-ly
flo-ra
  flo-ras
  flo-rae
flo-ral
flo-res-cence
  flo-res-cent
flo-ret
flo-ri-cul-ture
  flo-ri-cul-tur-al
  flo-ri-cul-tur-ist
flor-id
  flo-rid-i-ty
  flor-id-ly
  flor-id-ness
flo-rist
floss
  flossy
  floss-i-er
  floss-i-est
flo-ta-tion
flo-til-la
flot-sam
flounce
  flounced
  flounc-ing
floun-der
flour-y
  flour-i-er
  flour-i-est
flour-ish
  flou-rish-ing
flow-er
  flow-ered
  flow-er-ing
flow-ery
  flow-er-i-ness
flub
  flubbed
  flub-bing
fluc-tu-ate

fluc-tu-at-ed
fluc-tu-at-ing
fluc-tu-a-tion
flue
flu-ent
flu-ency
flu-ent-ly
fluff
fluff-i-ness
fluff-y
fluff-i-er
fluff-i-est
flu-id
flu-id-ly
flu-id-ness
fluke
fluky
fluk-i-er
fluk-i-est
flum-mer-y
flum-mer-ies
flun-ky
flunk-ies
flu-o-resce
flu-o-resced
flu-o-resc-ing
flu-o-res-cence
flu-o-res-sent
flur-ry
flur-ries
flur-ried
flur-ry-ing
flus-ter
flute
flut-ed
flut-ing
flut-ist
flut-ter
flut-ter-er
flut-ter-ing-ly
flut-tery
flut-ter-i-er
flut-ter-i-est

flux-ion
fly-brown
fly-by-night
fly-er
fly-ing
fly-leaf
fly-leaves
fly-pa-per
fly-speck
fly-wheel
foal
foam
foam-i-ness
foam-y
foam-i-er
foam-i-est
fob
fobbed
fob-bing
fo-cal
fo-cal-ize
fo-cal-lized
fo-cal-iz-ing
fo-cus
fo-cus-es
fo-cus-ing
fo-cus-er
fod-der
foe-tus
foe-tal
fog
fogged
fog-ging
fog-gy
fog-gi-er
fog-gi-est
fog-gi-ly
fog-gi-ness
fog-horn
fo-gy
fo-gies
fo-gy-ish
foi-ble

fold-er
fol-de-rol
fo-li-a-ceous
fo-li-age
fo-li-ate
fo-li-at-ed
fo-li-at-ing
fol-li-a-tion
fo-li-o
fol-li-os
fol-li-oed
fo-li-o-ing
folk-lore
folk-lor-ist
flok-sy
flok-si-er
flok-si-est
flok-si-ness
folk-ways
fol-li-cle
fol-lic-u-lar
fol-low
fol-low-er
fol-low-ing
fol-ly
fol-lies
fo-ment
fo-men-ta-tion
fo-ment-er
fon-dant
fon-dle
fond-led
fon-dling
fon-dler
fond-ly
fond-ness
fon-due
food-stuff
fool-er-y
fool-er-ies
fool-har-dy
fool-har-di-ness
fool-proof

fools-cap
foot-age
foot-ball
foot-board
foot-can-dle
foot-ed
foot-fall
foot-hill
foot-hold
foot-ing
foot-lights
foot-loose
foot-note
  foot-not-ed
  foot-not-ing
foot-path
foot-print
foot-sore
foot-step
foot-stool
foot-wear
foot-work
foo-zle
  foo-zled
  foo-zling
fop
  fop-pery
  fop-per-ies
  fop-pish
  fop-pish-ly
  fop-pish-ness
for-age
  for-aged
  for-ag-ing
for-ay
for-bear
  for-bore
  for-borned
  for-bear-ing
  for-bear-ance
  for-bear-ing-ly
for-bid
  for-bade

for-bid-den
for-bid-ding
force-ful
  force-ful-ly
for-ceps
for-ci-ble
  for-ci-bly
ford-a-ble
  fore-arm
fore-bear
fore-bode
  fore-bod-ed
  fore-bod-ing
  fore-bod-er
fore-brain
fore-cast
  fore-cast-ed
  fore-cast-ing
  fore-cast-er
fore-close
  fore-closed
  fore-clos-ing
  fore-clo-sure
fore-fa-ther
fore-fin-ger
fore-foot
  fore-feet
fore-front
fore-gath-er
fore-go
  fore-went
  fore-gone
  fore-go-ing
fore-ground
fore-hand
fore-hand-ed
  fore-hand-ed-ness
fore-head
fore-eign
  fore-eign-er
  fore-eign-ness
fore-leg
fore-lock

fore-man
  fore-men
fore-most
fo-ren-sic
fore-or-dain
fore-quar-ter
fore-run
  fore-ran
  fore-run-ning
fore-run-ner
fore-see
  fore-saw
  fore-seen
  fore-see-ing
  fore-see-a-ble
  fore-se-er
fore-shad-ow
  fore-shad-ow-er
fore-sight
  fore-sight-ed
  fore-sight-ed-ness
fore-skin
for-est
fore-stall
for-est-a-tion
for-es-ter
for-es-try
fore-taste
  fore-tast-ed
  fore-tast-ing
fore-tell
  fore-told
  fore-tell-ing
  fore-tell-er
fore-thought
for-ev-er
for-ev-er-more
fore-warn
fore-word
for-feit
  for-feit-er
for-fei-ture
for-gath-er

forge
forged
forg-ing
forg-er
for-ger-y
fog-er-ies
for-get
for-got
for-got-ten
for-get-ting
for-get-ta-ble
for-get-ter
for-get-ful
for-get-ful-ly
for-get-ful-ness
for-give
for-gave
for-giv-en
for-giv-ing
for-giv-a-ble
for-give-ness
for-giv-er
for-go
for-went
for-gone
for-go-ing
for-go-er
fork-loft
for-lorn
for-lorn-ly
for-lorn-ness
for-mal
for-mal-ly
for-mal-ism
for-mal-i-ty
for-mal-i-ties
for-mal-ize
for-mal-ized
for-mal-iz-ing
for-mal-i-za-tion
for-mat
for-ma-tion
form-a-tive

for-mer
for-mer-ly
for-mi-da-ble
for-mi-da-bly
form-less
form-less-ly
for-mu-la
for-mu-las
for-mu-lae
for-mu-lar-y
for-mu-lar-ies
for-mu-late
for-mu-lat-ed
for-mu-lat-ing
for-mu-la-tion
for-mu-la-tor
fort
forte
forth-com-ing
forth-right
forth-right-ness
forth-with
for-ti-fi-ca-tion
for-ti-fy
for-ti-fied
for-ti-fy-ing
for-ti-fi-er
for-tis-si-mo
for-ti-tude
fort-night
for-night-ly
for-night-lies
for-tress
for-tu-i-tous
for-tu-i-tous-ly
for-tu-i-tous-ness
for-tu-nate
for-tu-nate-ly
for-tune
for-tune-tell-er
for-tune-tell-ing
for-ty
for-ties

for-ty-nin-er
fo-rum
fo-rums
fo-ra
fos-sil
fos-sil-ize
fos-sil-ized
fos-sil-iz-ing
fos-sil-i-za-tion
fos-ter
fos-tered
fos-ter-ing
fought
fou-lard
found
foun-da-tion
foun-da-tion-al
found-er
found-ling
found-ry
found-ries
foun-tain
foun-tain-head
four-flush-er
four-square
four-teen
four-teenth
fourth
fourth-ly
fowl
fowl-er
foy-er
fra-cas
fra-cas-es
frac-tion
frac-tion-al
frac-tious
frac-tious-ly
frac-ture
frac-tured
frac-tur-ing
frag-ile
fra-gil-i-ty

frag-ment
frag-men-tal
frag-men-ter-i-ness
frag-men-tary
frag-men-ta-tion
frag-ment-ize
frag-ment-ized
frag-ment-iz-ing
fra-grance
fra-grant
fra-grant-ly
frail
frail-ty
frail-ness
frame
framed
fram-ing
fram-er
frame-up
frame-work
franc
fran-chise
fran-chised
frank-furt-er
frank-in-cense
fran-tic
fran-ti-cal-ly
fra-ter-nal
fra-ter-nal-ly
fra-ter-ni-ty
fra-ter-ni-ties
frat-er-nize
frat-ri-cide
frat-ri-cid-al
fraud-u-lent
fraud-u-lence
fraught
fraz-zle
fraz-zled
fraz-zling
freak
freak-ish
freck-le

freck-led
freck-li-er
free
fre-er
free-ly
free-bie
free-boot-er
free-dom
free-lance
free-lanced
free-lanc-ing
free-spoken
free-spo-ken-ness
free-stone
free-think-ing
free-way
freeze
froze
fro-zen
freez-ing
freez-er
fre-net-ic
fre-net-i-cal-ly
fren-zy
fren-zies
fren-zied
fren-zy-ing
fre-quen-cy
fre-quen-cies
fre-quent
fre-quent-er
fre-quent-ly
fresh
fresh-ly
fresh-ness
fresh-en
fresh-en-er
fresh-et
fresh-man
fresh-men
fret
fret-ted
fret-work

fri-ary
fri-ar-ies
fric-as-see
fric-as-seed
fric-tion
fric-tion-al
friend
friend-less
friend-ly
friend-li-er
friend-li-est
frieze
fright-ful
fright-ful-ly
frig-id
fri-gid-i-ty
frig-id-ly
frig-id-ness
frilly
frill-i-er
frill-i-est
fringe
fringed
fring-ing
frip-pery
frip-per-ies
frisky
frisk-i-er
fit-ter
friv-o-lous
fri-vol-i-ty
frizz
friz-zi-ness
friz-zi-er
friz-zle
friz-zled
friz-zling
frol-ic
frol-ick-ed
frol-ick-ing
frol-ic-some
front-al
fron-tal-ly

fron-tier
frost
  frost-ed
frost-ing
frost-y
  frost-i-er
froth
  frothy
  froth-i-er
  froth-i-est
frou-frou
fro-ward
frown
  frown-ing-ly
frow-zy
  frow-zi-er
fro-zen
  fro-zen-ly
  fro-zen-ness
fruc-ti-fy
  fruc-ti-fied
  fruc-ti-fy-ing
  fruc-ti-fi-ca-tion
fru-gal
  fru-gal-i-ty
  fru-gal-i-ties
  fru-gal-ly
fruit-ful
  fruit-ful-ly
fru-i-tion
  fruit-less-ly
fruity
frump
  frump-ish
  frump-i-est
frus-trate
  frus-trat-ed
  frus-trat-ing
  frus-tra-tion
fry-er
fud-dle
  fud-dled
  fud-dling

fudge
  fudged
  fudg-ing
fu-el
  fu-eled
  fu-el-ing
fu-gi-tive
  fu-gi-tive-ly
ful-crum
  ful-crums
  ful-cra
ful-fill
  ful-filled
  ful-fil-ling
  ful-fil-ment
full
  full-ness
  ful-ly
full-back
ful-mi-nate
  ful-mi-nat-ed
  ful-mi-nat-ing
  ful-mi-na-tion
ful-some
  ful-some-ly
fu-mi-gate
  fu-mi-gat-ed
  fu-mi-gat-ing
func-tion
  func-tion-less
func-tion-al
  func-tion-al-ly
func-tion-ary
  func-tion-ar-ies
fun-da-men-tal
  fun-da-men-tal-ly
fun-da-men-tal-ism
  fun-da-men-tal-ist
fu-ner-al
fu-ner-re-al
fun-gi-cide
  fun-gi-cid-al
  fun-gi-cid-al-ly

fun-gous
fun-gus
  fun-gi
  fun-gus-es
funic-u-lar
funk-y
  funk-i-er
  funk-i-est
fun-nel
  fun-neled
  fun-nel-ing
fur
  furred
  fur-ring
fur-bish
fu-ri-ous
  fu-ri-ous-ly
fur-long
fur-lough
fur-nace
fur-nish
fur-nish-ings
fur-ni-ture
for-row
fur-ry
  fur-ri-er
  fur-ri-est
fur-ther
fur-ther-more
fur-ther-most
fur-thest
fur-tive
  fur-tive-ly
fu-ry
  fu-ries
fuse
  fused
  fus-ing
fu-see
fu-se-lage
fu-si-bil-i-ty
fu-si-ble
fu-si-form

fu-si-lade
fu-si-lad-ed
fu-si-lad-ing
fu-sion
fussy
fuss-i-er
fuss-i-est
fuss-i-ly
fus-tian
fus-ty
fu-tile
fu-til-i-ty
fu-til-i-ties
fu-ture
fu-tur-is-tic
fu-tu-ri-ty
fuzz-y

G

gab
gabbed
gab-ber
gab-ar-dine
gab-ble
gab-bled
gab-bler
gab-by
gab-bi-er
gab-bi-est
ga-ble
ga-bled
ga-bling
gad
gad-ded
gad-ding
gad-a-bout
gad-fly
gad-flies
gad-get
gad-get-ry
gaffe
gaf-fer

gag
ga-ga
gai-e-ty
gai-e-ties
gai-ly
gain-ful
gain-say
gain-said
gain-say-ing
gait
ga-la
ga-lac-tic
gal-ax-y
gal-a-xies
gal-lant
gal-lant-ry
gal-lant-ries
gal-ler-y
gal-ler-ies
gal-ley
gal-li-cism
gal-li-mau-fry
gal-li-mau-fries
gall-ing
gal-li-vant
gal-lon
gal-lop
gal-lows
gal-lows-es
gall-stone
ga-loot
ga-lore
gal-van-ic
gal-va-nism
gal-va-nize
gal-va-nized
gal-va-nom-e-ter
gam-bit
gam-ble
gam-bled
gam-bling
gam-bol
gam-brel

game
gam-er
gam-est
gamed
gam-ing
game-keep-er
game-some
game-ster
gam-ete
ga-met-ic
gam-in
gam-ma
gam-mon
gam-ut
gam-y
gam-i-er
gam-i-ly
gam-i-ness
gan-der
gang-land
gan-gling
gan-gli-on
gan-glia
gan-gli-ons
gan-gly
gan-gli-er
gan-gli-est
gang-plank
gan-grene
gan-grened
gan-gren-ing
gan-gre-nous
gang-ster
gang-way
gant-let
gan-try
gan-tries
gap
gapped
gap-ping
gar-bage
gar-ble

gar-bled
gar-bling
gar-den
gar-gan-tu-an
gar-gle
gar-gled
gar-gling
gar-goyle
gar-ish
gar-land
gar-ment
gar-nish
gar-nish-ee
gar-nish-ee-ing
gar-nish-ment
gar-ni-ture
gar-ret
gar-ri-son
gar-rote
gar-rot-ed
gar-rot-ing
gar-rot-er
gar-ru-lous
gar-ter
gas-ket
gas-lit
gas-o-line
gas-ser
gas-sy
gas-si-er
gas-si-est
gas-tric
gas-ti-tis
gas-tro-in-tes-ti-nal
gas-tron-o-my
gas-tro-nom-ic
gas-tro-nom-i-cal
gas-tro-nom-i-cal-ly
gas-works
gate-crash-er
gate-crash-ing
gate-house
gate-keep-er

gate-post
gate-way
gath-er
gath-er-ing
gauche
gau-cho
gaud-y
gaud-i-er
gaud-i-est
gaud-i-ly
gaunt-let
gauze
gauz-i-er
gauz-i-est
gauzy
gay-e-ty
gaze
gazed
gaz-er
gaz-ing
ga-ze-bo
ga-ze-bos
ga-ze-boes
ga-zelle
ga-zette
gaz-et-teer
gear-ing
gear-shift
gear-wheel
gee
geed
gee-ing
gee-zer
gei-sha
gel
gelled
gel-ling
gel-a-tin
gel-lat-i-nous
ge-la-tion
geld
geld-ed
geld-ing

gelt
gel-id
gem
gemmed
gem-ming
gem-ol-o-gy
gem-o-log-i-cal
gem-ol-o-gist
gem-stone
gen-darme
gen-der
gene
ge-ne-al-o-gy
ge-ne-a-log-i-cal
ge-ne-al-o-gist
gen-er-al
gen-er-al-is-si-mo
gen-er-al-is-si-mos
gen-er-al-ist
gen-er-al-i-ty
gen-er-al-i-ties
gen-er-ate
gen-er-at-ed
gen-er-at-ing
gen-er-a-tive
gen-er-a-tive-ly
gen-er-a-tion
gen-er-a-tor
ge-ner-ic
ge-ner-i-cal
ge-ner-i-cal-ly
gen-er-ous
gen-er-os-i-ty
gen-er-os-i-ties
gen-e-sis
ge-net-ic
ge-net-i-cal-ly
ge-net-ics
ge-net-i-cist
gen-ial
ge-ni-al-i-ty
ge-nie
ge-nies

ge-nii
gen-i-tal
gen-i-ta-lia
gen-i-tals
gen-ius
gen-ius-es
gen-o-cide
gen-o-ci-dal
gen-re
gen-teel
gen-tian
gen-tile
gen-til-i-ty
gen-til-i-ties
gen-tle
gen-tler
gen-tlest
gen-tly
gen-tle-folk
gen-tle-man
gen-tle-mèn
gen-tle-wom-an
gen-tle-wom-en
gen-try
gen-u-flect
gen-u-flec-tion
gen-u-flec-tor
gen-u-ine
ge-nus
gen-e-ra
ge-nus-es
ge-o-cen-tric
ge-o-cen-tri-cal-ly
ge-o-chem-is-try
ge-o-chem-i-cal
ge-o-chem-ist
ge-ode
ge-o-des-ic
ge-o-gra-phy
ge-o-gra-phies
ge-o-gra-pher
ge-o-gra-phic
ge-o-graph-i-cal

ge-o-met-ric
ge-om-e-try
ge-om-e-tries
ge-o-phys-ics
ge-o-phys-i-cal
ge-o-phys-i-cist
ge-o-pol-i-tic
ge-o-pol-i-tics
ge-o-pol-o-tic
ge-o-po-lit-i-cal
ge-o-po-lit-i-cal-ly
ge-o-ther-mal
ger-bil
ger-i-at-ric
ger-i-at-rics
ger-i-a-tri-cian
ger-i-at-rist
ger-mane
ger-mi-cide
ger-mi-cid-al
ger-on-tol-o-gy
ger-on-tol-o-gist
ger-ry-man-der
ger-und
ges-so
ges-tate
ges-tat-ed
ges-tat-ing
ges-ta-tion
ges-tic-u-late
ges-tic-u-lat-ed
ges-tic-u-lat-ing
ges-tic-u-la-tion
ges-tic-u-la-tive
ges-tic-u-la-to-ry
ges-tic-u-la-tor
ges-ture
ges-tured
ges-tur-ing
ges-tur-er
ge-sund-heit
get-a-way
gew-gaw

gey-ser
ghast-ly
ghast-li-er
ghast-li-est
ghast-li-ness
gher-kin
ghet-to
ghe-tos
ghet-toes
ghoul
gi-ant
gib-ber-ish
gib-bon
gibe
gib-er
gib-ing-ly
gib-let
gid-dy
gid-di-er
gid-di-est
gid-di-ly
gid-di-ness
gi-gan-tic
gi-gan-tism
gig-gle
gig-gled
gig-gling
gig-gler
gig-gly
gig-gli-er
gig-gli-est
gig-o-lo
gild-ed
gilt-edged
gim-crack
gim-let
gim-mick
gin-ger
gin-ger-bread
gin-ger-ly
gin-ger-li-ness
gin-ger-snap
gin-ger-y

ging-ham
gird-er
gir-dle
  gir-dled
  gir-dling
girl-hood
girl-ish
girth
gist
give
  gave
  giv-en
  giv-ing
give-and-take
give-a-way
giz-zard
gla-cial
gla-cier
glad
  glad-der
  glad-dest
  glad-ly
  glad-ness
glad-den
glad-i-a-tor
  glad-i-a-to-ri-al
glad-i-o-lus
  glad-i-o-lus-es
  glad-i-o-la
glad-some
glam-or-ize
  glam-or-ized
  glam-or-iz-ing
  glam-or-i-za-tion
  glam-or-i-zer
glam-or-ous
  glam-or-ous-ly
  glam-or-ous-ness
glam-our
glance
  glanced
  glanc-ing
glan-du-lar

glare
  glared
  glar-ing
  glar-i-ness
  glar-y
  glar-i-er
  glar-i-est
glass-blow-ing
  glass-blow-er
glass-ful
glass-ware
glass-y
  glass-i-er
  glass-i-est
  glass-i-ly
  glass-i-ness
glau-co-ma
glaze
  glazed
  glaz-ing
gla-zier
gleam
  gleam-ing
  gleam-y
glean
  glean-er
  glean-ing
glee
  glee-ful
  glee-ful-ly
  glee-ful-ness
glen-gar-ry
glib
  glib-ber
  glib-best
  glib-ly
  glib-ness
glide
  glid-ed
  glid-ing
glim-mer
glimpse
  glimpsed

glis-san-do
  glis-san-di
  glis-san-dos
glis-ten
glit-ter
gloam-ing
gloat
  gloat-er
  gloat-ing
glob
glo-bal
  glob-al-ly
globe-trot-ter
  globe-trot-ting
glob-u-lar
glob-ule
glock-en-spiel
gloom-y
  gloom-i-er
  gloom-i-est
  gloom-i-ly
  gloom-i-ness
glo-ri-fy
  glo-ri-fied
  glo-ri-fy-ing
  glo-ri-fi-ca-tion
  glo-ri-fi-er
glo-ri-ous
  glo-ri-ous-ly
  glo-ri-ou-ness
glo-ry
  glo-ries
  glo-ried
  glo-ry-ing
glos-sa-ry
glos-sa-ries
glossy
  gloss-i-er
  gloss-i-est
  gloss-i-ly
  gloss-i-ness
glot-tis
  glot-tis-es

glot-ti-des
glove
  gloved
  glov-ing
glow
  glow-er
  glow-ing
glow-worm
glu-cose
glue
  glued
  glu-ing
glum
  glum-mer
  glum-mest
glut
  glut-ted
  glut-ting
glu-ten
glu-ti-nous
glut-ton
glut-ton-ous
  glut-tony
glyc-er-in
  glyc-er-ine
glyc-er-ol
gnarl
  gnarled
  gnarly
  gnarl-i-er
  gnarl-i-est
gnash
gnat
gnaw
  gnawed
  gnaw-ing
gneiss
gnome
gnu
  gnus
goad-ed
go-a-head
goal-keep-er

goat-ee
goat-herd
goat-skin
gob-ble
  gob-bled
  gob-bling
gob-ble-dy-ween
gob-let
gob-lin
go-cart
god-child
  god-chil-dren
  god-daugh-ter
  god-son
god-dess
good-fa-ther
god-head
god-less
  god-less-ness
god-like
god-ly
  god-li-er
  god-li-est
  god-li-ness
god-mo-ther
god-par-ent
god-send
go-get-ter
gog-gle
  gog-gled
  gog-gling
gog-gle-eyed
gog-gles
go-ing
goi-ter
gold-brick
gold-en
gold-smith
go-nad
gon-do-la
gon-do-lier
gon-er
gon-or-rhea

goo-ber
good-by
  good-bye
good-for-noth-ing
good-heart-ed
good-ish
good-look-ing
good-ly
  good-li-er
  good-li-est
good-na-tured
good-ness
good-tem-pered
good-y
  good-ies
goof-off
goof-y
  goof-i-er
  goof-i-est
  goof-i-ness
goose-ber-ry
  goose-ber-ries
gore
  gored
  gor-ing
gorge
  gorged
  gorg-ing
gor-geous
  gor-geous-ly
  gor-geous-ness
gor-y
  gor-i-er
  gor-i-est
gos-ling
gos-pel
gos-sa-mer
  gos-sa-mery
  gos-sa-mer-i-er
  gos-sa-mer-i-est
gos-sip
  gos-sip-ing
  gos-sipy

gouge
  gouged
  goug-ing
  goug-er
gou-lash
gourd
gour-met
  gour-mets
gout
  gouty
  gout-i-er
  gout-i-est
gov-ern
  gov-ern-a-ble
gov-ern-ess
gov-ern-ment
  gov-ern-men-tal
gov-er-nor
  gov-er-nor-ship
gow-and
gowned
grab
  grabbed
  grab-bing
  grab-ber
grace
  graced
  grac-ing
grace-ful
  grace-ful-ly
  grace-ful-ness
grace-less
gra-cious
gra-da-tion
grade
  grad-ed
  grad-ing
grad-er
gra-di-ent
grad-u-al
  grad-u-al-ly
  grad-u-al-ness
grad-u-ate

grad-u-at-ed
grad-u-at-ing
grad-u-ation
graf-fi-to
  graf-fi-ti
graft
  graft-age
  graft-er
  graft-ing
gra-ham
grain
grain-y
  grain-i-er
  grain-i-est
  grain-i-ness
gram
gram-mar
  gram-mar-i-an
gram-mat-i-cal
  gram-mat-i-cal-ly
gra-na-ry
  gra-na-ries
grand
  grand-ly
grand-child
  grand-daugh-ter
gran-dee
gran-deur
grand-fa-ther
gran-dil-o-quence
  gran-dil-o-quent
gran-di-ose
  gran-di-ose-ly
grand-moth-er
grand-par-ent
grand-son
grand-stand
grange
  grang-er
gran-ite
  gra-nat-ic
gran-ny
  gran-nies

gran-u-lar
  gran-u-lar-i-ty
gran-u-late
  gran-u-lat-ed
  gran-u-lat-ing
gran-u-la-tion
gran-ule
grape-fruit
grape-vine
graph-ic
  graph-i-cal
  graph-i-cal-ly
graph-ite
graph-ol-o-gy
  graph-ol-o-gist
grap-nel
grap-ple
  grap-pled
  grap-pling
  grap-pler
grass
  grass-y
  grass-i-er
  grass-i-est
grass-hop-per
grass-land
grate
  grat-ed
  grat-ing
grate-ful
  grate-ful-ly
  grate-ful-ness
grat-i-fy
  grat-i-fied
  grat-i-fy-ing
gra-tis
grat-i-tude
gra-tu-i-tous
gra-tu-i-ty
  gra-tu-i-ties
grave
  graved
  grav-en

grav-ing
grav-er
grave-ly
grave-ness
grav-el
grav-eled
grav-el-ing
grav-el-ly
grave-stone
grave-yard
grav-i-tate
grav-i-tat-ed
grav-i-tat-ing
grav-i-ta-tion
grav-i-ta-tion-al
grav-i-ty
grav-i-ties
gra-vy
grav-ies
gray
gray-ly
gray-ness
gray-ling
graze
grazed
graz-ing
grease
greas-ed
greas-ing
greas-y
greas-i-er
greas-i-ness
great
great-ly
great-coat
great-heart-ed
greed-y
greed-i-er
greed-i-est
greed-i-ly
greed-i-ness
green-back
green-er-y

green-er-ies
green-gro-cer
green-horn
green-house
green-hous-es
green-ing
green-ish
green-ish-ness
green-sward
greet
greet-er
greet-ing
gre-gar-i-ous
gre-gar-i-ous-ly
gre-gar-i-ous-ness
grem-lin
gren-a-dier
gren-a-dine
grey
grey-ly
grey-ness
grid-dle
grid-dle-cake
grid-i-ron
grief
griev-ance
grieve
grieved
griev-ing
griev-ous
griev-ous-ly
grif-fin
grif-fon
grill
gril-lage
grille
grill-room
grim
grim-mer
grim-mest
grim-ly
grim-ness
grim-ace

grim-aced
grim-ac-ing
grime
grimed
grim-ing
grim-y
grim-i-er
grim-i-est
grim-i-ly
grim-i-ness
grin
grin-ned
grin-ning
grin-ner
grind
ground
grind-ing
grind-er
grind-stone
grin-go
grin-gos
grip
gripped
grip-ping
gripe
griped
grip-er
grippe
gris-ly
gris-li-er
gris-li-est
gris-li-ness
gris-tle
gris-tly
gris-tli-er
gris-tli-est
grit
grit-ted
grit-ting
grit-ty
grit-ti-er
grit-ti-est
grit-ti-ly

grit-ti-ness
griz-zled
griz-zly
griz-zli-er
griz-zli-est
griz-zlies
groan
groan-er
gro-cer
gro-cer-y
gro-cer-ies
grog-gy
grog-gi-er
groin
grom-met
groom
groove
grooved
groov-er
groov-y
groov-i-er
groov-i-est
grope
groped
grop-ing
gros-grain
gross
gross-es
gross-ness
gro-tesque
gro-tesque-ly
gro-tesque-ness
grot-to
grot-toes
grot-tos
grouch
grouchy
grouch-i-er
grouch-i-est
ground-er
ground-less
ground-less-ly
ground-less-ness

ground-ling
ground-nut
ground-work
group-ie
grouse
groused
grous-ing
grous-er
grov-el
grov-eled
grov-el-er
grow
grow-ing
grow-er
growl
growl-er
grown-up
growth
grub
grubbed
grub-bing
grub-ber
grub-by
grub-bi-er
grub-bi-est
grub-stake
grub-staked
grub-stak-ing
grudge
grudged
grudg-ing
grudg-ing-ly
gru-el
gru-el-ing
grue-some
grue-some-ly
gruff
gruff-ly
gruff-ness
grum-ble
grum-bled
grum-bling
grum-bler

grump-y
grump-i-er
grump-i-ness
grunt
grunt-er
grunt-ing
gua-no
gua-nos
guar-an-tee
guar-an-teed
guar-an-tee-ing
guar-an-tor
guar-an-ty
guar-an-ties
guar-an-ty-ing
guard-ed
guard-ed-ly
guard-house
guard-i-an
guards-man
guards-men
gua-va
gu-ber-na-to-ri-al
gudg-eon
guer-ril-la
gue-ril-la
guess
gues-ser
guess-work
guest
guf-faw
guid-ance
guide
guid-ed
guid-ing
guide-book
guide-post
gui-don
guid-hall
guile
guile-ful
guile-ful-ly
guile-less

guile-less-ly
guil-to-tine
  guil-lo-tined
  guil-lo-tin-ing
guilt
  guilt-less
  guilt-less-ly
guilt-y
  guilt-i-er
  guilt-i-ness
guin-ea
guise
gui-tar
  gui-tar-ist
gul-let
gul-li-ble
  gul-li-bil-i-ty
  gul-li-bly
gum
  gummed
  gum-ming
gum-bo
  gum-bos
gum-drop
gum-my
  gum-mi-er
  gum-mi-est
gump-tion
gum-shoe
  gum-shoed
gun
  gunned
  gun-ning
gun-boat
gun-fight
  gun-fight-er
gun-fire
gun-man
  gun-men
gun-ner
  gun-ner-y
gun-ny
  gun-nies

gun-ny-bag
gun-pow-der
gun-stock
gun-wale
gup-py
  gup-pies
gur-gle
  gur-gling
gu-ru
gush-er
gush-ing
gush-y
  gush-i-er
  gush-i-est
gus-set
gus-ta-to-ry
  gus-to
gut-ter
gut-tur-al
  gut-tur-al-ly
guz-zle
  guz-zled
  guz-zling
  guz-zler
gym-na-si-um
  gym-na-si-ums
  gym-na-sia
gym-nast
gym-nas-tic
  gym-nas-tics
gy-ne-col-o-gy
  gy-ne-co-log-ic
  gy-ne-co-log-i-cal
  gy-ne-col-o-gist
gyp
  gypped
  gyp-ping
gyp-sum
gyp-sy
  gyp-sies
gy-ral
gy-rate
  gy-rat-ed

gy-rat-ing
gy-ra-tion
gy-ra-tor
gy-ra-to-ry
gyr-fal-con
gy-roi-dal
gy-rom-e-ter
gy-ro-plane
gy-ro-scope
  gy-ro-scop-ic
gy-rose
gy-rus
gyve
  gyved
  gyv-ing

H

hab-da-lah
ha-be-as cor-pus
hab-er-dash-er
  hab-er-dash-ery
  hab-er-dash-er-ies
ha-bil-i-ment
hab-it
hab-it-a-ble
ha-bi-tant
hab-i-ta-tion
ha-bit-u-al
  ha-bit-u-al-ly
  ha-bit-u-al-ness
ha-bit-u-ate
  ha-bit-u-at-ed
  ha-bit-u-at-ing
  ha-bit-u-a-tion
ha-ci-en-da
  ha-ci-en-das
hack-le
  hack-led
  hack-ling
hack-ney
  hack-neyed
hack-saw

hadn't	half-caste	ham-burg-er
had-ron	half-heart-ed	ham-let
hae-mo-glo-bin	half-heart-ed-ly	ham-mer
hae-mo-phil-i-a	half hour	ham-mer-head
haft	half--life	ham-mer-less
ha-gar	half-lives	ham-mock
hag-gard	half--mast	ham-my
hag-gard-ly	half--moon	ham-mi-er
hag-gle	half note	ham-mi-est
hag-gled	half step	hamp-er
hag-gling	half-tone	ham-ster
hag-gler	half-track	ham-string
ha-gi-ol-o-gy	half-truth	ham-strung
hag-i-ol-o-gies	half-way	ham-string-ing
hag-i-ol-o-gist	half--wit	hand-bag
hag-rid-den	half--wit-ted	hand-ball
haik	hal-i-but	hand-bill
hai-ku	hal-i-to-sis	hand-book
hail-fel-low	hall-mark	hand-cuff
hail-stone	hal-lo	hand-ed
hail-storm	hal-low	hand-ful
hair-breadth	hal-lowed	hand-fuls
hair-brush	hal-lu-ci-nate	hand-i-cap
hair-cut	hal-lu-ci-nat-ed	hand-i-capped
hair-do	hal-lu-ci-nat-ing	hand-i-cap-ping
hair-dress-er	hal-lu-ci-na-tion	hand-i-cap-per
hair-dress-ing	hal-lu-ci-na-to-ry	hand-i-craft
hair-line	hal-lu-cin-o-gen	hand-i-ly
hair-pin	hal-lu-cin-o-gen-ic	handi-ness
hair-split-ter	hal-lux	hand-i-work
hair-split-ting	hall-way	han-ker-chief
hair-spring	halo-phile	han-dle
hair-y	halt	han-dled
hair-i-er	halt-ing	han-dling
hair-i-est	halt-ing-ly	han-dler
ha-la-tion	hal-ter	han-dle-bar
hal-cy-on	hal-ter-break	hand-made
hale	halve	hand-maid-en
haled	halved	hand--me--down
hal-ing	halv-ing	hand-out
half-back	halv-ers	hand-pick
half-baked	halves	hand-picked
half-breed	hal-yard	hand-rail

hand-shake
hand-some
  hand-som-er
  hand-som-est
  hand-some-ly
  hand-some-ness
hand-spike
hand-spring
hand-to-hand
hand--to--mouth
hand-work
hand-writ-ing
handy
  hand-i-er
  hand-i-est
handy-man
  handy-men
hang
  hung
  hanged
  hang-ing
hang-ar
hang-dog
hang-er
hang-er--on
hang-man
  hanf-men
hang-nail
hang-out
hang-o-ver
hang--up
hank-er
han-som
hap-haz-ard
  hap-haz-ard-ly
  hap-haz-ard-ness
hap-less
  hap-less-ly
hap-ly
hap-pen
hap-pen-ing
hap-pen-stance
hap-pi-ness

hap-py
  hap-pi-er
  hap-pi-est
  hap-pi-ly
hap-py--go--lucky
hara-kiri
ha-rangue
  ha-rangued
  ha-rangu-ing
ha-rass
  ha-rass-ment
har-bin-ger
har-bor
hard--bit-ten
hard--boiled
hard--core
hard-cov-er
hard-en
  hard-en-er
hard hat
hard-head-ed
hard-heart-ed
har-di-hood
har-di-ness
hard-ly
  har-di-er
  har-di-est
  har-di-ly
hare-brained
hare-lip
har-em
har-le-quin
har-lot
  har-lot-ry
harm-ful
  harm-ful-ly
  harm-ful-ness
harm-less
  harm-less-ly
  harm-less-ness
har-mon-ic
  har-mon-i-cal-ly
har-mon-i-ca

har-mon-ics
har-mo-ni-ous
  har-mo-ni-ous-ly
har-mo-nize
  har-mo-nized
  har-mo-niz-ing
har-mo-ny
  har-mo-nies
har-ness
harp-ist
har-poon
harp-si-chord
har-py
  har-pies
har-que-bus
har-ri-dan
har-row
  har-row-ing
har-ry
  har-ried
  har-ry-ing
harsh
  harsh-ly
  harsh-ness
har-um-scar-um
har-vest
har-ves-ter
has--been
hash-ish
  hash-eesh
hasn't
has-sle
  has-sled
  has-sling
has-sock
has-ten
hasty
  hast-i-er
  hast-i-est
hatch-ery
  hatch-er-ies
hatch-et
hatch-way

hate
hat-ed
hat-ing
hat-er
hate-ful
hate-ful-ly
hate-ful-ness
ha-tred
hat-ter
haugh-ty
haugh-ti-er
haugh-ti-est
haugh-ti-ly
haught-ti-ness
haunch
haunch-es
haunt-ed
haunt-ing
hau-teur
ha-ven
have--not
haven't
hav-er-sack
havers
hav-oc
hawk
hawk-ish
haw-ser
hay-loft
hay-mak-er
hay-mow
hay-seed
hay-stack
hay-wire
haz-ard
haz-ard-ous
haz-ard-ous-ly
haze
hazed
haz-ing
ha-zel
ha-zel-nut
hazy

ha-zi-er
ha-zi-est
ha-zi-ly
ha-zi-ness
head-ache
head-band
head-dress
head-er
head-first
head-fore-most
head-gear
head-hunt-er
head-ing
head-land
head-less
head-light
head-line
head-lined
head-lin-ing
head-long
head-mas-ter
head-mis-tress
head-most
head--on
head-piece
head-quar-ters
head-set
head-stone
head-strong
head-wait-er
head-wa-ter
head-way
head-wind
heady
head-i-er
head-i-est
head-i-ly
head-i-ness
heal-er
health-ful
health-ful-ly
healthy
health-i-er

health-i-est
health-i-ness
heaped
hear
heared
hear-ing
hear-er
hear-ken
hear-say
hearse
heart-ache
heart-break
heart-break-ing
heart-brok-en
heart-burn
heart-en
heart-felt
hearth-stone
heart-less
heart-less-ly
heart-less-ness
heart-rend-ing
heart-sick
heart-strings
heart--to--heart
hearty
heart-i-er
heart-i-est
heart-i-ly
heart-i-ness
heat-ed
heat-er
heath
hea-then
heave
heaved
heav-ing
heav-en
heav-en-ly
heav-en-ward
heav-en-wards
heavy--du-ty
heavy--hand-ed

heavy-weight
heck-le
  heck-led
  heck-ling
  heck-ler
hect-are
hec-tic
  hec-ti-cal-ly
hec-to-gram
hec-to-li-ter
hec-to-me-ter
hedge
  hedged
  hedg-ing
  hedg-er
he-do-nism
  he-do-nist
  he-do-nis-tic
hee-haw
hefty
  heft-i-er
  heft-i-est
he-ge-mo-ny
  he-ge-mo-nies
  heg-e-mon-ic
he-gi-ra
heif-er
height-en
  height-en-er
hei-nous
  hei-nous-ly
heir-ess
heir-loom
heist
he-li-cop-ter
he-li-um
he-lix
  he-li-ces
  he-lix-es
hell--bent
hell-cat
hel-lion
hell-ish

hell-ish-ly
hell-ish-ness
hel-lo
  hel-los
helm
  helm-less
hel-met
  hel-met-ed
helms-man
  helms-men
help-er
help-ful
  help-ful-ly
  help-ful-ness
help-ing
help-less
  help-less-ly
help-mate
hel-er--skel-ter
hem
  hemmed
  hem-ming
he--man
  he--men
hemi-sphere
  hemi-spher-ic
  hemi-sper-i-cal
hem-lock
he-mo-glo-bin
he-mo-phil-ia
hem-or-rhage
  hem-or-rhag-ing
  hem-or-rhag-ic
hem-or-rhoid
  hem-or-rhoid-al
hemp-en
hem-stitch
hence-forth
hench-man
hench-men
  hench-man-ship
hen-na
hen-peck

hep-a-ti-tis
her-ald
  he-ral-dic
her-ald-ry
  her-ald-ries
herb-age
her-biv-o-rous
Her-cu-le-an
herd-er
herds-man
  herds-men
here-af-ter
he-red-i-tary
  he-red-i-tar-i-ly
he-red-i-ty
  he-red-i-ties
here-in
here-of
her-e-sy
  her-e-sies
her-e-tic
  he-ret-i-cal
  he-ret-i-cal-ly
here-to
here-to-fore
here-upon
here-with
her-i-ta-ble
  her-i-ta-bil-i-ty
  her-i-ta-bly
her-i-tage
her-maph-ro-dite
  her-maph-ro-dit-ic
  her-maph-ro-dit-ism
her-met-ic
  her-met-i-cal
  her-met-i-cal-ly
her-mit
  her-mit-age
her-nia
  her-ni-al
  her-ni-a-tion
he-ro

he-roes
he-ro-ic
he-ro-ical
he-ro-ical-ly
her-o-in
her-o-ine
her-o-ism
her-on
her-ring-bone
her-ring-boned
her-ring-bon-ing
her-self
hes-i-tant
hes-i-tan-cy
hes-i-tan-cies
hes-i-tant-ly
hes-i-ta-tion
het-ero-dox
het-ero-doxy
het-er-o-ge-neous
het-er-o-ge-ne-ity
het-ero-sex-u-al
het-ero-sex-u-al-i-ty
hew
hewed
hewn
hexa-gon
hex-ag-o-nal
hex-ag-o-nal-ly
hey-day
hey-dey
hi-a-tus
hi-a-tus-es
hi-ba-chi
hi-ber-nate
hi-ber-nat-ed
hi-ber-nat-ing
hi-ber-na-tion
hi-bis-cus
hic-cup
hic-cuped
hic-cup-ing
hid-den

hid-den-ness
hide
hid
hid-den
hid-er
hide-bound
hid-eous
hid-eous-ly
hid-eous-ness
hide-out
hi-er-ar-chy
hi-er-ar-chies
hi-er-ar-chal
hi-er-ar-chic
hi-er-ar-chi-cal
hi-er-ar-chi-cal-ly
hi-ero-glyph
hi-ero-glyph-ic
hi-ero-glyph-i-cal
hi--fi
high-ball
high-born
high-boy
high-brow
high-browed
high-brow-ism
high-er--up
high-fa-lu-tin
high-fa-lu-ting
high--flown
high--grade
high--hand-ed
high--hand-ed-ly
high--hand-ed-ness
high--hat
high-land
high-light
high--mind-ed
high--mind-ed-ly
high--mind-ed-ness
high-ness
high--pressure
high--pressured

high--pressur-ing
high school
high seas
high--spir-it-ed
high--spir-it-ed-ly
high--spir-it-ed-ness
high--strung
high-tail
high--tension
high--toned
high-way
high-way-man
high-way-men
hi-jack
hi-jack-er
hi-jack-ing
hike
hiked
hik-ing
hik-er
hi-lar-i-ous
hi-lar-i-ous-ly
hi-lar-i-ous-ness
hi-lar-i-ty
hill-bil-ly
hill-bil-lies
hill-ock
hill-side
hill-top
hilly
hill-i-er
hill-i-est
him-self
hin-der
hin-der-er
hind-most
hind-quar-ter
hin-drance
hind-sight
hinge
hinged
hing-ing
hint-er

hint-ing-ly
hin-ter-land
hipped
hip-pie
hip-po
hip-pos
hip-po-drome
hip-po-pot-a-mus
hip-po-pot-a-mus-es
hip-po-pot-a-mi
hire-ling
hir-sute
hir-sute-ness
hiss
hiss-er
his-ta-mine
his-ta-min-ic
his-to-ri-an
his-tor-ic
his-tor-i-cal
his-tor-i-cal-ly
his-tor-i-cal-ness
his-to-ry
his-to-ries
his-tri-on-ic
his-tri-on-i-cal
his-tri-on-i-cal-ly
his-tri-on-ics
hit
hit-ting
hit--and--run
hitch
hitch-er
hitch-hike
hitch-hiked
hitch-hik-ing
hitch-hik-er
hith-er-to
hive
hived
hiv-ing
hoary
hoar-i-er

hoar-i-est
hoar-i-ness
hoard
hoard-er
hoard-ing
hoar-frost
hoarse
hoarse-ly
hoars-en
hoarse-ness
hoax
hoax-er
hob-ble
hob-bled
hob-bling
hob-by
hob-bies
hob-by-horse
hob-gob-lin
hob-nail
hob-nail-ed
hob-nob
hob-nobbed
hob-nob-bing
ho-bo
ho-boes
ho-bos
ho-bo-ism
hock-er
hock-ey
ho-cus-po-cus
hodge-podge
hoe
hoed
hoe-ing
hoe-down
hog
hogged
hog-ging
hog-gish
hog-gish-ly
hog-gish-ness
hogs-head

hog--tie
hog--tied
hog--ty-ing
hog-wash
hoi pol-loi
hoist-er
ho-kum
hold-er
hold-ing
hold-out
hold-over
hold-up
hole
holed
hol-ing
holey
hol-i-day
ho-li-ness
Hol-land
hol-ler
hol-low
hol-low-ly
hol-low-ness
hol-ly
hol-lies
hol-ly-hock
hol-mi-um
ho-lo-caust
ho-lo-gram
hol-o-graph
hol-ster
ho-ly
ho-li-er
ho-li-est
ho-lies
hom-age
hom-bre
hom-bres
home-com-ing
home-less
home-less-ness
home-ly
home-li-er

home-li-est
home-li-ness
home-made
hom-er
home-sick
home-sick-ness
home-spun
home-stead
home-stead-er
home-ward
home-wards
home-work
homey
hom-i-er
hom-i-est
hom-i-ness
hom-i-cide
hom-i-let-ics
hom-i-ly
hom-i-lies
homing pigeon
hom-i-ny
ho-mo-ge-neous
ho-mo-ge-ne-ity
ho-mog-e-nize
ho-meg-e-nized
ho-mog-e-niz-ing
ho-mo-graph
ho-mol-o-gous
ho-mol-o-gy
ho-mol-o-gies
hom-onym
hom-onym-ic
ho-mo-phone
ho-mo-pho-nic
ho-mo-sex-u-al
ho-mo-sex-u-al-i-ty
hone
honed
hon-ing
hon-est
hon-est-ly
hon-es-ty

hon-es-ties
hon-ey
hon-eys
hon-eyed
hon-ied
hon-ey-ing
hon-ey-bee
hon-ey-comb
hon-ey-moon
hon-ey-moon-er
hon-ey-suck-le
hon-ey-suck-led
hon-ky--tonk
hon-or
hon-or-able
hon-or-ably
hon-o-rar-i-um
hon-o-rar-i-ums
hon-o-rar-ia
hon-or-ary
hon-or-if-ic
hood-ed
hood-lum
hoo-doo
hoo-doo-ism
hood-wink
hood-wink-er
hoo-ey
hoof
hoofs
hooves
hoofed
hooked
hook-er
hook-up
hoo-li-gan
hoo-li-gan-ism
hoop
hooped
hoop-like
hoop-la
hoo-ray
hoose-gow

hoot
hoot-er
hoot-ing-ly
hop
hopped
hop-ping
hop-er
hope-ful
hope-ful-ly
hope-ful-ness
hope-less
hope-less-ly
hope-less-ness
hop-head
hop-per
hop-scotch
horde
hord-ed
hord-ing
ho-ri-zon
hor-i-zon-tal
hor-i-zon-tal-ly
hor-mone
hor-mon-al
horn
horned
horn-like
horny
horn-i-er
horn-i-est
hor-net
horn-swog-gle
horn-swog-gled
horn-swog-gling
hor-rol-o-gy
ho-rol-o-ger
ho-rol-o-gist
horo-scope
hor-ren-dous
hor-ren-dous-ly
hor-ri-ble
hor-ri-bly
hor-rid

hor-rid-ly
hor-rid-ness
hor-ri-fy
hor-ri-fied
hor-ri-fy-ing
hor-ri-fi-ca-tion
hor-ror
horse
hors-es
horsed
hors-ing
horse-back
horse-fly
horse-flies
horse-hair
horse-laugh
horse-men
horse-man-ship
horse-wom-an
horse-wom-en
horse opera
horse-play
horse-pow-er
horse-rad-ish
horse-shoe
horse-sho-er
horse-whip
horse-whipped
horse-whip-ping
hors-ey
horsy
hors-i-er
hors-i-est
hors-i-ly
hors-i-ness
hor-ta-to-ry
hor-ti-cul-ture
hor-ti-cul-tur-al
hor-ti-cul-tur-ist
ho-san-na
hose
hos-es
hosed

hos-ing
ho-siery
hos-pice
hos-pi-ta-ble
hos-pi-ta-bly
hos-pi-tal
hos-pi-tal-i-ty
hos-pi-tal-i-ties
hos-pi-tal-iza-tion
hos-pi-tal-ize
hos-pi-tal-ized
hos-pi-tal-iz-ing
hos-tage
hos-tel
hos-tel-ry
hos-tel-ries
host-ess
hos-tile
hos-tile-ly
hos-til-i-ty
hos-til-i-ties
hos-tler
hot
hot-ter
hot-test
hot-ly
hot-bed
hot--blood-ed
ho-tel
hot-head
hot-head-ed
hot-head-ed-ness
hot-house
hot-shot
hound
hound-er
hour-glass
hour-ly
house
hous-es
housed
hous-ing
house-boat

house-bro-ken
house-break
house-broke
house-break-ing
house-fly
house-hold
house-keep-er
house-keep-ing
house-maid
house-warm-ing
house-wife
house-wives
house-wife-ly
house-wif-ery
house-work
hous-ing
hov-el
hov-eled
hov-el-ing
hov-er
hov-er-er
hov-er-ing
how-ev-er
how-it-zer
howl-er
how-so-ev-er
hoy-den
hoy-den-ish
hob-bub
huck-le-ber-ry
huck-le-ber-ries
huck-ster
hud-dle
hud-dled
hud-dling
hud-dler
huffy
huff-i-er
huff-i-est
huff-i-ly
huff-i-ness
hug
hugged

hug-ging
hug-ger
huge
  hug-er
  hug-est
  huge-ly
  huge-ness
hu-la
hulk-ing
hul-la-ba-loo
hum
  hummed
  hum-ming
  hum-mer
hu-man
  hu-man-ness
hu-mane
  hu-mane-ly
  hu-man-ness
hu-man-ism
  hu-man-ist
  hu-man-ist-ic
hu-man-i-ty
  hu-man-i-ties
hu-man-ize
  hu-man-ized
  hu-man-iz-ing
  hu-man-i-za-tion
  hu-man-iz-er
hu-man-kind
hu-man-ly
hum-ble
  hum-bler
  hum-blest
  hum-bled
  hum-bling
  hum-ble-ness
  hum-bly
hum-bug
  hum-bugged
  hum-bug-ging
  hum-bug-ger
  hum-bug-gery

hum-ding-er
hum-drum
hu-mer-us
hu-mid
  hu-mid-ly
hu-mid-i-fy
  hu-mid-i-fied
  hu-mid-i-fy-ing
  hu-mid-i-fi-er
hu-mid-i-ty
hum-ming-bird
hum-mock
  hum-mocky
  hum-mock-i-er
  hum-mock-i-est
hu-mor
hu-mor-ist
  hu-mor-is-tic
hu-mor-ous
  hu-mor-ous-ly
  hu-mor-ous-ness
hump
  humped
  humpy
  hump-i-er
  hump-i-est
hump-back
hu-mus
hunch-back
  hunch-backed
hun-dred
hun-ger
hun-gry
  hun-gri-er
  hun-gri-est
  hun-gri-ly
  hun-gri-ness
hunt
  hunt-er
  hunt-ing
  hunt-ress
  hunts-man
  hunts-men

hur-dle
  hur-dled
  hur-dling
  hur-dler
hur-dy--gur-dy
  hur-dy--gur-dies
hurl-er
hurl-y--burl-y
  hurl-y--burl-ies
hur-rah
hur-ri-cane
hur-ry
  hur-ried
  hur-ry-ing
  hur-ried-ly
  hur-ry-ing-ly
hurt-ful
  hurt-ful-ly
  hurt-ful-ness
hurt-ing
hur-tle
  hur-tled
  hur-tling
hurt-less
hus-band
  hus-band-er
  hus-band-less
  hus-band-ly
hus-band-man
hus-band-ry
hush
husk-er
husk-ing
husky
  husk-i-er
  husk-i-est
  husk-i-ly
  husk-i-ness
  husk-ies
hus-sar
hus-sy
  hussies
hus-tings

hus-tle
  hus-tled
  hus-tling
  hus-tler
hutch
hut-ment
huz-zah
  huz-za
hy-a-cinth
  hy-a-cin-thine
hy-a-line
hy-a-lite
hy-a-loid
hy-a-lo-plasm
hy-brid
  hy-brid-ism
  hy-brid-i-ty
hy-brid-ize
  hy-brid-ized
  hy-brid-iz-er
  hy-brid-iz-ing
  hy-brid-i-za-tion
hy-da-thode
hy-da-tid
hy-dra
  hy-dras
  hy-dae
hy-dral-azine
hy-dran-gea
hy-drant
hy-dra-ted
hy-dra-ting
hy-dra-tion
hy-dra-tor
hy-drau-lic
  hy-drau-li-cal-ly
hy-drau-lics
hy-dro-car-bon
hy-dro-chlo-ric acid
hy-dro-dy-nam-ics
  hy-dro-dy-na-mic
hy-dro-elec-tric
hy-dro-gen

hy-drog-e-nous
hy-dro-ly-sis
hy-drom-e-ter
  hy-dro-met-ric
  hy-dro-met-ri-cal
  hy-drom-e-try
hy-dro-pho-bia
hy-dro-plane
  hy-dro-plan-er
  hy-dro-plan-ing
hy-dro-pon-ics
hy-dro-ther-a-py
  hy-dro-ther-a-pist
hy-drous
hy-drox-ide
hy-drox-yl
hy-dro-zo-an
hy-e-na
hy-giene
  hy-gien-ic
  hy-gien-i-cal-ly
  hy-gien-ist
hy-men
hy-me-ne-al
  hy-me-ne-al-ly
hym-nal
hy-per-bo-la
hy-per-bo-le
  hy-per-bo-lize
  hy-per-bo-lized
  hy-per-bo-liz-ing
hy-per-bol-ic
hy-per-crit-i-cal
  hy-per-crit-i-cal-ly
hy-per-sen-si-tive
  -per-sen-si-tiv-i-ty
hy-per-sex-u-al
  hy-per-sex-u-al-ity
hy-per-ten-sion
hy-per-thy-roid-ism
hy-phen
hy-phen-ate
  hy-phen-at-ed

hy-phen-at-ing
hyp-no-sis
hyp-not-ic
hyp-no-tism
  hyp-no-tist
hyp-no-tize
  hyp-no-tized
  hyp-no-tiz-ing
hy-po
hy-po-chon-dria
hy-po-chon-dri-ac
hy-poc-ri-sy
  hy-poc-ri-sies
  hyp-o-crite
hy-po-der-mic
hy-po-sen-si-tize
  hy-po-sen-si-tized
  hy-po-sen-si-tiz-ing
hy-po-ten-sion
hy-pot-e-nuse
hy-poth-e-cate
  hy-poth-e-cat-ed
  hy-poth-e-cat-ing
  hy-poth-e-ca-tion
  hy-poth-e-ca-tor
hy-poth-e-sis
  hy-poth-e-ses
  hy-poth-e-size
  hy-poth-e-siz-ing
hy-po-thet-i-cal
  hy-po-thet-i-cal-ly
hyp-ox-emia
hyp-ox-ia
hyp-sog-ra-phy
hy-son
hys-sop
hys-ter-ec-to-my
  hys-ter-ec-to-mies
hys-ter-e-sis
hys-te-ria
  hys-ter-ic
  hys-ter-i-cal
  hys-ter-i-cal-ly

hys-ter-ics

I

iamb
iat-ric
ibid
ibi-dem
ibis
  ibis-es
ice-boat
ice--cream
ice-man
  ice-men
ice--skate
icon
icon-o-clasm
  icon-o-clas-tic
icon-o-clast
ide-al-ize
  ide-al-ized
  ide-al-iz-ing
  ide-al-i-za-tion
ide-al-ly
idem
iden-ti-cal
  iden-ti-cal-ly
iden-ti-fi-a-ble
  iden-ti-fy-ing
  iden-ti-fi-a-bly
iden-ti-fi-ca-tion
iden-ti-fy
  iden-ti-fied
  iden-ti-fy-ing
  iden-ti-fi-er
iden-ti-ty
  iden-ti-ties
ides
id-i-o-cy
  id-i-o-cies
id-i-om
  id-i-o-mat-ic
  id-i-o-mat-i-cal-ly

id-i-o-syn-cra-sy
  id-i-o-syn-cra-sies
  id-i-o-syn-crat-ic
id-i-ot
  id-i-ot-ic
  id-i-ot-i-cal-ly
idle
idol
idol-ize
idyll
  idyl-lic
  idyl-lic-al-ly
ig-ne-ous
ig-nite
ig-ni-tion
ig-no-ble
  ig-no-bil-i-ty
  ig-no-bly
ig-no-ra-mus
ig-no-rant
  ig-no-rance
  ig-no-rant-ly
ig-nore
  ig-nored
  ig-nor-ing
igua-na
ill--ad-vised
  ill--ad-vis-ed-ly
ill--bred
il-le-gal
  il-le-gal-i-ty
  il-le-gal-ly
il-leg-i-ble
  il-leg-i-bil-i-ty
  il-leg-i-bly
il-le-git-i-mate
  il-le-git-i-ma-cy
  il-le-git-i-ma-cies
  il-le-git-i-mate-ly
ill--fat-ed
ill--fa-vored
ill--got-ten
il-lib-er-al

il-lic-it
il-lim-it-able
il-lit-er-a-cy
  il-lit-er-a-cies
il-lit-er-ate
ill-ness
il-log-i-cal
ill-starred
ill-tem-pered
  ill-tem-pered-ly
il-lu-mi-na-tion
il-lu-mine
  il-lu-mined
  il-lu-min-ing
ill-use
il-lu-sion
il-lu-sive
  il-lu-sive-ly
  il-lu-sive-ness
il-lus-trate
  il-lus-trat-ed
  il-lus-trat-ing
il-lus-tra-tion
il-lus-tra-tive
  il-lus-tra-tive-ly
il-lus-tra-tor
il-lus-tri-ous
  il-lus-tri-ous-ly
im-age
  im-aged
im-ag-ing
  im-age-a-ble
  im-ag-er
im-ag-ery
  im-ag-eries
  im-ag-eri-al
imag-in-able
  imag-in-able-ness
  imag-in-ably
imag-i-nary
  imag-i-nar-ies
  imag-i-nar-i-ly
  imag-i-nar-i-ness

imag-i-na-tion
imag-i-na-tion-al
imag-i-na-tive
imag-i-na-tive-ly
imag-ine
imag-ined
imag-in-ing
im-bal-ance
im-be-cile
im-be-cil-ic
im-be-cile-ly
im-be-cil-i-ty
imbed
imbed-ded
im-bed-ding
im-bibe
im-bro-glio
im-brue
im-brued
im-bru-ing
im-i-ta-ble
im-i-tate
im-i-tat-ed
im-i-tat-ing
im-i-ta-tor
im-i-ta-tion
im-i-ta-tive
im-mac-u-late
im-mac-u-la-cy
im-mac-u-late-ly
im-ma-te-ri-al
im-ma-te-ri-al-ness
im-ma-te-ri-al-i-ty
im-ma-te-ri-al-ize
im-ma-ture
im-ma-ture-ly
im-ma-ture-ness
im-ma-tu-ri-ty
im-meas-ur-a-ble
im-meas-ur-a-bly
im-me-di-a-cy
im-me-di-a-cies
im-me-di-ate

im-me-di-ate-ly
im-me-di-ate-ness
im-me-mo-ri-al
im-me-mo-ri-al-ly
im-mense
im-mese-ly
im-mese-ness
im-men-si-ty
im-merge
im-merged
im-merse
im-mersed
im-mers-ing
im-mer-sion
im-mi-grant
im-mi-grat-ed
im-mi-gra-tion
im-mi-gra-tor
im-mi-nent
im-mi-nence
im-mo-bile
im-mo-bil-i-ty
im-mo-bi-lize
im-mod-er-ate
im-mod-er-ate-ly
im-mod-er-ate-ness
im-mod-est
im-mod-est-ly
im-mod-es-ty
im-mo-late
im-mo-lat-ed
im-mo-lat-ing
im-mo-la-tion
im-mo-la-tor
im-mor-al
im-mor-al-ist
im-mor-al-i-ty
im-mor-al-ly
im-mor-tal
im-mov-a-ble
im-mov-a-bli-i-ty
im-mov-a-bly
im-mune

im-mu-ni-ty
im-mu-ni-ties
im-mu-nize
im-mu-nized
im-mu-niz-ing
im-mu-ni-za-tion
im-mu-nol-o-gy
im-mure
im-mured
im-mur-ing
im-mu-ta-ble
im-mu-ta-bil-i-ty
im-mu-ta-bly
im-pact
im-pac-tion
im-pact-ed
im-pair
im-pair-er
im-pair-ment
im-pa-la
im-pal-as
im-pal-ae
im-pal-pa-ble
im-pal-pa-bil-i-ty
im-pal-pa-bly
im-pan-el
im-pan-eled
im-pan-el-ing
im-part
im-par-tial
im-par-ti-al-i-ty
im-par-tial-ly
im-pass-able
im-pass-abil-i-ty
im-pass-able-ness
im-pass-ably
im-passe
im-pas-si-ble
im-pas-si-bil-i-ty
im-pas-si-bly
im-pas-sion
im-pas-sioned
im-pas-sioned-ly

im-pas-sive
im-pas-sive-ly
im-pas-sive-ness
im-pas-siv-i-ty
im-pa-tience
im-pa-tient
im-pa-tient-ly
im-peach
im-peach-a-ble
im-peach-ment
im-pec-ca-ble
im-pec-ca-bil-i-ty
im-pec-ca-bly
im-pe-cu-nious
im-pe-cu-nious-ly
im-pe-cu-nious-ness
im-pede
im-ped-ed
im-ped-ing
im-ped-i-ment
im-pel
im-pelled
im-pel-ling
im-pend
im-pend-ing
im-pen-e-tra-bil-i-ty
im-pen-e-tra-ble
im-pen-e-tra-bly
im-pen-i-tent
im-pen-i-tence
im-pen-i-tent-ly
im-per-cep-ti-ble
im-per-cep-tive
im-per-fect
im-per-fect-ly
im-per-fect-ness
im-per-fec-tion
im-pe-ri-al
im-pe-ri-al-ly
im-pe-ri-al-ism
im-pe-ri-al-ist
im-pe-ri-al-is-tic
im-per-il

im-per-iled
im-per-il-ing
im-per-il-ment
im-pe-ri-ous
im-pe-ri-ous-ly
im-pe-ri-ous-ness
im-per-ish-able
im-per-ish-abil-i-ty
im-per-ish-ably
im-per-ma-nence
im-per-ma-nen-cy
im-per-ma-nent
im-per-ma-nent-ly
im-per-me-able
im-per-me-abil-i-ty
im-per-me-ably
im-per-son-al
im-per-son-al-i-ty
im-per-son-al-i-ties
im-per-son-al-ly
im-per-son-ate
im-per-son-at-ed
im-per-son-at-ing
im-per-son-a-tion
im-per-son-ator
im-per-ti-nent
im-per-ti-nence
im-per-ti-nent-ly
im-per-turb-able
im-per-turb-ably
im-per-vi-ous
im-per-vi-ous-ly
im-per-vi-ous-ness
im-pe-ti-go
im-pet-u-os-i-ty
im-pet-u-ous
im-pet-u-ous-ly
im-pet-u-ous-ness
im-pe-tus
im-pe-tus-es
im-pi-ety
im-pi-eties
im-pinge

im-pinged
im-ping-ing
im-pinge-ment
im-ping-er
im-pi-ous
im-pi-ous-ly
im-pi-ous-ness
im-pla-ca-ble
im-pla-ca-bil-i-ty
im-pla-ca-ble-ness
im-pla-ca-bly
im-plant
im-plan-ta-tion
im-plant-er
im-plau-si-ble
im-plau-si-bly
im-plau-si-bil-i-ty
im-ple-ment
im-ple-men-tal
im-ple-men-ta-tion
im-pli-cate
im-pli-cat-ed
im-pli-cat-ing
im-pli-ca-tion
im-plic-it
im-plic-it-ly
im-plic-it-ness
im-plode
im-plod-ed
im-plod-ing
im-plo-sion
im-plo-sive
im-ply
im-plied
im-ply-ing
im-po-lite
im-po-lite-ly
im-po-lite-ness
im-pol-i-tic
im-pol-i-tic-ly
im-pon-der-a-ble
im-pon-der-a-bly
im-pone

im-poned
im-port
im-port-a-ble
im-port-er
im-por-tance
im-por-tant
im-por-tant-ly
im-por-ta-tion
im-por-tu-nate
im-por-tu-nate-ly
im-por-tune
im-por-tuned
im-por-tun-ing
im-pose
im-posed
im-pos-ing
im-pos-ter
im-po-si-tion
im-pos-si-bil-i-ty
im-pos-si-bil-i-ties
im-pos-si-ble
im-pos-si-bly
im-post
im-pos-tor
im-pos-ture
im-po-tence
im-po-ten-cy
im-po-tent
im-po-tent-ly
im-pound
im-pound-age
im-pov-er-ish
im-pov-er-ish-ment
im-prac-ti-ca-ble
im-prac-ti-ca-bly
im-prac-ti-cal
im-pre-cate
im-pre-cat-ed
im-pre-cat-ing
im-pre-ca-tion
im-preg-na-ble
im-preg-na-bil-i-ty
im-preg-na-bly

im-pre-sa-rio
im-pre-sa-ri-os
im-press
im-press-er
im-press-i-ble
im-press-ment
im-pres-sion
im-pres-sion-ist
im-pres-sion-a-ble
im-pres-sion-a-bly
im-pres-sion-ism
im-pres-sion-ist
im-pres-sion-is-tic
im-pres-sive
im-pres-sive-ly
im-pres-sive-ness
im-pri-ma-tur
im-print
im-print-er
im-pris-on
im-pris-on-ment
im-prob-a-bil-i-ty
im-prob-a-ble
im-prob-a-ble-ness
im-prob-a-bly
im-promp-tu
im-prop-er
im-prop-er-ly
im-prop-er-ness
im-pro-pri-ety
im-pro-pri-eties
im-prove-ment
im-prov-i-dence
im-prov-i-dent
im-prov-i-dent-ly
im-pro-vi-sa-tion
im-pro-vi-sa-tion-al
im-pro-vise
im-pro-vised
im-pro-vis-ing
im-pro-vis-er
im-pru-dence
im-pru-dent

im-pru-dent-ly
im-pugn
im-pugn-er
im-pulse
im-pul-sion
im-pul-sive
im-pu-ni-ty
im-pure
im-pure-ly
im-pure-ness
im-pu-ri-ty
im-pu-ri-ties
in-a-bil-i-ty
in-ac-ces-si-ble
in-ac-ces-si-bly
in-ac-cu-rate
in-ac-cu-rate-ly
in-ac-cu-ra-cy
in-ac-cu-ra-cies
in-ac-tion
in-ac-tive
in-ac-tive-ly
in-ac-tiv-i-ty
in-ad-e-quate
in-ad-e-qua-cies
in-ad-e-qua-cy
in-ad-e-quate-ly
in-ad-mis-si-ble
in-ad-mis-si-bly
in-ad-ver-tence
in-ad-ver-ten-cy
in-ad-ver-tent
in-ad-ver-tent-ly
in-alien-a-ble
in-alien-a-bly
in-am-o-ra-ta
in-am-o-ra-tas
in-an-i-mate
in-ap-pro-pri-ate
in-ap-pro-pri-ate-ly
in-apt
in-apt-ti-tude
in-apt-ly

in-apt-ness
in-ar-tic-u-late
in-ar-tic-u-late-ly
in-ar-tic-u-late-ness
in-as-much as
in-at-ten-tion
in-at-ten-tive
in-at-ten-tive-ly
in-au-gu-ral
in-au-gu-rate
in-au-gu-rat-ed
in-au-gu-rat-ing
in-au-gu-ra-tion
in-aus-pi-cious
in-aus-pi-cious-ly
in-board
in-born
in-bred
in-breed
in-breed-ing
in-cal-cu-la-ble
in-cal-cu-la-bly
in-can-des-cent
in-can-des-cence
in-can-des-cent-ly
in-can-ta-tion
in-ca-pa-ble
in-ca-pa-bly
in-ca-pac-i-tate
in-ca-pac-i-tat-ed
in-ca-pac-i-tat-ing
in-ca-pac-i-ty
in-ca-pac-i-ties
in-car-cer-ate
in-car-cer-at-ed
in-car-cer-at-ing
in-car-cer-a-tion
in-car-nate
in-car-nat-ed
in-car-nat-ing
in-car-na-tion
in-cen-di-ary
in-cen-di-aries

in-cense
in-censed
in-ceas-ing
in-cen-tive
in-cep-tion
in-ces-sant
in-ces-sant-ly
in-cho-ate
in-cho-ate-ly
in-cho-ate-ness
in-ci-dence
in-ci-dent
in-ci-den-tal
in-ci-den-tal-ly
in-cin-er-ate
in-cin-er-at-ed
in-cin-er-at-ing
in-cin-er-a-tion
in-cin-er-a-tor
in-cip-i-ent
in-cip-i-ent-ly
in-cise
in-cised
in-cis-ing
in-ci-sion
in-ci-sive
in-ci-sive-ly
in-ci-sive-ness
in-ci-sor
in-cite
in-cit-ed
in-cit-ing
in-cite-ment
in-cit-er
in-clem-en-cy
in-clem-ent
in-clem-ent-ly
in-cli-na-tion
in-cline
in-clined
in-clin-ing
in-clin-er
in-clude

in-clud-ed
in-clud-ing
in-clud-a-ble
in-clu-sion
in-clu-sive
in-clu-sive-ly
in-clu-sive-ness
in-cog-ni-to
in-cog-ni-tos
in-co-her-ence
in-co-her-ent
in-co-her-ent-ly
in-come
in-com-ing
in-com-men-su-rate
in-com-mo-di-ous
in-com-pa-ra-ble
in-com-pa-ra-bly
in-com-pat-i-bil-i-ty
in-com-pat-i-ble
in-com-pat-i-bly
in-com-pe-tence
in-com-pen-ten-cy
in-com-pe-tent
in-com-pe-tent-ly
in-com-plete
in-com-plete-ly
in-com-plete-ness
in-com-ple-tion
in-com-pre-hen-si-ble
in-com-pre-hen-sion
in-con-ceiv-able
in-con-ceiv-ably
in-con-clu-sive
in-con-clu-sive-ly
in-con-clu-sive-ness
in-con-gru-ity
in-con-gru-ous
in-con-gru-ous-ly
in-con-gru-ous-ness
in-con-gru-i-ties

in-con-se-quen-tial
in-con-sid-er-able
  in-con-sid-er-ably
in-con-sid-er-ate
  in-con-sid-er-ate-ly
in-con-sis-tent
  in-con-sist-ent-ly
in-con-sol-able
  in-con-sol-able-ness
  in-con-sol-ably
in-con-spic-u-ous
  in-con-spic-u-ous-ly
in-con-stant
  in-con-stan-cy
  in-con-stan-cies
  in-con-stant-ly
in-con-test-able
  in-con-test-abil-i-ty
in-con-ti-nence
in-con-ti-nen-cy
in-con-ti-nent
  in-con-ti-nent-ly
in-con-trol-la-ble
in-con-tro-vert-ible
in-con-ve-nience
in-con-ve-nien-cy
in-con-ve-nient
  in-con-ve-nient-ly
  in-con-ven-ienc-ing
in-con-vert-ible
  in-con-vert-ibly
in-cor-po-rate
  in-cor-po-rat-ed
  in-cor-po-rat-ing
  in-cor-po-ra-tion
  in-cor-po-ra-tor
in-cor-po-re-al
in-cor-rect
  in-cor-rect-ly
in-cor-ri-gi-ble
  in-cor-ri-gi-bil-i-ty
  in-cor-ri-gi-ble-ness
  in-cor-ri-gi-bly

in-cor-rupt-ible
  in-cor-rupt-ibil-i-ty
  in-cor-rupt-ibly
in-crease
  in-creased
  in-creas-ing
  in-creas-able
  in-creas-ing-ly
in-cred-i-ble
  in-cred-i-bil-i-ty
  in-cred-i-ble-ness
  in-cred-i-bly
in-cre-du-li-ty
in-cred-u-lous
  in-cred-u-lous-ness
  in-cred-u-lous-ly
in-cre-ment
  in-cre-men-tal
in-crim-i-nate
  in-crim-i-nat-ed
  in-crim-i-nat-ing
  in-crim-i-na-tion
  in-crim-i-na-tor
  in-crim-i-na-to-ry
in-crust
  in-crus-ta-tion
in-cu-bate
  in-cu-bat-ed
  in-cu-bat-ing
  in-cu-ba-tion
  in-cu-ba-tor
in-cu-bus
  in-cu-bus-es
in-cul-cate
  in-cul-cat-ed
  in-cul-cat-ing
  in-cul-ca-tion
  in-cul-ca-tor
in-cul-pate
  in-cul-pat-ed
  in-cul-pat-ing
  in-cul-pa-tion
in-cum-ben-cy

in-cum-ben-cies
in-cum-bent
  in-cum-bent-ly
in-cur
  in-curred
  in-cur-ring
in-cur-able
  in-cur-a-bil-i-ty
  in-cur-a-ble-ness
  in-cur-a-bly
in-cur-sion
  in-cur-sive
in-debt-ed
  in-debt-ed-ness
in-de-cen-cy
  in-den-cies
in-de-cent
  in-de-cent-ly
in-de-ci-sion
in-de-ci-sive
  in-de-ci-sive-ly
  in-de-ci-sive-ness
in-deed
in-de-fat-i-ga-ble
  in-de-fat-i-ga-bly
in-def-i-nite
  in-def-i-nite-ly
  in-def-i-nite-ness
in-del-i-ble
  in-del-i-bil-ity
  in-del-i-ble-ness
  in-del-i-bly
in-del-i-ca-cy
in-del-i-cate
  in-del-i-cate-ness
  in-del-i-cate-ly
in-dem-ni-fi-ca-tion
in-dem-ni-fy
  in-dem-ni-fied
  in-dem-ni-fy-ing
  in-dem-ni-fi-er
in-dem-ni-ty
  in-dem-ni-ties

in-dent
in-den-ta-tion
in-dent-ed
in-den-ture
in-den-tured
in-den-tur-ing
in-de-pen-dence
in-de-pen-den-cy
in-de-pen-dent
in-de-pen-dent-ly
in-de-scib-able
in-de-scrib-abil-ity
in-de-scrib-ably
in-de-struc-ti-ble
in-de-struc-ti-bly
in-det-mi-na-cy
in-de-ter-mi-nate
in-de-ter-mi-nat-ly
in-de-ter-mi-na-tion
in-dex
in-dex-er
in-dex-es
in-di-ces
in-di-cate
in-di-cat-ed
in-di-cat-ing
in-di-ca-tion
in-dic-a-tive
in-dic-a-tive-ly
in-dic-a-tor
in-dic-a-tory
in-dict
in-dict-a-ble
in-dict-er
in-dict-or
in-dict-ment
in-dif-fer-ence
in-dif-fer-ent
in-dif-fer-ent-ist
in-dif-fer-ent-ly
in-dig-e-nous
in-dig-e-nous-ly
in-dig-e-nous-ness

in-di-gent
in-di-gent-ly
in-di-gest-ed
in-di-gest-ible
in-di-gest-ibil-i-ty
in-di-gest-ible-ness
in-di-ges-tion
in-di-ges-tive
in-dig-nant
in-dig-nant-ly
in-dig-na-tion
in-dig-ni-ty
in-dig-ni-ties
in-di-go
in-di-goes
in-di-gos
in-di-rect
in-di-rect-ly
in-di-rect-ness
in-dis-creet
in-dis-creet-ly
in-dis-creet-ness
in-dis-crete
in-dis-cre-tion
in-dis-crim-i-nate
in-dis-crim-i-nate-ly
-dis-crim-i-nat-ing
-dis-crim-i-na-tion
in-dis-pens-able
in-dis-pens-abil-i-ty
in-dis-pens-ably
in-dis-pose
in-dis-posed
in-dis-pos-ing
in-dis-po-si-tion
in-dis-sol-u-ble
in-dis-sol-u-bil-i-ty
in-dis-sol-u-bly
in-di-um
in-di-vid-u-al
in-di-vid-u-al-ly
in-di-vid-u-al-ism
in-di-vid-u-al-ist

in-di-vid-u-al-is-tic
in-di-vid-u-al-i-ty
in-di-vid-u-al-i-ties
in-di-vid-u-al-ize
in-di-vid-u-al-ized
in-di-vid-u-al-iz-ing
in-doc-tri-nate
in-doc-tri-nat-ed
in-doc-tri-nat-ing
in-doc-tri-na-tion
in-doc-tri-na-tor
in-do-lence
in-do-lent
in-do-lent-ly
in-dom-i-ta-ble
in-dom-i-ta-bil-i-ty
in-dom-ita-ble-ness
in-dom-i-ta-bly
in-door
in-doors
in-du-bi-ta-ble
in-du-bi-ta-bil-i-ty
in-dubi-ta-ble-ness
in-du-bi-tab-ly
in-duce
in-duced
in-duce-ment
in-duc-er
in-duc-i-ble
in-duc-ing
in-duct
in-duct-ee
in-duc-tion
in-duc-tive
in-dulge
in-dulged
in-dulg-ing
in-dul-gence
in-dul-gent
in-dul-gent-ly
in-dus-tri-al
in-dus-tri-al-ly
in-dus-tri-al-ness

in-dus-tri-al-ism
in-dus-tri-al-ize
  in-dus-tri-al-ist
  -dus-tri-al-i-za-tion
  in-dus-tri-al-ized
  in-dus-tri-al-iz-ing
in-dus-tri-ous
  in-dus-tri-ous-ly
in-dus-try
  in-dus-tries
ine-bri-ate
  ine-bri-at-ed
  ine-bri-at-ing
  ine-bri-a-tion
  ine-bri-e-ty
in-ed-u-ca-ble
in-ef-fa-ble
  in-ef-fa-bil-i-ty
  in-ef-fa-ble-ness
  in-ef-fa-bly
in-ef-fec-tive
  in-ef-fec-tive-ly
  in-ef-fec-tive-ness
in-ef-fec-tu-al
  in-ef-fec-tu-al-i-ty
  in-ef-fec-tu-al-ly
  in-ef-fec-tu-al-ness
in-ef-fi-cient
  in-ef-fi-cien-cy
  in-ef-fi-cien-cies
  in-ef-ffi-cient-ly
in-el-i-gi-ble
  in-el-i-gi-bil-i-ty
  in-el-i-gi-bly
in-e-luc-ta-ble
in-ept
  in-ept-i-tude
  in-ept-ly
in-ept-ness
in-e-qual-i-ty
in-eq-ui-ta-ble
in-eq-ui-ty
  in-eq-ui-ties

in-ert
in-ert-ly
in-ert-ness
in-er-tia
in-er-tial
in-es-cap-a-ble
in-es-cap-a-ble
in-es-ti-ma-ble
in-es-ti-ma-bly
in-ev-i-ta-ble
in-ev-i-ta-bil-i-ty
in-ev-i-ta-ble-ness
in-ev-i-ta-ble-ness
in-ev-i-ta-bly
in-ex-haust-i-ble
in-ex-haust-i-bly
in-ex-o-ra-ble
in-ex-o-ra-bil-i-ty
in-ex-o-ra-ble-ness
in-ex-o-ra-bly
in-ex-pe-ri-ence
in-ex-pe-ri-enced
in-ex-pert
in-ex-per-ly
in-ex-pert-ness
in-ex-pe-ri-ence
in-ex-pe-ri-enced
in-ex-pert
in-ex-pert-ly
in-ex-pert-ness
in-ex-pi-a-ble
in-ex-pi-a-ble-ness
in-ex-pi-a-bly
in-ex-pli-ca-ble
in-ex-pli-ca-bil-i-ty
in-ex-pli-ca-bly
in-fal-li-ble
in-fal-i-bil-i-ty
in-fal-li-ble-ness
in-fal-li-bly
in-fa-mous
in-fa-mous-ly
in-fa-mous-ness

in-fa-my
in-fa-mies
in-fan-cy
in-fan-cies
in-fant
in-fant-hood
in-fant-like
in-fan-tile
in-fan-tine
in-fan-til-i-ty
in-fan-try
in-fan-tries
in-fan-try-man
in-fan-try-men
in-fat-u-ate
in-fat-u-at-ed
in-fat-u-at-ing
in-fat-u-at-ed-ly
in-fat-u-a-tion
in-fect
in-fect-ed-ness
in-fect-er
in-fect-or
in-fec-tion
in-fec-tious
in-fec-tious-ly
in-fec-tious-ness
in-fec-tive
in-fer
inferred
in-fer-ring
in-fer-a-ble
in-fer-a-bly
in-fer-ence
in-fer-er
in-fe-ri-or
in-fe-ri-or-i-ty
in-fe-ri-or-ly
in-fer-nal
in-fer-no
in-fer-nos
in-fest
in-fes-ta-tion

in-fest-er
in-fi-del
in-fi-del-i-ty
  in-fi-del-i-ties
in-field
  in-field-er
in-fight-ing
  in-fight-er
in-fil-trate
  in-fil-trat-ed
  in-fil-trat-ing
  in-fil-tra-tion
  in-fil-tra-tive
  in-fil-tra-tor
in-fi-nite
  in-fi-nite-ly
  in-fi-nite-ness
  in-fin-i-tude
in-fin-i-tes-i-mal
  in-fin-i-tes-i-mal-ty
in-fin-i-tive
  in-fin-i-tive-ly
in-fin-i-ty
  in-fin-i-ties
in-firm
  in-firm-lly
  in-firm-ness
in-fir-ma-ry
  in-fir-ma-ries
in-fir-mi-ty
  in-fir-mi-ties
in-flame
  in-flamed
  in-flam-ing
  in-flam-er
in-flam-ma-ble
  in-flam-ma-bil-i-ty
  in-flam-ma-ble-ness
  in-flam-ma-bly
in-flam-ma-tion
in-flam-ma-to-ry
in-flate
  in-flat-ed

in-flat-ing
in-flat-a-ble
in-flat-ed-ness
in-fla-tor
in-flat-er
in-fla-tion
in-fla-tion-ary
in-fla-tion-ism
in-fla-tion-ist
in-flect
in-flec-tion
in-flec-tion-al
in-flec-tion-al-ly
in-flec-tion-less
in-flec-tive
in-flec-tor
in-flex-i-ble
in-flex-i-bil-i-ty
in-flex-i-ble-ness
in-flex-i-bly
in-flict
in-flict-a-ble
in-flict-er
in-flict-or
in-flic-tion
in-flic-tive
in-flu-ence
in-flu-enced
in-flu-enc-ing
in-flu-ence-a-ble
in-flu-enc-er
in-flu-en-tial
in-flu-en-tial-ly
in-flu-en-za
in-flu-en-zal
in-flu-en-za-like
in-flux
in-form
in-formed
in-for-mer
in-for-mal
in-for-mal-i-ty
in-for-mal-ly

in-for-mant
in-for-ma-tion
in-for-ma-tion-al
in-for-ma-tive
in-for-ma-tive-ly
in-for-ma-tive-ness
in-for-ma-to-ry
in-frac-tion
in-fran-gi-ble
in-fran-gi-bil-i-ty
in-fran-gi-ble-ness
in-fran-gi-bly
in-fra-red
in-fra-struc-ture
in-fre-quent
in-fre-quen-cy
in-fre-quent-ly
in-fringe
in-fringed
in-fring-ing
in-fringe-ment
in-fring-er
in-fu-ri-ate
in-fu-ri-at-ed
in-fu-ri-at-ing
in-fu-ri-at-ing-ly
in-fu-ri-a-tion
in-fuse
in-fused
in-fus-ing
in-fus-er
in-fus-i-bil-i-ty
in-fus-i-ble
in-fu-sion
in-fu-sive
in-gen-ious
in-gen-ious-ly
in-gen-ious-ness
in-gest
in-ges-tion
in-ges-tive
in-glo-ri-ous
in-glo-ri-ous-ly

in-glo-ri-ous-ness
in-got
in-grain
in-grained
in-grate
in-gra-ti-ate
in-gra-ti-at-ed
in-gra-ti-at-ing
in-gra-ti-a-tion
in-grat-i-tude
in-gre-di-ent
in-group
in-grow-ing
in-grown
in-growth
in-gulf
in-hab-it
in-hab-it-a-ble
in-hab-i-ta-tion
in-hab-it-er
in-hab-it-ed
in-hab-it-ant
in-hal-ant
in-ha-la-tion
in-ha-la-tor
in-hale
in-haled
in-hal-ing
in-hal-er
in-here
in-hered
in-her-ing
in-her-ence
in-her-ent
in-her-ent-ly
in-he-sion
in-her-it
in-her-i-tor
in-her-i-tance
in-hib-it
in-hib-i-tive
in-hib-o-to-ry
in-hib-i-ter

in-hib-it-or
in-hi-bi-tion
in-hos-pi-ta-ble
in-hos-pi-tal-i-ty
in-hu-man
in-hu-man-i-ty
in-hu-mane
in-im-i-cal
in-im-i-ta-ble
in-iq-ui-ty
in-iq-ui-ties
in-iq-ui-tous
in-i-tial
in-i-tialed
in-i-tial-ing
in-i-tial-ly
in-i-ti-ate
in-i-ti-at-ed
in-i-ti-at-ing
in-i-ti-a-tion
in-i-ti-a-tor
in-i-ti-a-tive
in-ject
in-jec-tion
in-jec-tor
in-ju-di-cious
in-junc-tion
in-junc-tive
in-jur
in-jured
in-jur-ing
in-ju-ri-ous
in-ju-ry
in-ju-ries
in-jus-tice
ink-blot
ink-ling
inky
in-law
in-lay
in-laid
in-lay-ing
in-let

in-me-mo-ri-an
in-most
in-nards
in-nate
in-ner
in-ner-most
in-ner-sole
in-ner-vate
in-ner-vat-ed
in-ner-vat-ing
in-ner-va-tion
in-nerve
in-ning
inn-keep-er
in-no-cence
in-no-cent
in-no-cent-ly
in-noc-u-ous
in-no-vate
in-no-vat-ed
in-no-vat-ing
in-no-va-tion
in-no-va-tive
in-no-va-tor
in-nu-en-do
in-nu-en-dos
in-nu-en-does
in-nu-mer-a-ble
in-nu-mer-ous
in-nu-mer-a-bly
in-ob-serv-ance
in-ob-serv-ant
in-ob-serv-ant-ly
in-oc-u-lant
in-oc-u-late
in-oc-u-lat-ed
in-oc-u-lat-ing
in-oc-u-la-tion
in-oc-u-la-tor
in-oc-u-lum
in-of-fen-sive
in-op-er-a-ble
in-op-er-a-tive

in-op-por-tune
  in-op-por-tun-i-ty
in-or-di-nate
in-pa-tient
in-pour
in-put
in-quest
in-qui-e-tude
in-quire
in-quiry
  in-quir-ies
in-qui-si-tion
in-qui-si-tive
  in-quis-i-tor
in-road
in-rush
in-sane
in-san-i-ty
  in-san-i-ties
in-sa-tia-ble
  in-sa-tia-bil-i-ty
  in-sa-tia-bly
in-sa-ti-ate
in-scribe
in-scru-ta-ble
  in-scru-ta-bil-i-ty
  in-scru-ta-bly
in-seam
in-sect
in-sec-ti-cide
  in-sec-ti-cid-al
in-se-cure
  in-se-cu-ri-ty
in-sem-i-nate
  in-sem-i-nat-ed
  in-sem-i-nat-ing
  in-sem-i-na-tion
in-sen-sate
in-sen-si-ble
in-sen-si-tive
  in-sen-si-tiv-i-ty
in-sen-ti-ent
in-sep-a-ra-ble

in-sep-a-ra-bil-i-ty
in-sep-a-ra-bly
in-sert
in-sert-er
in-ser-tion
in-set
  in-set-ting
in-shore
in-side
in-sid-er
in-sid-i-ous
in-sight
  in-sight-ful
in-sig-nia
in-sig-nif-i-cant
  in-sig-nif-i-cance
in-sin-cere
  in-sin-cer-i-ty
  in-sin-cer-i-ties
in-sin-u-ate
  in-sin-u-at-ed
  in-sin-u-at-ing
  in-sin-u-a-tor
in-sin-u-a-tion
in-sip-id
  in-si-pid-i-ty
  in-sip-id-ness
in-sist
  in-sist-ence
  in-sist-ent
in-so-bri-e-ty
in-so-cia-ble
  in-so-cia-bil-i-ty
  in-so-cia-bly
in-so-far
in-sole
in-so-lent
  in-so-lence
in-sol-u-ble
  in-sol-u-bil-i-ty
  in-sol-u-bly
in-solv-a-ble
in-sol-vent

in-sol-ven-cy
in-som-nia
  in-som-ni-ac
in-so-much
in-spect
in-spec-tion
in-spec-tor
in-spi-ra-tion
  in-spi-ra-tion-al
in-spire
  in-spir-ing
in-spir-it
in-sta-ble
  in-sta-bil-i-ty
in-stall
in-stan-ta-ne-ous
in-stant-ly
in-state
  in-stat-ed
  in-stat-ing
  in-state-ment
in-stead
in-step
in-sti-gate
  in-sti-gat-ed
  in-sti-gat-ing
  in-sti-ga-tion
  in-sti-ga-tor
in-still
in-stinct
in-stinc-tive
  in-stinc-tu-al
  in-stinc-tive-ly
in-sti-tute
  in-sti-tut-ed
  in-sti-tut-ing
  in-sti-tut-er
in-sti-tu-tor
in-sti-tu-tion
in-sti-tu-tion-al
  in-sti-tu-tion-al-ism
  in-sti-tu-tion-al-ize
  in-sti-tu-tion-al-ized

in-struct
in-struc-tion
in-struc-tive
in-struc-tor
in-stru-ment
in-stru-men-tal
in-stru-men-ta-list
in-stru-men-ta-tion
in-sub-or-di-nate
  in-sub-or-di-na-tion
in-sub-stan-tial
  in-sub-stan-ti-al-i-ty
in-suf-fer-a-ble
  in-suf-fer-a-bly
in-suf-fi-cient
  in-suf-fi-cien-cy
in-su-lar
  in-su-lar-i-ty
in-su-late
  in-su-lat-ed
  in-su-lat-ing
in-su-la-tion
in-su-la-tor
in-su-lin
in-sult
in-sop-port-a-ble
in-sup-press-i-ble
in-sur-ance
in-sure
  in-sured
  in-sur-ing
  in-sur-er
in-sur-gent
  in-sur-gence
  in-sur-gen-cy
in-sur-mount-a-ble
in-sur-rec-tion
  in-sur-rec-tion-ary
in-sus-cep-ti-ble
in-tact
in-take
in-tan-gi-ble
  in-tan-gi-bil-i-ty

in-tan-gi-bly
in-te-ger
in-te-gral
  in-te-gral-ly
in-te-grate
  in-te-grat-ed
  in-te-grat-ing
in-te-gra-tion
  in-te-gra-tion-ist
in-teg-ri-ty
in-tel-lect
in-tel-lec-tu-al
in-tel-lec-tu-al-ism
in-tel-li-gence
  in-tel-li-gent
  in-tel-li-gent-ly
in-tel-li-gent-sia
in-tel-li-gi-ble
  in-tel-li-gi-bil-i-ty
  in-tel-li-gi-bly
in-tem-per-ance
  in-tem-per-ate
in-tend
  in-tend-er
in-tend-ed
in-tense
  in-tense-ly
  in-tense-ness
in-ten-si-fy
  in-ten-si-fied
  in-ten-si-fy-ing
  in-ten-si-fi-ca-tion
  in-ten-si-fi-er
in-ten-sion
in-ten-si-ty
  in-ten-si-ties
in-ten-sive
  in-ten-sive-ly
  in-ten-sive-ness
in-tent
in-ten-tion
  in-ten-tion-al
  in-ten-tion-al-ly

in-ten-tioned
in-ter
in-ter-act
  in-ter-ac-tion
in-ter-breed
  in-ter-bred
in-ter-cede
  in-ter-ced-ed
  in-ter-ced-ing
  in-ter-ced-er
in-ter-cept
  in-ter-cep-ter
  in-ter-cep-tor
  in-ter-cep-tion
  in-ter-cep-tive
in-ter-ces-sion
in-ter-change
  in-ter-changed
  in-ter-chang-ing
  in-ter-chang-a-ble
  in-ter-chang-a-bly
in-ter-col-le-gi-ate
in-ter-com
in-ter-com-mun-i-cate
in-ter-con-nect
  in-ter-con-nec-tion
in-ter-con-ti-nen-tal
in-ter-course
in-ter-cul-tur-al
in-ter-cur-rent
in-ter-de-part-men-tal
in-ter-de-pend-ent
  in-ter-de-pend
  in-ter-de-pend-ence
  -ter-de-pend-en-cy
in-ter-dict
  in-ter-dic-tion
in-ter-dis-ci-pli-nary
in-ter-est
  in-ter-est-ed

in-ter-est-ed-ly
in-ter-est-ing
in-ter-face
in-ter-fa-cial
in-ter-faith
in-ter-fere
in-ter-ga-lac-tic
in-te-ri-or
in-ter-ject
in-ter-jec-tion
in-ter-jec-to-ry
in-ter-ly-er
in-ter-leaf
in-ter-leaves
in-ter-leave
in-ter-leaved
in-ter-leav-ing
in-ter-line
in-ter-lined
in-ter-lin-ing
in-ter-link
in-ter-lock
in-ter-lo-cu-tion
in-ter-loc-u-tor
in-ter-loc-u-to-ry
in-ter-lop-er
in-ter-lude
in-ter-nar
in-ter-na-ry
in-ter-mar-ry
in-ter-mar-ried
in-ter-mar-ry-ing
in-ter-mar-riage
in-ter-me-di-ary
in-ter-me-di-ar-ies
in-ter-me-di-ate
in-ter-me-di-at-ed
in-ter-me-di-at-ing
in-ter-me-di-a-tion
in-ter-me-di-a-tor
in-ter-mi-na-ble
in-ter-min-gle

in-ter-min-gledd
in-ter-min-gling
in-ter-mis-sion
in-ter-mis-sive
in-ter-mit
in-ter-mix
in-ter-mix-ture
in-tern
in-ter-ship
in-ter-nal
in-ter-nal-ly
in-ter-na-tion-al
in-ter-na-tion-al-i-ty
in-ter-na-tion-al-ize
in-tern-ee
in-tern-ist
in-tern-ment
in-tern-of-fice
in-ter-pen-e-trate
in-ter-pen-e-tra-tion
in-ter-plan-e-tary
in-ter-play
in-ter-po-late
in-ter-pose
in-ter-posed
in-ter-pos-ing
in-ter-pos-er
in-ter-po-si-tion
in-ter-pret
in-ter-pret-a-ble
in-ter-pret-er
in-ter-pre-tive
in-ter-pre-ta-tion
in-ter-pre-ta-tion-al
in-ter-pre-ta-tive
in-ter-ro-gate
in-ter-ro-gat-ed
in-ter-ro-gat-ing
in-ter-ro-ga-tion
in-ter-ro-ga-tion-al
in-ter-rog-a-tive
in-ter-ro-ga-tor

in-ter-rupt
in-ter-rup-tion
in-ter-rup-tive
in-ter-rupt-er
in-ter-rupt-or
in-terr-scho-las-tic
in-ter-sect
in-ter-sec-tion
in-ter-space
in-ter-spaced
in-ter-spac-ing
in-ter-state
in-ter-stel-lar
in-ter-tid-al
in-ter-twine
in-ter-twined
in-ter-twin-ing
in-ter-ur-ban
in-ter-val
in-ter-vence
in-ter-view
in-ter-view-er
in-ter-weave
in-ter-wove
in-ter-weav-ing
in-ter-wo-ven
in-tes-tate
in-tes-tine
in-tes-ti-nal
in-ti-mate
in-ti-mat-ed
in-ti-mat-ing
in-ti-mate-ly
in-ti-ma-tion
in-tim-i-date
in-tim-i-dat-ed
in-tim-i-dat-ing
in-tim-i-da-tion
in-tim-i-da-tor
in-ti-tled
in-ti-tling
in-to
in-tol-er-a-ble

in-tol-er-a-bly
in-tol-er-ant
in-tol-er-ance
in-tomb
in-to-mate
in-to-nat-ed
in-to-nat-ing
in-to-na-tion
in-tone
in-toned
in-ton-ing
in-ton-er
in-tox-i-cant
in-tox-i-cate
in-tox-i-cat-ed
in-tox-i-cat-ing
in-tox-i-ca-tion
in-trac-ta-ble
in-trac-ta-bil-i-ty
in-tra-mu-ral
in-tra-mu-ral-ly
in-tran-si-gent
in-tran-si-gence
in-tran-si-tive
in-tra-state
in-tra-ve-nous
in-trench
in-trep-id
in-tre-pid-i-ty
in-trique
in-tri-quing
in-trin-sic
in-trin-si-cal
in-trin-si-cal-ly
in-tro-spect
in-tro-spec-tion
in-tro-spec-tive
in-tro-ver-sion
in-tro-ver-sive
in-tro-vert
in-tro-vert-ed
in-trude
in-trust

in-tu-it
in-tu-i-tion
in-tu-i-tion-al
in-tu-i-tive
in-un-date
in-un-dat-ed
in-un-dat-ing
in-un-da-tion
in-un-da-tor
in-vade
in-val-id
in-va-lid-i-ty
in-va-lid-ism
in-val-u-a-ble
in-var-i-a-ble
in-var-i-a-bil-i-ty
in-var-i-ant
in-var-i-ance
in-va-sion
in-va-sive
in-vec-tive
in-ven-tion
in-ven-tive
in-ven-tive-ness
in-ven-to-ry
in-ven-to-ries
in-ven-to-ried
in-ven-to-ry-ing
in-verse
in-ver-sion
in-vert
in-ver-te-brate
in-vert-ed
in-vest
in-ves-tor
in-ves-ti-gate
in-ves-ti-gat-ed
in-ves-ti-gat-ing
in-ves-ti-ga-tion
in-ves-ti-ga-tor
in-ves-ti-ture
in-vest-ment
in-vet-er-ate

in-vid-i-ous
in-vig-or-ate
in-vig-or-at-ed
in-vig-or-at-ing
in-vig-or-ant
in-vig-or-a-tion
in-vig-or-a-tor
in-vin-ci-ble
in-vin-ci-bil-i-ty
in-vin-ci-bly
in-vi-o-la-ble
in-vi-o-la-bil-i-ty
in-vi-o-la-bly
in-vi-o-late
in-vis-i-ble
in-vis-i-bil-i-ty
in-vis-i-bly
in-vi-ta-tion
in-vi-ta-tion-al
in-vo-ca-tion
in-voice
in-voke
in-voked
in-vok-ing
in-vol-un-tary
in-vol-un-tar-i-ly
in-vo-lute
in-vo-lu-tion
in-volve
in-volved
in-volv-ing
in-volve-ment
in-volv-er
in-vul-ner-a-ble
in-ward
in-wards
in-ward-ly
in-waeve
in-wrought
io-dine
ion
ion-ic
ion-o-sphere

iota
ip-so fac-to
iras-ci-ble
  iras-ci-bil-i-ty
  iras-ci-bly
irate
ir-i-des-cent
  ir-i-des-cence
irid-i-um
iris
irk-some
iron
  iron-er
iron-clad
iron-ic
  iron-i-cal
iron-smith
iron-ware
iron-work
  iron-work-er
iro-ny
  iro-nies
ir-rad-i-ca-ble
ir-ra-tion-al
  ir-ra-tion-al-i-ty
ir-re-claim-a-ble
ir-rec-on-cil-a-ble
ir-re-cov-er-a-ble
ir-re-duc-i-ble
ir-ref-u-ta-ble
ir-re-gard-less
ir-reg-u-lar
  ir-reg-u-lar-i-ty
ir-rel-e-vant
  ir-rel-e-vance
  ir-rel-e-van-cy
ir-re-li-gion
  ir-re-li-gious
ir-re-mis-si-ble
ir-re-mov-a-ble
ir-rep-a-ra-ble
ir-re-plac-a-ble
ir-re-press-i-ble

ir-re-press-i-bil-i-ty
ir-re-press-i-bly
ir-re-proach-a-ble
ir-re-sist-i-ble
  ir-re-sist-i-bil-i-ty
ir-res-o-lute
  ir-res-o-lu-tion
ir-re-spec-tive
ir-re-spon-si-ble
  ir-re-spon-si-bil-i-ty
ir-re-spon-sive
ir-re-triev-a-ble
  ir-re-triev-a-bil-i-ty
  ir-re-trieev-a-bly
ir-rev-o-ca-ble
  ir-rev-o-ca-bil-i-ty
ir-ri-gate
  ir-ri-gat-ed
ir-ri-ta-ble
ir-ri-tant
ir-ri-tate
ir-rupt
is-land
isle
iso-bar
iso-gloss
iso-late
  iso-lat-ed
iso-met-ric
ison-o-my
iso-ton-ic
is-su-ance
is-sue
item
it-er-ate
ivo-ry

J

jab
  jabbed
  jab-bing
jab-ber

jab-ber-er
jac-a-mar
jac-a-ram-da
jack-al
jack-ass
jack-boot
jack-et
  jack-et-ed
jack-ham-mer
jack-knife
  jack-kives
  jack-knifed
  jack-knif-ing
jack--o'--lan-tern
jack-pot
jack rab-bit
jac-o-net
jac-quard
jade
  jad-ed
  jad-ing
Jaf-fa
jag
  jag-ged
  jag-ging
jag-uar
jail-bird
jail-break
jail-er
ja-lopy
  ja-lop-ies
jal-ou-sie
jam
  jammed
  jam-ming
  jam-mer
jamb
jam-bo-ree
jan-gle
  jan-gled
  jan-gling
  jan-gler
  jan-gly

jan-i-tor
  jan-i-to-ri-al
jar
  jar-ful
  jarred
  jar-ring
jar-di-niere
jar-red
jar-gon
  jar-gon-ize
jas-mine
jas-sid
jaun-dice
  jaun-diced
  jaun-dic-ing
jaunt
  jaun-ty
  jaun-ti-er
  jaun-ti-est
  jaun-ti-ly
  jaun-ti-ness
jav-e-lin
jaw-bone
jaw-break-er
jay-gee
jay-walk
  jay-walk-er
jazz
  jazz-ist
  jazz-man
jazzy
  jazz-i-er
  jazz-i-est
  jazz-i-ly
  jazz-i-ness
jeal-ous
  jeal-ous-ies
jeep
jeer-er
je-hu
jel-li-fy
  jel-li-fies
  jel-li-fy-ing

jel-ly
  jel-lied
  jel-lies
  jel-ly-ing
  jel-ly-like
jel-ly bean
jel-ly-fish
jen-ny
  jen-nies
jeop-ar-dy
  jeop-ar-dize
  jeop-ar-dized
  jeop-ar-diz-ing
jerk
  jerk-er
  jerk-i-ly
  jerk-y
  jerk-i-er
  jerk-i-est
jer-kin
jer-sey
jes-sa-mine
jest-er
  jest-ing
Je-sus
jet
  jet-ted
  jet-ting
jet-lin-er
jet-port
jet-pro-polled
jet-sam
jet-ti-son
jet-ty
  jet-ties
jew-el
  jew-eled
  jew-el-ing
jew-el-er
jew-el-ry
jibe
  jibed
  jib-ing

jig
  jigged
  jig-ging
jig-ger
jig-gle
  jig-gled
  jig-gling
  jig-gly
jig-saw
jilt-er
jim-dan-dy
jim-my
  jim-mies
  jim-mied
  jim-my-ing
jin-gle
  jin-gled
  jin-gling
jinx
jit-ney
  jit-neys
jit-ter
  jit-ters
  jit-tery
jit-ter-bug
  jit-ter-bugged
job
  jobbed
  job-bing
job-ber
job-hold-er
jock-ey
  jock-eys
  jock-ey-ing
jock-strap
jo-cose
  jo-cos-i-ty
jo-cund
  jo-cun-di-ty
jodh-pur
jog
  jogged
  jog-ging

jog-ger
jog-gle
jog-gled
jog-gling
join-able
join-er
joint
joint-ed
joint-ly
joist
joke
joked
jok-ing
joke-ster
jok-ing-ly
jok-er
jolt
jolt-er
jolt-ing-ly
jolty
jon-quil
jos-tle
jos-tled
jos-tling
jos-tler
jot
jott-ed
joule
jour-nal
jour-nal-ism
jour-nal-ist
jour-na-lis-tic
jour-nal-ize
jour-ney
jour-ney-man
jour-ney-men
joust
jo-vi-al
jo-vi-al-i-ty
jowl
jowled
jowy
joy-ful

joy-less
joy-ous
joy-ride
ju-bi-lant
ju-bi-lance
ju-bi-lan-cy
ju-bi-lar-i-an
ju-bi-la-tion
ju-bi-late
ju-bi-lat-ed
ju-bi-lat-ing
ju-bi-lee
judge
judged
judg-ing
judge-ment
judge-men-tal
ju-di-ca-ture
ju-di-cial
ju-di-cia-ry
ju-di-cious
Ju-dith
ju-do
jug
jugged
jug-gin
jug-ful
jug-gler
ju-gate
jug-u-lar
jug-u-lum
ju-gum
juice
juic-i-er
juic-i-est
juic-i-ly
ju-jit-su
juke-box
ju-lep
ju-li-enne
Ju-lius
Ju-ly
jum-ble

jum-bled
jum-bling
jum-bo
jum-bos
jump
jump-ing
jumpy
jump-er
jump--off
junc-tion
junc-ture
jun-gle
jun-ior
ju-ni-per
junk
junk-man
junky
jun-ket
junk-ie
jun-ta
Ju-pi-ter
ju-ris-dic-tion
ju-ris-dic-tion-al
ju-ris-pru-dence
ju-ris-pru-den-tial
ju-ris-pru-dent
ju-rist
ju-ris-tic
ju-ror
ju-ry
ju-ries
ju-ry-man
just
just-ly
just-ness
jus-tice
jus-tice-less
jus-tice-like
jus-ti-fi-ca-tion
jus-ti-fy
jus-ti-fied
jus-ti-fy-ing
jus-ti-fi-a-ble

jus-tif-i-ca-to-ry
jut
  jut-ted
  jut-ting
jute
ju-ve-nes-cence
  ju-ve-nes-cent
ju-ve-nile
  ju-ve-nil-i-ty
jux-ta-pose
  jux-ta-posed
  jux-ta-pos-ing
  jux-ta-po-si-tion

K

ka-bob
kai-ser
ka-lei-do-scope
  ka-lei-do-scop-ic
ka-mi-ka-ze
kan-ga-roo
ka-olin
  ka-oline
ka-pok
ka-put
ka-ra-te
kar-ma
  kar-mic
ka-ty-did
kay-ak
kay-o
kedge
  kedged
  kedg-ing
keel-haul
keel-son
keen-ly
  keen-ness
keep-ing
keep-sake
keg-ler
kelp

ken-nel
  ken-neled
  ken-nel-ing
ke-no
ker-a-tin
ker-chief
ker-mis
ker-nel
ker-o-sene
kes-trel
ketch-up
ke-tone
ket-tle
ket-tle-drum
key
  keyed
key-board
key-hole
key-note
key-stone
kha-ki
  khak-is
kha-lif
khan
kib-butz
  kib-but-zim
ki-bitz-er
ki-bosh
kick-off
kid
kid-nap
kid-ney
  kid-neys
kill-deer
kill-ing
kill-joy
kiln
kilo
  kil-os
kilo-cy-cle
ki-lo-gram
ki-lo-me-ter
ki-lo-ton

kil-o-watt
kilt
ki-mo-no
kin-der-gar-ten
kin-dle
  kin-dled
  kin-dling
kind-ly
  kind-li-er
  kind-li-est
kin-dred
kin-e-mat-ic
kin-e-scope
ki-net-ic
  ki-net-ics
kin-folk
king-bird
king-dom
king-ly
king-pin
king--size
  king--sized
kink-y
  kink-i-er
  kink-i-est
kins-folk
kins-man
  kins-men
  kins-wom-an
ki-osk
kip-per
kir-mess
kis-met
kiss-a-ble
kiss-er
kitch-en
kitch-en-ette
kite
  kit-ed
  kit-ing
kitsch
kit-ten
kit-ten-ish

kit-ten-ish-ly
kit-ty
  kit-ties
kit-ty--cor-ner
ki-wi
klatch
  klatsch
klep-to-ma-nia
  klep-to-ma-ni-ac
knack
knap-sack
knave
knav-ery
knav-ish
  knav-ish-ly
knead
knee
  kneed
  knee-ing
knee-cap
knee--deep
kneel
  knelt
  kneel-ing
  kneel-er
knee-pan
knell
knick-knack
knife
  knives
  knifed
  knif-ing
  knife-like
knight
  knight-hood
  knight-ly
knit
  knit-ted
  knit-ting
  knit-ter
knob
  knobbed
  knob-by

knob-bi-er
knob-bi-est
knock
knock-a-bout
knock-down
knock-er
  knock--knee
  knock--kneed
knock-out
knoll
knot
  knot-ted
  knot-ting
  knot-like
  knot-ty
knot-hole
knout
know
  knew
  known
  know-ing
  know-a-ble
  know-er
know--how
know-ing-ly
knowl-edge
knowl-edge-able
know--noth-ing
knuck-le
  knuck-led
  knuck-ling
ko-ala
ko-bold
ko-el
ko-gas-in
kohl-ra-bi
  kohl-ra-bies
ko-la
ko-lin-sky
  ko-lin-skies
kook
  kooky
  kook-i-er

kook-i-est
kook-a-bur-ra
ko-peck
ko-ru-na
ko-sher
kou-mis
kow-tow
kro-na
kro-ne
kryp-ton
ku-dos
ku-miss
kum-quat

L

la-bel
  la-beled
  la-bel-ing
  la-bel-er
la-bi-al
  la-bi-al-ly
la-bi-ate
la-bi-o-den-tal
la-bi-um
  la-bia
la-bor
  la-bor-er
lab-o-ra-to-ry
la-bored
la-bo-ri-ous
  la-bo-ri-ous-ly
  la-bo-ri-ous-ness
la-bor-sav-ing
la-bur-num
lab-y-rinth
  lab-y-rin-thine
  lab-y-rin-thi-an
lace
lac-er-ate
  lac-er-at-ed
  lac-er-at-ing
  lac-er-a-tion

lace-wing
la-ches
lach-ry-mal
lach-ry-mose
 lach-ry-mose-ly
lac-ing
lack-a-dai-si-cal
 lack-a-dai-si-cal-ly
lack-ey
lack-lus-ter
la-ci-nia
la-con-ic
 la-con-i-cal-ly
lac-quer
 lac-quer-er
la-crosse
lac-tate
 lac-tat-ed
 lac-tat-ing
 lac-ta-tion
lac-te-al
lac-tic
lac-tose
la-cu-na
 la-cu-nas
 la-cu-nae
lad-der
lad-die
lade
 lad-ed
 lad-en
 lad-ing
la-dle
 la-dled
 la-dling
la-dy
 la-dy-bug
la-dy-fin-ger
la-dy--in--wait-ing
la-dy-like
la-dy-love
lag
 lagged

lag-ging
la-ger
lag-gard
la-gniappe
la-goon
la-ic
 la-i-cal
 la-i-cal-ly
lair
laird
la-i-ty
 la-i-ties
lake-side
lal-la-tion
la-lop-a-thy
lam
 lammed
 lam-ming
la-ma
la-ma-sery
 la-ma-ser-ies
lam-baste
 lam-bast-ed
 lam-bast-ing
lam-ben-cy
lam-bent
 lam-bent-ly
lam-bre-quin
lamb-skin
lame
la-ment
 lam-en-ta-ble
 lam-en-ta-bly
 lam-en-ta-tion
lam-i-na
 lam-i-nae
 lam-i-nas
lam-i-nate
 lam-i-nat-ed
 lam-i-nat-ing
 lam-i-na-tion
lam-poon
lam-prey

lam-preys
lance
 lanced
 lanc-ing
lance-wood
lan-dau
land-ed
land-ing
land-la-dy
 land-la-dies
land-locked
land-lord
land-lub-ber
land-own-er
 land-own-ing
 land-own-er-ship
land-slide
land-ward
 land-wards
lang syne
lan-gauge
lan-quid
 lan-quid-ly
lan-quish
 lan-quish-ing
 lan-quish-ing-ly
lan-quor
 lan-guor-ous
 lan-guor-ous-ly
lan-o-lin
lan-tern
lan-tha-num
lan-yard
la-pel
lap-ful
 lap-fuls
 laps-ful
lap-i-dary
 lap-i-dar-ies
lap-in
lap-pet
lapse
 lapsed

laps-ing
lar-board
lar-ce-ny
  lar-ce-nies
  lar-ce-nous
larch
lar-der
large
  larg-er
  larg-est
large-ly
lar-gess
lar-ghet-to
  lar-ghet-tos
larg-ish
lar-go
  lar-gos
lar-i-at
lar-rup
lar-va
  lar-vae
  lar-val
lar-yn-gi-tis
lar-ynx
  lar-ynx-es
  lar-ynx-ges
  la-ryn-ge-al
las-civ-i-ous
  las-ci-v-i-ous-ly
las-sie
las-si-tude
las-so
  las-sos
  las-soes
  las-so-er
last-ing
  last-ing-ly
last-ly
latch-key
late
  lat-er
  lat-est
  late-ness

late-ly
la-tent
  la-ten-cy
  la-tent-ly
lat-er-al
  lat-er-al-ly
la-tex
  la-tex-es
lathe
lath-er
  lath-er-er
  lath-ery
lath-ing
lat-i-tude
  lat-i-tu-di-nal
  lat-i-tu-di-nar-i-an
la-trine
lat-ter
lat-tice
  lat-tied
  lat-tic-ing
lat-tice-work
laud-able
  laud-ably
lau-da-num
lau-da-to-ry
  lau-da-tive
laugh
  laugh-ter
launch
  launch-er
laun-der
  laun-der-er
  laun-dress
laun-der-ette
laun-dry
  laun-dries
lau-re-ate
lau-rel
la-va
la-a-liere
lav-a-to-ry
  lav-a-to-ries

lav-en-der
lav-ish
  lav-ish-ly
  la-vish-ness
law-abid-ing
law-break-er
  law-break-ing
law-ful
  law-ful-ly
  law-ful-ness
law-less
  law-less-ly
  law-less-ness
law-mak-er
  law-mak-ing
lawn
law-ren-ci-um
law-suit
law-yer
lax
  lax-i-ty
  lax-ly
  lax-ness
lax-a-tive
lay-er
lay-ette
lay-man
  lay-men
lay-off
lay-out
lay-over
laze
  lazed
  laz-ing
la-zy
  la-zi-er
  la-zi-est
  la-zi-ly
la-zy-bones
lea
leach
lead
  lead-ing

lead-en
lead-en-ly
lead-er
lead-er-less
lead-er-ship
leaf-age
leafy
leaf-i-er
leaf-i-est
leaque
leaqued
leaqu-ing
leak
leak-age
leak-i-ness
leaky
leak-i-er
leak-i-est
lean
lean-ly
lean-ness
lean-ing
lean--to
lean--tos
leap
leaped
leapt
leap-ing
leap-er
leap-frog
learn
learn-ed
learnt
learn-ing
learn-er
learn-ed-ly
learn-ed-ness
lease
leased
leas-ing
leash
least-wise
least-ways

leath-er
leath-er-neck
leath-ery
leave
left
leav-ing
lev-er
leav-en
leaves
leave-talk-ing
lech-er
lech-er-ous
lech-er-ous-ly
lech-ery
lech-er-ies
lec-tern
lec-ture
lec-tured
lec-tur-ing
lec-tur-er
ledge
ledg-er
leech
leek
leer-ing-ly
leery
lee-ward
lee-way
left--hand-ed
left--hand-ed-ly
left--hand-ed-ness
left-ist
left-over
left--wing
left--wing-er
leg
legged
leg-ging
leg-a-cy
leg-a-cies
le-gal
le-gal-ly
le-gal-ist

le-gal-is-tic
le-gal-i-ty
le-gal-i-ties
le-gal-ize
le-gal-ized
le-gal-iz-ing
le-gal-i-za-tion
leg-ate
leg-a-tee
le-ga-tion
le-ga-to
leg-end
leg-end-ary
leg-er-de-main
leg-gy
leg-gi-er
leg-gi-est
leg-horn
leg-i-ble
leg-i-bil-i-ty
leg-i-bly
le-gion
le-gion-ary
le-gion-ar-ies
le-gion-naire
leg-is-late
leg-is-lat-ed
leg-is-la-tive
leg-is-la-tor
leg-is-la-tion
leg-is-la-ture
le-git
le-git-i-mate
le-git-i-mat-ed
le-git-i-mat-ing
le-git-i-ma-cy
le-git-i-mate-ly
le-git-i-mist
le-git-i-mize
le-git-i-mized
le-git-i-miz-ing
le-gume
le-gu-mi-nous

lei
  leis
lei-sure
lei-sure-ly
  lei-sure-li-ness
leit-mo-tif
lem-ming
lem-on
lem-on-ade
le-mur
lend
  lent
  lend-ing
  lend-er
length
length-en
length-wise
lengthy
  length-i-er
  length-i-est
  length-i-ly
  length-i-ness
le-nient
  le-ni-ence
  le-ni-en-cy
  le-ni-ent-ly
len-i-tive
len-i-ty
lens
len-til
len-to
le-o-nine
leop-ard
  leop-ard-ess
le-o-tard
lep-er
lep-i-dop-ter-ous
lep-re-chaun
lep-ro-sy
lep-rous
les-bi-an
  les-bi-an-ism
le-sion

les-see
less-en
les-sor
least
let-down
le-thal
  le-thal-ly
leth-ar-gy
  leth-ar-gies
  le-thar-gic
  le-thar-gi-cal
let-ter
  let-ter-ed
let-ter-head
  let-ter-ing
let-ter--per-fect
let-ter-press
let-tuce
let-up
leu-ke-mia
leu-ko-cyte
lev-ee
lev-el
  lev-eled
  lev-el-ing
  lev-el-er
  lev-el-ly
  lev-el-ness
lev-el-head-ed
  lev-el-head-ed-ness
lev-er
lev-er-age
le-vi-a-than
lev-i-tate
  lev-i-tat-ed
  lev-i-tat-ing
  lev-i-ta-tion
lev-i-ty
levy
  lev-ies
  lev-ied
  lev-y-ing
lewd

lewd-ly
lewd-ness
lex-i-cog-ra-phy
  lex-i-cog-ra-pher
  lex-i-co-graph-ic
  lex-i-co-graph-i-cal
lex-i-con
li-a-bil-i-ty
  li-a-bil-i-ties
li-a-ble
li-ai-son
li-ar
li-ba-tion
li-bel
  li-beled
  li-bel-ing
  li-bel-er
li-bel-ous
  li-bel-ous-ly
lib-er-al
  lib-er-al-ly
  lib-er-al-ness
lib-er-al-ism
lib-er-al-i-ty
  lib-er-al-i-ties
lib-er-al-ize
  lib-er-al-ized
  lib-er-al-iz-ing
  lib-er-al-i-za-tion
lib-er-ate
  lib-er-at-ed
  lib-er-at-ing
  lib-er-a-tion
  lib-er-a-tor
lib-er-tar-i-an
lib-er-tine
  lib-er-tin-ism
lib-er-ty
  lib-er-ties
li-bid-i-nous
  li-bid-i-nous-ly
  li-bid-i-nous-ness
li-bi-do

li-bid-in-al
li-brar-i-an
  li-brar-ies
li-brary
  li-brar-ies
li-bret-to
  li-bret-tos
  li-bret-ist
li-cense
  li-censed
  li-cens-ing
  li-cen-see
  li-cens-er
li-cen-ti-ate
li-cen-tious
  li-cen-tious-ly
  li-cen-tious-ness
li-chee
li-chen
lic-it
lick-e-ty--split
lick-spit-tle
lic-o-rice
lid-ded
lief
liege
lien
lieu
lieu-ten-an-cy
lieu-ten-ant
life-blood
life-boat
life-guard
life-less
  life-less-ly
  life-less-ness
life-like
life-line
lif-er
life-sav-er
life--size
life--style
life-time
life-work

lift-off
lig-a-ment
lig-a-ture
  lig-tured
  lig-a-tur-ing
light-en
light-er
light-fin-gered
light-foot-ed
  light-foot-ed-ly
light-head-ed
  light-head-ed-ly
  light-head-ed-ness
light-heart-ed
  light-heart-ed-ly
  light-heart-ed-ness
light-house
light-ing
light-ly
light--mind-ed
  light--mind-ed-ly
  light--mind-ed-ness
light-ning
light-weight
light--year
lig-nite
like
  liked
  lik-ing
  lik-a-ble
  lik-a-ble-ness
  lik-a-ble-ness
like-li-hood
like-ly
  like-li-er
  like-li-est
like--mind-ed
lik-en
like-ness
like-wise
lik-ing
li-lac
lilt-ing

lily
  lil-lies
lil-y--liv-ered
li-ma
limb
limb-er
  lim-ber-ness
lim-bo
lime
  limed
  lim-ing
  limy
  lim-i-er
  lim-i-est
  lime-like
lime-light
  lime-light-er
lim-er-ick
lime-stone
lim-it
lim-it-a-ble
lim-i-ta-tive
lim-i-ter
lim-it-less
lim-i-ta-tion
lim-it-ed
  lim-it-ed-ly
  lim-it-ed-ness
lim-ou-sine
limp
  limp-er
  limp-ing-ly
  limp-ly
  limp-ness
lim-pet
lim-pid
  lim-pid-i-ty
  lim-pid-ly
  lim-pid-ness
lin-age
lin-den
line
  lined

lin-ing
lin-e-age
lin-eal
lin-ea-ment
lin-ear
lin-ear-ly
line-back-er
line-back-ing
line-man
line-men
lin-en
lin-er
line-up
lin-ger
lin-ger-er
lin-ger-ing-ly
lin-ge-rie
lin-go
lin-goes
lin-gua fran-ca
lin-qual
lin-qual-ly
lin-quist
lin-quis-tic
lin-quis-tics
lin-quis-ti-cal
lin-quis-ti-cal-ly
lin-i-ment
lin-ing
link
linked
link-er
link-age
lin-net
li-no-leum
lin-seed
lint
linty
lint-i-er
lint-i-est
lin-tel
li-on
li-on-ess

li-on-like
li-on-heart-ed
li-on-ize
li-on-ized
li-on-iz-ing
li-on-i-za-tion
li-on-iz-er
lip-py
lip-pi-er
lip-pi-est
lip-stick
liq-ue-fy
liq-ue-fied
liq-ue-fy-ing
liq-ue-fac-tion
liq-ue-fi-able
liq-ue-fi-er
li-queur
liq-uid
li-quid-i-ty
li-quid-ness
li-quid-ly
liq-ui-date
liq-ui-dat-ed
liq-ui-dat-ing
liq-ui-da-tion
liq-ui-da-tor
liq-uor
lisle
lisp
lisp-ing-ly
lis-some
lis-some-ly
lis-some-ness
list
list-ed
list-er
list-ing
lis-ten
lis-ten-er
list-less
list-less-ly
list-less-ness

lit-a-ny
lit-a-nies
li-tchi
li-tchis
li-ter
lit-er-a-cy
lit-er-al
lit-er-al-i-ty
lit-er-al-ness
lit-er-al-ly
lit-er-ary
lit-er-ar-i-ly
lit-er-ar-i-ness
lit-er-ate
lit-er-ate-ly
lit-e-ra-ti
lit-er-a-ture
lithe
lithe-some
lithe-ly
lithe-ness
lith-i-um
lith-o-graph
lith-o-gra-pher
lith-o-graph-ic
lith-o-graph-i-cal-ly
li-thog-ra-phy
lit-i-gate
lit-i-gat-ed
lit-i-gat-ing
lit-i-ga-tion
lit-i-ga-tor
lit-ter
lit-ter-bug
lit-tle
lit-tler
lit-tlest
lit-to-ral
lit-ur-gy
lit-ur-gies
lit-ur-gist
lit-ur-gic
li-tur-gi-cal

liv-able
  live-able
live-li-hood
live-long
live-ly
  live-li-er
  live-li-est
liv-en
  liv-en-er
liv-er
liv-er-wurst
liv-ery
  liv-er-ies
  liv-er-ied
  liv-er-y-man
  liv-er-y-men
live-stock
liv-id
  li-vid-i-ty
  liv-id-ness
  liv-id-ly
liv-ing
  liv-ing-ly
  liv-ing-ness
liz-ard
lla-ma
lla-no
  lla-mos
loamy
loath
  loath-ness
loathe
  loathed
  loath-ing
  loath-ing-ly
loath-some
  loath-some-ly
  loath-some-ness
lob
  lobbed
  lob-bing
lobe
  lo-bar

lo-bate
lobed
lob-ster
lo-cal
  lo-cal-ly
lo-cale
lo-cal-i-ty
  lo-cal-i-ties
lo-cal-i-ties
lo-cal-ize
  lo-cal-ized
  lo-cal-iz-ing
  lo-cal-i-za-tion
lo-cate
  lo-cat-ed
  lo-cat-ing
  lo-ca-tor
lo-ca-tion
loch
lock-able
lock-er
lock-et
lock-jaw
lock-out
lock-smith
lock-up
lo-co
lo-co-mo-tion
lo-co-mo-tive
lo-co-weed
lo-cus
  lo-ci
lo-cust
lo-cu-tion
lode-stone
lodge
  lodged
  lodg-ing
  lodg-er
lofty
  loft-i-er
  loft-i-est
  loft-i-ly

lo-gan-ber-ry
  lo-gan-ber-ries
log-a-rithm
  log-a-rith-mic
  log-a-rith-mi-cal
  log-a-rith-mi-cal-ly
log-book
loge
log-ger
log-ger-hed
log-ic
  lo-gi-cian
log-i-cal
  log-i-cal-i-ty
  log-i-cal-ly
lo-gis-tic
  lo-gis-tics
  lo-gis-ti-cal
loin-cloth
loi-ter
  loi-ter-er
lol-li-pop
lone-ly
  lone-li-er
  lone-li-est
  lone-li-ly
lon-er
lone-some
  lone-some-ly
  lone-some-ness
lon-gev-i-ty
long-ing
  long-ing-ly
lon-gi-tude
lon-gi-tu-di-nal
  lon-gi-tu-di-nal-ly
long-lived
long--play-ing
long-shore-man
  long-shore-men
long--suf-fer-ing
long--term
long--wind-ed

long--wind-ed-ly
long-wise
look-out
loose
loos-er
loos-est
loos-en
loot-er
lop
looped
lop-ping
lope
loped
lop-ing
lop-er
lop-sid-ed
lo-qua-cious
lo-qua-cious-ly
lo-quac-i-ty
lo-quac-i-ties
lord-ly
lord-li-er
lord-li-est
lord-ship
lor-gnette
lor-ry
lor-ries
lose
lost
los-ing
los-a-ble
los-er
lot
lo-tion
lot-tery
lot-ter-ies
lot-to
lo-tus
lo-tus-es
loud
loud-ly
loud-ness
loud-mouthed

loud-speak-er
lounge
lounged
loung-ing
loung-er
louse
lice
lou-ver
lou-vered
love
loved
lov-ing
lov-able
love-lorn
lov-er
lov-ing
loving-ly
low-er
low-er-case
low-er-ing
low-er-ing-ly
low-ery
low--key
low--keyed
low-ly
low-li-er
low-li-est
loy-al
loy-al-ist
loy-al-ly
loy-al-ties
loz-enge
lu-au
lub-ber
lub-ber-ly
lu-beak
lu-bri-cate
lu-bri-cat-ed
lu-bri-cat-ing
lu-bri-ca-tion
luck
luck-i-er
luck-i-est

lu-cra-tive
lu-cra-tive-ly
lu-cre
lu-cu-brate
lu-cu-brat-ed
lu-cu-brat-ing
lu-cu-bra-tion
lu-cu-bra-tor
lu-di-crous
lu-di-crous-ly
lug-gage
lug-ger
lug-sail
lu-gu-bri-ous
lu-gu-bri-ous-ly
luke-warm
luke-warm-ly
lull-a-by
lull-a-bies
lum-ba-go
lum-bar
lum-ber
lum-ber-ing-ly
lum-ber-er
lum-ber-ing
lum-ber-jack
lum-ber-man
lum-ber-men
lu-men
lu-mi-nary
lu-mi-nar-ies
lu-mi-nes-cence
lu-mi-nes-cent
lu-mi-nous
lu-mi-nos-i-ty
lu-mi-nous-ly
lum-mox
lumpy
lu-na-cy
lu-na-cies
lu-nar
lu-nate
lu-na-tic

lunch
lunch-er
lun-cheon
lunge
lunged
lung-ing
lu-pine
lurch
lure
lured
lur-ing
lu-rid
lu-rid-ly
lurk
lurk-er
lurk-ing-ly
lus-cious
lus-cious-ly
lust
lust-ful
lust-ful-ly
lust-er
lusty
lut-ist
lux-u-ri-ant
lux-u-ri-ance
lux-u-ri-an-cy
lux-u-ri-ant-ly
lux-u-ri-ate
lux-u-ri-at-ed
lux-u-ri-at-ing
lux-u-ri-a-tion
lux-u-ri-ous
lux-u-ri-ous-ly
lux-u-ry
lux-u-ries
ly-ce-um
ly-ing
ly-ing--in
lymph
lym-phoid
lym-phat-ic
lynch

lynch-er
lynch-ing
lynx
lynx-es
lynx-eyed
lyre
ly-ric
lyr-i-cal
lyr-i-cal-ly
ly-ser-gic acid
ly-sine

M

ma-ca-bre
ma-ca-bre-ly
mac-ad-am
mac-ad-am-ize
mac-ad-am ised
mac-ad-am-iz-ing
mac-ad-am-i-za-tion
ma-caque
mac-a-ro-ni
ma-caw
mace
maced
mac-ing
mac-er-ate
mac-er-at-ed
mac-er-at-ing
mac-er-a-tion
mac-er-a-tor
ma-chete
mach-i-nate
ma-chine
ma-chin-ery
ma-chin-er-ies
ma-chin-ist
mack-er-el
mack-i-naw
mack-in-tosh
mac-in-tosh
mac-ro-cosm

mac-ro-cos-mic
ma-cron
mad
mad-der
mad-ly
mad-ness
mad-am
mes-dames
mad-cap
mad-den
mad-den-ing
mad-den-ing-ly
mad-e-moi-selle
mes-de-moi-selles
made-up
mad-house
mad-man
mad-men
ma-dras
mad-ri-gal
mad-ri-gal-ist
mael-strom
mae-stro-so
mag-a-zine
ma-gen-ta
mag-got
mag-goty
mag-ic
mag-i-cal
mag-i-cal-ly
ma-gi-cian
mag-is-te-ri-al
mag-is-te-ri-al-ly
mag-is-te-ri-al-ness
mag-is-tra-cy
mag-is-tra-cies
mag-is-trate
mag-ma
mag-mas
mag-ma-ta
mag-mat-ic
mag-nan-i-mous
mag-nan-i-mous-ly

mag-na-nim-i-ty
mag-na-nim-i-ties
mag-nate
mag-ne-sia
mag-ne-sian
mag-ne-sium
mag-net
mag-net-ic
mag-net-i-cal-ly
mag-net-ism
mag-net-ize
mag-net-ized
mag-net-iz-ing
mag-net-iz-a-ble
mag-net-i-za-tion
mag-net-iz-er
mag-ne-to
mag-ne-tos
mag-ne-tom-e-ter
mag-ne-to-met-ric
mag-ne-tom-e-try
mag-nif-i-cent
mag-nif-i-cence
mag-nif-i-cent-ly
mag-ni-fy
mag-ni-fied
mag-ni-fy-ing
maf-ni-fi-a-ble
mag-ni-fi-ca-tion
mag-ni-fi-er
mag-ni-tude
mag-no-lia
mag-num
mag-uey
ma-ha-ra-jah
ma-ha-ra-ni
ma-hat-ma
ma-hat-ma-ism
ma-hoe
ma-hog-a-ny
ma-hog-a-nies
ma-hout
maid-en

mail-a-ble
mail-box
mail-man
mail-men
maim
maim-er
main-land
main-land-er
main-ly
main-mast
main-sail
main-tain
main-tain-a-ble
main-te-nance
maize
maj-es-ty
maj-es-ties
ma-jes-tic
ma-jes-ti-cal
ma-jol-i-ca
ma-jor
ma-jor-do-mo
ma-jor-do-mos
ma-jor-i-ty
ma-jor-i-ties
make
mak-a-ble
mak-er
mak-ing
make-shift
make-up
mal-a-dapt-ed
mal-ad-just-ment
mal-ad-just-ed
mal-ad-min-is-ter
mal-adroit
mal-adroit-ly
mal-adroit-ness
mal-a-dy
mal-a-dies
mal-aise
mal-a-prop
mal-a-prop-ism

ma-lar-ia
ma-lar-i-al
ma-lar-i-an
ma-lar-i-ous
ma-lar-key
mal-con-tent
male-dict
male-dic-tion
male-dic-to-ry
male-frac-tion
male-frac-tor
ma-lev-o-lent
ma-lev-o-lence
ma-lev-o-lent-ly
mal-fea-sance
mal-fea-sant
mal-for-ma-tion
mal-formed
mal-func-tion
mal-ice
ma-li-cious
ma-li-cious-ly
ma-lign
ma-lign-er
ma-lign-ly
ma-lig-nant
ma-lig-nan-cy
ma-lig-nan-cies
ma-lig-nant-ly
ma-lin-ger
ma-lin-ger-er
mal-lard
mal-lea-ble
mal-lea-bil-i-ty
mal-let
ma-low
mal-nour-ished
mal-nu-tri-tion
mal-oc-clu-sion
mal-odor
mal-odor-ous
mal-odor-ous-ly
mal-prac-tice

mal-prac-ti-tion-er
malt
  malty
  malt-i-er
mal-treat
  mal-treat-ment
mam-ma
  ma-ma
mam-mal
  mam-ma-li-an
mam-mam-ries
mam-mon
mam-moth
mam-my
  mam-mies
man
  manned
  man-ning
man-a-cle
  man-a-cled
  man-a-cling
man-age
  man-aged
  man-a-ging
  man-age-a-ble
  man-age-a-bil-i-ty
  man-age-a-bly
man-age-ment
man-ag-er
  man-ag-er-ship
man-a-ge-ri-al
  man-a-ge-ri-al-ly
man-a-tee
man-da-la
man-da-rin
man-date
  man-dat-ed
  man-dat-ing
man-da-to-ry
  man-da-to-ries
  man-da-to-ri-ty
man-di-ble
  man-dib-u-lar

man-dib-u-lary
man-dib-u-late
man-do-lin
  man-do-lin-ist
man-drakes
man-drill
man-eat-er
  man-eat-ing
ma-neu-ver
  ma-neu-ver-a-ble
  ma-neu-ver-er
man-ga-nese
mange
man-ger
man-gle
  man-gled
  man-gling
man-go
  man-goes
  man-gos
man-grove
man-gy
  man-gi-er
  man-gi-est
  man-gi-ly
man-han-dle
  man-han-dled
  man-han-dling
man-hole
man-hood
man--hour
man-hunt
  man-hunt-er
ma-nia
  man-ic
ma-ni-ac
  ma-ni-a-cal
  ma-ni-a-cal-ly
man-ic-de-pres-sive
man-i-cure
  man-i-cur-eed
  man-i-cur-ing
  man-i-cur-ist

man-i-fest
  man-i-fest-er
  man-i-fest-ly
man-i-fes-ta-tion
man-i-fes-to
  man-i-fes-tos
  man-i-fes-toes
man-i-fold
man-i-kin
  man-a-kin
  man-ni-kin
ma-nila
  ma-nil-la
ma-nip-u-late
man-kind
man-ly
  man-li-er
  man-li-est
man--made
man-na
man-ne-quin
man-ner
man-nered
man-ner-ism
man-ner-ly
  man-ner-li-ness
man-nish
man-of--war
  men-of--war
ma-nom-e-ter
man-or
  ma-no-ri-al
man pow-er
man-sard
man-ser-vant
man-sion
man-sized
man-slaugh-ter
man-slay-er
man-til-la
man-tle
  man-tled
  man-tling

man-trap
man-u-al
  man-u-al-ly
man-u-fac-ture
  man-u-fac-tured
  man-u-fac-tur-ing
  man-u-fac-tur-a-ble
  man-u-fac-tur-al
  man-u-fac-tur-er
ma-nure
manu-script
many
man-y-sid-ed
map
mapped
  map-ping
  map-per
ma-ple
mar
  marred
  mar-ring
ma-ra-ca
mar-a-schi-no
mar-a-thon
ma-raud
  ma-raud-er
mar-ble
  mar-bled
  mar-bling
  mar-ble-ize
  mar-ble-ized
  mar-ble-iz-ing
  mar-bly
mar-cel
  mar-celled
  mar-cel-ling
march-er
mar-chio-ness
mare's tail
mar-ga-rine
mar-gin
mar-gi-nal
  mar-gi-na-lia

mar-gin-al-i-ty
mar-gin-al-ly
mar-gin-ate
  mar-gin-ated
  mar-gin-at-ing
  mar-gin-a-tion
mar-gue-rite
mar-i-cul-ture
mari-gold
mar-i-jua-na
ma-rim-ba
ma-ri-na
mar-i-nade
  mar-i-nad-ed
  mar-i-nad-ing
  mar-i-na-tion
mar-i-nate
  mar-i-nat-ed
  mar-i-nat-ing
  mar-i-na-tion
ma-rine
mar-i-ner
mar-i-o-nette
mar-i-tal
mar-i-time
mar-jo-ram
marked
  mark-ed-ly
mark-er
mar-ket
  mar-ket-er
mar-ket-able
  mar-ket-abil-i-ty
mar-ket-ing
mar-ket-place
mark-ing
marks-man
  marks-men
  marks-man-ship
mar-lin
mar-ma-lade
mar-mo-set
mar-mot

ma-roon
mar-quee
mar-quis
  mar-quis-es
  mar-quess
mar-quise
  mar-quis-es
mar-riage
  mar-riage-able
  mar-riage-abil-i-ty
mar-ried
mar-row
  mar-rowy
mar-row-bone
mar-ry
  mar-ried
  mar-ry-ing
mar-shall
  mar-shaled
  mar-shal-ing
marsh-mal-low
marshy
  marsh-i-er
  marsh-i-est
  marsh-i-ness
mar-su-pi-al
mar-tial
mar-tin
mar-ti-ni
  mar-ti-nis
mar-tyr
  mar-tyr-ize
  mar-tyr-ized
  mar-tyr-iz-ing
  mar-tyr-dom
mar-vel
  mar-veled
  mar-vel-ing
mar-vel-ous
  mar-vel-ous-ly
mar-zi-pan
mas-cara
mas-cu-line

mas-cu-line-ness
mas-cu-lin-i-ty
mas-cu-lin-ize
  mas-cu-lin-ized
  mas-cu-lin-iz-ing
mash-er
mask
  mask-like
masked
mas-och-ism
  mas-och-ist
  mas-och-is-tic
ma-son
  ma-son-ic
ma-son-ary
  ma-son-ries
masque
mas-quer-ade
  mas-quer-ad-ed
  mas-quer-ad-ing
  mas-quer-ad-er
mas-sa-cre
  mas-sa-cred
  mas-sa-cring
  mas-sa-cre
mas-sage
  mas-saged
  mas-sag-ing
  mas-sag-er
  mas-sag-ist
mas-seur
mas-sause
  mas-seus-es
mas-sive
mass-pro-duce
  mass-pro-duced
  mass-pro-duc-ing
  mass-pro-duc-er
  mass-pro-duc-tion
massy
  masss-i-er
  mass-i-est
  mass-i-ness

mas-tec-to-my
  mas-tec-to-mies
mas-ter
mas-ter-ful
mas-ter-mind
mas-ter-piece
mas-tery
  mas-ter-ies
mast-head
mas-tic
mas-ti-cate
  mas-ti-ca-ted
  mas-ti-ca-ting
  mas-ti-ca-ble
  mas-ti-ca-tion
  mas-ti-ca-tor
mas-tiff
mast-odon
mas-toid
mas-tur-bate
  mas-tur-bat-ed
  mas-tur-bat-ing
  mas-tur-ba-tion
mat
  mat-ted
  mat-ting
mat-a-dor
match-book
match-mak-er
  match-mak-ing
mate
  mat-ed
  mat-ing
  mate-less
ma-te-ri-al
  ma-te-ri-al-ly
ma-te-ri-al-ism
  ma-te-ri-al-ist
  ma-te-ri-al-is-tic
ma-te-ri-al-ize
  ma-te-ri-al-ized
  ma-te-ri-al-iz-ing
ma-te-ri-el

ma-ter-nal
  ma-ter-nal-ism
  ma-ter-nal-is-tic
  ma-ter-nal-ly
ma-ter-ni-ty
  ma-ter-ni-ties
math-e-mat-i-cal
  math-e-mat-ic
  math-e-mat-i-cal-ly
math-e-ma-ti-cian
math-e-mat-ics
ma-tin
  mat-in-al
mat-i-nee
ma-tri-arch
  ma-tri-ar-chal-ism
  ma-tri-ar-chy
  ma-tri-ar-chies
ma-tri-cide
ma-tric-u-lant
ma-tric-u-late
  ma-tric-u-lat-ed
  ma-tric-u-lat-ing
  ma-tric-u-la-tion
ma-tri-lin-eal
mat-ri-mo-ny
  mat-ri-mo-nies
  mat-ri-mo-ni-al
ma-trix
  ma-tri-ces
  ma-trix-es
ma-tron
ma-tron-ly
mat-ter
mat-ter-of-course
mat-ter--of--fact
  mat-ter--of--fact-ly
mat-ting
mat-tress
mat-u-rate
  mat-u-rat-ed
  mat-u-rat-ing
  mat-u-ra-tion

ma-ture
ma-tur-i-ty
mat-zo
  mat-zoth
  mat-zos
maud-lin
mau-so-le-um
  mau-so-le-ums
  mau-so-lea
mauve
mav-er-ick
mawk-ish
max-im
max-i-mal
  max-i-mal-ly
max-i-mize
  max-i-mized
  max-i-miz-ing
max-i-mum
  max-i-mums
  max-i-ma
may-be
may-flow-er
may-fly
  may-flies
may-hem
may-on-naise
may-or
  may-or-al
may-or-al-ty
  may-or-al-ties
maze
  mazed
  maz-ing
ma-zy
  ma-zi-er
  ma-zi-est
  ma-zi-ly
  ma-zi-ness
mead-ow
mead-ow-lark
mea-ger
  mea-ger-ly

mea-ger-ness
meal-time
meal-worm
mealy
  meal-i-er
  meal-i-est
  meal-i-ness
meal-y-mouthed
mean
  mean-ing
  mean-ly
  mean-ness
me-an-der
mean-ing-ful
  mean-ing-ful-ly
mean-ing-less
  mean-ing-less-ly
  mean-ing-less-ness
meant
mean-time
mean-while
mea-sles
mea-sly
  mea-sli-er
  mea-sli-est
meas-ur-a-ble
  meas-ur-a-bil-i-ty
  meas-ur-a-bly
meas-ure
  meas-ur-er
mea-sured
mea-sure-ment
meaty
  meat-i-er
  meat-i-est
  meat-i-ness
mec-ca
me-chan-ic
mech-a-nism
mech-a-nis-tic
  mech-a-nis-ti-cal-ly
mech-a-nize
  mech-a-nized

mech-a-niz-ing
mech-a-ni-za-tion
mech-a-niz-er
med-al
  med-aled
  med-al-ing
  me-dal-ic
me-dal-lion
med-dle
  med-dled
  med-dling
  med-dler
med-dle-some
me-dia
me-di-al
me-di-an
  me-di-an-ly
me-di-ate
  me-di-at-ed
  me-di-at-ing
me-di-a-tion
  me-di-a-tive
  me-di-a-to-ry
me-di-a-tor
med-ic
med-i-ca-ble
  med-i-ca-bly
med-i-cal
  med-i-cal-ly
me-di-ca-ment
med-i-cate
  med-i-cat-ed
  med-i-cat-ing
med-i-ca-tion
me-dic-i-nal
  me-dic-i-nal-ly
med-i-cine
  med-i-cined
  med-i-cin-ing
med-i-co
me-di-e-val
  me-di-e-val-ism
me-di-o-cre

me-di-oc-ri-ty
  me-di-oc-ri-ties
med-i-tate
  med-i-tat-ed
  med-i-tat-ing
  med-i-tat-ing-ly
  med-i-ta-tor
med-i-ta-tion
  med-i-ta-tive
Med-i-ter-ra-ne-an
me-di-um
  me-dia
  me-di-ums
med-ley
  med-leys
meet-ing
meet-ing-house
meg-a-city
  meg-a-cit-ies
mega-cy-cle
meg-a-lo-ma-nia
  meg-a-lo-ma-ni-ac
meg-a-lop-o-lis
  meg-a-lo-pol-i-tan
mega-phone
  mega-phoned
  mega-phon-ing
mega-ton
mega-watt
mei-o-sis
  mei-ot-ic
mel-a-mine
mel-an-cho-lia
  mel-an-cho-li-ac
mel-an-choly
  mel-an-chol-ies
  mel-an-chol-ic
  mel-an-chol-i-cal-ly
  mel-an-chol-i-ty
  mel-an-chol-i-ness
mel-a-nin
mel-a-no-ma
  mel-a-no-mas

mel-a-no-ma-ta
me-lee
me-lio-rate
  me-lio-rat-ed
  me-lio-rat-ing
  me-lio-ra-ble
  me-lio-ra-tion
  me-lio-ra-tor
mel-lif-lu-ous
  mel-lif-lu-nt
  mel-lif-lu-ous-ly
mel-low
me-lo-de-on
melo-dra-ma
  melo-dra-mat-ic
  melo-dra-mat-ics
mel-o-dy
  mel-o-dies
  me-lod-ic
  me-lod-i-cal-ly
  me-lo-di-ous
  me-lo-di-ous-ness
mel-on
melt
  melt-ed
  melt-ing
  melt-a-bil-i-ty
  melt-a-ble
  melt-er
mem-ber
  mem-bered
  mem-ber-less
mem-ber-ship
mem-brane
  mem-bra-nous
me-men-to
  me-men-tos
  me-men-toes
memo
mem-oir
mem-o-ra-bil-ia
mem-o-ra-ble
  mem-o-ra-bly

mem-o-ran-dum
  mem-o-ran-dums
  mem-o-ran-da
me-mo-ri-al
  me-mo-ri-al-ly
me-mo-ri-al-ize
  me-mo-ri-al-ized
  me-mo-ri-al-iz-ing
  me-mo-ri-al-iz-er
  me-mo-ri-al-ly
mem-o-rize
  mem-o-rized
  mem-o-riz-ing
  mem-o-riz-a-ble
  mem-o-ri-za-tion
mem-o-ry
  mem-o-ries
men-ace
  men-aced
  men-ac-ing
me-nag-er-ie
mend
  mend-able
men-da-cious
  men-da-cious-ly
  men-da-cious-ness
men-dac-i-ty
men-de-le-vi-um
men-di-cant
me-ni-al
  me-ni-al-ly
men-in-ges
men-in-gi-tis
me-nis-cus
  me-nis-cus-es
  me-nis-ci
men-o-pause
  men-o-pau-sal
me-nor-ah
men-sal
men-ses
men-stru-al
men-stru-a-tion

men-stru-ate
men-stru-at-ed
men-stru-at-ing
men-sur-a-ble
men-tal
men-tal-ly
men-tal-i-ty
men-tal-i-ties
men-thol
men-tho-lat-ed
men-tion
men-tion-a-ble
men-tion-er
men-tor
menu
me-ow
mep-ro-bam-ate
mer-can-tile
mer-can-til-ism
mer-can-til-ist
mer-ce-nary
mer-ce-nar-ies
mer-ce-nar-ily
mer-cer-ize
mer-cer-ized
mer-cer-iz-ing
mer-chan-dise
mer-chan-dised
mer-chan-dis-ing
mer-chan-dis-er
mer-chant
mer-chant-man
mer-chant-men
mer-cu-ri-al
mer-cu-ry
mer-cu-ries
mer-cy
mer-cies
mer-ci-ful
mer-ci-ful-ly
mer-ci-less
mere-ly
mer-e-tri-cious

mer-e-tri-cious-ly
mer-e-tri-cious-ness
merge
merged
merg-ing
mer-gence
merg-er
me-rid-i-an
me-rid-i-o-nal
me-ringue
mer-it
mer-it-ed
mer-it-ed-ly
mer-it-less
mer-i-to-ri-ous
mer-maid
mer-man
mer-men
mer-ri-ment
mer-ry
mer-ri-er
mer-ri-est
mer-ri-ness
mer-ry--go--round
mer-ry-mak-er
mer-ry-mak-ing
me-sa
mes-cal
mes-dames
mes-de-moi-selles
mesh-work
me-si-al
mes-mer-ism
mes-mer-ic
mes-mer-i-cal-ly
mes-mer-ist
mes-mer-ize
mes-mer-ized
mes-mer-iz-ing
mes-mer-i-za-tion
mes-mer-iz-er
mes-o-morph
mes-o-mor-phic

mes-o-mor-phism
mes-o-mor-phy
me-son
mes-o-sphere
mes-quite
mess
mess-i-ly
mess-i-ness
messy
mess-i-er
mess-i-est
mes-sage
mes-sen-ger
mes-ti-zo
me-tab-o-lism
met-a-bol-ic
met-a-bol-i-cal
me-tab-o-lize
me-tab-o-lized
me-tab-o-liz-ing
met-al
met-aled
met-al-ing
met-al-ize
met-al-ized
met-al-iz-ing
me-tal-lic
me-tal-li-cal-ly
met-al-loid
met-al-lur-gy
met-al-lur-gic
met-al-lur-gi-cal
met-al-lur-gi-cal-ly
met-al-lur-gist
met-al-work
met-al-work-er
met-al-work-ing
meta-mor-phism
meta-mor-phic
meta-mor-phose
meta-mor-phosed
meta-mor-phos-ing
meta-mor-pho-sis

meta-mor-pho-ses
met-a-phor
  met-a-phor-ic
  met-a-phor-i-cal
meta-phys-ic
meta-phys-ics
  meta-phys-i-cal
meta-tar-sus
  meta-tar-si
  meta-tar-sal
meta-zo-an
  meta-zo-al
  meta-zo-ic
mete
  met-ed
  met-ing
me-te-or
me-te-or-ic
me-te-or-ite
  me-te-or-it-ic
me-te-or-oid
me-te-o-rol-o-gy
  me-te-o-ro-log-i-cal
  me-te-o-rol-o-gist
me-ter
met-es-trus
meth-a-done
meth-ane
meth-a-nol
meth-od
me-thodi-cal
  me-thodi-cal-ly
meth-od-ize
  meth-od-ized
  meth-od-iz-ing
  meth-od-iz-er
meth-od-ol-o-gy
  meth-od-ol-o-gies
  meth-od-o-log-i-cal
  meth-od-ol-o-gist
me-tic-u-lous
  me-tic-u-los-i-ty
  me-tic-u-lous-ly

met-ric
met-ri-cal
  met-ri-cal-ly
met-ri-fi-ca-tion
met-ro
met-ro-nome
  met-ro-nom-ic
me-trop-o-lis
met-ro-pol-i-tan
met-tle
met-tle-some
mez-za-nine
mez-zo
mi-as-ma
  mi-as-mas
  mi-as-ma-ta
  mi-as-mat-ic
  mi-as-mic
mi-ca
mi-crobe
  mi-cro-bi-al
  mi-cro-bi-an
  mi-cro-bic
mi-cro-bi-ol-o-gy
  mi-cro-bi-ol-o-gist
mi-cro-copy
  mi-cro-cop-ies
mi-cro-cosm
  mi-cro-cos-mos
  mi-cro-cos-mic
  mi-cro-cos-mi-cal
mi-cro-film
mi-cro-gram
mi-cro-groove
mi-crom-e-ter
mi-crom-e-try
mi-cro-mi-cron
mi-cro-min-ia-ture
mi-cro-mil-li-me-ter
mi-cron
  mi-crons
  mi-cra
mi-cro-or-gan-ism

mi-cro-phone
  mi-cro-phon-ic
m i - c r o - p h o - t o -
graph
mi-cro-read-er
mi-cro-scope
  mi-cro-scop-i-cal
  mi-cro-scop-i-cal-ly
mi-cros-co-py
  mi-cros-co-pist
mi-cro-sec-ond
mi-cro-wave
mid-day
mid-dle
  mid-dles
  mid-dling
mid-dle--aged
mid-dle-man
  mid-dle-men
mid-dle-most
mid-dle-weight
mid-dy
  mid-dies
midg-et
mid-land
mid-night
mid-sec-tion
mid-ship
mid-ship-man
  mid-ship-men
midst
mid-sum-mer
mid-term
mid-way
mid-wife
  mid-wives
mid-wife-ry
mid-year
mien
mighty
  might-i-er
  might-i-est
  might-i-ly

might-i-ness
mi-graine
mi-grant
mi-grate
mi-grat-ed
mi-grat-ing
mi-gra-tion
mi-gra-tor
mi-gra-to-ry
mi-la-dy
mi-la-dies
mild
mild-ly
mild-ness
mil-dew
mil-dewy
mile-age
mil-er
mile-stone
mi-lieu
mi-lieus
mil-i-tant
mil-i-tan-cy
mil-i-tant-ness
mil-i-ta-rism
mil-i-ta-ris-tic
mil-i-ta-ris-ti-cal-ly
mil-i-ta-rize
mil-i-ta-rized
mil-i-ta-riz-ing
mil-i-ta-ri-za-tion
mil-i-tary
mil-i-tar-i-ly
mi-li-tia
milk
milk-er
milky
milk-i-er
milk-i-est
milk-maid
milk-man
milk-men
milk-weed

mill-board
mil-len-ni-um
mil-len-nia
mil-len-ni-al
mil-ler
mil-let
mil-li-am-pere
mil-li-bar
mil-li-gram
mil-li-li-ter
mil-li-me-ter
mil-li-ner
mil-li-nery
mill-ing
mil-lion
mil-lionth
mill-lion-aire
mil-li-sec-ond
mill-pond
mill-run
mill-stone
mill-stream
mi-lord
milt
mime
mimed
mim-ing
mim-er
mim-e-o-graph
mim-ic
mim-icked
mim-ick-ing
mim-i-cal
mim-i-cal
mim-ick-r
mim-ic-ry
mim-ic-ries
min-able
mine-able
min-e-ret
mince
minced

minc-ing
minc-er
minc-ing-ly
mince-meat
mind-ed
mind-less
mind-less-ly
mind-less-ness
min-er
mine-field
min-er-al
min-er-al-ize
min-er-al-ized
min-er-al-iz-ing
min-er-al-i-za-tion
min-er-al-o-gy
min-er-al-og-ical
min-er-al-o-gist
min-e-stro-ne
mine-sweep-er
mine-sweep-ing
min-gle
min-gled
min-gling
min-i-a-ture
min-i-a-tur-ize
min-i-a-tur-ized
min-i-a-tur-iz-ing
min-i-a-tur-i-za-tion
min-im
min-i-mal
min-i-mal-ly
min-i-mize
min-i-mized
min-i-miz-ing
min-i-mi-za-tion
min-i-miz-er
min-i-mum
min-i-mums
min-i-ma
min-ing
min-ion
min-is-ter

min-is-te-ri-al
min-is-trant
min-is-tra-tion
min-is-tries
min-now
mi-nor
mi-nor-i-ty
  mi-nor-i-ties
min-strel
mint-age
  mint-er
min-u-end
mi-nus
mi-nus-cule
min-ute
  min-ut-ed
  min-ut-ing
mi-nut-er
  mi-nut-est
min-ute-man
  min-ute-men
mi-nu-tia
  mi-nu-ti-ae
minx
mir-a-cle
mi-rac-u-lous
mi-rage
mire
  mired
  mir-ing
mir-ror
mirth
  mirth-ful
  mirth-ful-ly
  mirth-ful-ness
  mirth-less
mis-ad-ven-tage
mis-ad-vise
  mis-ad-vised
  mis-ad-vis-ing
mis-al-li-ance
mis-an-thrope
mis-an-tho-pist

mis-an-throp-ic
mis-an-throp-i-cal
  mis-an-thro-py
mis-ap-ply
  mis-ap-plied
  mis-ap-ply-ing
  mis-ap-pli-ca-tion
mis-ap-pre-hend
  mis-ap-pre-hen-sion
mis-ap-pro-pri-ate
  mis-ap-pro-pri-at-ed
  -ap-pro-pri-at-ing
  -ap-pro-pri-a-tion
mis-be-have
  mis-be-haved
  mis-be-hav-ing
  mis-be-hav-er
  mis-be-ha-vior
mis-cal-cu-late
  mis-cal-cu-lat-ed
  mis-cal-cu-lat-ing
  mis-cal-cu-la-tion
  mis-cal-cu-la-tor
mis-call
mis-car-riage
mis-car-ry
  mis-car-ried
  mis-car-ry-ing
mis-ce-ge-na-tion
  mis-ce-ge-net-ic
mis-cel-la-neous
  mis-cel-la-ny
  mis-cel-la-nies
mis-chance
mis-chief
mis-chie-vous
  mis-chie-vous-ly
  mis-chie-vous-ness
mis-ci-ble
  mis-ci-bil-i-ty
mis-con-ceive
mis-con-ceived
  mis-con-ceiv-ing

mis-con-ceiv-er
mis-con-cep-tion
mis-con-duct
mis-con-strue
  mis-con-strued
  mis-con-stru-ing
  mis-con-struc-tion
mis-count
mis-cre-ant
mis-cue
  mis-cued
  mis-cu-ing
mis-deal
  mis-dealt
  mis-deal-ing
mis-deed
mis-de-mean-or
mis-di-rect
  mis-di-rec-tion
mis-do
  mis-did
  mis-done
  mis-do-ing
mis-em-ploy
  mis-em-ploy-ment
mi-ser
  mi-ser-li-ness
  mi-ser-ly
mis-er-a-ble
  mis-er-a-ble-ness
  mis-er-a-bly
mis-ery
  mis-er-ies
mis-fea-sance
mis-fire
  mis-fired
  mis-fir-ing
mis-fit
  mis-fit-ted
  mis-fit-ting
mis-for-tune
mis-giv-ing
mis-gov-ern

mis-gov-ern-ment
mis-guide
 mis-guid-ed
 mis-guid-ing
 mis-guid-ance
mis-han-dle
 mis-han-dled
 mis-han-dling
mis-hap
mish-mash
mis-in-form
 mis-in-form-ant
 mis-in-form-er
 mis-in-for-ma-tion
mis-in-ter-pret
 -in-ter-pre-ta-tion
 mis-in-ter-pret-er
mis-judge
 mis-judged
 mis-judg-ing
 mis-judg-ment
mis-lay
 mis-laid
 mis-lay-ing
mis-lead
 mis-led
 mis-lead-ing
 mis-lead-er
mis-man-age
 mis-man-aged
 mis-man-ag-ing
 mis-man-age-ment
mis-match
mis-mate
 mis-mat-ed
 mis-mat-ing
mis-name
 mis-named
 mis-nam-ing
mis-no-mer
mi-sog-a-my
mi-sog-y-ny
 mi-sog-y-nist

mi-sog-y-nous
mis-place
 mis-placed
 mis-plac-ing
 mis-place-ment
mis-play
mis-print
mis-pri-sion
mis-prize
 mis-prized
 mis-priz-ing
mis-pro-nounce
 mis-pro-nounced
 mis-pro-nouc-ing
 -pro-nun-ci-a-tion
mis-quote
 mis-quoted
 mis-quot-ing
 mis-quo-ta-tion
mis-read
 mis-read-ing
mis-rep-re-sent
 -rep-re-sen-ta-tion
 -rep-re-sen-ta-tive
mis-rule
 mis-ruled
 mis-rul-ing
mis-sal
mis-shape
 mis-shaped
 mis-shap-ing
 mis-shap-en
mis-sile
miss-ing
mis-sion
mis-sion-ary
 mis-sion-ar-ies
mis-sive
mis-spell
 mis-spelled
 mis-spel-ling
mis-spend
 mis-spent

mis-spend-ing
mis-state
 mis-stat-ed
 mis-stat-ing
 mis-state-ment
mis-step
mist
 mist-i-ly
 mist-i-ness
mis-ta-a-ble
mis-take
 mis-took
 mis-tak-en
 mis-tak-ing
 mis-tak-en-ly
 mis-tak-er
mis-tle-toe
mis-tral
mis-treat
 mis-treat-ment
mis-tress
mis-tri-al
mis-trust
 mis-trust-ful
 mis-trust-ful-ly
 mis-trust-ing-ly
misty
 mist-i-er
 mist-i-est
mis-un-der-stand
 mis-un-der-stood
 -un-der-stand-ing
mis-us-age
mis-use
 mis-used
 mis-us-ing
 mis-us-er
mis-val-ue
 mis-val-ued
 mis-val-u-ing
mi-ter
 mi-tre
mi-ti-cide

mi-ti-cid-al
mit-i-gate
mit-i-gat-ed
mit-i-gat-ing
mit-i-ga-tion
mit-i-ga-tive
mit-i-ga-tor
mit-i-ga-to-ry
mi-to-sis
mi-tral
mit-ten
mix
mixed
mix-ing
mix-er
mix-ture
mix-up
miz-pah
miz-zen
mne-mon-ic
mne-mon-ics
moa
mob
mobbed
mob-bing
mob-bish
mo-bile
mo-bil-i-ty
mo-bi-lize
mo-bi-lized
mo-bi-liz-ing
mo-bi-li-za-tion
mob-ster
moc-ca-sin
mo-cha
mock
mock-er
mock-ing-ly
mock-ery
mock-er-ies
mock-ing-bird
mock-up
mod-al

mo-dal-i-ty
mod-al-ly
mod-el
mod-eled
mod-el-ing
mod-el-er
mod-er-ate
mod-er-at-ed
mod-er-at-ing
mod-er-ate-ly
mod-er-ate-ness
mod-er-a-tion
mod-er-a-tor
mod-er-a-tor-ship
mod-ern
mod-ern-ism
mod-er-ist
mod-er-ist-ic
mod-ern-ize
mod-ern-ized
mod-ern-iz-ing
mod-ern-iz-er
mod-ern-i-za-tion
mod-est
mod-est-ly
mod-est-ty
mod-es-ties
mod-i-cum
mod-i-fi-ca-tion
mod-i-fy
mod-i-fied
mod-i-fy-ing
mod-i-fi-a-ble
mod-i-fi-er
mod-ish
mod-ish-ly
mod-ish-ness
mo-diste
mod-u-late
mod-u-lat-ed
mod-u-lat-ing
mod-u-la-tion
mod-u-la-tor

mod-u-la-to-ry
mod-ule
mod-u-lar
mo-gulmo-hair
moi-ety
moi-eties
moil
moil-er
moil-ing-ly
mois-ten
moist-en-er
mo-lar
mo-las-ses
mold
mold-able
mold-er
mold-board
mold-ing
moldy
mold-i-er
mold-i-est
mold-i-ness
mol-e-cule
mole-hill
mole-skin
mo-lest
mo-les-ta-tion
mo-lest-er
mol-li-fy
mol-li-fied
mol-li-fy-ing
mol-li-fi-ca-tion
mol-li-fi-er
mol-li-fy-ing-ly
mol-lusk
mol-ly-cod-dle
mol-ly-cod-dled
mol-ly-cod-dling
molt
moult
molt-er
mol-ten
mol-ten-ly

mo-lyb-de-num
mo-ment
me-men-tary
  mo-men-tar-i-ly
mo-men-tous
  mo-men-tous-ly
mo-men-tum
mon-arch
  mo-nar-chal
  mo-nar-chal-ly
mo-nar-chi-cal
  mo-nar-chic
  mo-nar-chi-cal-ly
mon-ar-chism
  mon-ar-chist
  mon-ar-chis-tic
mo-nas-tic
mo-nas-ti-cal
  mo-nas-ti-cal-ly
mo-nas-ti-cism
mon-au-ral
  mon-au-ral-ly
mon-e-tary
  mon-e-tar-i-ly
mon-e-tize
  mon-e-tized
  mon-e-tiz-ing
  mon-e-ti-za-tion
mon-ey
mon-ey-chang-er
mon-eyed
  mon-ied
mon-ey--mak-er
  mon-ey--mak-ing
mon-ger
mon-goose
  mon-gooses
mon-grel
mon-i-ker
mo-ni-tion
mon-i-tor
  mon-i-to-ri-al
monk

monk-ish
monk-ish-ly
mon-key
  mon-keys
  mon-keyed
  mon-key-ing
mon-key-shine
mon-chro-mat-ic
mon-o-chrome
  mon-o-chro-mic
  mon-o-chro-mi-cal
  mon-o-chrom-ist
mon-o-cle
  mon-o-cled
mon-o-cli-nal
mon-o-cline
  mon-o-cli-nal-ly
mon-o-cli-nous
mon-o-dist
mon-o-dy
  mon-o-dies
  mo-nod-ic
mo-noe-cious
  mo-noe-cious-ly
mo-nog-a-my
  mo-nog-a-mist
  mo-nog-a-mous
mon-o-gram
  mon-o-grammed
  mon-o-gram-ming
  mon-o-gram-mat-ic
mon-o-graph
  mo-nog-ra-pher
  mon-o-graph-ic
mon-o-lith
mon-o-logue
  mon-o-log
  mon-o-logu-ist
  mon-o-log-ist
mon-o-ma-nia
  mon-o-ma-ni-ac
  mon-o-ma-ni-a-cal
mon-o-met-al-lism

mon-o-me-tal-lic
mo-no-mi-al
mon-nu-cle-o-sis
mon-o-pho-nic
mono-plane
mo-nop-o-lize
  mo-nop-o-lized
  mo-nop-o-liz-ing
  mo-nop-o-li-za-tion
  mo-nop-o-liz-er
mo-nop-o-ly
  mo-nop-o-lies
mono-rail
mon-o-syl-lab-ic
mon-o-syl-la-ble
mon-o-the-ism
  mon-o-the-ist
  mon-o-the-is-tic
mon-o-tone
mo-not-o-nous
  mo-not-o-nous-ly
  mo-not-o-nous-ness
mo-not-o-ny
mone-treme
mono-type
  mon-o-typ-er
  mon-o-typ-ic
mon-o-va-lent
  mon-o-va-lence
  mon-o-va-len-cy
mon-ox-ide
mon-sei-gneur
  mes-sei-gneurs
mon-sieur
mon-soon
mon-ster
mon-stros-i-ty
  mon-stro-i-ties
mon-strous
  mon-strous-i-ties
mon-tage
month-ly
  month-lies

mon-u-ment
mon-u-men-tal
  mon-u-men-tal-ly
mooch
  mooch-er
moon-beam
moon-light
moon-light-er
  moon-light-ing
moon-scape
moon-shine
  moon-shiner
moon-stone
moon-struck
moony
  moon-i-er
  moon-i-est
moor-ing
moot-ness
mop
  mopped
  mop-ping
mop-pet
mo-raine
  mo-rain-al
  mo-rain-ic
mor-al
  mor-al-ly
mo-rale
mor-al-ist
  mor-al-is-tic
mo-ral-i-ty
  mo-ral-i-ties
mor-al-ize
  mor-al-ized
  mor-al-iz-ing
  mor-al-i-za-tion
  mor-al-iz-er
mo-rass
mor-a-to-ri-um
  mor-a-to-ri-ums
  mor-a-to-ria
mo-ray

mor-bid
  mor-bid-ly
  mor-bid-i-ty
  mor-bid-ness
mor-dant
  mor-dan-cy
  mor-dant-ly
more-over
mo-res
mor-ga-nat-ic
  mor-ga-nat-i-cal-ly
morque
mor-i-bund
mo-ri-on
morn-ing
morn-ing glo-ry
  morn-ing glo-ries
mo-roc-co
mo-rose
  mo-rose-ly
mor-pheme
mor-phine
mor-phol-o-gy
  mor-pho-log-ic
  mor-pho-log-i-cal
  mor-phol-o-gist
mor-row
mor-sel
mor-tal
  mor-tal-ly
mor-tal-i-ty
  mor-tal-i-ties
mor-tar
mort-gage
  mort-gaged
  mort-gag-ing
  mort-gag-ee
  mort-gag-er
mor-ti-cian
mor-ti-fy
  mor-ti-fied
  mor-ti-fy-ing
  mor-ti-fi-ca-tion

mor-tise
  mor-tised
  mor-tising
mort-main
mor-tu-ary
  mor-tu-ar-ies
mo-sa-ic
mo-sey
  mo-seyd
  mo-sey-ing
mosque
mos-qui-to
  mos-qui-toes
  mos-qui-tos
moss
most-ly
mo-tel
mo-tet
moth-ball
moth-eat-en
moth-er
moth-er-hood
moth-er-in-law
moth-er-ly
mo-tif
mo-tile
  mo-til-i-ty
mo-tion
  mo-tion-less
mo-ti-vate
  mo-ti-vat-ed
  mo-ti-vat-ing
  mo-ti-va-tion
mo-tive
mot-ley
mo-tor
mo-tor-bike
mo-tor-boat
mo-tor-bus
mo-tor-cade
mo-tor-cy-cle
  mo-tor-cy-cling
  mo-tor-cy-clist

mo-tor-ist
mo-tor-ize
  mo-tor-ized
  mo-tor-iz-ing
  mo-tor-i-za-tion
mo-tor-man
  mo-tor-men
mound
mount
  mount-able
  mount-er
moun-tain
moun-tain-eer
moun-tain-ous
moun-te-bank
mount-ing
mourn
  mourn-er
mourn-ful
  mourn-ful-ly
mourn-ing
  mourn-ing-ly
mouse
  moused
  mous-ing
mous-er
mous-tache
mousy
  mous-i-er
  mous-i-est
mouth
  mouthed
  mouth-er
mouth-ful
  mouth-fuls
mouth-piece
mouthy
  mouth-i-er
  mouth-i-est
mou-ton
mov-able
  mov-a-bil-i-ty
  mov-a-bly

move
  moved
  mov-ing
move-ment
mov-ie
mow
mox-ie
mu-ci-lage
  mu-ci-lag-i-nous
muck
  mucky
mu-cous
  mu-cos-i-ty
mu-cus
mu-ez-zin
muf-fin
muf-ti
mug
  mugged
  mug-ging
  mug-ger
mug-gy
  mug-gi-er
  mug-gi-est
mu-lat-to
  mu-lat-toes
mul-ber-ry
  mul-ber-ries
mulch
mu-le-teer
mul-ish
  mul-ish-ly
mul-let
mul-li-gan
mul-li-ga-taw-ny
mul-lion
  mul-lioned
mul-ti-far-i-ous
  mul-ti-far-i-ous-ly
mul-ti-lat-er-al
mul-ti-ple
mul-ti-i-cand
mul-ti-pli-ca-tion

mul-ti-plic-i-ty
mul-ti-pli-er
mul-ti-ply
  mul-ti-plied
  mul-ti-ply-ing
  mul-ti-pli-a-ble
mul-ti-tude
mul-ti-tu-di-nous
  mul-ti-tu-di-nous-ly
mum-ble
mum-mer
mum-mery
mum-mi-fy
  mum-mi-fied
  mum-mi-fy-ing
  mum-mi-fi-ca-tion
mum-my
  mum-mies
  mum-mied
  mum-my-ing
munch
  munch-er
mun-dane
  mun-dane-ly
mu-nic-i-pal
  mu-nic-i-pal-ly
mu-nic-i-pal-i-ty
mu-nif-i-cent
  mu-nif-i-cence
  mu-nif-i-cent-ly
mu-ni-tion
mu-ral
  mu-ral-ist
mur-der
  mur-der-er
  mur-der-ess
mur-der-ous
  mur-der-ous-ly
mu-ri-at-ic ac-id
murky
  murk-i-er
  murk-i-est
  murk-i-ly

mur-mur
mur-rain
mus-cat
  mus-ca-tel
mus-cle
  mus-cled
  mus-cling
mus-cle--bound
mus-cu-lar
  mus-cu-lar-i-ty
  mus-cu-lar-ly
mus-cu-lar dys-tro-
phy
mus-cu-la-ture
muse
  mused
  mus-ing
  mus-ing-ly
mu-se-um
mush-room
mu-sic
mu-si-cal
  mu-si-cal-ly
mu-si-cale
mu-si-cian
musk
  musky
  musk-i-er
  misk-i-est
mus-ket
mus-ke-teer
musk-mel-on
musk-rat
mus-lin
muss
  mussy
  muss-i-er
mus-sel
mus-tache
mus-tang
mus-ter
mus-ty
  mus-ti-er

mus-ti-est
mus-ti-ly
mu-ta-ble
mu-ta-bil-i-ty
mu-ta-bly
mu-tant
mu-ta-tion
mu-tate
mu-tat-ed
mu-tat-ing
mu-ta-tion-al
mute
  mut-ed
mu-ti-late
mu-ti-ny
  mu-ti-nies
  mu-ti-nied
  mu-ti-nous
mut-ter
  mut-ter-er
mut-ton
mu-tu-al
  mu-tu-al-i-ty
  mu-tu-al-ly
muz-zle
my-col-o-gy
  my-col-o-gist
my-na
  my-nah
my-o-pia
  my-op-ic
myr-i-ad
myr-mi-don
myrrh
myr-tle
mys-te-ri-ous
  mys-te-ri-ous-ly
mys-tery
  mys-ter-ies
mys-tic
mys-ti-cal
  mys-ti-cal-ly
mys-ti-cism

mys-ti-fy
  mys-ti-fied
  mys-ti-fy-ing
  mys-ti-fi-ca-tion
mys-tique
myth
  myth-ic
  myth-i-cal
  myth-i-cal-ly
  myth-i-cist
  myth-i-cize
my-thol-o-gy
  my-thol-o-gies
  myth-o-log-ic
  myth-o-log-i-cal
  my-thol-o-gist

N

nab
  nabbed
  nab-bing
na-bob
na-cre
na-cre-ous
na-dir
nag
  nagged
  nag-ging
  nag-ger
nail-er
na-ive
  na-ive-ly
  na-ive-te
na-ked
  na-ked-ly
  na-ked-ness
nam-by-pam-by
name
  named
  nam-ing
  name-less
  name-ly

name-sake
nan-keen
  nan-kin
nan-ny
  nan-nies
nap
  napped
  nap-ping
  nap-per
na-palm
nape
naph-tha
naph-tha-lene
nap-kin
nar-cis-sism
  nar-cism
  nar-cis-sist
nar-co-sis
nar-cot-ic
  nar-co-tize
  nar-co-tized
nar-is
  nar-es
nar-rate
  nar-ra-ted
  nar-ra-ting
  nar-ra-tor
  nar-ra-tion
nar-ra-tive
  nar-ra-tive-ly
nar-row
  nar-row-ly
nar-row--mind-ed
nary
na-sal
na-scent
  na-scence
  na-scen-cy
na-stur-tium
nas-ty
  nas-ti-er
  nas-ti-est
na-tal

na-tion
  na-tion-hood
na-tion-al
  na-tion-al-ly
na-tion-al-ism
  na-tion-al-ist
  na-tion-al-is-tic
na-tion-al-i-ty
  na-tion-al-i-ties
na-tion-al-ize
  na-tion-al-ized
  na-tion-al-iz-ing
  na-tion-al-i-za-tion
na-tion-wide
na-tive
  na-tive-ly
na-tiv-i-ty
  na-tiv-i-ties
nat-ty
  nat-ti-er
nat-u-ral
  nat-u-ral-ly
  nat-u-ral-ness
nat-u-ral-ism
nat-u-ral-ist
  nat-u-ral-is-tic
  nat-u-ral-ized
  nat-u-ral-iz-ing
  nat-u-ral-i-za-tion
na-ture
naught
naugh-ty
  naugh-ti-er
  naugh-ti-est
nau-sea
nau-se-ate
  nau-se-at-ed
  nau-se-at-ing
nau-seous
  nau-seous-ly
nau-ti-cal
  nau-ti-cal-ly
nau-ti-lus

  nau-ti-lus-es
nau-ti-li
na-val
na-vel
nav-i-ga-ble
nav-i-gate
  nav-i-gat-ed
  nav-i-gat-ing
nav-i-ga-tion
  nav-i-ga-tion-al
nav-i-ga-tor
na-vy
  na-vies
near
  near-ly
  near-ness
near-by
neat
  neat-ly
  neat-ness
neb-bish
neb-u-la
nec-es-sary
  nec-es-sar-ies
  nec-es-sar-i-ly
  ne-ces-si-tate
  ne-ces-si-ta-ting
ne-ces-si-ty
  ne-ces-si-ties
neck-er-chief
neck-ing
neck-lace
neck-tie
ne-crol-o-gy
  ne-crol-o-gies
nec-ro-man-cy
  nec-ro-man-cer
ne-cro-sis
  ne-crot-ic
nec-tar
  nec-tar-ine
need-ful
  need-ful-ly

need-ful-ness
nee-dle
  nee-dled
  nee-dling
  nee-dle-like
  nee-dler
nee-dle-point
need-less
  need-less-ly
nee-dle-work
  nee-dle-work-er
needy
  need-i-er
  need-i-est
  need-i-ness
ne'er--do--well
ne-far-i-ous
  ne-far-i-ous-ly
  ne-far-i-ous-ness
ne-gate
  ne-ga-ted
  ne-ta-ting
ne-ga-tion
neg-a-tive
  neg-a-tive-ly
  neg-a-tive-ness
  neg-a-tive-i-ty
  neg-a-tiv-ism
ne-glect
  ne-glec-ter
  ne-glec-tor
  ne-glect-ful-ness
  ne-glect-ful
  ne-glect-ful-ly
neg-li-gee
neg-li-gent
  neg-li-gence
  neg-li-gent-ly
neg-li-gi-ble
  neg-li-gi-bly
  neg-li-gi-bil-i-ty
ne-go-tia-ble
  ne-go-tia-bil-i-ty

ne-go-ti-ate
  ne-go-ti-at-ed
  ne-go-ti-at-ing
  ne-go-ti-a-tion
  ne-go-ti-a-tor
neigh-bor
  neigh-bor-ing
  neigh-bor-ly
  neigh-bor-li-ness
  neigh-bor-hood
nei-ther
nem-e-sis
  nem-e-ses
neo-clas-sic
  neo-clas-si-cism
neo-lith-ic
ne-ol-o-gism
ne-ol-o-gy
ne-on
ne-o-phyte
nep-en-the
  ne-pen-the-an
neph-ew
ne-phri-tis
  ne-phrit-ic
nep-o-tism
  nep-o-tist
nep-tu-ni-um
nerve
  nerved
  nerv-ing
  nerve-less
nerve--rack-ing
  nerve--wrack-ing
ner-vous
  ner-vous-ly
  ner-vous-ness
nervy
  nerv-i-er
  nerv-i-est
  nerv-i-ness
nes-tle
  nes-tled

nes-tling
nes-tler
net
net-ted
net-ting
neth-er
neth-er-most
net-tle
net-tled
net-tling
net-work
neu-ral
  neu-ral-ly
  neu-ral-gia
  neu-ral-gic
neu-ras-the-nia
  neu-ra-then-ic
neu-ri-tis
  neu-rit-ic
neu-rol-o-gy
  neu-ro-log-i-cal
  neu-rol-o-gist
neu-ron
  neu-ron-ic
neu-ro-sis
  neu-ro-ses
neu-rot-ic
  neu-rot-i-cal-ly
neu-ter
neu-tral
  neu-tral-i-ty
  neu-tral-ly
neu-tral-ism
  neu-tral-ist
neu-tral-ize
  neu-tral-ized
  neu-tral-iz-ing
neu-tral-i-za-tion
neu-tral-iz-er
neu-tri-no
neu-tron
nev-er
nev-er-more

nev-er-the-less
new
new-ish
new-ness
new-born
new-com-er
new-el
new-fan-gled
new-ly
new-ly-wed
news-boy
news-cast
news-cast-er
news-pa-per
news-pa-per-man
news-print
news-reel
news-stand
newsy
news-i-er
news-i-est
newt
nex-us
ni-a-cin
nib-ble
nib-bled
nib-bling
nib-bler
nib-lick
nice
nic-er
nic-est
nice-ly
nice-ness
nice-ty
nice-ties
niche
nick-el
nick-el-ode-on
nick-name
nick-named
nick-nam-ing
nic-o-tine

nic-o-tin-ic
niece
nif-ty
nif-ti-er
nif-ti-est
nig-gard
nig-gard-li-ness
nig-gard-ly
nigh
nigh-er
nigh-est
night-cap
night-dress
night-fall
night-gown
night-hawk
night-in-gale
night-ly
night-mare
night-mar-ish
night-shade
night-shirt
night-time
ni-hil-ism
ni-hil-ist
ni-hil-is-tic
nim-ble
nim-bler
nim-blest
nim-ble-ness
nim-bly
nim-bus
nin-com-poop
nine-pin
nine-teen
nine-teenth
nine-ty
nine-ties
nine-ti-eth
nin-ny
nin-nines
ninth
nip

nipped
nip-ping
nip-per
nip-ple
nip-py
nip-pi-er
nip-pi-est
nir-va-na
nit
nit-ty
nit-ti-er
nit-ti-est
ni-ter
nit-pick
ni-trate
ni-trat-ed
ni-trat-ing
ni-tra-tion
ni-tra-tor
ni-tric
ni-tro-gen
ni-trog-e-nous
ni-tro-glyc-er-in
ni-trous ox-ide
nit-ty-grit-ty
nit-wit
no-be-li-um
no-bil-i-ty
no-bil-i-ties
no-ble
no-body
noc-tur-nal
noc-turne
node
nod-al
nod-ule
nod-u-lar
no-el
nog-gin
noise
noised
nois-ing
noise-less

no-mad
no-mad-ic
no-mad-i-cal-ly
no-mad-ism
nom de plume
noms de plume
no-men-cla-ture
nom-i-nal
nom-i-nal-ly
nom-i-nee
non-age
nonce
non-cha-lant
non-cha-lance
non-cha-lant-ly
non-com
non-com-bat-ant
non-com-mit-tal
non-com-mit-tal-ly
non-con-duc-tor
non-con-duc-ing
non-con-form-ist
non-con-form-i-ty
non-de-script
non-en-ti-ty
non-en-ti-ties
none-the-less
non-in-ter-ven-tion
non-met-al
non-me-tal-lic
non-pa-reil
non-par-ti-san
non-par-ti-san-ship
non-plus
non-plused
non-plus-ing
non-prof-it
non-res-i-dent
non-res-i-dence
non-res-i-den-cy
non-res-i-den-cies
non-re-stric-tive
non-sec-tar-i-an

non-sense
non-sen-si-cal
non-sen-si-cal-ly
non se-qui-tur
non-stop
non-union
non-union-ism
non-union-ist
non-vi-o-lence
non-vi-o-lent
non-vi-o-lent-ly
noo-dle
noon
noon-day
noon-time
nor-mal
nor-mal-cy
nor-mal-i-ty
nor-mal-ly
nor-mal-ize
nor-mal-ized
nor-mal-iz-ing
nor-mal-i-za-tion
north-east
north-east-ern
north-east-er
north-er
north-ern
north-ern-most
north-ern-er
north-ward
north-wards
north-ward-ly
north-west
nose
nosed
nos-ing
nose-gay
nos-tal-gia
nos-tal-gic
nos-tril
nos-trum
no-ta-ble

no-ta-rize
no-ta-rized
no-ta-riz-ing
no-ta-ri-za-tion
no-ta-ry
no-ta-ries
no-ta-tion
no-ta-tion-al
notch
notched
note
not-ed
not-ed-ly
note-wor-thy
note-wor-thi-ness
noth-ing
noth-ing-ness
no-tice
no-ticed
no-tic-ing
no-tice-a-ble
no-tice-a-bly
no-ti-fy
no-ti-fied
no-ti-fy-ing
no-ti-fi-ca-tion
no-ti-fi-er
no-tion
no-to-ri-ous
no-to-ri-ous-ly
no-to-ri-e-ty
no-trump
nought
nour-ish
nour-ish-er
nour-ish-ing
nour-ish-ment
no-va
no-vas
nov-el
nov-el-ist
nov-el-is-tic

nov-el-ette
nov-el-ty
nov-el-ties
no-ve-na
no-ve-nae
nov-ice
no-vi-tiate
no-where
no-wise
nox-ious
nox-ious-ly
noz-zle
nu-ance
nub-bin
nu-bile
nu-cle-ar
nu-cle-us
nu-cle-us-es
nu-clei
nudge
nudged
nudg-ing
nudg-er
nud-ism
nud-ist
nug-get
nui-sance
null
nul-li-ty
nul-li-ties
nul-li-fy
nul-li-fied
nul-li-fy-ing
nul-li-fi-ca-tion
nul-li-fi-er
num-ber
num-ber-er
num-ber-less
numb-skull
nu-mer-al
num-er-al-ly
nu-mer-ate
nu-mer-at-ed

nu-mer-at-ing
nu-mer-a-tion
nu-mer-a-tor
nu-mer-i-cal
nu-mer-i-cal-ly
nu-mer-ous
nu-mer-ous-ly
nu-mis-mat-ics
nu-mis-mat-ic
nu-mis-mat-i-cal
nu-mis-ma-tist
num-skull
nun-cio
nun-ci-os
nun-nery
nun-ner-ies
nup-tial
nup-tial-ly
nurse
nursed
nurs-ing
nurs-er
nurse-maid
nurs-ery
nurs-er-ies
nut
nut-ted
nut-ting
nut-crack-er
nut-hatch
nut-meg
nu-tri-ent
nu-tri-ment
nu-tri-tion
nu-tri-tion-al
nu-tri-tion-al-ly
nu-tri-tion-ist
nu-tri-tious
nu-tri-tious-ly
nu-tri-tive
nu-tri-tive-ly
nut-shell
nut-ty

nut-ti-er
nut-ti-est
nuz-zle
nuz-zled
nuz-zling
ny-lon
nymph
nym-phal
nym-pho-ma-nia
nym-pho-ma-ni-ac

O

oaf
oaf-ish
oaf-ish-ly
oak-en
oa-kum
oar
oared
oars-man
oars-men
oar-lock
oa-sis
oa-ses
oat-en
oath
oat-meal
ob-bli-ga-to
ob-bli-ga-tos
ob-du-rate
ob-du-ra-cy
ob-du-rate-ly
obe-di-ence
obe-di-ent
obe-di-ent-ly
obei-sance
obei-sant
obe-lisk
obese
obese-ness
obes-i-ty
obey

obey-er
ob-fus-cate
ob-fus-ca-ted
ob-fus-ca-ting
ob-fus-ca-tion
obit
obit-u-ary
obit-u-ar-ies
ob-ject
ob-ject-less
ob-ject-or
ob-jec-tion
ob-jec-tion-a-ble
ob-jec-tion-a-bly
ob-jec-tive
ob-jec-tive-ly
ob-jec-tive-ness
ob-jec-tiv-i-ty
ob-jur-gate
ob-jur-gat-ed
ob-jur-gat-ing
ob-jur-ga-tion
ob-jur-ga-to-ry
ob-late
ob-late-ly
ob-late-ness
ob-li-gate
ob-li-gat-ed
ob-li-gat-ing
ob-li-ga-tion
ob-lig-a-to-ry
oblige
obliged
oblig-ing
oblig-er
ob-lique
ob-liqued
ob-liqu-ing
ob-lique-ly
oblit-er-ate
oblit-er-at-ed
oblit-er-at-ing
oblit-er-a-tion

oblit-er-a-tive
obliv-i-on
obliv-i-ous
obliv-i-ous-ly
ob-long
ob-lo-quy
ob-lo-quies
ob-nox-ious
ob-nox-ious-ly
oboe
obo-ist
ob-scene
ob-scene-ly
ob-scen-ity
ob-scen-i-ties
ob-se-qui-ous
ob-se-qui-ous-ly
ob-se-quy
ob-se-quies
ob-serv-able
ob-serv-ably
ob-ser-vance
ob-ser-vant
ob-ser-vant-ly
ob-ser-va-tion
ob-ser-va-tion-al
ob-ser-va-to-ry
ob-ser-va-to-ries
ob-sess
ob-ses-sive
ob-ses-sive-ly
ob-ses-sion
ob-sid-i-an
ob-so-les-cent
ob-so-les-cence
ob-so-les-cent-ly
ob-so-lete
ob-sta-cle
ob-ste-tri-cian
ob-stet-rics
ob-stet-ric
ob-stet-ri-cal
ob-sti-nate

ob-sti-na-cy
ob-sti-na-cies
ob-sti-nat-ly
ob-strep-er-ous
ob-strep-er-ous-ly
ob-struct
ob-struc-tive
ob-struc-tor
ob-struc-tion
ob-struc-tion-ism
ob-struc-tion-ist
ob-tain
ob-tain-a-ble
ob-tain-er
ob-tain-ment
ob-trude
ob-trud-ed
ob-trud-ing
ob-trud-er
ob-tru-sion
ob-tru-sive
ob-tuse
ob-tuse-ly
ob-verse
ob-verse-ly
ob-vi-ate
ob-vi-ated
ob-vi-at-ing
ob-vi-a-tion
ob-vi-a-tor
ob-vi-ous
ob-vi-ous-ly
oc-ca-sion
oc-ca-sion-al
oc-ca-sion-al-ly
oc-ci-dent
oc-ci-den-tal
oc-clude
oc-clud-ed
oc-clud-ing
oc-clu-sive
oc-clu-sion
oc-cult

oc-cult-ism
oc-cult-ist
oc-cu-pan-cy
oc-cu-pan-cies
oc-cu-pant
oc-cu-pa-tion
oc-cu-pa-tion-al
oc-cu-pa-tion-al-ly
oc-cu-py
oc-cu-pied
oc-cu-py-ing
oc-cu-pi-er
oc-cur
oc-curred
oc-cur-ring
oc-cur-rence
oc-cur-rent
ocean
oce-an-ic
ocean-og-ra-phy
ocean-og-ra-pher
ocean-o-graph-ic
oce-lot
ocher
ocher-ous
ochery
o'clock
oc-ta-gon
oc-tag-o-nal
oc-tag-o-nal-ly
oc-ta-he-dron
oc-ta-he-drons
oc-ta-he-dra
oc-ta-he-dral
oc-tane
oc-tave
oc-ta-vo
oc-tet
oc-to-ge-nar-i-an
oc-tog-e-nary
oc-to-pus
oc-u-lar
oc-u-lar-ly

oc-u-list
odd
odd-ly
odd-ness
odd-ball
odd-i-ty
odd-i-ties
od-ic
odi-ous
odi-ous-ly
odi-um
odom-e-ter
odor
odored
odor-less
odor-ous
odor-ous-ly
odor-if-er-ous
odor-if-er-ous-ly
od-ys-sey
oe-di-pal
of-fal
off-beat
off--col-or
of-fend
of-fend-er
of-fense
of-fense-less
of-fen-sive
of-fen-sive-ly
of-fen-sive-ness
of-fer
of-fer-er
of-fer-ing
of-fer-to-ry
of-fer-to-ri-al
of-fer-to-ries
off-hand
off-hand-ed-ly
off-hand-ed-ness
of-fice
of-fice-hold-er
of-fi-cer

of-fi-cial
of-fi-cial-dom
of-fi-cial-ism
of-fi-cial-ly
of-fi-ci-ate
of-fi-ci-at-ed
of-fi-ci-at-ing
of-fi-ci-a-tion
of-fi-ci-a-tor
of-fi-cious
of-fi-cious-ly
of-fi-cious-ness
off-ing
off-set
off-set-ting
off-shoot
off-shore
off-side
off-spring
off-stage
off--the--cuff
of-ten
of-ten-times
ogle
ogled
ogler
ogling
ogre
ogre-ish
ohm
ohm-ic
ohm-age
ohm-me-ter
oil-cloth
oil-er
oil-skin
oily
oil-i-er
oil-i-est
oil-i-ness
oint-ment
okra
old

old-en
old-er
old-est
old-ish
old-ness
old--fash-ioned
old-ster
old--time
old-tim-er
old--world
ole-ag-i-nous
ole-ag-i-nous-ly
ole-ag-i-nous-ness
oleo
oleo-mar-ga-rine
ol-fac-tion
ol-fac-to-ry
ol-fac-to-ries
oli-garch
oli-gar-chic
oli-gar-chi-cal
oli-gar-chy
oli-gar-chies
oli-gop-oly
ol-ive
om-buds-man
om-buds-men
om-elet
omen
om-i-nous
om-i-nous-ly
om-i-nous-ness
omis-sion
omit
omit-ted
omit-ting
om-ni-bus
om-ni-bus-es
om-nip-o-tence
om-nip-o-tent-ly
om-ni-pres-ence
om-ni-pres-ent
om-ni-pres-ent-ly

om-ni-science
om-ni-scient
om-ni-scient-ly
om-ni-vore
om-niv-o-rous
om-niv-o-rous-ly
om-niv-o-rous-ness
onan-ism
onan-ist
onan-is-tic
once--over
on-com-ing
oner-ous
oner-ous-ly
oner-ous-ness
one-self
one--sid-ed
one--sid-ed-ly
one--sid-ed-ness
one-time
one--track
one--way
on-go-ing
on-ion
on-ion-like
on-iony
on-ion-skin
on--line
on-look-er
on-look-ing
on-ly
on-o-mato-poe-ia
on-o-mato-poe-ic
on-o-mato-po-et-ic
on-rush
on-rush-ing
on-set
on-shore
on-slaught
onto-
onus
on-ward
on-yx

oo-dles
ooze
oozed
oo-zi-er
oo-zi-est
oo-zi-ness
ooz-ing
oo-zy
opac-i-ty
opac-i-ties
opal
opal-es-cence
opal-es-cent
opaque
opaque-ly
opaque-ness
open
open-er
open-ly
open-ness
open--air
open door
open--end
open--eyed
open-hand-ed
open-hand-ed-ly
open house
open-ing
open--mind-ed
open--mind-ed-ly
open-mouthed
open ses-a-me
open-work
opera
op-er-at-ic
op-er-at-i-cal-ly
op-er-a-ble
op-er-a-bil-i-ty
op-er-a-bly
opera glass
opera house
op-er-ate
op-er-at-ed

op-er-at-ing
op-er-a-tion
op-er-a-tive
op-er-a-tive-ly
op-er-a-tor
op-er-et-ta
oph-thal-mic
oph-thal-mo-log-ic
oph-thal-mol-o-gist
oph-thal-mol-o-gy
opi-ate
opine
opined
opin-ing
opin-ion
opin-ion-at-ed
opin-ion-at-ed-ly
opi-um
opos-sum
op-po-nent
op-por-tune
op-por-tune-ly
op-por-tune-ness
op-por-tun-ism
op-por-tun-ist
op-por-tun-is-tic
op-por-tu-ni-ty
op-por-tu-ni-ties
op-pos-able
op-pos-a-bil-i-ty
op-pose
op-posed
op-pos-er
op-pos-ing
op-pos-ing-ly
op-po-site
op-po-site-ly
op-po-si-tion
op-po-si-tion-al
op-press
op-pres-si-ble
op-pres-sor
op-pres-sion

op-pres-sive
op-pres-sive-ly
op-pres-sive-ness
op-pro-bri-ous
op-pro-bri-ous-ly
op-pro-bri-um
op-tic
op-ti-cal
op-ti-cal-ly
op-ti-cian
op-tics
op-ti-mal
op-ti-mism
op-ti-mist
op-ti-mis-tic
op-ti-mis-ti-cal-ly
op-ti-mize
op-ti-mi-za-tion
op-ti-mized
op-ti-miz-ing
op-ti-mum
op-ti-ma
op-tion
op-tion-al
op-tion-al-ly
op-tom-e-trist
op-tom-e-try
op-to-met-ric
op-to-met-ri-cal
op-u-lence
op-u-lent
op-u-lent-ly
opus
opus-es
or-a-cle
orac-u-lar
orac-u-lar-i-ty
orac-u-lar-ly
oral
oral-ly
or-ange
or-ange-ade
orang-utan

orate
orat-ed
orat-ing
ora-tion
or-a-tor
or-a-tor-i-cal
or-a-tor-i-cal-ly
or-a-to-rio
or-a-to-ri-os
or-a-to-ry
or-bic-u-lar
or-bic-u-lar-i-ty
or-bic-u-lar-ly
or-bic-u-late
or-bit
or-bit-al
or-bit-er
or-chard
or-ches-tra
or-ches-tral
or-ches-tral-ly
or-ches-trate
or-ches-trat-ed
or-ches-trat-ing
or-ches-tra-tion
or-chid
or-dain
or-dain-er
or-dain-ment
or-deal
or-der
or-dered
or-der-li-ness
or-der-ly
or-di-nal
or-di-nance
or-di-nari-ly
or-di-nary
or-di-nari-ness
or-di-na-tion
ord-nance
or-dure
oreg-a-no

or-gan
or-gan-dy
or-gan-ic
  or-gan-i-cal-ly
or-gan-ism
  or-gan-is-mal
  or-gan-is-mic
or-gan-ist
or-ga-ni-za-tion
  or-gan-i-za-tion-al
or-ga-nize
  or-ga-niz-able
  or-ga-nized
  or-ga-niz-er
  or-ga-niz-ing
  or-ga-niz-a-ble
or-gasm
  or-gas-mic
or-gi-as-tic
  or-gi-as-ti-cal-ly
or-gy
  or-gies
ori-ent
Ori-en-tal
ori-en-tal-ism
  ori-en-tal-ist
  ori-en-tal-ly
ori-en-tate
  ori-en-tat-ed
  ori-en-tat-ing
ori-en-ta-tion
or-i-fice
ori-ga-mi
orig-i-nal
  orig-i-nal-i-ty
  orig-i-nal-ly
orig-i-nate
  orig-i-nat-ed
  orig-i-nat-ing
  orig-i-na-tion
  orig-i-na-tive
  orig-i-na-tive-ly
  orig-i-na-tor

or-i-son
or-na-ment
  or-na-men-tal
  or-na-men-ta-tion
or-nate
  or-nate-ly
  or-nate-ness
or-nery
  or-ner-i-ness
or-ni-thol-o-gy
  or-ni-tho-log-ic
  or-ni-tho-log-i-cal
  or-ni-thol-o-gist
oro-tund
  oro-tun-di-ty
or-phan
  or-phan-hood
or-phan-age
orth-odon-tics
  orth-odon-tic
  orth-odon-tist
or-tho-dox
  or-tho-dox-ly
  or-tho-dox-ness
or-tho-doxy
  or-tho-dox-ies
or-tho-gen-ic
or-thog-o-nal
  or-thog-o-nal-ly
or-thog-ra-phy
  or-tho-graph-ic
  or-tho-graph-i-cal
  or-thog-ra-phies
  or-thog-ra-pher
or-tho-pe-dic
  or-tho-pe-dics
  or-tho-pe-dist
os-cil-late
  os-cil-lat-ed
  os-cil-lat-ing
  os-cil-la-tion
  os-cil-la-tor
  os-cil-la-to-ry

os-cil-lo-scope
os-cu-late
  os-cu-lat-ed
  os-cu-lat-ing
  os-cu-la-tion
  os-cu-la-to-ry
os-mi-um
os-mose
  os-mosed
  os-mos-ing
os-mo-sis
  os-mot-ic
  os-mot-i-cal-ly
os-prey
os-si-fy
  os-si-fied
  os-si-fi-er
  os-si-fy-ing
os-ten-si-ble
  os-ten-si-bly
os-ten-sive
  os-ten-sive-ness
os-ten-ta-tion
os-ten-ta-tious
  os-ten-ta-tious-ly
os-te-op-a-thy
  os-teo-path
  os-teo-path-ic
  os-teo-path-i-cal-ly
os-tra-cism
os-tra-cize
  os-tra-cized
  os-tra-ciz-ing
os-trich
oth-er
  oth-er-ness
oth-er-wise
oth-er-world
  oth-er-world-ly
oti-ose
  oti-ose-ly
  oti-os-i-ty
ot-ter

ot-to-man
ought
ounce
our-self
our-selves
oust-er
out-bid
  out-bid-den
  out-bid-ding
  out-bid-der
out-board
out-bound
out-brave
  out-braved
  out-brav-ing
out-break
out-build-ing
out-burst
out-cast
out-come
out-cry
  out-cries
out-dat-ed
out-dis-tance
  out-dis-tanced
  out-dis-tanc-ing
out-do
  out-did
  out-do-ing
  out-done
out-door
out-er
out-er-most
outer space
out-face
  out-faced
  out-fac-ing
out-field
  out-field-er
out-flank
out-fox
out-grow
  out-grew

out-grow-ing
out-grown
out-growth
out-guess
out-ing
out-land-ish
  out-land-ish-ly
out-last
out-law
  out-law-ry
out-lay
  out-laid
  out-lay-ing
out-let
out-line
  out-lined
  out-lin-ing
out-live
  out-lived
  out-liv-ing
out-look
out-ly-ing
out-mod-ed
out-num-ber
out--of--date
out-post
out-put
out-rage
  out-raged
  out-rag-ing
out-ra-geous
  out-ra-geous-ly
out-range
  out-ranged
  out-rang-ing
out-rank
out-rig-ger
out-right
out-run
  out-ran
  out-run-ning
out-set
out-shine

out-shin-ing
out-shone
out-side
out-sid-er
out-smart
out-spo-ken
  out-spo-ken-ly
out-stand-ing
  out-stand-ing-ly
out-strip
  out-stripped
  out-strip-ping
out-ward
  out-ward-ly
  out-wards
out-weigh
out-wit
  out-wit-ted
  out-wit-ting
ova
oval
  oval-ly
ova-ry
  ovar-i-an
  ova-ries
ovate
ova-tion
ov-en
over
over-act
over-age
over-all
over-awe
  over-awed
  over-aw-ing
over-bear-ing
  over-bear-ing-ly
over-blown
over-board
over-build
  over-build-ing
  over-built
over-cast

over-charge
 over-charged
 over-charg-ing
over-coat
over-come
 over-came
over-con-fi-dence
 over-con-fi-dent
over-do
 over-did
 over-do-ing
 over-done
over-dose
 over-dos-age
over-draft
over-draw
 over-draw-ing
 over-drawn
 over-drew
over-drive
over-due
over-em-pha-sis
 over-em-pha-size
 over-em-pha-sized
 over-em-pha-sizing
over-es-ti-mate
 over-es-ti-mat-ed
 over-es-ti-mat-ing
 over-es-ti-ma-tion
over-flow
 over-flowed
 over-flowing
 over-flown
over-gen-er-ous
over-grow
 over-grew
 over-grow-ing
 over-grown
over-growth
over-hand
 over-hand-ed
over-hang
 over-hang-ing

over-hung
over-haul
 over-haul-ing
over-head
over-land
over-lap
 over-lapped
 over-lap-ping
over-lay
 over-laid
 over-lay-ing
over-look
over-lord
over-ly
over-much
over-night
over-pass
over-play
over-pow-er
 over-pow-er-ing
over-reach
over-ride
 over-rid-den
 over-rid-ing
 over-rode
over-rule
 over-ruled
 over-rul-ing
over-run
over-seas
over-see
 over-saw
 over-see-ing
 over-seen
over-seer
over-shad-ow
over-shoe
over-shoot
 over-shoot-ing
 over-shot
over-sight
over-sim-pli-fy
 -sim-pli-fi-ca-tion

over-sim-pli-fied
over-sim-pli-fy-ing
over-size
over-sleep
 over-sleep-ing
 over-slept
over-spread
 over-spread-ing
over-stay
over-step
 over-stepped
 over-step-ping
over-strung
over-stuff
overt
 overt-ly
over-tax
over--the--coun-ter
over-time
over-tone
over-ture
over-turn
over-view
over-ween-ing
 over-ween-ing-ly
over-weight
over-whelm
 over-whelm-ing
over-wrought
ovi-duct
ovip-a-rous
 ovip-ar-ous-ly
ovoid
 ovoi-dal
ovule
 ovu-lar
ovum
ova
owe
 owed
 ow-ing
owl-ish
own-er

ox-al-ic ac-id
ox-bow
ox-en
ox-ford
ox-i-da-tion
  ox-i-da-tive
  ox-i-dant
ox-ide
ox-i-dize
  ox-i-dized
  ox-i-diz-ing
ox-y-a-cet-y-lene
ox-y-gen
ox-y-gen-ate
  ox-y-gen-at-ed
  ox-y-gen-at-ing
  ox-y-gen-a-tion
oys-ter
ozone

P

pab-u-lum
pace
  paced
  pac-ing
  pac-er
pace-mak-er
pa-cif-ic
pa-cif-i-ca-tion
  pa-cif-i-ca-tor
  pa-cif-i-ca-to-ry
pac-i-fi-er
pac-i-fism
  pac-i-fist
pac-i-fy
  pac-i-fied
  pac-i-fy-ing
pack-age
  pack-ag-er
pack-er
pack-et
pack-ing

pad
  pad-ded
  pad-ding
pad-dle
pad-dock
pad-dy
  pad-dies
pad-lock
pae-an
  pe-an
pe-gan
  pe-gan-ism
pag-eant
  pag-ent-ry
pag-i-nate
  pag-i-nat-ed
  pag-i-nat-ing
pa-go-da
pains-tak-ing
  pains-tak-ing-ly
paint-er
pais-ley
pa-ja-mas
pal-ace
pal-at-a-ble
  pal-at-a-bil-i-ty
  pal-at-a-bly
pal-ate
pa-la-tial
  pa-la-tial-ly
pal-a-tiner
  pa-lat-i-nate
pa-lav-er
pale
pa-le-on-tol-o-gy
  pa-le-on-to-log-ic
  pa-le-on-to-log-i-cal
pal-ette
pal-imp-sest
pal-in-drome
pal-ing
pal-i-sade
  pal-i-sad-ed

pal-i-sad-ing
pal-la-di-um
pall-bear-er
pal-let
pal-li-ate
  pal-li-at-ed
  pal-li-at-ing
  pal-li-a-tion
pal-lid
pal-lor
palm
  pal-ma-ceous
pal-mate
  pal-mate-ly
palm-er
palm-is-try
  palm-ist
pal-o-mi-no
  pal-o-mi-nos
pal-pa-ble
  pal-pa-bil-i-ty
  pal-pa-bly
pal-pate
  pal-pat-ed
  pal-pat-ing
pal-ter
  pal-ter-er
pal-try
  pal-tri-er
  pal-tri-est
pam-pas
  pam-pe-an
pam-per
  pam-per-er
pam-phlet
pan-a-ce-a
  pan-a-ce-an
pa-nache
pan-cake
pan-cre-as
  pan-cre-at-ic
pan-dem-ic
pan-de-mo-ni-um

pan-der
pan-el
  pan-eled
  pan-el-ing
pan-el-ist
pang
pan-ic
  pan-icked
  pan-ick-ing
pan-nier
  pan-ier
pan-ta-loon
pan-the-ism
  pan-the-is-tic
pan-the-on
pan-ther
pan-ties
pan-to-mime
  pan-to-mimed
pan-try
  pan-tries
pant-suit
pant-y-hose
pa-pa
pa-pa-cy
  pa-pa-cies
pa-pal
pa-per
  pa-per-er
  pa-pery
pa-per-back
pa-pil-la
  pa-pil-pae
pa-poose
pap-ri-ka
pa-py-rus
par-a-ble
par-a-digm
  par-a-dig-mat-ic
par-a-dise
  par-a-di-si-a-cal
par-a-dox
  par-a-dox-i-cal

par-af-fin
par-a-gon
par-a-graph
  par-a-graph-er
par-a-keet
par-al-lax
  par-al-al-lac-tic
par-al-lel
  par-al-leled
  par-al-lel-ing
par-al-lel-o-gram
pa-ral-y-sis
  pa-ral-y-ses
  par-a-lyt-ic
par-a-lyze
  par-a-lyzed
  par-a-lyz-ing
par-a-me-cium
par-a-med-ic
par-am-e-ter
par-a-mount
  par-a-mount-cy
  par-a-mount-ly
par-amour
para-noia
  para-noid
par-a-pet
par-a-pher-nal-ia
para-phrase
  para-phrased
  para-phras-ing
para-ple-gia
  para-ple-gic
para-psy-chol-o-gy
par-a-site
  par-a-sit-ic
para-sol
para-thi-on
para-troop-er
par-ty-phoid
par-boil
par-cel
  par-celed

par-cel-ing
parch-ment
par-don
  par-don-a-ble
  par-don-a-bly
pare
  pared
  par-ing
par-e-gor-ic
par-ent
  pa-ren-tal
par-ent-age
pa-ren-the-sis
pa-re-sis
  pa-ret-ic
par-fait
pa-ri-ah
par-i-mu-tu-el
par-ish
  pa-rish-ion-er
par-i-ty
par-ka
par-lance
par-lay
  par-lay-ed
  par-lay-ing
par-ley
  par-leyed
  par-ley-ing
par-lia-ment
par-lia-men-tar-ian
par-lia-men-ta-ry
par-lor
pa-ro-chi-al
par-o-dy
  par-o-dies
  par-o-died
pa-role
  pa-roled
par-ot-id
par-ox-ysm
  par-ox-ys-mal
par-quet

par-queted
par-quet-ing
par-quet-ry
par-rot
par-rot-like
par-roty
parse
par-si-mo-ny
par-si-mo-ni-ous
par-si-mo-ni-ous-ly
pars-ley
pars-nip
par-son-age
par-take
par-took
par-tak-en
part-ed
par-the-no-gen-e-sis
par-tial
par-tial-ly
par-tial-i-ty
par-tial-i-ties
par-tic-i-pant
par-tic-i-pate
par-tic-i-pat-ed
par-tic-i-pat-ing
par-ti-cip-i-al
par-ti-ci-ple
par-ti-cle
par-ti--col-ored
par-tic-u-lar
par-tic-u-lar-ly
par-tic-u-lar-i-ties
par-tic-u-lar-ize
par-tic-u-lar-ized
par-tic-u-lar-iz-ing
par-tic-u-late
part-ing
par-ti-san
par-ti-san-ship
par-tite
par-ti-tion
par-ti-tive

part-ly
part-ner
part-ner-ship
par-tridge
par-tridg-es
part--time
par-tu-ri-ent
par-tu-ri-tion
par-ty
par-ties
par-ve-nu
pas-chal
pa-sha
pass-able
pass-ably
pas-sen-ger
pass-er-by
pass-ers-by
pass-ing
pas-sion
pas-sion-ies
pas-sion-ate
pas-sion-ate-ly
pas-sive
pas-ta
paste
pas-ted
pas-ting
paste-board
pas-tel
pas-teur-ize
pas-teur-ized
pas-teur-iz-ing
pas-teur-i-za-tion
pas-tille
pas-time
pas-tor
pas-to-ral
pas-to-ral-ly
pas-tor-ate
pas-tra-mi
past-ry
pas-tries

pas-ture
pas-ty
past-i-er
past-i-est
pat-ent
pa-ten-cy
pat-ent-ly
pat-en-tee
pat-er-nal
pat-ter-nal-ly
pa-ter-nal-ism
pa-ter-ni-ty
pa-thet-ic
path-find-er
pa-thol-o-gy
pa-thos
pa-tience
pa-tient
pa-tient-ly
pat-i-na
pa-tio
pa-tios
pa-tri-arch
pa-tri-ar-chy
pa-tri-ar-chies
pa-tri-cian
pat-ri-mo-ny
pat-ri-mo-nies
pa-tri-ot
pa-tri-ot-ic
pa-tri-ot-ism
pa-trol
pa-trolled
pa-trol-ling
pa-trol-man
pa-trol-men
pa-tron
pa-tron-ess
pa-tron-age
pa-tron-ize
pa-tron-ized
pa-tron-iz-ing
pa-tron-iz-ing-ly

pat-ro-nym-ic
pat-sy
  pat-sies
pat-ter
pat-tern
  pat-terned
pat-ty
  pat-ties
pau-ci-ty
paunch
pau-per
  pau-per-ism
pause
  paused
  paus-ing
pa-vil-ion
pawn
  pawn-er
pawn-bro-ker
pay-a-ble
pay-off
peace
peace-able
  peace-ably
peace-ful
  peace-ful-ly
peach
pea-cock
peak-ed
pea-nut
pearl
  pear-ly
peas-ant
  peas-ant-ly
peaty
peb-ble
pe-can
pec-ca-dil-lo
  pec-ca-dil-loes
pec-ca-dil-los
peck-er
pec-tin
pec-to-ral

pec-u-late
  pec-u-lat-ed
  pec-u-lat-ing
pe-cu-liar
  pe-cu-liar-ly
  pe-cu-li-ar-i-ty
  pe-cu-li-ar-i-ties
pe-cu-ni-ary
ped-a-go-gue
ped-a-go-gy
ped-al
  ped-aled
  ped-al-ing
ped-dle
ped-es-tal
pe-des-tri-an
  pe-des-tri-an-ism
pe-di-at-ric
  pe-di-at-rics
pe-di-a-tri-cian
  pe-di-at-rist
ped-i-cure
  ped-i-cur-ist
ped-i-gree
  ped-i-greed
ped-i-ment
  ped-i-men-tal
  ped-i-ment-ed
pe-dom-e-ter
peep-hole
peer
peer-less
  peer-less-ly
peeve
  peeved
peev-ing
pee-vish
  pee-vish-ly
pee-wee
pe-jo-ra-tive
  pe-jo-ra-tive-ly
pe-koe
pel-let

pell--mell
pel-lu-cid
  pel-lu-cid-i-ty
  pel-lu-cid-ly
pelt-er
  pelt-ry
pel-vis
  pel-vis-es
  pel-ves
  pel-vic
pem-mi-can
  pem-i-can
pe-nal
pe-nal-ize
  pe-nal-ized
  pe-nal-iz-ing
pen-al-ty
  pen-al-ties
pen-ance
pen-chant
pen-cil
pend-ant
pend-ent
  pend-en-cy
  pend-ent-ly
pend-ing
pen-du-lous
  pen-du-lous-ly
pen-du-lum
pen-a-tra-ble
  pen-a-tra-bil-i-ty
  pen-a-tra-bly
pen-e-trate
  pen-e-trat-ed
  pen-e-trat-ing
pen-e-tra-tion
pen-i-cil-lin
pen-in-su-la
  pen-in-su-lar
pe-nis
pen-i-tent
  pen-i-tence
  pen-i-ten-tial

pen-i-ten-tia-ry
  pen-i-ten-tia-ries
pen-knife
  pen-knives
pen-man-ship
pen-nant
pen-non
pen-ny
  pen-nies
pen-ny an-te
pe-nol-o-gy
  pe-no-log-i-cal
  pe-nol-o-gist
pen-sion
pen-sive
  pen-sive-ly
pen-ta-gon
  pen-tag-o-nal
  pen-tag-o-nal-ly
pen-tam-e-ter
pen-tath-lon
pent-up
pe-nult
  pe-nul-ti-ma
  pe-nul-ti-mate
pe-nu-ri-ous
  pe-nu-ri-ous-ly
pen-u-ry
pe-on
  pe-on-age
pe-o-ny
  pe-on-ies
peo-ple
pep
  pepped
  pep-ping
pep-per
pep-pery
pep-py
  pep-pi-er
  pep-pi-est
pep-sin
pep-tic

per-am-bu-late
per-am-bu-la-tor
per an-num
per-cale
per cap-i-ta
per-ceive
  per-ceived
  per-ceiv-ing
  per-ceiv-a-ble
per-cent
  per-cent-age
per-cen-tile
per-cep-ti-ble
  per-cep-ti-bil-i-ty
  per-cep-ti-bly
per-cep-tion
  per-cep-tion-al
  per-cep-tu-al
  per-cep-tu-al-ly
perch
per-co-late
  per-co-lat-ed
  per-co-lat-ing
  per-co-la-tion
per-co-la-tor
per-cus-sion
  per-cus-sion-ist
per di-em
per-di-tion
per-e-gri-nate
pe-remp-to-ry
  pe-remp-to-ri-ly
pe-ren-ni-al
  pe-ren-ni-al-ly
per-fec-tion
  per-fec-tion-ist
per-fect-ly
per-fi-dy
  per-fid-i-ous
  per-fid-i-ous-ly
per-fo-rate
  per-fo-rat-ed
per-force

per-form
  per-form-a-ble
  per-form-er
per-for-mance
per-fume
  per-fumed
per-func-to-ry
  per-func-to-ri-ly
per-haps
per-i-gee
  per-i-ge-al
  per-i-ge-an
peri-he-li-on
  peri-he-lia
per-il
  per-il-ous
  per-il-ous-ly
pe-rim-e-ter
  per-i-met-ic
  per-i-met-ri-cal
pe-ri-od
pe-ri-od-ic
  pe-ri-o-dic-i-ty
pe-ri-od-i-cal
  pe-ri-od-i-cal-ly
pe-riph-ery
  pe-riph-er-ies
  pe-riph-er-al
  pe-riph-er-al-ly
per-i-phrase
peri-scope
  peri-scopic
  peri-scop-i-cal
per-ish
per-ish-able
  per-ish-abil-i-ty
  per-ish-ably
peri-stal-sis
  peri-stal-ses
  peri-style
peri-to-ne-um
  peri-to-ne-ums
  peri-to-nea

peri-to-ne-al
peri-to-ni-tis
peri-wig
peri-win-kle
per-jure
  per-jured
  per-jur-ing
  per-jur-er
per-ju-ry
  per-ju-ries
perky
  perk-i-er
  perk-i-est
per-ma-nent
per-me-able
  per-me-abil-i-ty
  per-me-ably
per-mis-si-ble
  per-mis-si-bil-i-ty
  per-mis-si-bly
per-mis-sion
per-mis-sive
  per-mis-sive-ly
per-mu-ta-tion
per-ni-cious
  per-ni-cious-ly
per-ora-tion
per-ox-ide
  per-ox-id-ed
  per-ox-id-ing
per-pen-dic-u-lar
  per-pen-dic-u-lar-ly
per-pe-trate
  per-pe-trat-ed
  per-pe-trat-ing
  per-pe-tra-tion
  per-pe-tra-tor
per-pet-u-al
  per-pet-u-al-ly
per-pet-u-ate
  per-pet-u-at-ed
  per-pet-u-at-ing
  per-pet-u-a-tion

per-pet-ua-tor
per-pe-tu-ity
  per-pe-tu-ities
per-plex
  per-plexed
  per-plex-ing
  per-plex-ing-ly
  per-plex-ed-ly
  per-plex-i-ty
  per-plex-i-ties
per-qui-site
per-se-cute
  per-se-cut-ed
  per-se-cut-ing
  per-se-cu-tive
  per-se-cu-tor
  per-se-cu-tion
per-se-vere
  per-se-vered
  per-se-ver-ing
  per-sse-ver-ance
  per-se-ver-ing-ly
per-si-flage
per-sim-mon
per-sist
  per-sist-ence
  per-sis-ten-cy
per-sist-ent
  per-sist-ent-ly
per-snick-e-ty
per-son
per-son-age
per-son-al-i-ty
  per-son-al-i-ties
per-son-al-ize
  per-son-al-ized
  per-son-al-iz-ing
per-son-al-ly
per-so-na non gra-ta
per-son-ate
  per-son-at-ed

  per-son-at-ing
  per-son-a-tion
  per-son-a-tor
per-son-i-fy
  per-son-i-fied
  per-son-i-fy-ing
  per-son-i-fi-ca-tion
  per-son-i-fi-er
per-son-nel
per-spec-tive
  per-spec-tive-ly
per-spi-ca-cious
  per-spi-ca-cious-ly
  per-spi-cac-i-ty
per-spi-cu-i-ty
  per-spic-u-ous
  per-spic-u-ous-ly
per-spi-ra-tion
per-spire
  per-spired
  per-spiring
per-suade
  per-suad-ed
  per-suad-ing
  per-suad-a-ble
  per-suad-er
per-sua-sion
per-sua-sive
  per-sua-sive-ly
  per-sua-sive-ness
pert
  pert-ly
  pert-ness
per-tain
per-ti-na-cious
  per-ti-na-cious-ly
  per-ti-nac-i-ty
per-ti-nent
  per-ti-nence
  per-ti-nen-cy
  per-ti-nent-ly
per-turb
  per-turb-a-ble

per-tur-ba-tion
pe-ruke
pe-ruse
pe-rused
pe-rus-ing
pe-rus-al
pe-rus-er
per-vade
per-vad-ed
per-vad-ing
per-vad-er
per-va-sion
per-va-sive
per-va-sive-ly
per-verse
per-verse-ly
per-verse-ness
per-ver-si-ty
per-ver-sion
per-vert
per-vi-ous
per-vi-ous-ness
pes-si-mism
pes-si-mist
pes-si-mist
pes-si-mis-tic
pes-si-mis-ti-cal-ly
pes-ter
pest-hole
pest-i-cide
pes-tif-er-ous
pes-tif-er-ous-ly
per-ti-lence
pes-ti-len-tial
pes-ti-lent
pes-ti-lent-ly
pes-tle
pes-tled
pes-tling
pet-al
pet-aled
pet-cock
pe-ter

pet-i-ole
pe-tite
pe-tite-ness
pet-it four
pe-ti-tion
pe-ti-tion-ary
pe-ti-tion-er
pet-rel
pet-ri-fy
pet-ri-fied
pet-ri-fy-ing
pe-tri-fac-tion
pe-tro-chem-is-try
pe-tro-chem-i-cal
pet-rol
pet-ro-la-tum
pe-trol-eum
pet-ti-coat
pet-tish
pet-tish-ly
pet-tish-ness
pet-ty
pet-u-lant
pet-u-lance
pet-u-lan-cy
pet-u-lant-ly
pe-tu-nia
pew-ter
pey-o-te
pey-o-tes
pha-lanx
pha-lanx-es
pha-lang-es
pal-lus
pal-li
pahl-lus-es
phal-lic
phan-tasm
phan-tas-ma
phan-tas-mal
phan-tas-mic
phan-tas-ma-go-ria
phan-tas-ma-gor-ic

phan-ta-sy
phan-ta-sies
phan-tom
phar-aoh
phar-ma-ceu-ti-cal
phar-ma-cue-tic
phar-ma-cue-tics
phar-ma-cist
phar-ma-col-o-gy
phar-ma-co-log-ic
phar-ma-co-log-i-ca
phar-ma-col-o-gist
phar-ma-co-poe-ia
phar-ma-co-poe-ial
phar-ma-cy
phar-ma-cies
phar-ynx
pha-ryn-ges
pha-ryn-ge-al
pha-ryn-gal
phase
phased
phas-ing
pha-sic
pheas-ant
phe-no-bar-bi-tal
phe-nol
phe-nol-ic
phe-nom-e-non
phe-nom-e-na
phe-nom-e-nons
phe-nom-e-nal
phe-nom-e-nal-ly
phi-al
phi-lan-der
phi-lan-der-er
phi-lan-thro-py
phi-lan-thro-pies
phil-an-throp-ic
phil-an-throp-i-cal
phil-an-thro-pist
phi-late-ly
phil-a-tel-ic

phil-a-tel-i-cal
phi-lat-e-list
phil-har-mon-ic
phil-o-den-dron
  phil-o-den-drons
  phil-o-den-dra
phi-log-o-gy
  phi-lol-o-gist
  phil-lol-o-ger
  phil-o-lo-gi-an
  phil-o-log-i-cal
  phil-o-log-ic
  phil-o-log-i-cal-ly
phi-los-o-pher
phil-o-soph-i-cal
  phil-o-soph-ic
  phil-o-soph-i-cal-ly
phi-los-o-phize
  phil-los-o-phized
  phil-los-o-phiz-ing
  phil-los-o-phiz-er
phi-los-o-phy
  phi-los-o-phies
phil-ter
  phil-tered
  phil-ter-ing
phle-bi-tis
  phle-bit-ic
phle-bot-o-my
  phle-bot-o-mist
phlegm
phleg-mat-ic
  phleg-mat-i-cal
  phleg-mat-i-cal-ly
phlox
pho-bia
  pho-bic
phoe-be
phoe-nix
phone
  phoned
  phon-ing
pho-neme

pho-ne-mic
pho-net-ic
  pho-net-ics
  pho-net-i-cal
  pho-net-i-cal-ly
phon-ic
phon-ics
pho-no-graph
  pho-no-graph-ic
pho-nol-o-gy
  pho-no-log-ies
  pho-no-log-ic
  pho-no-log-i-cal
  pho-no-log-i-cal-ly
  pho-nol-o-gist
pho-ny
  pho-ni-er
  pho-ni-est
  pho-nies
  pho-ni-ness
phos-phate
phos-pho-res-cence
  phos-pho-resce
  phos-pho-resced
  phos-pho-resc-ing
  phos-pho-res-cent
phos-pho-rus
pho-to
  pho-tos
pho-to-copy
  pho-to-cop-ies
  pho-to-cop-ied
  pho-to-cop-y-ing
pho-to-e-lec-tric
pho-to-en-grav-ing
  pho-to-en-grave
  pho-to-en-graved
  pho-to-en-grav-er
pho-to-flash
pho-to-gen-ic
pho-to-graph
  pho-to-graph-er
pho-tog-ra-phy

pho-to-graph-ic
pho-to-graph-i-cal
pho-to-gra-vure
pho-to--off-set
pho-to-stat
  pho-to-stat-ed
  pho-to-stat-ing
  pho-to-stat-ic
pho-to-syn-the-sis
phrase
  phrased
  phras-ing
  phras-al
phrase-ol-o-gy
phre-net-ic
phre-nol-o-gy
  phre-nol-o-gist
phy-lac-tery
  phy-lac-ter-ies
phy-log-e-ny
  phy-lo-gen-e-sis
  phy-lo-ge-net-ic
  phy-lo-gen-ic
  phy-log-e-nist
phy-lu
phys-ic
  phys-icked
  phys-ick-ing
phys-i-cal
  phys-i-cal-ly
phy-si-cian
phys-ics
  phys-i-cist
phys-i-og-no-my
  phys-i-og-no-mies
  phys-i-og-nom-ic
  phys-i-og-nom-i-cal
  phys-i-og-no-mist
phys-i-og-ra-phy
  phys-i-o-graph-ic
  phys-i-o-graph-i-cal
phys-i-ol-o-gy
  phys-i-o-log-ic

phys-i-o-log-i-cal
phys-i-o-log-i-cal-ly
phys-i-ol-o-gist
phys-i-o-ther-a-py
phy-sique
pi-a-nis-si-mo
pi-an-ist
pi-ano
pia-nos
pi-ano-forte
pi-az-za
pi-ca
pic-a-dor
pic-a-resque
pic-a-yune
pic-a-yun-ish
pic-ca-lil-li
pic-co-lo
pic-co-los
pic-co-lo-list
pick-ax
picked
pick-er-el
pick-et
pick-et-er
pick-ing
pick-le
pick-led
pick-ling
pick-pock-et
pick-up
picky
pick-i-er
pick-i-est
pic-nic
pic-nicked
pic-nick-ing
pic-nick-er
pic-to-ri-al
pic-to-ri-al-ly
pic-ture
pic-tured
pic-tur-ing

pic-tur-esque
pic-tur-esque-ly
pid-dle
pid-dled
pid-dling
pid-gin
pie-bald
piece
piec-er
piece-meal
piece-work
piece-worker
pied
pier
pierce
pierc-ed
pierc-ing
pierc-ing-ly
pi-etism
pi-etis-tic
pi-etis-ti-cal
pi-ety
pi-eties
pif-fle
pig
pigged
pig-ging
pi-geon
pe-geon-hole
pi-geon-holed
pi-geon-hol-ing
pi-geon--toed
pig-gish
pig-ish-ly
pig-gis-ness
pig-head-ed
pig-head-ed-ly
pig-head-ed-ness
pig-ment
pig-men-tary
pig-men-ta-tion
pig-pen
pig-skin

pig-sty
pig-sties
pig-tail
pike
piked
pik-ing
pik-er
pi-las-ter
pil-chard
pile
piled
pil-ing
pil-fer
pil-fer-age
pil-fer-er
pil-grim
pil-grim-age
pil-grim-aged
pil-grim-ag-ing
pil-lage
pil-laged
pil-lag-ing
pil-lag-er
pil-lar
pill-box
pil-lion
pil-lo-ry
pil-lo-ries
pil-lo-ry-ing
pil-low
pil-low-case
pi-lot
pi-lot-age
pi-lot-less
pi-lot-house
pi-men-to
pi-men-tos
pim-ple
pim-pled
pim-ply
pin
pinned
pin-ning

pin-afore
pince-nez
pin-cers
pinch
pinch-er
pinch-beck
pin-cush-ion
pin-dling
pine
pine-like
piney
pin-ing
pi-ne-al
pine-ap-ple
pin-feath-er
pin-feath-ered
pin-feath-ery
pin-fold
pin-head
pin-head-ed
pin-hole
pin-ion
pink-eye
pink-ie
pinko
pink-os
pink-oes
pin-na
pin-nas
pin-nae
pin-nal
pin-na-cle
pin-na-cled
pin-na-cling
pi-nate
pin-nate-ly
pin-na-tion
pi-noch-le
pi-noc-le
pin-point
pin-prick
pin-set-ter
pin-tail

pin-tailed
pin-tle
pin-to
pin-tos
pin-up
pin-wheel
pin-worm
pi-o-neer
pi-ous
pi-ous-ly
pi-ous-ness
pip
pipped
pip-ping
pipe-line
pipe-lined
pipe-lin-ing
pip-er
pip-ing
pip-it
pip-pin
pip-squek
pi-quant
pi-quan-cy
pi-quant-ly
pique
piqued
pi-quing
pi-ra-cy
pi-ra-cies
pi-ra-nha
pi-rate
pi-rat-ed
pi-rat-ing
pi-rat-i-cal
pi-rat-i-cal-ly
pi-roque
pir-ou-ette
pir-ou-et-ted
pir-ou-et-ting
pi-sci-cul-ture
pis-ta-chio
pis-ta-chi-os

pis-til
pis-til-late
pis-tol
pis-toled
pis-tol-ing
pis-ton
pit
pit-ted
pit-ting
pitch--blake
pitch-blend
pitch-er
pitch-fork
pitchy
pitch-i-er
pitch-i-est
pit-e-ous
pit-e-ous-ly
pit-fall
pith
pith-i-er
pith-i-est
pith-i-ly
piti-a-ble
piti-anle-ness
piti-a-bly
piti-ful
piti-ful-ly
piti-ful-ness
piti-less
piti-less-ly
pit-man
pit-men
pit-tance
pi-tu--tar-ies
pity
pit-ies
pit-ied
pit-y-ing
pit-y-ing-ly
piv-ot
piv-ot-al
piv-ot-al-ly

pix-i-lat-ed
pixy
  pix-ie
  pix-ies
piz-za
piz-ze-ria
piz-zi-ca-to
place-a-ble
  plac-a-bil-i-ty
  plac-a-bly
plac-ard
pla-cate
  pla-cat-ed
  pla-cat-ing
  pla-ca-tion
  pla-ca-tive
  pla-ca-to-ry
place
  placed
  plac-ing
pla-ce-bo
  pla-ce-bos
  pla-ce-boes
place-ment
pla-cen-ta
  pla-cen-tas
  pla-cen-tae
  pla-cen-tal
plac-er
plac-id
  pla-cid-i-ty
  plac-id-ness
pla-gal
pla-gia-rism
  pla-gia-rized
  pla-gia-riz-ing
  pla-gia-riz-er
pla-gia-ry
  pla-gia-ries
plaque
  plaqued
  pla-quing
  pla-quer

pla-guy
  pla-guey
  pla-gui-ly
plaid
plain
  plain-ly
  plain-ness
plain-song
plain-spo-ken
plain-tiff
plain-tive
  plain-tive-ly
plait
  plait-ing
plan
  planned
  plan-ning
  plan-less
  plan-ner
plane
  planed
  plan-ing
plan-er
plan-et
plan-e-tar-i-um
  plan-e-tar-i-ums
  plan-e-tar-ia
plan-e-tary
plan-e-toid
plan-ish
  plan-ish-er
plank-ing
plank-ton
  plank-ton-ic
plant
  plant-able
  plant-like
plan-tain
plan-ta-tion
plant-er
plaque
plasm
plas-ma

plas-mic
plas-mat-ic
plas-ter
  plas-ter-er
  plas-ter-ing
  plas-ter-work
plas-ter-board
plas-tered
plas-tic
  plas-ti-cal-ly
  plas-tic-i-ty
  plas-ti-ciz-er
plat
  plat-ted
  plat-ting
plate
  plat-ed
  plat-ing
  plat-er
pla-teau
  pla-teaus
  pla-teaux
plate-ful
  plate-fuls
plate-let
plat-form
plat-i-num
plat-i-tude
  plat-i-tu-di-nal
  plat-i-tu-di-nous
plat-i-tu-di-nize
  plat-i-tu-di-nized
  plat-i-tu-di-niz-ing
pla-ton-ic
  pla-ton-i-cal-ly
pla-toon
plat-ter
platy-pus
  platy-pus-es
  platy-pi
plau-dut
plau-si-ble
  plau-si-bil-i-ty

plau-si-bly
play-act
play-act-ing
play-back
play-bill
play-boy
play-er
play-ful
play-ful-ly
play-ful-ness
play-go-er
play-ground
play-house
play-hous-es
play-let
play-mate
play--off
play-pen
play-thing
play-time
play-wright
pla-za
plea
plead
plead-ed
plead-ing
plead-a-ble
plead-er
pleas-ant
pleas-ant-ly
pleas-ant-ness
pleas-ant-ry
pleas-an-trioes
please
pleased
pleas-ing
pleas-ing-ly
pleas-ing-ness
plea-sur-a-ble
plea-sur-able-ness
plea-sur-ably
pleas-ure
pleat

pleat-ed
pleat-er
plebe
ple-be-ian
pleb-i-scite
pledge
pledged
pledg-ing
pledg-ee
pledg-er
ple-na-ry
pleni-po-ten-tia-ry
pleni-po-ten-tia-ries
plen-i-tude
plen-te-ous
plen-te-ous-ly
plen-ti-ful
plen-ti-ful-ly
plen-ty
pleth-o-ra
ple-thor-ic
pleu-ra
pleu-rae
pleu-ral
pleu-ri-sy
pleu-rit-ic
plex-us
plex-us-es
pli-able
pli-a-bil-i-ty
pli-a-ble-ness
pli-a-bly
pli-ant
pli-an-cy
pli-ant-ness
pli-ant-ly
pli-ca-tion
pli-ers
plight
plink
plod
plod-ded
plod-ding

plod-der
plop
plopped
plop-ping
plot
plot-ted
plot-ting
plot-ter
plow
plow-a-ble
plow-er
plow-man
plow-share
pluck
pluck-er
plucky
pluck-i-er
pluck-i-est
pluck-i-ly
pluck-i-ness
plug
plugged
plug-ging
plug-ger
plum-age
plumb-er
plumb-ing
plume
plumed
plum-ing
plume-like
plumy
plum-i-er
plum-i-est
plum-met
plump
plump-er
plump-ly
plump-ness
plun-der
plun-der-er
plun-der-ous
plunge

plunged
plung-ing
plung-er
plunk-er
plu-ral
plu-ral-ly
plu-ral-ize
plu-ral-ized
plu-ral-iz-ing
plu-ral-ism
plu-ral-ist
plu-ral-is-tic
plu-ral-i-ty
plu-ral-i-ties
plush
plush-i-ness
plushy
plush-i-er
plush-i-est
plu-toc-ra-cy
plu-toc-ra-cies
plu-ta-crat
plu-to-cart-ic
plu-to-ni-um
plu-vi-al
ply
plied
ply-ing
ply-wood
pneu-mat-ic
pneu-mat-i-cal-ly
pneu-mat-ics
pneu-mo-nia
pneu-mon-ic
poach
poach-er
pock-et
pock-et-book
pock-et-ful
pock-et-knife
pock-et-knives
pock-mark
pock-marked

pod
pod-ded
pod-ding
pod-like
podgy
podg-i-er
podg-i-est
po-di-trist
po-di-a-try
po-di-um
po-dia
po-di-ums
po-esy
po-esies
po-et
po-et-ess
po-et-ize
po-et-ized
po-et-iz-ing
po-et-iz-er
po-et lau-re-ate
po-ets lau-re-ate
po-et-ry
po-go
po-grom
poi-gnant
poi-gnan-cy
poi-gnant-ly
poin-set-tia
point--blank
point-ed
point-ed-ly
point-ed-ness
point-er
poin-til-lism
poin-til-list
point-less
poise
poised
pois-ing
poi-son
poi-son-er
poi-son-ing

poi-son-ous
poi-son--pen
poke
poked
pok-ing
pok-er
poky
pok-i-er
pok-i-est
pok-i-ly
pok-i-ness
po-lar
po-lar-i-ty
po-lar-i-ties
po-lar-i-za-tion
po-lar-ize
po-lar-ized
po-lar-iz-ing
po-lar-iz-a-ble
po-lar-iz-er
pole
poled
pol-ing
pole-less
pole-cat
po-lem-ic
po-lem-i-cal
po-lem-i-cal-ly
po-lem-i-cist
po-lem-ics
pole-star
po-lice
po-liced
po-lic-ing
pol-i-cy
pol-i-cies
pol-i-o-my-e-li-tis
pol-ish
pol-ish-er
po-lite
po-lite-ly
po-lite-ness
pol-i-tic

po-lit-i-cal
  po-lit-i-cal-ly
pol-i-ti-cian
po-lit-i-cize
  po-lit-i-cized
  po-lit-i-ciz-ing
pol-i-tick
  pol-i-tick-er
pol-i-tics
pol-i-ty
  pol-i-ties
pol-ka
  pol-kaed
  pol-ka-ing
poll
  poll-ee
  poll-er
pol-len
pol-li-nate
  pol-li-nat-ed
  pol-li-nat-ing
  pol-li-na-tion
  pol-li-na-tor
pol-li-wog
poll-ster
pol-lu-tant
pol-lute
  pol-lut-ed
  pol-lut-ing
  pol-lut-er
  pol-lu-tion
po-lo
  po-lo-ist
pol-o-naise
po-lo-ni-um
pol-ter-geist
poly-an-dry
  poly-an-drous
poly-chro-mat-ic
poly-chrome
poly-es-ter
poly-eth-yl-ene
polyg-a-mist

polyg-a-my
  polyg-a-mous
poly-glot
poly-gon
  polyg-o-nal
  polyg-o-nal-ly
poly-graph
  poly-graph-ic
po-lyg-y-ny
  po-lyg-y-nous
poly-he-dron
  poly-he-drons
  poly-he-dra
  poly-he-dral
poly-mer
po-ly-mer-ize
  po-ly-mer-ized
  po-ly-mer-iz-ing
  po-lym-er-ism
  po-lym-er-i-za-tion
pol-y-mor-phism
  pol-y-mor-phic
  pol-y-mor-phous
poly-no-mi-al
pol-yp
poly-phon-ic
  po-lyph-o-ny
poly-sty-rene
poly-syl-lab-ic
  poly-syl-lab-i-cal-ly
poly-syl-la-ble
poly-tech-nic
poly-the-ism
  poly-the-ist
  poly-the-is-tic
  poly-the-is-ti-cal
poly-un-sat-u-rat-
ed
pom-ace
po-made
  po-mad-ed
  po-mad-ing
pome-gran-ate

pom-mel
  pom-meled
  pom-mel-ing
pom-pa-dour
pom-pon
pomp-ous
  pom-pos-i-ty
  pom-pous-ly
pon-cho
pon-der
  pon-der-a-ble
  pon-der-er
pon-der-ous
  pon-der-ous-ly
  pon-der-ou-ness
pon-iard
pon-tiff
pon-tif-i-cal
  pon-tif-i-cal-ly
pon-tif-i-cate
  pon-tif-i-cat-ed
  pon-tif-i-cat-ing
pon-toon
po-ny
  po-nies
  po-nied
  po-ny-ing
po-ny-tail
poo-dle
pool-room
poor
  poor-ish
  poor-ly
pop-corn
pop-ery
  pop-ish
pop-eyed
pop-gun
pop-in-jay
pop-lar
pop-lin
pop-per
pop-py

pop-pies
pop-pied
pop-py-cock
pop-u-lace
pop-u-lar
pop-u-lar-ly
pop-u-lar-i-ty
pop-u-lar-ize
pop-u-lar-ized
pop-u-lar-iz-ing
pop-u-lar-i-za-tion
pop-u-lar-iz-er
pop-u-late
pop-u-lat-ed
pop-u-lat-ing
pop-u-la-tion
pop-u-lism
pop-u-list
pop-u-lous
pop-u-lous-ly
por-ce-lain
por-cine
por-cu-pine
pore
pored
por-ing
pork-er
por-nog-ra-phy
por-nog-ra-pher
por-no-graph-ic
po-rous
po-rous-i-ty
po-rous-ly
po-rous-ness
por-poise
por-pios-es
por-ridge
port-a-ble
port-a-bil-i-ty
port-a-bly

por-tal
por-tend
por-tent
por-ten-tous
por-ter
por-ter-house
port-fo-lio
port-fo-lios
port-hole
por-ti-co
por-ti-coes
por-ti-cos
por-tion
por-tion-less
port-ly
port-li-er
port-li-est
por-trait
por-trat-ist
por-trai-ture
por-tray
por-tray-er
por-tray-al
pose
posed
pos-ing
pos-er
po-suer
pos-it
po-si-tion
po-si-tion-al
po-si-tion-er
pos-i-tive
pos-i-tive-ly
pos-i-tive-ness
pos-i-tiv-ism
pos-i-tron
pos-se
pos-sess
pos-ses-sor
pos-sessed
pos-ses-sion
pos-ses-sive

pos-ses-sive-ly
pos-ses-sive-ness
pos-si-bil-i-ty
pos-si-ble
pos-si-bly
pos-sum
post-age
post-box
post-date
post-dat-ed
post-dat-ing
post-er
pos-te-ri-or
pos-te-ri-or-i-ty
pos-ter-i-ty
post-grad-u-ate
post-haste
post-hu-mous
post-hu-mous-ly
post-lude
post-man
post-men
post-mark
post-mas-ter
post-mis-tress
post me-ri-di-em
post-mor-tem
post-na-sal
post-na-tal
post-na-tal-ly
post-paid
post-par-tum
post-pone
post-poned
post-pon-ing
post-pon-a-ble
post-pone-ment
post-pon-er
post-scipt
pos-tu-lant
pos-tu-late
pos-tu-lat-ed
pos-tu-lat-ing

pos-tu-la-tion
pos-tu-la-tor
pos-ture
pos-tured
pos-tur-ing
pos-tur-al
pos-tur-er
post-war
po-sy
po-sies
pot
pot-ted
pot-ting
po-ta-ble
pot-ash
po-tas-si-um
po-ta-to
po-ta-toes
pot-bel-ly
pot-bel-lied
pot-boil-er
po-tent
po-ten-cy
po-tent-ly
po-ten-tate
po-ten-tial
po-ten-ti-al-i-ty
po-ten-tial-ly
pot-hole
po-tion
pot-luck
pot-pour-ri
pot-sherd
pot-tage
pot-ter
pot-tery
pot-ter-ies
pot-ty
pot-ties
pot-ty--chair
pouch
pouched
pouchy

pouch-i-er
pouch-i-est
poul-tice
poul-ticed
poul-tic-ing
poul-try
pounce
pounced
pounc-ing
pound-age
pound--fool-ish
pour
pour-a-ble
pour-er
pout
pov-er-ty
pov-er-ty--strick-en
pow-der
pow-dery
pow-er
pow-er-boat
pow-er-ful
pow-er-ful-ly
pow-er-ful-ness
pow-er-house
pow-er-less
Pow-ha-tan
pow-wow
prac-ti-ca-ble
prac-ti-ca-bil-i-ty
prac-ti-ca-bly
prac-ti-cal
prac-ti-cal-i-ty
prac-ti-cal-ly
prac-tice
prac-ti-tio-ner
prae-di-al
pre-di-al
prag-mat-ic
prag-mat-i-cal
prag-mat-i-cal-ly
prag-ma-tism
prag-ma-tist

prag-ma-tis-tic
prai-rie
praise
praised
prais-ing
prais-er
praise-wor-thy
praise-wor-thi-ly
praise-wor-thi-ness
pra-line
prance
pranced
pranc-ing
pranc-er
prank
prank-ish
prank-ster
prate
prat-ed
prat-ing
prat-er
prat-ing-ly
prat-fall
prat-tle
prat-tled
prat-tling
prat-tler
prat-tling-ly
prawn
prawn-er
pray-er
pray-er-ful
preach
prach-er
preach-ify
preach-ified
preach-ify-ing
preach-ment
preachy
preach-i-er
preach-i-est
pre-ad-o-les-cence
pre-ad-o-les-cent

pre-am-ble
pre-ar-range
  pre-ar-ranged
  pre-ar-rang-ing
  pre-ar-range-ment
pre-as-signed
pre-can-cel
  pre-can-celed
  pre-can-cel-ing
  pre-can-cel-la-tion
pre-car-i-ous
  pre-car-i-ous-ly
  pre-car-i-ous-ness
pre-cau-tion
  pre-cau-tion-ary
pre-cede
  pre-ced-ed
  pre-ced-ing
prec-e-dence
prec-e-dent
pre-cept
pre-cep-tive
pre-cep-tor
  pre-cep-to-ri-al
pre-ces-sion
  pre-ces-sion-al
pre-cinct
pre-cious
  pre-ci-os-i-ty
  pre-cious-ness
prec-i-pice
  pre-cip-i-tous
pre-cip-i-tant
  pre-cip-i-tant-ly
pre-cip-i-tate
  pre-cip-i-tat-ed
  pre-cip-i-tat-ing
  pre-cip-i-ta-tive
  pre-cip-i-ta-tor
pre-cip-i-ta-tion
pre-cip-i-tous
  pre-cip-i-tous-ly
pre-cise

pre-cise-ness
pre-ci-sion
  pre-ci-sion-ist
pre-clude
  pre-clud-ed
  pre-clud-ing
  pre-clu-sion
  pre-clu-sive
pre-co-cious
  pre-coc-cious-ly
  pre-coc-cious-ness
  pre-coc-i-ty
pre-cog-ni-tion
  pre-cog-ni-tive
pre-con-ceive
  pre-con-ciev-ed
  pre-con-ceiv-ing
  pre-con-cep-tion
pre-cook
pre-cur-sor
  pre-cur-so-ry
pre-date
pred-a-tor
pred-a-to-ry
  pred-a-to-ri-ly
pre-dawn
pre-de-ces-sor
pre-des-ti-nate
  pre-des-ti-nat-ed
  pre-des-ti-nat-ing
pre-des-ti-na-tion
pre-des-tine
  pre-des-tined
  pre-des-tin-ing
pre-de-ter-mine
  pre-de-ter-mined
  pre-de-ter-min-ing
  -de-ter-mi-na-tion
pred-i-ca-ble
  pred-i-ca-bil-i-ty
pre-dic-a-ment
pred-i-cate
  pred-i-cat-ed

  pred-i-cat-ing
  pred-i-ca-tion
  pred-i-ca-tive
pre-dict
  pre-dict-a-ble
  pre-dict-a-bly
  pre-dict-a-bil-i-ty
pre-dic-tion
  pre-dic-tive
pre-di-lec-tion
pre-dis-po-si-tion
  pre-dis-pose
  pre-dis-posed
  pre-dis-pos-ing
pre-dom-i-nant
  pre-dom-i-nance
  pre-dom-i-nan-cy
pre-dom-i-nate
  pre-dom-i-nat-ed
  pre-dom-i-nat-ing
  pre-dom-i-na-tion
pre-em-i-nent
  pre-em-i-nence
pre-empt
  pre-emp-tor
pre-emp-tion
  pre-emp-tive
preen-er
pre-ex-ist
  pre-ex-ist-ence
  pre-ex-ist-ent
pre-fab-ri-cate
  pre-fab-ri-cat-ed
  pre-fab-ri-cat-ing
  pre-fab-ri-a-tion
pref-ace
  pref-aced
  pref-ac-ing
  pref-a-to-ry
pre-fer
  pre-ferred
  pre-fer-ring
  pre-fer-rer

pref-er-a-ble
pre-fer-a-bil-i-ty
pref-er-a-bly
pref-er-ence
pref-er-en-tial
pref-er-en-tial-ly
pre-fer-ment
pre-fix
pre-flight
pre-form
preg-n-able
preg-na-bil-i-ty
preg-nan-cy
preg-nan-cies
preg-nant
pre-heat
pre-hen-sile
pre-hen-sil-i-ty
pre-his-tor-ic
prej-u-dice
prej-u-diced
prej-u-dic-ing
prej-u-di-cial
prej-u-di-cial-ly
prel-ate
prel-ate-ship
prel-a-ture
pre-lim-i-nar-y
pre-lim-i-nar-ies
pre-lim-i-nar-i-ly
prel-ude
prel-uded
prel-ud-ing
pre-ma-ture
pre-na-tu-ri-ty
pre-med-i-cal
pre-med-i-tate
pre-med-i-tat-ed
pre-med-i-ta-tion
pre-men-stru-al
pre-mier
pre-mier-ship
pre-miere

prem-ise
prem-ised
prem-is-ing
pre-mi-um
pre-mo-ni-tion
pre-mon-i-to-ry
pre-mon-i-to-ri-ly
pre-na-tal
pre-na-tal-ly
pre-oc-cu-pa-tion
pre-oc-cu-py
pre-oc-cu-pied
pre-oc-cu-py-ing
prep-a-ra-tion
pre-par-a-to-ry
pre-par-a-to-ri-ly
pre-plan
pre-planned
pre-plan-ning
pre-pon-der-ant
pre-pon-der-ance
pre-pon-der-an-cy
pre-pon-der-ant-ly
pre-pon-der-ate
pre-pon-der-at-ed
pre-pon-der-at-ing
pre-pon-der-a-tion
prep-o-si-tion
prep-o-si-tion-al
pre-pos-sess
pre-pos-sess-ing
pre-pos-sess-ing-ly
pre-pos-ter-ous
pre-puce
pre-pu-tial
pre-re-cord
pre-re-ui-site
pre-rog-a-tive
pres-age
pres-aged
pres-ag-ing
pres-ag-er
pres-by-ter-y

pres-by-ter-ies
pre-school
pre-script
pre-scrip-tion
pre-scrip-tive
pre-sea-son
pres-ence
pre-sent
pre-sent-er
pres-ent
pre-sent-a-ble
pre-sent-a-bil-i-ty
pre-sent-a-ble-ness
pre-sent-a-bly
pres-en-ta-tion
pres-ent-day
pres-ent-ly
pre-serv-a-tive
per-serve
pre-served
pre-serv-ing
pre-serv-a-ble
pres-er-va-tion
pre-serv-er
pre-side
pre-sid-ed
pre-sid-ing
pre-sid-er
pres-i-den-cy
pres-i-den-cies
pres-i-dent
pres-i-den-tial
press-board
press-ing
pres-sure
pres-sured
pres-sur-ing
press-work
pres-ti-dig-i-ta-tion
pres-ti-dig-i-ta-tor
pres-tige
pres-tig-ious
pres-to

pre-sum-a-ble
  pre-sum-a-bly
pre-sump-tion
pre-sump-tive
pre-sump-tu-ous
pre-sup-pose
  pre-sup-posed
  pre-sup-pos-ing
  pre-sup-po-si-tion
pre-tend
  pre-tend-ed
pre-tend-er
pre-tense
pre-ten-sion
pre-ten-tious
  pre-ten-tious-ness
pre-test
pre-text
pret-ti-fy
  pret-ti-fied
  pret-ti-fy-ing
  pret-ti-fi-ca-tion
pret-zel
pre-vail
pre-vail-ing
prev-a-lent
  prev-a-lence
pre-vent
  pre-vent-a-ble
  pre-vent-a-bil-i-ty
  pre-vent-er
pre-ven-tion
pre-view
pre-vi-ous
pre-war
prey
  prey-er
price-less
prick-er
prick-le
prick-ly
  prick-li-er
  prick-li-est

prick-li-ness
pride
  prid-ed
  prid-ing
pride-ful
pri-er
priest
  priest-ess
  priest-hood
pri-ma-cy
  pri-ma-cies
pri-ma don-na
  pri-ma don-nas
pri-mal
pri-ma-ri-ly
pri-ma-ry
  pri-mar-ies
pri-mate
prime
  primed
  prim-ing
prime me-rid-i-an
  prim-er
pr-me-val
prim-i-tive
pri-mo-gen-i-tor
pri-mo-gen-i-ture
pri-mor-di-al
  pri-mor-di-al-ly
primp
prim-rose
prince-ly
  prince-li-er
  prince-li-est
prin-cess
prin-ci-pal
  prin-ci-pal-ly
prin-ci-pal-i-ty
  prin-ci-pal-i-ties
prin-ci-ple
prin-ci-pled
print-a-ble
print-ing

print-out
pri-or
  pri-or-ate
pri-or-ess
pri-or-i-ty
  pri-or-i-ties
pri-or-y
  pri-or-ies
prism
  pris-mat-ic
  pris-mat-i-cal-ly
pris-on
pris-on-er
pris-tine
pri-va-cy
pri-vate
pri-va-tion
priv-et
priv-i-ledge
  priv-i-ledged
  priv-i-leg-ing
prize
  prized
prize-fight
prob-a-bil-i-ty
  prob-a-bil-i-ties
prob-a-ble
  prob-a-bly
pro-bate
  pro-bat-ed
  pro-bat-ing
pro-ba-tion
  pro-ba-tion-al
  pro-ba-tion-ary
pro-na-tion-er
pro-ba-tive
probe
  probed
  prob-ing
  prob-er
prob-lem
prob-lem-at-ic
  pro-lem-at-i-cal

pro-bos-cis
  pro-bos-cis-es
  pro-bos-ci-des
pro-ce-dure
  pro-ce-dur-al
  pro-ce-dur-al-ly
pro-ceed
pro-ceed-ing
pro-ceeds
pro-ces-sion
pro-ces-sion-al
pro-claim
  pro-claim-er
proc-la-ma-tion
pro-cliv-i-ty
  pro-cliv-i-ties
pro-cre-ate
  pro-cre-at-ed
  pro-cre-at-ing
  pro-cre-a-tion
proc-tor
  proc-to-ri-al
proc-u-ra-tor
  proc-u-ra-to-ri-al
  proc-u-ra-tor-ship
pro-cure
  pro-cured
  pro-cur-ing
  pro-cure-ment
prod-i-gal
  prod-i-gal-i-ty
  prod-i-gal-ly
pro-di-gious
  pro-di-gious-ness
prod-i-gy
  prod-i-gies
pro-duce
  pro-duced
  pro-duc-ing
pro-duc-er
prod-uct
pro-duc-tion
pro-duc-tive

pro-duc-tive-ness
  pro-duc-tiv-i-ty
pro-fane
  pro-faned
pro-fan-i-ty
pro-fess
  pro-fessed
  pro-fess-ed-ly
pro-fes-sion
pro-fes-sion-al
  pro-fes-sion-al-ism
pro-fes-sion-al-ize
  pro-fes-sion-al-ized
pro-fes-sor
  pro-fes-so-ri-al
  pro-fes-sor-ship
prof-fer
  prof-fer-er
pro-fi-cien-cy
pro-fi-cient
pro-file
  pro-filed
  pro-fil-ing
prof-it
  prof-it-less
prof-it-able
  prof-it-a-bil-i-ty
  prof-it-ably
prof-i-teer
prof-li-gate
  prof-li-ga-cy
pro-found
pro-fun-di-ty
  pro-fun-di-ties
pro-fuse
pro-fu-sion
pro-gen-i-tor
prog-e-ny
  prog-e-nies
pro-ges-ter-one
prog-no-sis
  prog-no-ses
  prog-nos-tic

pro-gram
prog-ress
pro-gres-sion
pro-gres-sive
  pro-gres-siv-ism
pro-hib-it
pro-hi-bi-tion
pro-hi-bi-tion-ist
pro-hib-i-tive
pro-ject
pro-jec-tile
pro-jec-tion
pro-jec-tion-ist
pro-jec-tive
  pro-jec-tive-ly
  pro-jec-tiv-i-ty
pro-jec-tor
pro-le-tar-i-at
  pro-le-tar-i-an
pro-lif-er-ate
  pro-lif-er-at-ed
pro-lif-ic
  pro-lif-i-ca-cy
pro-lix
  pro-lix-i-ty
pro-logue
  pro-logued
  pro-logu-ing
pro-long
  pro-lon-ga-tion
  pro-long-er
prom-i-nence
prom-i-nent
  prom-i-nent-ly
pro-mis-cu-ity
  pro-mis-cu-i-ties
pro-mis-cu-ous
  pro-mis-cu-ous-ly
prom-ise
  prom-ised
  prom-is-ing
prom-is-so-ry
prom-on-to-ry

prom-on-to-ries
pro-mot-er
pro-mo-tion
pro-mo-tive
pro-mul-gate
pro-mul-gat-ed
pro-mul-ga-tion
prone
prong
pro-noun
pro-nounce
pro-nounced
pro-nounce-ment
pron-to
pro-nun-ci-a-tion
proof
proof-read
prop
pro-pa-gan-da
pro-pa-gate
pro-pa-ga-tion
pro-pa-ga-tion-al
pro-pane
pro-pel
pro-pelled
pro-pel-ling
pro-pel-lant
pro-pel-ler
pro-pen-si-ty
pro-pen-si-ties
prop-er
proph-e-cy
proph-e-cies
proph-e-sy
proph-e-sied
proph-e-sy-ing
proph-et
pro-phet-ic
pro-phet-i-cal-ly
pro-phy-lax-is
pro-pin-qui-ty
pro-pi-ti-ate
pro-pi-ti-at-ed

pro-pi-ti-a-tion
pro-pi-tious
pro-pi-tious-ly
pro-po-nent
pro-por-tion
pro-por-tion-a-ble
pro-por-tion-a-bly
pro-por-tion-al
pro-por-tion-al-i-ty
pro-por-tion-ate
pro-por-tion-at-ed
pro-por-tion-at-ing
pro-pos-al
pro-pose
pro-posed
prop-o-si-tion
prop-o-si-tion-al
pro-pound
pro-pound-er
pro-pri-e-tary
pro-pri-e-tar-ies
pro-pri-etor
pro-pri-e-tor-ship
pro-pri-ety
pro-pul-sion
pro-pul-sive
pro-rate
pro-rat-ed
pro-sa-ic
pro-sa-i-cal-ly
pro-scrip-tion
pro-srip-tive
prose
pros-e-cute
pros-e-cute-a-ble
pros-e-cu-tion
pros-e-cu-tor
pros-pect
pros-pec-tor
pro-spec-tive
pro-spec-tus
pros-per-i-ty
pros-per-ous

pros-tate
pros-the-sis
pros-the-ses
pros-thet-ic
pros-thet-ics
pros-the-tis
prosth-odon-tics
prosth-odon-tist
pros-ti-tute
pros-trate
pros-trat-ing
pros-tra-tor
pros-tra-tive
pro-tag-o-nist
pro-te-an
pro-tect
pro-tect-ing
pro-tec-tive
pro-tec-tor
pro-tec-tion
pro-tec-tion-ism
pro-tec-tion-ist
pro-tec-tor-ate
pro-tein
pro-test
prot-es-ta-tion
pro-tist
pro-tis-tan
pro-to-col
pro-ton
pro-to-plasm
pro-to-plas-mic
pro-to-type
pro-to-typ-i-cal
pro-to-typ-ic
pro-to-typ-i-cal-ly
pro-to-zo-an
pro-to-zo-ic
pro-tract
pro-trac-tion
pro-trac-tive
pro-trac-tile
pro-trac-tor

pro-trude
 pro-trud-ed
 pro-trud-ing
pro-tru-sion
pro-tru-sive
pro-tu-ber-ance
pro-tu-ber-ant
proud
 proud-ly
prov-erb
pro-ver-bi-al
 pro-ver-bi-al-ly
prov-i-dence
 prov-i-den-tial
prov-i-dent
prov-ince
pro-vin-cial
pro-vin-cial-ism
pro-vi-sion
 pro-vi-sion-er
pro-vi-sion-al
 pro-vi-sion-ary
prov-o-ca-tion
pro-voc-a-tive
 pro-voc-a-tive-ly
 pro-voc-a-tive-ness
pro-vost
prow-ess
prowl
 prowl-er
prox-i-mal
prox-i-mate
 prox-i-mate-ly
prox-im-i-ty
proxy
 prox-ies
prude
pru-dence
 pru-dent
 pru-den-tial
prud-ish
prune
 pruned

 prun-ing
psalm-book
psalm-ist
pseu-do
pseud-onym
 pseud-on-y-mous
pseu-do-preg-nant
pseu-do-sci-ence
 pseu-do-sci-en-tif-ic
pshaw
psil-o-cy-bin
pso-ri-a-sis
 pso-ri-at-ic
psych
 psyched
 psych-ing
psy-che-del-ic
psy-chi-a-trist
psy-chi-a-try
 psy-chi-at-ric
 psy-chi-at-ri-cal-ly
psy-chic
 psy-chi-cal
 psy-chi-cal-ly
psy-cho
psy-cho-anal-y-sis
 -cho-an-a-lyt-ic
psy-cho-bi-ol-o-gy
 -cho-bi-o-log-i-cal
psy-cho-dra-ma
psy-cho-dy-nam-ic
 psy-cho-dy-nam-ics
psy-cho-gen-e-sis
 psy-cho-ge-net-ic
psy-cho-gen-ic
 psy-cho-gen-i-cal-ly
psy-cho-log-i-cal
 psy-cho-log-ic
 psy-cho-log-i-cal-ly
psy-chol-o-gist
psy-chol-o-gy

psy-cho-mo-tor
psy-cho-neu-ro-sis
 psy-cho-neu-rot-ic
psy-cho-path
psy-cho-pa-thol-o-gy
psy-chop-a-thy
 psy-cho-path-ic
 -chop-ath-i-cal-ly
psy-cho-ther-a-py
 psy-cho-ther-a-pist
pto-maine
pu-ber-ty
pu-bes-cence
 pu-bes-cen-cy
 pu-bes-cent
pu-bic
pub-lic
 pub-lic-ly
pub-li-ca-tion
pub-li-cist
pub-lic-i-ty
pub-li-cize
 pub-li-cized
 pub-li-ciz-ing
pub-lish
 pub-lish-a-ble
pub-lish-er
puce
puck-er
pud-ding
pud-dle
 pud-dled
 pud-dling
pueb-lo
 pueb-los
pu-er-ile
 pu-er-il-i-ty
puff
 puffy
puff-er
pu-gi-lism
 pu-gi-list

pu-gi-lis-tic
pug-na-cious
pug-nac-i-ty
pulke
puked
puk-ing
pull-back
pul-let
pul-ley
pul-mo-nary
pulp
pul-pit
pulp-wood
pul-sate
pul-sat-ed
pul-sat-ing
pul-sa-tion
pul-sa-tor
pul-sa-to-ry
pulse
pulsed
puls-ing
pul-ver-ize
pu-ma
pu-mas
pum-ice
pu-mi-ceous
pum-mel
pum-per-nick-el
pump-kin
pun
punned
pun-ning
punch
punch-er
punc-tu-al
punc-tu-ate
punc-tu-at-ed
punc-tu-at-ing
punc-tu-a-tor
punc-tu-a-tion
punc-ture
punc-tured

punc-tur-ing
pun-dit
pun-gent
pun-gen-cy
pun-gent-ly
pun-ish
pun-ish-able
pun-ish-ment
pu-ni-tive
pun-ster
punt-er
pu-ny
pu-ni-er
pu-ni-est
pup
pupped
pup-ping
pu-pil
pep-pet-ry
pup-pet-ries
pure
pure-ly
pur-ga-tive
pur-ga-to-ry
pur-ga-to-ries
pur-ga-to-ri-al
purge
purged
pu-ri-fy
pur-ism
pur-ist
pu-ris-tic
pu-ri-ty
purl
pur-loin
pur-loin-er
pur-port
pur-port-ed
pur-port-ed-ly
pur-pose
pur-posed
pur-pos-ing
pur-pose-ly

pur-pos-ive
purse
pursed
purs-ing
purs-er
pur-su-ant
pur-sue
pur-sued
pur-su-ing
pur-suit
pur-sy
pu-ru-lent
pu-ru-lence
pu-ru-len-cy
pur-vey
pur-vey-or
pur-vey-ance
pur-view
pushy
pu-sil-lan-i-mous
pu-sil-la-nim-i-ty
-sal-lan-i-mous-ly
pus-sy
pussy-foot
pussy-wil-low
pus-tule
pus-tu-lar
pus-tu-late
pu-ta-tive
pu-ta-tive-ly
put--on
pu-tre-fac-tion
pu-tre-fy
pu-tre-fied
pu-tre-fy-ing
pu-trid
pu-trid-i-try
putt
putt-ed
putt-ing
putt-er
put-ter-er
put--up

puz-zle
puz-zle-ment
py-lon
pyr-a-mid
  py-ra-mi-dal
pyre
py-ric
py-ro-ma-nia
  py-ro-ma-ni-ac
  py-ro-ma-ni-a-cal
py-ro-tech-nics
  py-ro-tech-nic
  py-ro-tech-ni-cal
py-thon

Q

quack-ery
  quack-er-ies
quad-ran-gle
  quad-ran-gu-lar
quad-rant
  quad-ran-tal
quad-ra-phon-ic
quad-rate
  quad-rat-ed
  quad-rat-ing
qua-drat-ic
  qua-drat-i-cal-ly
qua-drat-ics
quad-ra-ture
quad-ri-lat-er-al
qua-drille
qua-dril-lion
  qua-dril-lionth
qua-droon
quad-ru-ped
  quad-ru-pe-dal
qua-dru-ple
  qua-dru-pled
  qua-dru-pling
qua-dru-plet
qua-dru-pli-cate

qua-dru-pli-cat-ed
qua-dru-pli-cat-ing
quaff
  quaff-er
quag-mire
  quag-mired
  quag-miry
quail
quaint
quake
qual-i-fi-ca-tion
qual-i-fied
  qual-i-fied-ly
qual-i-fy
  qual-i-fy-ing
  qual-i-fi-a-ble
  qual-i-fier
qual-i-ta-tive
qual-i-ty
  qual-i-ties
qualm
  qualm-ish
quan-da-ry
  quan-dar-ies
quan-ti-fy
  quan-ti-fy-ing
  quan-ti-fi-ca-tion
quan-ti-ta-tive
quan-ti-ty
  quan-ti-ties
quan-tum
  quan-ta
quar-an-tine
  quar-an-tin-able
quar-rel
  quar-reled
  quar-rel-ing
  quar-rel-er
quar-rel-some
quar-ri-er
quar-ry
  quar-ries
  quar-ried

quar-ry-ing
quart
quar-ter
quar-ter-back
quar-ter-ing
quar-ter-ly
  quar-ter-lies
quar-ter-mas-ter
quar-tet
quartz
quash
qua-si
qua-ter-na-ry
qua-train
qua-ver
  quav-er-ing-ly
  qua-very
quay
quea-sy
  quea-si-er
  quea-si-est
  quea-si-ly
queen
quell
  quell-er
quench
  quench-able
  quench-er
que-ry
  que-ries
  que-ried
quest
ques-tion
  ques-tion-er
ques-tion-able
  ques-tion-ably
ques-tion-naire
queue
  queued
  queu-ing
quib-ble
quick
quick-en

quick--en-er
quick--freeze
quick--wit-ted
  quick--wit-ted-ly
qui-es-cent
  qui-es-cence
qui-et
  qui-et-ly
  qui-et-er
qui-e-tude
quill
quilt
quilt-ing
quince
quin-til-lion
quin-tu-ple
  quin-tu-pled
  quin-tu-pling
quin-tu-plet
quip
  quipped
  quip-ping
quirk
  quirky
quis-ling
quit
  quit-ed
  quit-ing
quit-claim
quite
quit-er
quiv-er
quix-ot-ic
quiz
quiz-zi-cal
  quiz-zi-cal-ly
quoin
quoit
quon-dam
quo-rum
quo-ta
quot-able
  quot-a-bil-i-ty

quo-ta-tion
quote
quo-tid-i-an
quo-tient

R

rab-bet
  rab-bet-ted
  rab-bet-ting
rab-bi
  rab-bis
ra-bin-ate
rab-bin-i-cal
  rab-bin-i-al-ly
rab-bit
rab-ble
  rab-bled
  rab-bling
ra-bid
  ra-bid-ly
ra-bies
rac-coon
race-horse
ra-ceme
rac-er
ra-ce-ric
ra-ce-ri-za-tion
race-track
ra-chis
  ra-chis-es
  rach-i-des
ra-cial
  ra-cial-ism
  ra-cial-ly
rac-ism
  ra-cial-ism
  rac-ist
rack-et
rack-e-teer
ra-con-teur
racy
  rac-i-ly

ra-dar
ra-di-al
  ra-di-al-ly
ra-di-ance
  ra-di-an-cy
ra-di-ant
ra-di-ate
  ra-di-at-ed
  ra-di-at-ing
ra-di-a-tion
ra-di-a-tor
rad-i-cal
  rad-i-cal-ly
rad-i-cal-ism
ra-dio
ra-dio-ac-tive
ra-dio-ac-tive-i-ty
ra-dio-gram
ra-dio-graph
  ra-diog-ra-phy
ra-di-ol-o-gy
  ra-di-ol-o-gist
rad-ish
ra-di-um
ra-di-us
  ra-dii
  ra-di-us-es
ra-don
raf-fia
raf-fi-nose
raff-ish
raf-fle
  raf-fled
  raf-fling
raft
raft-er
rag
rag-ged
rag-gle
rail-ing
rail-lery
  rail-ler-ies
rail-road

rail-road-er
rail-road-ing
rail-way
rai-ment
rain-bow
rain-fall
rainy
raise
raised
rai-sin
rake
raked
rak-ing
rake--off
rak-ish
rak-ish-ly
ral-li-form
ral-ly
ral-lied
ram
rammed
ram-ble
ram-bled
ram-bling
ram-bler
ram-bunc-tious
ram-bu-tan
ram-i-fi-ca-tion
ram-i-fy
ram-i-fied
ram-i-fy-ing
ram-page
ram-paged
ram-pag-ing
ram-pan-cy
ram-pant
ram-pant-ly
ram-part
ram-rod
ram-shack-le
ranch-er
ran-cid
ran-cid-i-ty

ran-cor
ran-cor-ous
ran-dom
ran-dom-ly
range
ranged
rang-ing
rang-er
rangy
rang-i-er
rang-i-est
ran-sack
rant-er
ran-u-la
rape
rap-ist
ra-phe
raph-ide
rap-id
ra-pi-er
rap-ine
rap-pel
rap-proche-ment
rap-scal-lion
rap-to-ri-al
rap-ture
rap-tur-ous
rare
rar-er
rar-est
rare-bit
rar-efy
rar-efied
rar-efy-ing
rare-ly
rar-i-ty
rar-i-ties
rash
ra-so-ri-al
rasp
rasp-ber-ry
rat-able
ratch-et

rate
rat-ed
rat-ing
rath-er
rat-icide
rat-i-fy
rat-i-fi-ca-tion
ra-tio
ra-tios
ra-ti-o-ci-na-tion
ra-tion
ra-tio-nal
ra-tio-nal-i-ty
ra-tio-nal-ly
ra-tion-able
ra-tio-nal-ism
ra-tio-nal-ize
ra-tio-nal-iz-ing
ra-tio-nal-i-za-tion
rat-line
rat-tan
rat-tle
rat-tled
rat-tling
rat-tle-snake
rat-ty
rat-ti-er
rat-ti-est
rau-cous
rau-cous-ly
rav-age
rav-aged
rave
rav-el
ra-ven
rav-en-ous
rav-en-ous-ly
ra-vine
rav-i-o-li
rav-ish
rav-ish-ment
rav-ish-ing
raw

raw-hide
ray-on
raze
  razed
  raz-ing
ra-zor
raz-zle--daz-zle
re-act
  re-ac-tive
re-ac-tion
re-ac-tion-ary
  re-ac-tion-ar-ies
re-ac-ti-vate
  re-ac-ti-vat-ed
  re-ac-ti-vat-ing
re-ac-tor
read-able
read-er
read-ing
re-ad-just
  re-ad-just-ment
ready--made
re-agent
re-al
re-al-ism
  re-al-ist
  re-al-is-tic
  re-al-is-ti-cal-ly
re-al-ly
realm
Re-al-tor
re-al-ty
ream-er
re-an-i-mate
  re-an-i-mat-ed
  re-an-i-mat-ing
  re-an-i-ma-tion
reap-er
re-ap-pear
  re-ap-pear-ance
re-ap-por-tion
re-ap-por-tion-ment
rear ad-mir-ral

re-arm
  re-ar-ma-ment
re-ar-range
  re-ar-ranged
  re-ar-rang-ing
  re-ar-range-ment
rear-ward
rea-son
  rea-son-er
rea-son-able
  rea-son-abil-i-ty
  rea-son-able-ness
  rea-son-ably
rea-son-ing
re-as-sem-ble
  re-as-sem-bled
  re-as-sem-bling
  re-as-sem-bly
re-as-sume
  re-as-sump-tion
re-as-sure
  re-as-sured
  re-as-sur-ing
  re-as-sur-ance
  re-as-sur-ing-ly
re-bate
  re-bat-ed
  re-bat-ing
  re-bat-er
reb-el
re-bel
  re-belled
  re-bel-ling
re-bel-lion
re-bel-lious
  re-bel-lious-ly
re-birth
re-born
re-bound
re-buff
re-build
  re-built
  re-build-ing

re-buke
re-bus
  re-bus-es
re-but
re-but-tal
re-cal-ci-trant
  re-cal-ci-trance
  re-cal-ci-tran-cy
re-call
re-cant
  re-can-ta-tion
re-ca-pit-u-late
re-cap-ture
  re-cap-tured
re-cede
  re-ced-ed
  re-ced-ing
re-ceipt
re-ceiv-able
re-ceive
  re-ceiv-ed
  re-ceiv-ing
re-ceiv-er
re-ceiv-er-ship
re-cent
  re-cent-ly
  re-cen-cy
re-cep-ta-cle
re-cep-tion
  re-cep-tion-ist
re-cep-tive
re-cess
re-ces-sion
  re-ces-sion-ary
re-ces-sion-al
re-ces-sive
re-charge
  re-charg-ed
  re-charg-ing
rec-i-pe
re-cip-i-ent
  re-cip-i-ence
  re-cip-i-en-cy

re-cip-ro-cal
re-cip-ro-cal-ly
re-cip-ro-cate
rec-i-proc-i-ty
re-cit-al
rec-i-ta-tion
rec-i-ta-tive
re-cite
re-cited
re-cit-ing
reck-less
reck-less-ly
reck-on
re-claim
rec-la-ma-tion
re-cline
re-clined
rec-luse
rec-og-ni-tion
re-cog-ni-zance
rec-og-nize
rec-og-nized
rec-og-niz-ing
rec-og-niz-a-ble
re-coil
re-coil-less
re-col-lect
re-col-lect
re-col-lec-tion
rec-om-mend
rec-om-mend-able
rec-om-mend-er
rec-om-men-da-tion
rec-om-pense
rec-om-pensed
rec-om-pens-ing
rec-on-cile
rec-on-ciled
rec-con-dite
re-con-di-tion
re-con-firm
re-con-nais-sance
re-con-noi-ter

re-con-noi-tered
re-con-noi-ter-ing
re-con-sid-er
re-con-sid-er-a-tion
re-con-struct
re-con-struc-tion
re-cord
re-cord-er
re-count
re-coup
re-course
re-cov-er
re-cov-ery
re-cov-er-ies
rec-re-ant
re-cre-ate
re-cre-at-ed
re-cre-at-ing
re-cre-a-tion
rec-re-ation
rec-re-ation-al
re-crim-i-nate
re-crim-i-nat-ed
re-crim-i-nat-ing
re-cruit
re-cruit-er
re-cruit-ment
rec-tal
rect-an-gle
rect-an-gu-lar
rec-ti-fi-er
rec-ti-fy
rec-ti-fied
rec-ti-fy-ing
rec-ti-fi-ca-tion
rec-ti-lin-ear
rec-ti-tude
rec-tor
rec-to-ry
rec-to-ries
rec-tum
rec-tums
rec-ta

re-cum-bent
re-cum-ben-cy
re-cum-bent-ly
re-cu-per-ate
re-cur
re-cur-ring
re-cur-rence
re-cur-rent
red-bird
red--blood-ed
re-dec-o-rate
re-dec-o-rat-ed
re-dec-o-ra-tion
re-ded-i-cate
re-ded-i-cat-ed
re-ded-i-ca-tion
re-deem
re-deem-able
re-deem-er
re-demp-tion
re-demp-tive
red--hand-ed
red--hot
re-di-rect
re-di-rec-tion
red--let-ter
red--neck
re-do
red-o-lence
red-o-len-cy
red-o-lent
re-dou-ble
re-dou-bled
re-dou-bling
re-doubt-able
re-doubt-ably
re-dound
re-dress
red-start
re-duce
re-duc-tion
re-dun-dance
re-dun-dant

re-du-pli-cate
re-du-pli-cat-ed
re-du-pli-ca-tion
red-wood
re-echo
re-ech-oed
reedy
reed-i-er
reef-er
re-elect
re-elec-tion
re-em-pha-sie
re-em-pha-sized
re-em-pha-siz-ing
re-en-force
re-en-forced
re-en-forc-ing
re-en-force-ment
re-en-list
re-en-list-ment
re-en-ter
re-en-trance
re-en-try
re-en-tries
re-es-tab-lish
re-es-tab-lish-ment
re-ex-am-ine
re-ex-am-i-na-tion
re-fec-to-ry
re-fec-to-ries
re-fer
re-fer-ral
ref-er-ee
ref-er-ence
ref-er-enced
ref-er-enc-ing
ref-er-en-dum
ref-er-en-dums
ref-er-en-da
ref-er-ent
re-fill
re-fill-able
re-fine

re-fined
re-fin-ing
re-fine-ment
re-fin-ery
re-fin-er-ies
re-fin-ish
re-fit
re-fit-ted
re-fit-ting
re-flect
re-flec-tion
re-flec-tive
re-flec-tive-ly
re-flec-tive-ness
re-flec-tor
re-flex
re-flex-ive
re-for-est
re-for-est-a-tion
re-form
re-form-a-tory
re-fract
re-frac-tive
re-frac-tion
re-frac-to-ry
re-frac-to-ri-ly
re-frain
re-fresh
re-fresh-ing
re-fresh-ment
re-frig-er-ant
re-frig-er-ate
re-frig-er-at-ed
re-frig-er-a-tor
re-fu-el
ref-uge
ref-u-gee
re-ful-gence
re-ful-gent
re-fund
re-fur-bish
re-fus-al
re-fuse

re-fused
re-fus-ing
ref-use
re-fute
re-gain
re-gal
re-gal-ly
re-gale
re-galed
re-gal-ing
re-ga-lia
re-gard
re-gard-ful
re-gard-ing
re-gard-less
re-gard-less-ly
re-gat-ta
re-gen-cy
re-gen-cies
re-gen-er-ate
re-gen-er-at-ed
re-gen-er-at-ing
re-gen-er-a-vy
re-gen-er-a-tion
re-gen-er-a-tive
re-gent
re-grime
reg-i-men
reg-i-ment
reg-i-men-tal
reg-i-men-ta-tion
re-gion
re-gion-al
re-gion-al-ly
reg-is-ter
reg-is-tered
reg-is-trant
reg-is-trar
reg-is-tra-tion
reg-is-try
reg-is-tries
re-gress
re-gres-sion

re-gres-sor
re-gret
  re-gret-ted
  re-gret-ting
  re-gret-ta-ble
  re-gret-ta-bly
  re-gret-er
  re-gret-ful
  re-gret-ful-ly
reg-u-lar
  reg-u-lar-i-ty
reg-u-late
  reg-u-lat-ed
  reg-u-lat-ing
  reg-u-la-tive
  reg-u-la-tor
  reg-u-la-to-ry
reg-u-la-tion
re-gur-gi-tate
  re-gur-gi-tat-ed
  re-gur-gi-tat-ing
  re-gur-gi-ta-tion
re-ha-bil-i-tate
  re-ha-bil-i-tat-ed
  re-ha-bil-i-tat-ing
  re-ha-bil-i-ta-tion
  re-ha-bil-i-ta-tive
re-hash
re-hears-al
re-hearse
  re-hearsed
  re-hears-ing
  re-hears-er
reign
re-im-burse
  re-im-bursed
  re-im-burs-ing
  re-im-burse-meny
rein
re-in-car-na-tion
rein-deer
re-in-force
  re-in-forced

re-in-forc-ing
re-in-force-ment
re-in-state
  re-in-stat-ed
  re-in-stat-ing
  re-in-state-ment
re-it-er-ate
  re-it-er-at-ed
  re-it-er-at-ing
  re-it-er-a-tion
re-ject
  re-jec-tion
re-joice
  re-joiced
  re-joic-ing
  re-joic-er
  re-joic-ing-ly
re-join
re-join-der
re-ju-ve-nate
  re-ju-ve-nat-ed
  re-ju-ve-nat-ing
  re-ju-ve-na-tion
  re-ju-ve-na-tor
re-kin-dle
  re-kin-dled
  re-kin-dling
re-lapse
  re-lapsed
  re-laps-ing
  re-laps-er
re-late
  re-lat-ed
  re-lat-ing
  re-lat-er
  re-lat-or
re-la-tion
  re-la-tion-al
re-la-tion-ship
rel-a-tive
  rel-a-tive-ly
rel-a-tiv-ism
  rel-a-tiv-ist

rel-a-tiv-is-tic
rel-a-tiv-i-ty
rel-a-tiv-ize
re-la-tor
re-lax
  re-lax-er
re-lax-ation
re-lay
  re-laid
  re-lay-ing
re-lay
  re-layed
  re-lay-ing
re-lease
  re-leas-ed
  re-leas-ing
  re-leas-a-ble
  re-leas-er
rel-e-gate
  rel-e-gat-ed
  rel-e-ga-tion
re-lent
re-lent-less
rel-e-vant
  rel-e-vance
  rel-e-van-cy
  rel-e-vant-ly
re-li-able
  re-li-abil-i-ty
  re-li-able-ness
  re-li-ably
re-li-ance
  re-li-ant
rel-ic
re-lief
re-leive
  re-liev-ed
  re-liev-ing
  re-liev-able
  re-liev-er
re-li-gion
re-li-gi-os-i-ty
re-li-gious

re-lin-quish
rel-ish
re-live
  re-lived
  re-liv-ing
re-lo-cate
  re-lo-ct-ed
  re-lo-cat-ing
  re-lo-ca-tion
re-luc-tance
  re-luc-tant
re-ly
  re-lied
  re-ly-ing
re-main
re-main-der
re-mand
re-mark
re-mark-able
  re-mark-able-ness
  re-mark-ably
re-me-di-a-ble
re-me-di-al
rem-e-dy
  rem-e-dies
  rem-e-died
  rem-e-dy-ing
re-mem-ber
re-mem-brance
re-mind
  re-mind-er
re-mind-ful
rem-i-nisce
  rem-i-nisced
  rem-i-nisc-ing
rem-i-nis-cence
rem-i-nis-cent
re-miss
re-mis-sion
re-mit
  re-mit-ted
  re-mit-ting
re-mit-tance

rem-nant
re-mod-el
re-mon-strance
re-mon-strate
  re-mon-strat-ed
  re-mon-strat-ing
re-morse
  re-morse-ful
  re-morse-ful-ly
  re-morse-less
re-mote
  re-mot-er
  re-mot-est
re-mount
re-mov-able
re-mov-al
re-move
  re-moved
  re-mov-ing
re-mu-ner-ate
  re-mu-ner-at-ed
  re-mu-ner-at-ing
  re-mu-ner-a-tion
re-nais-sance
re-na-scence
  re-na-scent
rend
rend-er
ren-dez-vous
  ren-dez-voused
  ren-dez-vous-ing
ren-di-tion
ren-e-gade
re-nege
  re-neged
  re-neg-ing
re-new
re-new-al
ren-net
re-nounce
  re-nounced
  re-nounc-ing
ren-o-vate

ren-o-vat-ed
ren-o-vat-ing
ren-o-va-tion
re-nown
re-nowned
rent-al
re-nun-ci-a-tion
re-or-ga-ni-za-tion
re-or-ga-nize
  re-or-ga-niz-ed
  re-or-gan-iz-ing
re-pair
re-pair-man
  re-pair-men
rep-a-ra-ble
rep-a-ra-tion
rep-ar-tee
re-pa-tri-ate
  re-pa-tri-at-ed
re-pay
  re-paid
  re-pay-ing
  re-pay-ment
re-peal
re-peat
  re-peat-able
  re-peat-ed
re-peat-er
re-pel
  re-pelled
  re-pel-ling
re-pel-lent
re-pent
  re-pent-ance
  re-pen-tant
re-per-cus-sion
rep-er-toire
rep-er-to-ry
  rep-er-to-ries
rep-e-ti-tion
  rep-e-ti-tious
  re-pet-i-tive
re-place

re-placed
re-plac-ing
re-plac-able
re-place-ment
re-plen-ish
re-plete
re-ple-tion
rep-li-ca
re-ply
re-plied
re-ply-ing
re-plies
re-port
re-port-age
re-port-ed-ly
re-port-er
rep-or-to-ri-al
re-pos-al
re-pose
re-posed
re-pos-ing
re-pose-ful
re-pos-it
re-po-si-tion
re-pos-i-to-ry
re-pos-i-tor-ies
re-pos-sess
re-pos-ses-sion
re-pow-er
rep-re-hend
rep-re-hen-si-ble
rep-re-hen-sive
rep-re-sent
rep-re-sen-ta-tion
rep-re-sen-ta-tive
re-press
re-press-ed
re-pres-sion
re-pres-sive-ness
re-prieve
re-prieved
re-priev-ing
rep-ri-mand

re-print
re-pris-al
re-prise
re-proach
re-proach-ful
rep-ro-bate
rep-ro-ba-tion
re-pro-cess
re-pro-duce
re-pro-duced
re-pro-duc-ing
re-pro-duc-tion
re-pro-duc-tive
re-proof
re-prove
re-proved
re-prov-ing
rep-tile
rep-til-ian
re-pub-lic
re-pub-li-can
re-pub-li-can-ism
re-pu-di-ate
re-pu-di-at-ed
re-pu-di-at-ing
re-pu-di-a-tion
re-pu-di-a-tion-ist
re-pugn
re-pug-nance
re-pug-nan-cy
re-pug-nant
re-pulse
re-pulsed
re-puls-ing
re-pul-sion
re-pul-sive
re-pul-sive-ly
rep-u-ta-ble
rep-u-ta-bly
rep-u-ta-bil-i-ty
rep-u-ta-tion
re-pute
re-put-ed

re-put-ing
re-put-ed-ly
re-quest
re-qui-em
re-quire
re-quired
re-quir-ing
re-quire-ment
req-ui-site
req-ui-site-ly
req-ui-si-tion
re-quit-al
re-quite
re-quit-a-ble
re-quit-ed
re-quit-ing
rere-dos
re-run
re-run-ning
re-sale
re-sal-a-ble
re-scind
re-scind-a-ble
re-scis-sion
res-cue
res-cued
res-cu-ing
res-cu-er
re-search
re-search-er
re-sec-tion
re-se-da
re-seed
re-sem-blance
re-sem-ble
re-sem-bled
re-sem-bling
re-send
re-sent
re-sent-ful
re-sent-ment
re-ser-va-tion
re-serve

re-served
re-serv-ing
re-serve clause
re-serv-ist
res-er-voir
re-set
re-set-ting
re-shape
re-side
re-sid-ed
re-sid-ing
res-i-dence
res-i-den-cy
res-i-den-cies
res-i-dent
res-i-den-tial
re-sid-u-al
res-i-due
re-sign
res-ig-na-tion
re-signed
re-sil-ient
re-sil-ience
re-sil-ien-cy
res-in
res-in-ous
re-sist
re-sis-ti-ble
re-sist-er
re-sist-or
re-sist-ance
re-sis-tant
re-sist-less
re-sis-tor
res ju-di-ca-ta
res-o-lute
res-o-lu-te-ly
re-so-lu-tion
re-solve
re-solv-a-ble
re-solved
re-solv-er
re-solv-ing

res-o-nance
res-o-nant
res-o-nate
res-o-nat-ed
res-o-nat-ing
res-o-na-tor
re-sort
re-sound
re-sound-ing
re-sound-ing-ly
re-source
re-source-ful
re-spect
re-spect-ful
re-spect-ful-ly
re-spect-a-ble
re-spect-a-bly
re-spect-a-bil-i-ty
re-spect-ing
re-spec-tive
re-spec-tive-ly
res-pi-ra-tion
res-pi-ra-ble
res-pi-ra-to-ry
res-pi-ra-tor
re-spire
re-spired
re-spir-ing
res-pi-ro-me-ter
re-spite
re-splend-ent
re-splen-dent-ly
re-splend-ence
re-spond
re-spon-dent
re-sponse
re-spon-si-bil-i-ty
re-spon-si-bil-i-ties
re-spon-si-ble
re-spon-si-bly
re-spon-sive
re-spon-sum
rest

res-tau-rant
res-tau-ran-teur
rest-ful
rest home
res-ti-tu-tion
res-tive
res-tive-ly
res-tive-ness
rest-less
res-to-ra-tion
re-stor-a-tive
re-store
re-stored
re-stor-ing
re-strain
re-strain-er
re-strain-ing or-der
re-straint
re-strict
re-strict-ed
re-strict-ed-ly
re-stric-tion
re-stric-tive
re-stric-tive-ly
re-sult
re-sul-tant
re-sume
re-sumed
re-sum-ing
res-u-me
re-sump-tion
re-su-pi-nate
re-su-pine
re-sur-gence
re-sur-gent
re-sur-rect
re-sur-rec-tion
re-sus-ci-tate
re-sus-ci-tat-ed
re-sus-ci-tat-ing
re-sus-ci-ta-tion
re-sus-ci-ta-tor
re-tail

re-tail-er
re-tain
re-tainer
re-take
re-took
re-tak-en
re-tak-ing
re-tal-i-ate
re-tal-i-at-ed
re-tal-i-at-ing
re-tal-i-a-tion
re-tal-i-a-to-ry
re-tard
re-tard-ant
re-tar-da-tion
re-tard-ed
re-ten-tion
re-ten-tive
ret-i-cence
ret-i-cent
ret-i-cent-ly
ret-i-cu-lar
ret-i-cu-late
ret-i-cu-la-tion
ret-i-na
ret-i-nal
ret-i-nue
re-tire
re-tired
re-ti-ree
re-tir-ing
re-tire-ment
re-tool
re-tort
re-touch
re-trace
re-traced
re-trac-ing
re-tract
re-trac-tion
re-trac-ta-ble
re-trac-tor
re-trac-tile

re-tral
re-tread
re-treat
re-trench
re-trench-ment
re-tri-al
ret-ri-bu-tion
re-trib-u-tive
re-trie-val
re-trieve
re-triev-a-ble
re-trieved
re-triev-ing
re-triev-er
ret-ro-ac-tive
ret-ro-ac-tive-ly
ret-ro-ac-ti-vi-ty
ret-ro-grade
ret-ro-grad-ed
ret-ro-grad-ing
ret-ro-gra-da-tion
ret-ro-gress
ret-ro-gres-sion
ret-ro-gres-sive
ret-ro-pack
ret-ro-rock-et
ret-ro-spect
ret-ro-spec-tion
ret-ro-spec-tive
re-turn
re-turn-a-ble
re-turn-ee
re-turn-er
re-un-ion
re-u-nite
re-u-nit-ed
re-u-nit-ing
re-us-a-ble
re-use
rev
rev-ved
rev-ving
re-val-u-ate

re-val-u-a-tion
re-val-ue
re-vamp
re-veal
rev-eil-le
rev-el
rev-el-er
rev-e-la-tion
rev-el-ry
rev-el-ries
re-venge
re-venged
re-veng-ing
re-venge-ful
re-venge-ful-ly
rev-e-nue
rev-e-nu-er
re-verb
re-ver-ber-ate
re-ver-ber-at-ed
re-ver-ber-at-ing
re-ver-ber-a-tion
re-vere
re-vered
re-ver-ing
rev-er-ence
rev-er-enced
rev-er-enc-ing
rev-er-end
rev-er-ent
rev-er-en-tial
rev-er-ie
rev-er-sal
re-verse
re-versed
re-ver-ser
re-vers-ing
re-vers-i-ble
re-ver-sion
re-vert
re-view
re-view-er
re-vile

re-viled
re-vil-ing
re-vise
re-vised
re-vis-ing
re-vi-sion
re-vi-sion-ist
re-vi-sion-ism
re-vi-tal-ize
re-vi-ta-li-za-tion
re-viv-al
re-viv-al-ist
re-vive
re-vived
re-vi-ver
re-viv-ing
re-vo-ca-ble
re-vo-ca-tion
re-voke
re-voked
re-vok-ing
re-volt
rev-o-lu-tion
rev-o-lu-tion-ary
rev-o-lu-tion-ar-ies
rev-o-lu-tion-ist
rev-o-lu-tion-ize
rev-o-lu-tion-ized
rev-o-lu-tion-iz-ing
re-volve
re-volved
re-volv-ing
re-volv-er
re-vue
re-vul-sion
re-ward
re-write
re-wrote
re-writ-ten
re-writ-ing
rhab-do-man-cy
rham-na-ceous
rhap-sod-ic

rhap-so-di-cal
rhap-so-di-cal-ly
rhap-so-dize
rhap-so-dized
rhap-so-diz-ing
rhap-so-dy
rhap-so-dies
rhap-so-dist
rhat-a-ny
rhea
rhe-ni-um
rhe-ol-o-gy
rhe-o-me-ter
rheo-stat
rhe-sus
rhe-tor
rhet-o-ric
rhe-tor-i-cal
rhet-o-ri-cian
rheum
rheu-mat-ic
rheu-mat-i-cal-ly
rheu-ma-tism
rhi-nal
rhine-stone
rhi-ni-tis
rhi-no
rhi-noc-er-os
rhi-noc-er-os-es
rhi-zan-thous
ri-zo-bi-um
rhi-zo-ceph-a-lan
rhi-zoid
rhi-zome
rhi-zo-mor-phous
rhi-zo-pus
rho-da-mine
Rhode Is-land
rho-di-um
rho-do-chro-site
rho-do-den-dron
rho-do-lite
rho-do-ra

rhom-bic
rhom-boid
rhom-boi-dal
rhom-bus
rhom-bus-es
rhom-bi
rhon-chus
rhu-barb
rhyme
rhymed
rhymer
rhym-ing
rhyme-ster
rhythm
rhyth-mic
rhyth-mi-cal
rhyth-mi-cal-ly
rhyth-mics
ri-al-to
ri-ant
rib
ribbed
rib-ber
rib-bing
rib-ald
rib-ald-ry
rib-ald-ries
rib-band
rib-bon
ri-bo-fla-vin
ri-bo-nu-cle-ase
ri-bo-nu-cle-ic
rib-wort
rice
riced
ric-ing
rice bird
rice pa-per
ric-er
rich
rich-ly
rich-es
rich-ness

ri-cin
rick-ets
rick-ett-si-a
rick-et-y
  rick-et-i-er
  rick-et-i-est
rick-rack
rick-shaw
  ricksha
ric-o-chet
ri-cot-ta
rid
  rid-ded
  rid-ding
rid-dance
rid-dle
  rid-dled
  rid-dling
ride
  rid-den
  rid-ing
  rid-er
ridge
  ridged
  ridg-ing
ridge-pole
rid-i-cule
  rid-i-culed
  rid-i-cul-ing
ri-dic-u-lous
  ridiculously
  ridiculousness
rid-ley
ri-dot-to
rife
  rifely
rif-fle
  rif-fled
  riffler
  rif-fling
riff-raff
ri-fle
ri-fle-man

ri-fling
rift
rig
  rigged
  rig-ging
rig-a-doon
rig-a-to-ni
rig-ger
right
  right-ly
right an-gle
right-eous
  righteously
  righteousness
right-ful
right-hand
right--hand-ed
right-ism
rig-id
  ri-gid-i-ty
  ri-gid-ness
ri-gid-i-fy
  ri-gid-i-fi-ca-tion
rig-ma-role
rig-or
  rig-or-ous
  rigorously
rig-or-ism
rig-or mor-tis
rile
  riled
  ril-ing
rill
rim
rime
ri-mose
  rimosely
  rimosity
rim-rock
rind
rin-der-pest
ring
ring-er

ring-lead-er
ring-let
ring-mas-ter
ring-side
ring-worm
rink
rinse
  rinsed
  rins-ing
ri-ot
  ri-ot-ous
rip
ripped
  rip-ping
  rip-per
ri-par-i-an
ripe
  ripe-ly
  ripe-ness
rip-en
rip--off
ri-poste
rip-ple
  rip-pled
  rip-pling
rip-rap
rip-roar-ing
rip saw
rip tide
rise
  rose
  ris-en
  ris-ing
ris-er
ris-i-ble
  ris-i-bil-i-ty
risk
risk-y
  risk-i-ness
ri-sot-to
rite
rit-u-al
rit-u-al-ism

rit-u-al-ist
 rit-u-al-is-tic
 rit-u-al-is-ti-cal-ly
ritz-y
 ritz-i-er
 ritz-i-est
ri-val
ri-val-ry
 ri-val-ries
rive
riv-er
riv-er-bed
riv-er-ine
riv-er-side
riv-er-weed
riv-et
 riv-et-er
riv-i-era
riv-u-let
roach
road
road-a-bil-i-ty
road-bed
road-block
road-run-ner
road-side
road-ster
road-way
roam
 roam-er
roan
roar
 roar-er
 roar-ing
roast
roast-er
rob
 robbed
 rob-bing
 rob-ber
rob-a-lo
ro-band
rob-ber-y

rob-ber-ies
robe
 robed
 rob-ing
rob-in
ro-ble
ro-bot
ro-bot-ics
ro-bot-ize
 ro-bot-i-za-tion
ro-bust
 ro-bust-ly
 ro-bust-ness
roc-am-bole
roch-et
rock
rock-er
rock-et
rock-e-teer
rock-et-ry
rock-fish
rock-ling
rock-oon
rock-ribbed
rock-rose
rock-y
 rock-i-er
 rock-i-est
 rock-i-ness
ro-co-co
rod
rode
ro-dent
ro-den-ti-cide
ro-de-o
 ro-de-os
rod-man
rod-o-mon-tade
roe
roe-buck
roent-gen
roent-gen-o-gram
rog-er

rogue
 ro-guish
 ro-guish-ly
rogu-er-y
 rogu-er-ies
roil
roist-er
role
roll
roll-er
roll-er bear-ing
roll-er coast-er
roll-er skate
rol-lick
 rol-lick-ing
roll-ing pin
ro-ly--po-ly
 ro-ly--po-lies
ro-maine
ro-mance
 ro-manced
 ro-manc-ing
ro-man-tic
 ro-man-ti-cal-ly
ro-man-ti-cism
ro-man-ti-cize
 ro-man-ti-ciz-ing
romp
romp-er
ron-dure
rood
roof
roof-ing
rook
rook-er-y
 rook-er-ies
rook-ie
room
room-er
room-ful
room-mate
room-y
 room-i-er

room-i-est
room-i-ly
room-i-ness
roost
roos-ter
root
root-age
root-less
root-let
root-stock
root-y
rope
  roped
  rop-ing
rop-y
  rop-i-er
  rop-i-est
ro-que-laure
ror-qual
ro-sa-ry
  ro-sa-ries
rose
ro-se-ate
  ro-se-ate-ly
rose-bay
rose-bud
rose--col-ored
rose-mar-y
  rose-mar-ies
ro-se-o-la
ro-sette
rose-wood
ros-in
ros-ter
ros-trum
  ros-tra
  ros-trums
ros-y
  ros-i-ly
  ros-i-er
  ros-i-est
rot
ro-ta-ry

ro-tar-ies
ro-tate
  ro-tat-ed
  ro-tat-ing
  ro-ta-ta-ble
ro-ta-tion
ro-ta-tor
ro-te-none
ro-tis-ser-ie
ro-tor
rot-ten
  rot-ten-ness
  rot-ten-ly
rot-ter
ro-tund
  ro-tun-di-ty
  ro-tun-di-ties
ro-tun-da
rouge
  rouged
  roug-ing
rough
  rough-ly
  rough-ness
rough-age
rough--and--ready
rough-en
rough-house
rough-neck
rough-shod
rou-leau
rou-lette
round
  roundly
  roundness
round-a-bout
round-er
round-ish
round-up
rouse
  roused
  rous-ing
  rous-er

roust
roust-a-bout
rout
route
  rout-ed
  rout-ing
rout-er
rou-tine
rou-tin-ize
  rou-tin-ized
  rou-tin-iz-ing
row
row-boat
row-dy
  row-dies
  row-di-er
  row-di-est
  row-di-ness
roy-al
roy-al-ist
roy-al-ty
  roy-al-ties
rub
  rubbed
  rub-bing
rub-ber
  rub-ber-y
rub-ber-ize
  rub-ber-ized
  rub-ber-iz-ing
rub-ber-neck
rub-bish
  rub-bish-y
rub-ble
  rub-bly
  rub-bli-er
  rub-bli-est
rub-down
ru-be-fa-cient
ru-bel-la
ru-bel-lite
ru-be-o-la
  ru-be-o-lar

ru-bi-cund
ru-bi-cun-di-ty
ru-bid-i-um
ru-bi-ous
ru-bric
ru-bri-cate
ru-by
ru-bies
ruche
ruck
ruck-sack
ruck-us
rud-der
rud-dock
rud-dy
rud-di-er
rud-di-est
rud-di-ly
rude
rudely
rudeness
ru-di-ment
ru-di-ment-al
ru-di-men-ta-ry
rue
rue-ful
rue-ful-ly
rue-ful-ness
ru-fes-cent
ruff
ruffed
ruf-fi-an
ruf-fle
ruf-fled
ruf-fling
rug
ru-ga
rug-by
rug-ged
rug-ged-ly
rug-ged-ness
ru-gose
ru-in

ru-in-a-tion
ru-in-ous
rule
ruled
rul-ing
rul-er
rum
rum-ba
rum-baed
rum-ba-ing
rum-ble
rumbler
rumbling
rumbly
ru-men
ru-mi-nant
ru-mi-nate
ru-mi-na-tion
ru-mi-na-tive
ru-mi-na-tor
rum-mage
rum-maged
rum-mag-ing
rum-mag-er
rum-my
rum-mies
ru-mor
ru-mor-mon-ger
rump
rum-ple
rum-pled
rum-pling
rum-pus
run
run-ning
run-about
run-around
run-away
run-nel
run-ner
run-ner--up
run-ning
run-ny

run-ni-er
run-ni-est
run-off
run--on
run-way
rup-ture
rup-tured
rup-tur-ing
ru-ral
ru-ral-ize
ruse
rush
rusk
rus-set
rust
rus-tic
rus-ti-cate
rus-ti-cat-ed
rus-ti-cat-ing
rus-ti-ca-tion
rus-tle
rus-tled
rus-tling
rus-tler
rust-proof
rus-ty
rust-i-er
rust-i-est
rut
rut-ted
rut-ting
ru-ta-ba-ga
ru-the-ni-um
ruth-ful
ruth-less
ruth-less-ly
ru-ti-lant
rut-ty
rye

S

sab-a-dil-la
sab-bat

Sab-bath
sab-bat-i-cal
sa-ber
sa-ber-toothed
sa-ble
sa-ble-fish
sa-bot
sab-o-tage
  sab-o-taged
  sab-o-tag-ing
sab-o-teur
sa-bra
sac-cade
sac-cate
sac-cha-rate
sac-char-i-fy
sac-cha-rim-e-ter
sac-cha-rin
sac-cha-roi-dal
sac-cha-rom-e-ter
sac-cu-lar
sac-cu-late
sac-cule
sac-er-do-tal
sa-chem
sa-chet
sack
sack-cloth
sack-ful
  sack-fuls
sack-ing
sacque
sa-cral
sac-ra-ment
  sac-ra-men-tal
sa-crar-i-um
sa-cred
  sa-cred-ly
  sa-cred-ness
sac-ri-fice
  sac-ri-ficed
  sac-ri-fic-ing
  sac-ri-fic-er

sac-ri-fi-cial
sac-ri-lege
sac-ri-le-gious
sac-ris-ty
sc-ro-il-li-ac
sac-ro-sanct
sac-ro-sanc-i-ty
sac-rum
  sac-rums
sac-ra
sa-cral
sad
sad-den
sad-dle
  sad-dled
  sad-dling
sad-dle-backed
sad-dle-bag
sad-dler
  sad-dler-y
sad-i-ron
sad-ism
  sad-ist
  sa-dis-tic
sad-o-mas-o-chism
  sad-o-mas-o-chist
sa-fa-ri
  sa-fa-ris
safe
  saf-er
  saf-est
safe--con-duct
safe-crack-er
  safe-crack-ing
safe--de-pos-it
safe-guard
safe-keep-ing
safe-ty
  safe-ties
safe-ty match
safe-ty pin
safe-ty valve
safe-ty zone

saf-flow-er
saf-fron
saf-ra-nine
saf-role
sag
  sagged
  sag-ging
sa-ga
sa-ga-cious
sa-gac-i-ty
sa-gac-i-ty
sag-a-more
sage
  sag-er
  sag-est
sage-brush
sag-ger
sag-it-tal
Sag-it-ta-ri-us
sag-it-tate
sa-go
sa-gua-ro
said
sail
sail-er
sail-fish
sail-ing
sail-or
sail-plane
sain-foin
saint
  saint-hood
saint-ed
saint-ly
  saint-li-er
  saint-li-est
sa-ke
sal-a-ble
  sal-a-ble
  sal-a-bil-i-ty
  sal-a-bly
sa-la-cious
sal-ad

sal-a-man-der
sa-la-mi
sa-lar-i-at
sal-a-ry
  sal-a-ries
sale
sales-man
  sales-men
sales-man-ship
sales-per-son
  sales-peo-ple
sales-room
sal-i-cin
sa-lic-y-late
sa-li-ence
sa-li-ent
  sa-li-ence
  sa-li-en-cy
  sa-li-ent-ly
sa-line
  sa-lin-i-ty
sa-li-nize
sa-li-nom-e-ter
sa-li-va
  sal-i-var-y
  sal-i-vate
sal-low
  sal-low-ish
sal-ly
  sal-lies
salm-on
sa-lon
sa-loon
sal-si-fy
salt
  salt-ed
  salt-er
  salt-ing
salt-cel-lar
sal-tine
salt-shak-er
salt-wa-ter
salt-wort

salt-y
  salt-i-er
  salt-i-est
  salt-i-ness
sa-lu-bri-ous
  sa-lu-bri-ous-ly
sal-u-tar-y
  sal-u-tar-i-ly
sal-u-ta-tion
sa-lu-ta-to-ry
  sa-lu-ta-to-ries
sa-lute
  sa-luted
  sa-lut-ing
  sa-lut-er
salv-a-ble
sal-vage
sal-va-tion
salve
  salved
  salv-ing
  salv-er
sal-ver
sal-vi-a
sal-vo
sa-mar-i-tan
sa-mar-i-um
sam-ba
  sam-baed
  sam-ba-ing
same
same-ness
sam-o-var
samp
sam-pan
sam-ple
  sam-pled
  sam-pling
sam-pler
sam-u-rai
san-a-to-ri-um
sanc-ti-fy
  sanc-ti-fied

sanc-ti-fy-ing
sanc-ti-fi-ca-tion
sanc-ti-fi-er
sanc-ti-mo-ny
sanc-ti-mo-ni-ous
sanc-tion
  sanc-tion-a-ble
  sanc-tion-er
sanc-ti-ty
  sanc-ti-ties
sanc-tu-ary
  sanc-tu-ar-ies
sanc-tum
  sanc-ta
sand
  san-ded
  san-der
san-dal
san-dal-wood
san-dar-ac
sand-bag
  sand-bagged
  sand-bag-ger
  sand-bag-ging
sand-bank
sand-blast
sand-box
sand-cast
  sand-cast-ed
  sand-cast-ing
sand-lot
sand-man
  sand-men
sand-pa-per
sand-pi-per
sand-stone
sand-wich
  sand-wiched
  sand-wiches
san-dy
  san-di-er
  san-di-est
sane

san-er
san-est
sane-ly
sang-froid
san-gui-na-ria
san-guine
san-guine-ly
san-i-cle
san-i-ous
san-i-tar-i-an
san-i-tar-i-um
san-i-tar-i-ums
san-i-tar-ia
san-i-tar-y
san-i-tar-i-ly
san-i-tate
san-i-ta-tion
san-i-tize
san-i-tized
san-i-tiz-er
san-i-tiz-ing
san-i-ty
sank
sap
sapped
sap-ping
sap-head
sap-head-ed
sa-pid
sa-pi-ent
sa-pi-ence
sa-pi-en-cy
sap-less
sap-ling
sa-pon-i-fy
sa-pon-i-fied
sa-pon-i-fy-ing
sap-per
sa-por
sap-phire
sap-phism
sap-py
sap-pi-er

sap-pi-est
sap-suck-er
sap-wood
sa-ran
sar-casm
sar-cas-tic
sar-cas-ti-cal-ly
sar-co-ma
sar-co-mas
sar-co-ma-ta
sar-co-ma-tous
sar-coph-a-gus
sar-coph-a-gus-es
sar-dine
sar-don-ic
sar-don-i-cal-ly
sar-gas-sum
sa-ri
sa-ris
sa-rong
sar-sa-pa-ril-la
sar-to-ri-al
sash
sashed
sash-es
sa-shay
sa-shayed
sass
sas-sa-fras
sas-sy
sas-si-er
sas-si-est
sa-tan-ic
sa-tan-i-cal
sa-tan-ism
sa-tan-ist
satch-el
sate
sat-ed
sat-ing
sa-teen
sat-el-lite
sa-ti-a-ble

sa-ti-a-bly
sa-ti-a-bil-i-ty
sa-ti-ate
sa-ti-at-ed
sa-ti-at-ing
sa-ti-a-tion
sa-ti-e-ty
sat-in
sat-in-y
sat-ire
sa-tir-i-cal
sa-tir-i-cal-ly
sat-i-rist
sat-i-rize
sat-i-rized
sat-i-riz-ing
sat-i-riz-er
sat-is-fac-tion
sat-is-fac-to-ry
sat-is-fa-to-ri-ly
sat-is-fy
sat-is-fied
sat-is-fy-ing
sat-is-fi-a-ble
sat-is-fi-er
sat-is-fy-ing-ly
sat-u-ra-ble
sat-u-rate
sat-u-rat-ed
sat-u-rat-ing
sat-u-ra-tion
Sat-ur-day
sat-ur-na-li-a
sat-ur-nine
sa-tyr
sa-tyr-ic
sauce
sauced
sauc-ing
sau-cer
sau-cy
sau-ci-er
sau-ci-est

sau-er-bra-ten
sau-er-kraut
sau-na
saun-ter
 saun-tered
 saun-ter-er
sau-ro-pod
sau-sage
 sau-sages
sau-te
sav-age
 sav-age-ly
 sav-age-ry
 sav-age-ries
sa-van-na
sa-vant
save
 saved
 sav-ing
 sav-er
sav-ior
sa-voir-faire
sa-vor
 sa-vor-er
sa-vor-y
 sa-vor-i-er
 sa-vor-i-est
sav-vy
saw
 sawed
 saw-ing
saw-buck
saw-dust
sawed--off
saw-horse
saw-mill
saw-toothed
saw-yer
sax-o-phone
 sax-o-phon-ist
say
 said
 say-ing

say-a-ble
say-er
say-so
scab
 scabbed
 scab-bing
scab-bard
scab-by
 scab-bi-er
 scab-bi-est
sca-bies
sca-brous
 sca-brous-ly
scads
scaf-fold
scaf-fold-ing
scal-a-ble
sca-lar
sca-lar-i-form
scal-a-wag
scald
 scald-ing
scale
 scaled
 scal-er
 scal-ing
 scale-less
sca-lene
sca-le-nus
scal-lion
scal-lop
scalp
scal-pel
scaly
 sca-li-er
 sca-li-est
scamp
scamp-er
scam-pi
scan
 scanned
 scan-ner
scan-dal

scan-dal-ize
 scan-dal-ized
 scan-dal-iz-ing
scan-dal-mon-ger
scan-dal-ous
 scan-dal-ous-ly
scan-dent
scan-sion
scant
 scant-ness
scan-ties
scant-y
 scant-i-er
 scant-i-est
 scant-i-ly
scape-goat
scape-grace
scaph-oid
sca-pose
scap-u-la
 scap-u-las
 scap-u-lae
scap-u-lar
scar
 scarred
 scar-ring
scar-ab
scarce
 scar-ci-ty
 scarce-ly
 scarce-ness
scare
 scared
scare-crow
scared-y-cat
scare-mon-ger
scarf
 scarfs
 scarves
scarf-skin
scar-i-fy
 scar-i-fied
 scar-i-fi-ca-tion

scar-i-fy-ing
scar-i-ous
scar-let
scarp
scar-y
  scar-i-er
  scar-i-est
scat
  scat-ted
  scat-ting
scathe
scath-ing
  scath-ing-ly
scat-o-log-i-cal
scat-ter
  scat-tered
  scat-ter-a-ble
  scat-ter-er
scat-ter-a-tion
scat-ter-brain
scav-enge
  scav-enged
  scav-eng-ing
scav-en-ger
sce-nar-i-o
  sce-nar-i-os
sce-nar-ist
scene
scen-er-y
  scen-er-ies
sce-nic
  sce-ni-cal
scent
  scent-ed
scep-ter
  scep-tered
  scep-ter-ing
sched-ule
  sched-ul-ed
  sched-ul-ing
sche-ma
sche-ma-tic
  sche-ma-ti-cal-ly

sche-ma-tize
  sche-ma-tized
  sche-ma-tiz-ing
scheme
  schem-er
  schem-ing
scher-zo
  scher-zos
  scher-zi
schil-ler
schism
schis-mat-ic
  schis-mat-i-cal
schist
  schis-tose
schiz-o
  schiz-os
schiz-oid
schiz-o-phre-ni-a
  schiz-o-phren-ic
schle-miel
schmaltz
  schmalt-zy
schmo
schnapps
schnau-zer
schnit-zel
schnook
schnor-kel
schnoz-zle
schol-ar
schol-ar-ly
  schol-ar-li-ness
schol-ar-ship
scho-las-tic
  scho-las-ti-cal-ly
scho-las-ti-cism
school
school board
school-house
school-child
  school-chil-dren
school-ing

school-room
school-teach-er
  school-teach-ing
school-work
schoon-er
schuss
schwa
sci-ae-nid
sci-at-ic
sci-at-i-ca
sci-ence
sci-en-tif-ic
  sci-en-tif-i-cal-ly
sci-en-tist
scil-la
scim-i-tar
scin-tig-ra-phy
scin-til-la
scin-til-lant
scin-til-late
  scin-til-lat-ed
  scin-til-lat-ing
  scin-til-la-tion
sci-on
scir-rhus
scis-sion
scis-sor
  scis-sored
  scis-soring
scis-sors
scle-ra
  scle-rot-i-ca
scler-ite
scle-ro-der-ma
scle-rom-e-ter
scle-ro-sis
  scle-ro-ses
scle-rot-ic
scle-rous
scoff
  scoffed
  scoff-er
  scoff-ing-ly

scold
scold-er
scold-ing
sco-lex
sco-li-o-sis
sco-li-ot-ic
sconce
scone
scoop
scooped
scoop-er
scoop-ful
scoot-er
scope
scop-u-la
scop-u-las
scop-u-lae
scop-u-late
scor-bu-tic
scorch
scorched
scorch-ing
scorch-er
score
scored
scor-ing
score-less
scor-er
score-board
score-keep-er
sco-ri-a
scor-i-fy
scor-i-fi-ca-tion
scorn
scorn-er
scorn-ful
scorn-ful-ly
scor-pi-oid
scor-pi-on
scotch
scotched
scotch-ing
scot--free

sco-to-ma
sco-to-ma-tous
scot-tie
scoun-drel
scoun-drel-ly
scour
scoured
scour-er
scourge
scourged
scourg-ing
scourg-er
scour-in
scout
scout-ed
scout-ing
scout-mas-ter
scow
scowed
scow-ing
scow-man
scowl
scowl-er
scowled
scowl-ing
srab-ble
scrab-bled
scrab-bling
scrab-bler
scrag
scragged
scrag-ging
scrag-gly
scrag-gli-er
scrag-gli-est
scrag-gy
scrag-gi-er
scrag-gi-est
scram
scrammed
scram-ming
scram-ble
scram-bled

scram-bling
scram-bler
scrap
scrapped
scrap-ping
scrap-book
scrape
scraped
scrap-ing
scrap-er
scra-pie
scrap-per
scrap-py
scrap-pi-er
scrap-pi-est
scrap-pi-ly
scrap-pi-ness
scrap-ple
scratch
scratch-a-ble
scratch-er
scratch-y
scratch-i-er
scratch-i-est
scratch-i-ly
scratch-i-ness
scrawl
scrawled
scrawl-ing
scrawn-y
scrawn-i-er
scrawn-i-est
scrawn-i-ness
scream
screamed
scream-ing
scream-ing-ly
scream-er
scree
screech
screech-er
screed
screen

screen-a-ble
screened
screen-er
screen-ing
screen-play
screw
screwed
screw-ing
screw-ball
screw-driv-er
screw-y
screw-i-er
screw-i-est
scrib-ble
scrib-bled
scrib-bling
scrib-bler
scribe
scribed
scrib-ing
scrib-al
scrib-er
scrim
scrim-mage
scrim-maged
scrim-mag-ing
scrimp
scrimped
scrimp-ing
scrimp-y
scrimp-i-er
scrimp-i-est
scrim-shaw
scrip
script
scrip-tur-al
scrip-ture
script-writ-er
scrive-ner
scrod
scrof-u-la
scrof-u-lous
scroll

scrolled
scroll-ing
scroll-work
scrooge
scro-tum
scro-ta
scro-tal
scrounge
scroung-er
scrounged
scroung-ing
scrub
scrubbed
scrub-bing
scrub-ber
scrub-by
scrub-bi-er
scrub-bi-est
scrub-wom-an
scrub-wom-en
scruff
scruff-y
scruff-i-er
scruff-i-est
scrump-tious
scru-ple
scru-pled
scru-pling
scru-pu-lous
scru-pu-los-i-ty
scru-pu-lous-ly
scru-ta-ble
scru-ti-nize
scru-ti-nized
scru-ti-niz-ing
scru-ti-ny
scru-ti-nies
scu-ba
scud
scud-ded
scud-ding
scuff
scuf-fle

scuf-fled
scuf-fling
scull
scul-ler-y
scul-ler-ies
scul-lion
sculpt
sculp-tor
sculp-ture
sculp-tured
sculp-tur-ing
sculp-tur-al
* **scum**
scummed
scum-ming
scum-ble
scum-bled
scum-bling
scum-my
scum-mi-er
scum-mi-est
scup-per
scurf
scurf-y
scurf-i-er
scurf-i-est
scur-ri-lous
scur-ril-i-ty
scur-ril-i-ties
scur-ry
scur-ri-ed
scur-ry-ing
scur-vy
scur-vi-ly
scur-vi-er
scur-vi-est
scut
scut-age
scute
scu-tel-late
scu-tel-lum
scut-tle
scut-tled

scut-tling
scut-tle-butt
scythe
scythed
scyth-ing
sea-bed
sea-coast
sea-drome
sea-far-ing
sea-far-er
sea-food
sea gull
sea horse
seal
seal-er
sealed
seal-ing
sea-lam-prey
seal-ant
sea legs
sea lev-el
seal-ing wax
sea li-on
seal-skin
seam
seamed
seam-ing
seam-er
sea-maid
sea-man
sea-men
sea-man-ship
seam-stress
seam-stress-es
seam-y
seam-i-er
seam-i-est
sea ot-ter
sea-plane
sea-port
sear
seared
sear-ing

search
search-a-ble
search-er
search-ing
search-light
search war-rant
sea-scape
sea ser-pent
sea-shell
sea-shore
sea-sick
sea-sick-ness
sea-side
sea-son
sea-son-er
sea-son-a-ble
sea-son-al
sea-son-al-ly
sea-son-ing
seat
seat-ed
seat-ing
sea ur-chin
sea-ward
sea-weed
sea-wor-thy
sea-wor-thi-ness
se-ba-ceous
se-cant
se-cede
se-ced-ed
se-ced-ing
se-ced-er
se-ces-sion
se-ces-sion-ist
se-clude
se-clud-ed
se-clud-ing
se-clu-sion
se-clu-sive
sec-ond
sec-ond-ar-y
sec-ond-ar-i-ly

sec-ond--best
sec-ond--class
sec-ond-hand
sec-ond-rate
sec-ond--sto-ry man
se-cre-cy
se-cre-cies
se-cret
se-cret-ly
sec-re-tar-i-at
sec-re-tary
sec-re-tar-ies
sec-re-tar-i-al
se-crete
se-cret-ed
se-cret-ing
se-cre-tion
se-cre-tive
se-cre-to-ry
se-cre-to-ries
sec-tar-i-an
sec-tar-i-an-ism
sec-tion
sec-tion-al
sec-tion-al-ly
sec-tor
sec-to-ri-al
sec-u-lar
sec-u-lar-ism
sec-u-lar-ize
sec-u-lar-ized
sec-u-lar-iz-ing
se-cure
se-cured
se-cur-ing
se-cu-ri-ty
se-cu-ri-ties
se-dan
se-date
se-dat-ed
se-dat-ing
se-date-ly
se-da-tion

sed-a-tive
sed-en-tar-y
  sed-en-tar-i-ness
sedge
sed-i-ment
  sed-i-men-tal
  sed-i-men-ta-ry
  sed-i-men-ta-tion
se-di-tion
  se-di-tion-ary
se-di-tious
se-duce
  se-duced
  se-duc-ing
  se-duc-er
se-duc-tive
  se-duc-tive-ness
  se-duc-tive-ly
sed-u-lous
  se-du-li-ty
  sed-u-lous-ness
see
  saw
  see-ing
seed
  seed-ed
  seed-ing
seed-bed
seed-case
seed-pod
seed-y
  seed-i-er
  seed-i-est
seek
  sought
  seek-ing
  seek-er
seem
  seemed
seem-ing
  seem-ing-ly
  seem-ing-ness
seem-ly

seep-y
  seep-i-er
  seep-i-est
seep-age
seer
  seer-ess
seer-suck-er
see-saw
seethe
  seethed
  seeth-ing
seg-ment
  seg-men-tal
  seg-men-tary
seg-men-ta-tion
seg-re-gate
  seg-re-gat-ed
  seg-re-gat-ing
seg-re-ga-tion
seg-re-ga-tion-ist
sei-gneur
seine
  seined
  sein-ing
seis-mic
  seis-mal
  seis-mi-cal
  seis-mi-cal-ly
seis-mo-graph
  seis-mog-ra-pher
  seis-mo-graph-ic
  seis-mog-ra-phy
seis-mol-o-gy
  seis-mo-log-ic
  seis-mo-log-i-cal
  seis-mol-o-gist
seize
  seized
  seiz-ing
  seiz-er
sei-zure
sel-dom

se-lect
  se-lect-ed
  se-lec-tor
se-lec-tion
se-lec-tive
  se-lec-tiv-i-ty
se-le-ni-um
self
  selves
self-a-base-ment
self-a-buse
self--ad-dressed
self-ag-gran-diz-ing
self--as-sur-ance
  self--as-sured
self--cen-tered
  self--cen-tered-ness
self--com-mand
self--com-posed
self--con-fessed
self--con-fi-dence
  self--con-fi-dent
self--con-scious
self--con-tained
self--con-trol
  self--con-trolled
self--cor-rect-ing
self--crit-i-cal
self--crit-i-cism
self--de-cep-tion
  self--de-cep-tive
self--de-fense
self--de-ni-al
  self--de-ny-ing
self--dis-ci-pline
  self--dis-ci-plined
self--ed-u-cate-ed
  self--ed-u-ca-tion
self--ef-fac-ing
self--em-ployed
  self--em-ploy-ment
self--es-teem
self--ev-i-dent

self--ev-i-dence
self--ex-plan-a-to-ry
self--ex-pres-sion
self--ex-pres-sive
self--ful-fill-ing
self--ful-fill-ment
self--gov-ern-ment
self--gov-erned
self--gov-ern-ing
self--help
self--im-age
self--im-por-tance
self--im-por-tant
self--im-posed
self--im-prove-ment
self--in-duced
self--in-dul-gence
self--in-dul-gent
self--in-flict-ed
self--in-ter-est
self--in-ter-est-ed
self--ish
self--ish-ness
self--kow-ledge
self--less
self--less-ness
self--love
self--lov-ing
self--made
self--per-pet-u-at-ing
self--per-pet-u-a-tion
self--pity
self--pit-y-ing
self--pol-li-na-tion
self--pos-sessed
self--pos-sess-ed-ly
self--pos-ses-sion
self--pres-er-va-tion
self--pro-pelled
self--pro-pel-ling
self--re-al-i-za-tion
self--re-li-ance

self--re-li-ant
self--re-spect
self--re-spect-ing
self--re-straint
self--re-strain-ing
self--right-eous
--right-eous-ness
self--sac-ri-fice
self--sac-ri-fic-ing
self--same
self--sat-is-fied
self--sat-is-fac-tion
self--sat-is-fy-ing
self--ser-vice
self--serv-ing
self--start-er
self--start-ing
self--styled
self--suf-fi-cient
self--suf-fic-ing
self--suf-fi-cien-cy
self--sup-port
self--sup-port-ing
self--taught
self--will
self--willed
sell
sell-ing
sell-er
sell-out
sel-vage
sel-vaged
se-man-tics
se-man-tic
se-man-ti-cal
se-man-ti-cal-ly
sem-a-phore
sem-a-phor-ed
sem-a-phor-ing
sem-blance
se-men
se-mes-ter
sem-i-an-nu-al

sem-i-an-nu-al-ly
sem-i-ar-id
sem-i-au-to-mat-ic
sem-i-cir-cle
sem-i-cir-cu-lar
sem-i-clas-si-cal
sem-i-clas-sic
sem-i-co-lon
sem-i-con-duc-tor
sem-i-con-duct-ing
sem-i-con-scious
-i-con-sious-ness
sem-i-de-tached
sem-i-fi-nal
sem-i-fi-nal-ist
sem-i-flu-id
sem-i-for-mal
sem-i-gloss
sem-i-liq-uid
sem-i-month-ly
sem-i-nal
sem-i-nal-ly
sem-i-nar-y
sem-i-nar-ies
sem-i-nar-ian
sem-i-of-fi-cial
sem-i-of-fi-cial-ly
sem-i-per-ma-nent
sem-i-per-me-a-ble
sem-i-pre-cious
sem-i-pri-vate
sem-i-pro-fes-sion-al
sem-i-pro
sem-i-pub-lic
sem-i-skilled
sem-i-sol-id
sem-i-trail-er
sem-i-trop-ic
sem-i-trop-i-cal
sem-i-trop-ics
sem-i-vow-el
sem-i-week-ly

sem-i-week-lies
sem-i-year-ly
sen-a-ry
sen-ate
sen-a-tor
sen-a-tor-ship
sen-a-to-ri-al
sen-a-to-ri-al-ly
send--off
se-nile
se-nil-i-ty
sen-ior
sen-ior-i-ty
sen-na
sen-sate
san-sa-tion
sen-sa-tion-al
sen-sa-tion-al-ly
sen-sa-tion-al-ism
sense
sensed
sens-ing
sense-less
sense-less-ness
sen-si-bil-i-ty
sen-si-ble-ness
sen-si-ble
sen-si-ble-ness
sen-si-bly
sen-si-tive
sen-si-tiv-i-ty
sen-si-tiv-i-ties
sen-si-tize
sen-si-tized
sen-si-tiz-ing
sen-si-ti-za-tion
sen-si-tizer
sen-sor
sen-so-ry
sen-so-ri-al
sen-su-al
sen-su-al-i-ty
sen-su-al-ly

sen-su-al-ism
sen-su-al-ist
sen-su-al-ize
sen-su-al-ized
sen-su-al-iz-ing
sen-su-al-i-za-tion
sen-su-ous
sen-tence
sen-tenced
sen-tenc-ing
sen-tient
sen-ti-ment
sen-ti-men-tal
sen-ti-men-tal-ly
sen-ti-men-til-i-ty
sen-ti-men-tal-i-ties
sen-ti-men-tal-ist
sen-ti-men-tal-ize
sen-ti-men-tal-ized
-ti-men-tal-iz-ing
sen-ti-nel
sen-ti-neled
sen-ti-nel-ing
sen-try
sen-tries
se-pal
se-paled
se-palled
sep-a-ra-ble
sep-a-ra-bil-i-ty
sep-e-ra-bly
sep-a-rate
sep-a-rat-ed
sep-a-rat-ing
sep-a-ra-tion
sep-a-ra-tist
sep-a-ra-tism
sep-a-ra-tive
sep-a-ra-tor
se-pi-a
sep-sis
sep-ses
sep-ten-ni-al

sep-tet
sep-tic
sep-ti-cal-ly
sep-tic-i-ty
sep-tu-a-ge-nar-i-an
sep-tum
sep-ta
sep-tu-ple
sep-tu-pled
sep-tu-pling
sep-ul-cher
sep-u-chered
sep-u-cher-ing
se-pul-chral
se-quel
se-quence
se-quent
se-quen-tial
se-quen-tial-ly
se-ques-ter
se-ques-tered
se-ques-tra-ble
se-ques-tra-tion
se-quin
se-quined
se-quoi-a
se-ra-pe
ser-aph
ser-aphs
ser-a-phim
se-raph-ic
ser-e-nade
ser-e-nad-ed
ser-e-nad-ing
ser-e-nad-er
ser-en-dip-i-ty
ser-en-dip-i-tous
se-rene
se-rene-ness
se-ren-i-ty
se-ren-i-ties
serf
serge

ser-geant
ser-geant at arms
ser-geant ma-jor
se-ri-al
  se-ri-al-ly
  se-ri-al-ist
  se-ri-al-i-za-tion
  se-ri-al-ize
  se-ri-al-ized
  se-ri-al-iz-ing
se-ries
se-ri-ous
  se-ri-ous-ly
  se-ri-ous-ness
se-ri-ous--mind-ed
  se-ri-us--mind-ed-ly
ser-mon
  ser-mon-ize
  ser-mon-ized
  ser-mon-iz-ing
se-rol-o-gy
  se-ro-log-ic
  se-ro-log-i-cal
  se-rol-o-gist
se-rous
ser-pent
ser-pen-tine
ser-rate
  ser-rat-ing
ser-ra-tion
se-rum
  se-rums
  se-ra
serv-ant
serve
  served
  serv-ing
serv-er
serv-ice
  serv-iced
  serv-ic-ing
serv-ice-a-ble
  serv-ice-a-bil-i-ty

serv-ice-a-ble-ness
serv-ice-a-bly
serv-ice-man
ser-vile
  ser-vil-i-ty
  ser-vile-ness
ser-vi-tude
ser-vo-mech-an-ism
ses-a-me
ses-qui-cen-ten-ni-al
ses-sion
set-back
set-in
set-off
set-ter
set-ting
set-tle
  set-tled
  set-tling
set-tle-ment
set-tler
set-to
set-up
sev-en
sev-enth
sev-en-teen
  sev-en-teenth
sev-en-ty
  sev-en-ti-eth
sev-er
  sev-er-a-bil-i-ty
  sev-er-a-ble
sev-er-al
  sev-er-al-ly
sev-er-al-fold
sev-er-ance
se-vere
  se-ver-er
  se-ver-est
  se-vere-ness
se-ver-i-ty
  se-ver-i-ties

sew
sew-age
sew-ing
sew-ing ma-chine
sex-less
sex-ol-o-gy
  sex-o-log-i-cal
  sex-ol-o-gist
sex-tant
sex-tet
sex-ton
sex-tu-ple
  sex-tu-pled
  sex-tu-pling
sex-tu-plet
sex-u-al
  sex-u-al-ly
  sex-u-al-i-ty
sex-y
  sex-i-er
  sex-i-est
shab-by
  shab-bi-er
  shab-bi-est
  shab-bi-ly
shack-le
  shack-led
  shack-ling
  shack-ler
shade
  shad-ed
  shad-ing
  shade-less
shad-ow
shad-ow-box
shad-owy
shad-y
  shad-i-er
  shad-i-est
  shad-i-ly
shaft-ing
shag
  shagged

shag-ging
shag-gi-ly
shake
shak-en
shak-ing
shake-down
shak-er
shake-up
shak-y
shak-i-er
shak-i-est
shak-i-ly
shal-lot
shal-low
shal-low-ness
sham
shammed
sham-ming
sha-man
sha-man-ism
sha-man-ist
sham-bles
shame
shamed
sham-ing
shame-faced
shame-fac-ed-ly
shame-ful
shame-ful-ly
shame-ful-ness
sham-mer
sham-my
sham-poo
sham-pooed
sham-poo-ing
sham-poo-er
sham-rock
shan-tey
shan-ties
shan-ty-town
shape
shaped
shap-ing

shap-a-ble
shap-er
shape-less
shape-ly
shape-li-er
shape-li-est
share
shared
shar-ing
shar-er
share-crop-per
share-crop
share-cropped
share-crop-ping
share-hold-er
shark-skin
sharp-en
sharp-en-er
sharp-er
sharp-eyed
sharp-ie
sharp-shoot-er
sharp-shoot-ing
sharp-tongued
sharp-wit-ted
sharp-wit-ted-ly
sharp-wit-ted-ness
shat-ter
shat-ter-proof
shave
shaved
shav-ing
shav-er
shawl
sheaf
sheaves
shear
sheared
shear-ing
shear-er
sheath
sheath-less
sheathe

sheathed
sheath-ing
sheath-er
shed
shed-ding
sheen
sheeny
sheen-i-er
sheep-dog
sheep-herd-er
sheep-herd-ing
sheep-ish
sheep-skin
sheer
sheer-ly
sheet-ing
sheik
shelf
shelves
shell
shelled
shel-lac
shel-lacked
shel-lack-ing
shell-fire
shell-fish
shell shock
shel-ter
shel-ter-er
shelve
shelved
shelv-ing
she-nan-i-gan
shep-herd
shep-herd-ess
sher-bet
sher-iff
sher-ry
sher-ries
shib-bo-leth
shield
shield-er
shift

shift-er
shift-less
shift-y
shift-i-er
shift-i-est
shift-i-ly
shil-ly--shal-ly
shil-ly-shal-lied
shil-ly-shal-ly-ing
shim-mer
shim-mery
shim-mer-i-er
shim-mer-i-est
shim-my
shim-mies
shim-mied
shim-my-ing
shin
shinned
shin-ning
shin-bone
shin-dig
shine
shined
shone
shin-ing
shin-er
shin-gle
shin-gled
shin-gling
shin-gler
shin-gles
shin-ing
shin-ing-ly
shin-ny
shin-nied
shin-ny-ing
shin-y
shin-i-er
shin-i-est
ship
shipped
ship-ping

ship-a-ble
ship-board
ship-build-er
ship-build-ing
ship-mate
ship-ment
ship-per
ship-yard
shirk
shirker
shirt-tail
shirt-waist
shish ke-bab
shiv-er
shiv-ery
shiv-er-i-er
shiv-er-i-est
shoal
shock-er
shock-ing
shod-dy
shod-di-er
shod-di-ly
shod-di-ness
shoe-horn
shoe-lace
shoe-mak-er
sho-er
shoe-string
shoo--in
shoot
shot
shoot-ing
shoot-er
shop
shopped
shop-ping
shop-keep-er
shop-lift-er
shop-lift-ing
shop-per
shop-talk
shop-worn

shore
shore-line
short
short-ly
short-ness
short-age
short--change
short--changed
short--chang-ing
short-com-ing
short-cut
short-cut-ting
short-en
short-en-er
short-en-ing
short-hand
short--hand-ed
short--lived
short--sight-ed
short--sight-ed-ly
short--sight-ed-nes
short--tem-pered
short--term
short--wave
short--wind-ed
shot-gun
shot-gunned
shot-gun-ning
shoul-der
shoul-der blade
shout-er
shout-ing
shove
shoved
shov-ing
shov-er
shov-el
shov-eled
shov-el-ing
shov-el-ful
show
showed
shown

show-ing
show-bill
show-boat
show-case
show-cased
show-cas-ing
show-down
show-er
show-ery
show-man
show-men
show-man-ship
show-off
show-piece
show-place
show-room
show-y
show-i-er
show-i-est
show-i-ly
shrap-nel
shred
shred-ded
shred-ding
shred-der
shrew
shrewd
shrewd-ly
shrewd-ness
shrew-ish
shriek
shrill
shirl-ly
shrimp
shrine
shrined
shrin-ing
shrink
shrunk-ed
shrink-a-ble
shrink-er
shrink-age
shriv-el

shriv-eled
shriv-el-ing
shroud
shrub-bery
shrub-ber-ies
shrub-by
shrub-bi-er
shrub-bi-est
shrug
shrugged
shrug-ging
shuck-er
shud-der
shud-dery
suf-fle
shuf-fled
shuf-fling
shuf-fler
shuf-fle-board
shun
shunned
shun-ning
shun-ner
shunt
shunt-er
shut-down
shut-eye
shut-in
shut-off
shut-out
shut-ter
shut-tle
shut-tled
shut-tling
shut-tle-like
shy
shi-er
shy-est
shy-ness
shy-ster
sib-i-lant
sib-i-lance
sib-ling

sick
sicked
sick-ing
sick-bed
sick-en
sick-en-ing
sick-ish
sick-le
sick-ly
sick-li-er
sick-li-est
sick-ness
sick-room
side-arm
side-board
sid-ed
side-kick
side-line
side-lined
side-lin-ing
side--long
side-show
side-split-ting
side-step
side-step-ped
side-step-ping
side-swipe
side-swiped
side-swip-ing
side-track
side-ways
sid-ing
si-dle
si-dled
si-dling
siege
si-en-na
si-er-ra
si-es-ta
sieve
sieved
siev-ing
sift-er

sift-ings
sigh-er
sight-ed
sight-less
sight-ly
sight-read
  sight-read-ing
sight-see-ing
  sight-see-er
sig-nal
  sig-naled
  sig-nal-ing
  sig-nal-er
sig-nal-man
  sig-nal-men
sig-na-to-ry
  sig-na-to-ries
sig-na-ture
sign-board
sig-net
sig-nif-i-cance
sig-nif-i-cant
sig-ni-fi-ca-tion
sig-ni-fy
  sig-ni-fied
  sig-ni-fy-ing
  sig-ni-fi-a-ble
  sig-ni-fi-er
sign-post
si-lage
si-lence
  si-lenced
  si-lenc-ing
si-lenc-er
si-lent
si-lent part-ner
sil-hou-ette
  sil-hou-et-ted
  sil-hou-et-ting
sil-ic-a
sil-i-con
sil-i-cone
silk-en

silk-like
silk-weed
silk-worm
silk-y
  silk-i-er
  silk-i-est
  silk-i-ly
sil-ly
  sil-li-er
  sil-li-est
  sil-li-ness
si-lo
  si-los
  si-loed
  si-lo-ing
silt
  sil-ta-tion
silt-y
  silt-i-er
  silt-i-est
sil-ver
sil-ver-fish
sil-ver-fox
sil-ver-ware
sil-ver-y
sim-i-an
sim-i-lar
  sim-i-lar-i-ty
  sim-i-lar-i-ties
sim-i-le
si-mil-i-tude
sim-mer
si-mon-ize
  si-mon-ized
  si-mon-iz-ing
sim-pa-ti-co
sim-per
  sim-per-er
  sim-per-ing-ly
sim-ple
  sim-pler
  sim-plest
  sim-ple-ness

sim-ple--mind-ed
sim-ple sen-tence
sim-ple-ton
sim-plex
sim-plic-i-ty
  sim-plic-i-ties
sim-pli-fy
  sim-pli-fied
  sim-pli-fy-ing
  sim-pli-fi-ca-tion
  sim-pli-fi-er
sim-plism
  sim-plis-tic
  sim-plis-ti-cal-ly
sim-ply
sim-u-late
  sim-u-lat-ed
  sim-u-lat-ing
  sim-u-la-tion
  sim-u-la-tive
  sim-u-la-tor
si-mul-cast
  si-mul-cast-ing
si-mul-ta-ne-ous
  si-mul-ta-ne-ous-ly
  si-mul-ta-ne-i-ty
sin
  sin-ned
  sin-ning
sin-cere
sin-cer-i-ty
si-ne-cure
si-ne qua non
sin-ew
sin-ew-y
sin-ful
  sin-ful-ly
  sin-ful-ness
sing
  sing-ing
  sing-a-ble
singe
  singed

singe-ing
sing-er
sin-gle
sin-gled
sin-gling
sin-gle-ness
sin-gle-brest-ed
sin-gle--hand-ed
sin-gle-hand-ed-ly
sin-gle--mind-ed
sin-gle--mind-ed-ly
sin-gle--space
sin-gle--spaced
sin-gle--spac-ing
sin-gle-ton
sin-gle--track
sin-gly
sing-song
sin-gu-lar
sin-gu-lar-i-ty
sin-gu-lar-i-ties
sin-is-ter
sin-is-ter-ness
sink-a-ble
sink-er
sink-hole
sin-less
sin-ner
sin-u-ate
sin-u-at-ed
sin-u-at-ing
sin-u-ous
sin-u-os-i-ty
sin-u-ous-ness
si-nus
si-nus-i-tis
sip
sipped
sip-ping
sip-per
si-phon
sire
sired

sir-ing
si-ren
sir-loin
sis-sy
sis-sies
sis-si-fied
sis-sy-ish
sis-ter
sis-ter-li-ness
sis-ter-ly
sis-ter-in-law
sis-ters-in-law
si-tar
sit-in
sit-ter
sit-ting
sit-u-ate
sit-u-at-ed
sit-u-at-ing
sit-u-a-tion
six--pack
six--shoot-er
six-teen
six-teenth
sixth
six-ty
six-ti-eth
siz-a-ble
siz-a-ble-ness
siz-a-bly
size
sized
siz-ing
siz-zle
siz-zled
siz-zling
siz-zler
skate
skat-ed
skat-ing
skat-er
ske-dad-dle
ske-dad-dled

ske-dad-dling
skein
skel-e-ton
skel-e-tal
skep-tic
skep-ti-cal
skep-ti-cism
sketch
sketch-er
sketch-book
sketch-y
sketch-i-er
sketch-i-est
sketch-i-ly
skew-er
skew-ness
ski
skied
ski-ing
ski-er
skid
skid-ded
skid-ding
skid-der
skilled
skil-let
skill-ful
skill-ful-ly
skill-ful-ness
skim
skimmed
skim-ming
skim-mer
skimp
skimp-i-ly
skimp-y
skimp-i-er
skimp-i-est
skin
skinned
skin-ning
skin--deep
skin dive

skin div-ing
skin div-er
skin-flint
skin-less
skin-ner
skin-ny
skin-ni-er
skin-ni-est
skin-tight
skip-per
skir-mish
skir-mish-er
skirt-er
skirt-ing
skit-ter
skit-tish
skiv-vy
skiv-vies
skoal
skul-dug-ger-y
skulk-er
skull-cap
skunk
sky
skies
skied
sky-ing
sky-blue
sky-cap
sky-div-ing
sky-rock-et
sky-svap-er
sky-ward
sky-way
sky-writ-ing
sky-writ-er
slab
slabbed
slab-bing
slack
slack-ness
slack-en
slack-er

slack-jawed
slake
slaked
slak-ing
sla-lom
slam
slammeed
slam-ming
slam-bang
slan-der
slan-der-er
slan-der-ous
slang
slang-i-er
slang-i-est
slant
slant-ways
slant-wise
slap
slapp-ed
slap-ping
slap-per
slap-dash
slap-hap-py
slap-hap-pi-er
slap-hap-pi-est
slap-stick
slash-er
slash-ing
slat
slat-ted
slat-ting
slate
slat-ed
slat-ing
slath-er
slat-tern
slat-tern-ly
slaugh-ter
slaugh-ter-er
slaugh-ter-house
slave
slaved

slav-ing
slav-er
slav-er-y
slav-ish
sla-vish-ly
slay
slain
slay-ing
slay-er
slea-zy
slea-zi-er
slea-zi-est
sled
sled-ded
sled-ding
sled-der
sledge
sledged
sledg-ing
sleek
sleek-er
sleek-ness
sleep-er
sleep-less
sleep-less-ness
sleep-walk
sleep-walk-er
sleep-walk-ing
sleep-y
sleep-i-er
sleep-i-est
sleep-i-ly
sleep-y-head
sleet
sleet-y
sleet-i-ness
sleeve
sleeved
sleev-ing
sleeve-less
sleigh
sleigh-er
sleight

slen-der
slen-der-ness
slen-der-ize
slen-der-ized
slen-der-iz-ing
sleuth
slice
sliced
slic-ing
slic-er
slick-er
slick-ness
slide
slid
slid-ing
slid-er
slight
slight-er
slight-ing
slim
slim-mer
slim-mest
slimmed
slim-ming
slim-ness
slime
slimed
slim-ing
slimy
slim-i-er
slim-i-est
slim-i-ly
sling-er
sling-shoot
slink-y
slink-i-er
slink-i-est
slip
slipped
slip-ping
slip-cov-er
slip-knot
slip--on

slip-o-ver
slip-page
slip-per
slip-per-y
slip-per-i-er
slip-per-i-est
slip-py
slip-shod
slip-stick
slip-up
slit
slit-ting
slit-ter
slith-er
slith-ery
sliv-er
sliv-er-er
sliv-er-like
slob-ber
slob-ber-er
slob-ber-ing-ly
sloe--eyed
slo-gan
slo-gan-eer
slop
slopped
slop-ping
slope
sloped
slop-ing
slop-er
slop-py
slop-pi-er
slop-pi-est
slo-pi-ly
slop-pi-ness
slosh-y
slosh-i-er
slosh-i-est
slot
slot-ted
slot-ting
sloth

sloth-ful
sloth-ful-ly
slouch
slouch-er
slouch-i-ly
slouch-i-ness
slouch-y
slouch-i-er
slouch-i-est
slough
slough-y
slough-i-er
slough-i-est
slov-en
slov-en-ly
slov-en-li-ness
slow-down
slow--mo-tion
slow-poke
slow--wit-ted
sludge
slug-y
sludg-i-er
sludg-i-est
slug
slugged
slug-ging
slug-ger
slug-gard
slug-gard-li-ness
slug-gish
slug-gish-ness
sluice
sluiced
sluic-ing
slum
slummed
slum-ming
slum-ber
slum-ber-er
slum-ber-ous
slur
slurred

slur-ring
slush
slush-i-ness
slush-y
slush-i-er
slush-i-est
slut
slut-tish
sly
smack
smack-ing
small--mind-ed
--mind-ed-ness
small-pox
small--time
small--tim-er
smart
smart-ness
smart al-eck
smart-al-eck-y
smart-en
smash
smash-ing
smash--up
smat-ter
smat-ter-er
smat-ter-ing
smear
smear-er
smear-y
smear-i-er
smear-i-est
smell
smelled
smel-ling
smell-er
smell-y
smell-i-er
smell-i-est
smelt
smelt-er
smelt-ery
smid-gen

snile
smil-er
smil-ing-ly
smirch
smirk
smirk-er
smirk-ing-ly
smite
smote
smit-ten
smit-ting
smit-er
smith-er-eens
smit-ten
smock-ing
smog-gy
smog-gi-er
smog-gi-est
smoke
smoked
smok-ing
smoke-less
smoke-house
smok-er
smoke-stack
smok-ing jack-et
smok-y
smok-i-er
smok-i-est
smok-i-ly
smol-der
smooth
smooth-er
smooth-ness
smooth-en
smooth-ie
smoth-er
smoth-er-y
smoth-er-i-er
smoth-er-i-est
smudge
smudged
smudg-ing

smudg-i-ly
smug
smug-ger
smug-gest
smug-ly
smug-ness
smug-gle
smug-gled
smug-gling
smug-gler
smut
smut-ted
smut-ting
smut-ty
smut-ti-er
smut-ti-est
smut-ti-ly
sna-fu
sna-fued
sna-fu-ing
snag
snagged
snag-ging
snag-gy
snag-gle-tooth
snag-gle-teeth
snag-gle-toothed
snail
snail-like
snail-paced
snake
snake-bite
snake-skin
snak-y
snak-i-er
snak-i-est
snap
snapped
snap-ping
snap-back
snap-drag-on
snap-per
snap-pish

snap-pish-ness
snap-py
  snap-pi-er
  snap-pi-est
  snap-pi-ly
snap-shot
snare
  snared
  snar-ing
  snar-er
snarl
  snarl-er
  snarl-y
  snarl-i-er
  snarl-i-est
snatch
  snatch-i-er
  snatch-i-est
  snatch-i-ly
snaz-zy
  snaz-zi-er
  snaz-zi-est
sneak-er
sneak-ing
sneak-y
  sneak-i-er
  sneak-i-est
  sneak-i-ly
sneer
  sneer-er
  sneer-ing-ly
sneeze
  sneezed
  sneez-ing
  sneez-er
  sneez-y
  sneez-i-er
  sneez-i-est
snick-er
snif-fle
  snif-fled
  snif-fling
  snif-fler

snif-fy
  snif-fi-er
  snif-fi-est
  snif-fi-ly
snif-ter
snip
  snipped
  snip-ping
  snip-per
snipe
  sniped
  snip-ing
  snip-er
snip-py
  snip-pi-er
  snip-pi-est
  snip-pi-ly
snitch-er
sniv-el
  sniv-eled
  sniv-el-ing
  sniv-el-er
snob
  snob-ber-y
  snob-bish
  snob-bish-ness
snoop
  snoop-y
  snoop-i-er
  snoop-i-est
  snoop-er
snoot-y
  snoot-i-er
  snoot-i-est
  snoot-i-ly
  snoot-i-ness
snooze
  snoozed
  snooz-ing
  snooz-er
snore
  snored
  snor-ing

snor-er
snor-kel
snort
  snort-er
snot-ty
  snot-ti-er
  snot-ti-est
snout
  snout-ed
  snout-y
  snout-i-er
  snout-i-est
snow-ball
snow-blow-er
snow-bound
snow-cap
snow-drift
snow-fall
snow-flake
snow-man
  snow-men
snow-mo-bile
snow-plow
snow-shoe
  snow-shoed
  snow-shoe-ing
snow-suit
snow--white
snow-y
  snow-i-er
  snow-i-est
snub
  snubbed
  snub-bing
  snub-ber
snub-by
  snub-bi-er
  snub-bi-est
  snub-bi-ness
snub--nosed
snuf-fle
snuff-y
  snuff-i-er

snuff-i-est
snug
snug-gle
snug-gled
snug-gling
soak
soak-age
soak-er
soak-ing-ly
so--and--so
soap-box
soap-suds
soap-y
soap-i-er
soap-i-est
soap-i-ly
soap-i-ness
soar-er
sob
sobbed
sob-bing
sob-ber
so-ber
so-ber-ing-ly
so-ber-ness
so-bri-e-ty
so-bri-quet
so--called
soc-cer
so-cia-ble
so-cia-bil-i-ty
so-cia-bly
so-cial
so-cial-i-ty
so-cial-ly
so-cial-ism
so-cial-ist
so-cial-is-tic
so-cial-is-ti-cal-ly
so-cial-ite
so-cial-ize
so-cial-ized
so-cial-iz-ing

so-cial-i-za-tion
so-cial-iz-er
so-ci-e-ty
so-ci-e-ties
so-ci-e-tal
so-ci-o-ec-o-nom-ic
so-ci-ol-o-gy
so-ci-o-log-i-cal
so-ci-ol-o-gist
so-ci-o-po-lit-i-cal
sock-et
sod
sod-ded
sod-ding
so-da
so-dal-i-ty
so-dal-i-ties
sod-den
sod-den-ness
so-di-um
sod-om-y
so-ev-er
so-fa
soft
soft-ness
soft-ball
soft--boiled
sof-ten
sof-ten-er
soft--head-ed
soft--heart-ed
soft--heart-ed-ness
soft ped-al
soft-ped-aled
soft-ped-al-ing
soft--shell
soft--shoe
soft--spok-en
soft-ware
soft-wood
soft-y
sof-ties
sog-gy

sog-gi-er
sog-gi-est
sog-gi-ly
sog-gi-ness
so-journ
so-journ-er
sol-ace
sol-aced
sol-ac-ing
sol-ac-er
so-lar
so-lar-i-um
so-lar-i-ums
so-lar-ia
so-lar-ize
so-lar-ized
so-lar-iz-ing
so-lar-i-za-tion
sol-der
sol-der-er
sol-dier
sol-dier-y
sol-e-cism
sole-ly
sol-emn
sol-emn-ly
sol-emn-less
so-lem-ni-ty
so-lem-ni-ties
sol-em-nize
sol-em-nized
sol-em-niz-ing
sol-em-ni-za-tion
sole-ness
so-lic-it
so-lic-i-ta-tion
so-lic-i-tor
so-lic-i-tous
so-lic-i-tous-ness
so-lic-i-tude
sol-id
so-lid-i-ty
sol-id-ness

sol-i-dar-i-ty
  sol-i-dar-i-ties
so-lid-i-fy
  so-lid-i-fied
  so-lid-i-fy-ing
  so-lid-i-fi-ca-tion
so-lil-o-quize
  so-lil-o-quized
  so-lil-o-quiz-ing
  so-lil-o-quist
so-lil-o-quy
  so-lil-o-quies
sol-i-taire
sol-i-tar-y
  sol-i-tar-ies
  sol-i-tar-i-ly
  sol-i-tar-i-ness
sol-i-tude
so-lo
  so-loed
  so-lo-ing
  so-lo-ist
sol-stice
sol-u-ble
  sol-u-bil-i-ty
  sol-u-bly
sol-ute
so-lu-tion
solve
  solved
  solv-ing
  solv-a-ble
  solv-a-bil-i-ty
  solv-er
sol-vent
  sol-ven-cy
so-mat-ic
so-ma-to-type
som-ber
  som-ber-ly
  som-ber-ness
som-bre-ro
  som-bre-ros

some-bod-y
  some-bod-ies
some-day
some-how
some-place
som-er-sault
some-thing
some-time
  some-times
some-way
some-what
some-where
sosm-nam-bu-late
som-no-lent
  som-no-lence
  som-no-len-cy
so-nar
so-na-ta
song-bird
song-fest
song-ster
  song-stress
song-writ-er
son-ic
son--in--law
  sons--in--law
son-net
son-ny
  son-nies
so-no-rous
  so-nor-i-ty
  so-no-rous-ness
soon-er
soothe
  soothed
  sooth-ing
  sooth-er
sooth-say-er
  sooth-say-ing
soot-y
  soot-i-er
  soot-i-est
  soot-i-ly

sop
  sopped
  sop-ping
soph-ist
  soph-ism
  so-phis-tic
  so-phis-ti-cal
so-phis-ti-cate
  so-phis-ti-cat-ed
  so-phis-ti-cat-ing
  so-phis-ti-ca-tion
  so-phis-ti-ca-tor
soph-ist-ry
  soph-ist-ries
soph-o-more
soph-o-mor-ic
  soph-o-mor-i-cal
  soph-o-mor-i-cal-ly
sop-o-rif-ic
sop-py
  sop-pi-er
  sop-pi-est
so-pran-o
  so-pran-os
sor-cer-er
  sor-cer-ess
sor-cer-y
  sor-cer-ies
  sor-cer-ous
sor-did
  sor-did-ness
sore
  sor-er
  sor-est
  sore-ly
  sore-ness
sore-head
  sore-head-ed
sor-ghum
so-ror-i-ty
  so-ror-i-ties
sor-rel
sor-row

sor-row-er
sor-row-ful
sor-ry
sor-ri-er
sor-ri-est
sor-ri-ly
sort-a-ble
sort-er
sor-tie
so--so
sot
sot-ted
sot-tish
sot-tish-ness
sot-vo vo-ce
sought
soul-ful
soul-ful-ly
soul-ful-ness
soul-less
soul-searching
sound
sound-a-ble
sound-ly
sound-ness
sound-box
sound-er
sound-ing
sound-less
sound-less-ly
sound-proof
soup-y
soup-i-er
soup-i-est
sour
sour-ish
sour-ness
sour-ball
source
souse
soused
sous-ing
south-bound

south-east
south-east-er
south-east-er-ly
south-east-ern
south-east-ward
south-east-ward-ly
south-er
south-er-ly
south-ern
south-ern-most
south-ern-er
south-paw
south-ward
south-ward-ly
south-west
south-west-er
south-west-ern
south-west-ern-er
south-west-ward
south-west-ward-ly
sou-ve-nir
sov-er-eign
sov-er-eign-ty
sov-er-eign-ties
so-vi-et
sow-er
soy-bean
space
spaced
spac-ing
space-less
spac-er
space-craft
space-man
space-men
space-ship
space-walk
spa-cious
spa-cious-ness
spade
spad-ed
spad-ing
spade-ful

spad-er
spade-work
spa-ghet-ti
span
spanned
span-ning
span-gle
span-gled
span-gling
span-iel
spank-er
spank-ing
spar
sparred
spar-ring
spare
spared
spar-ing
spar-er
spar-est
spar-a-ble
spare-ness
spare-rib
spar-ing
spar-ing-ness
spark-er
spar-kle
spar-kled
spar-kling
spar-kler
spar-row
spar-row-grass
sparse
spars-er
spars-est
spasm
spas-mod-ic
spas-mod-i-cal
spas-mod-i-cal-ly
spas-tic
spas-ti-cal-ly
spat
spat-ted

spat-ting
spa-tial
  spa-cial
  spa-ti-al-i-ty
  spa-tial-ly
spat-ter
spat-u-la
spawn
speak
  spok-en
  speak-ing
  speak-a-ble
speak-eas-y
  speak-eas-ies
speak-er
  speak-er-ship
spear-er
spear-head
spear-mint
spe-cial
  spe-cial-ly
spe-cial-ist
spe-cial-ize
  spe-cial-ized
  spe-cial-iz-ing
  spe-cial-i-za-tion
spe-cial-ty
  spe-cial-ties
spe-cie
spe-cies
spec-i-fia-ble
spe-cif-ic
  spe-cif-i-cal-ly
  spec-i-fic-i-ty
spec-i-fi-ca-tion
spec-i-fy
  spec-i-fied
  spec-i-fy-ing
  spec-i-fi-er
spec-i-men
spe-cious
  spe-ci-os-i-ty
  spe-ci-os-i-ties

spe-cious-ness
speck-le
  speck-led
  speck-ling
spec-ta-cle
  spec-ta-cled
spec-tac-u-lar
  spec-tac-u-lar-ly
spec-ta-tor
spec-ter
spec-tral
spce-tro-scope
  spec-tro-scop-ic
  spec-tro-scop-i-cal
  spec-tros-co-py
spec-trum
  spec-tra
  spec-trums
spec-u-late
  spec-u-lat-ed
  spec-u-lat-ing
  spec-u-la-tion
  spec-u-la-tive
  spec-u-la-tor
speech-i-fy
  speech-i-fie
  speech-i-fy-ing
speech-less
  speech-less-ness
speed
  speed-ed
  speed-ing
  speed-er
  speed-ster
speed-boat
  speed-boat-ing
speed-om-e-ter
speed--up
speed-way
speed-y
  speed-i-er
  speed-i-est
  speed-i-ly

speed-i-ness
spe-le-ol-o-gy
  spe-le-ol-o-gist
spell
  spelled
  spell-ing
spell-bind
  spell-bouns
  spell-bind-ing
  spell-bind-er
spell-er
spe-lun-ker
spend
  spent
  spend-ing
  spend-a-ble
  spend-er
spend-thrift
sper-ma-cet-i
sper-mat-ic
sper-ma-to-zo-on
  sper-ma-to-zo-a
  sper-ma-tozo-ic
spew-er
sphag-num
sphere
  sphered
  spher-ing
  spher-ic
  sphe-ric-i-ty
sphe-roid
  sphe-roi-dal
sphinc-ter
  sphin-ter-al
  sphin-ter-ic
sphinx
  sphinxes
  sphin-ges
spice
  spiced
  spic-ing
spi-cule
  spic-u-lar

spic-u-late
spic-y
  spic-i-er
  spic-i-esst
  spic-i-ly
spi-der
spi-der-y
spiel
  spiel-er
spi-er
spiff-y
  spiff-i-er
  spiff-i-est
spig-ot
spike
  spiked
  spik-ing
spik-y
  spik-i-er
  spik-i-est
spill
  spilled
  spill-ing
spil-lage
spill-way
spin
  spun
  spin-ning
spin-ach
spi-nal
  spi-nal-ly
spin-dle
  spin-dled
  spin-dling
spin-dle-legs
  spin-dle-leg-ged
spin-dly
  spin-dli-er
  spin-dli-est
spine-less
spin-et
spin-na-ker
spin-ner

spin-ning wheel
spin--off
spi-nose
spi-nous
spin-ster
spin-y
  spin-i-ness
spi-ra-cle
spi-ral
  spi-raled
  spi-ral-ing
  spi-ral-ly
spire
  spired
  spir-ing
spir-it
spir-it-ed
spir-it-ism
  spir-ir-ist
spir-it-less
  spir-it-les-ness
spir-i-tous
spir-it-u-al
  spir-it-u-al-ly
spir-it-u-al-ism
  spir-it-u-al-ist
  spir-it-u-al-is-tic
spir-it-u-al-i-ty
  spir-it-u-al-i-ties
spir-it-u-al-ize
  spir-it-u-al-ized
  spir-it-u-al-iz-ing
  spir-it-u-al-i-za-tion
spir-it-u-ous
  spir-it-u-os-i-ty
spi-ro-chete
spit
  spat
  spit-ting
  spit-ter
spite
  spit-ed
  spit-ing

spite-ful
spit-fire
spit-tle
spit-toon
splash
  splash-er
  splashy
  splash-i-er
  splash-i-est
  splash-i-ly
splash-board
splash-down
splat-ter
splay-foot
  splay-feet
  splay-foot-ed
spleen
  spleen-ful
splen-did
splen-dif-er-ous
sple-net-ic
splice
  spliced
  splic-ing
  splic-er
splin-ter
  splin-tery
split
  split-ting
  split-a-ble
  split-ter
split--lev-el
split--sec-ond
splotch
  spotch-y
  splotch-i-er
  splotch-i-est
splurge
  splurged
  splurg-ing
splut-ter
  splut-ter-er
spoil

spoil-ed
spoil-ing
spoil-age
spoil-er
spoil-sport
spoke
spoked
spok-ing
spo-ken
spokes-man
spokes-men
spokes-wom-an
spokes-wom-en
sponge
sponged
spong-ing
spong-er
spon-gy
spon-gi-er
spon-gi-est
spon-gi-ness
spon-sor
spon-sor-ship
spon-ta-ne-i-ty
spon-ta-ne-i-ties
spon-ta-ne-ous
spon-ta-ne-ous-ly
spon-ta-ne-ous-ness
spook
spook-ish
spook-y
spook-i-er
spook-i-est
spook-i-ly
spoon-er-ism
spoon-er-is-tic
spoon--fed
spoon--feed
spoon--feed-ing
spoon-ful
spoon-fuls
spo-rad-ic
spo-rad-i-cal

spo-rad-i-cal-ly
spo-ran-gi-um
spo-ran-gia
spore
spored
spor-ing
sport
sport-ing
sport-ing-ly
spor-tive
sports-cast
sports-cast-er
sports-man
sports-wear
sports-writ-er
sport-y
sport-i-er
sport-i-est
sport-i-ly
spot
spot-ted
spot-ting
spot-less
spot-less-ly
spot-light
spot-ted
spot-ted fe-ver
spot-ter
spot-ty
spot-ti-er
spot-ti-est
spot-ti-ly
spouse
spout
spout-er
sprain
sprawl
spray
spray-er
spread
spread-ing
spread--ea-gle
spread--ea-gled

spread--ea-gling
spread-er
sprig
sprigged
sprig-ging
spright-ly
spright-li-er
spright-li-est
spring
spring-ing
spring-board
spring--clean-ing
spring-time
spring-y
spring-i-er
spring-i-est
spring-i-ly
sprin-kle
sprin-kled
sprin-kling
sprink-ler
sprint
sprint-er
sprock-et
spruce
spruc-er
spruc-est
spruced
spruc-ing
spry
spry-er
spry-est
spry-ly
spue
spued
spu-ing
spume
spumed
spum-ing
spum-ous
spunk-y
spunk-i-er
spunk-i-est

spunk-i-ly
spunk-i-ness
spur
spurred
spur-ring
spu-ri-ous
spu-ri-ous-ness
spurner
spurt
spurt-er
spur-tive
sput-nik
sput-ter
sput-ter-er
spu-tum
spu-ta
spy
spies
spied
spy-ing
spy-glass
squad-ron
squal-id
squal-id-ly
squal-id-ness
squall
squally
squall-i-er
squall-i-est
squal-or
squan-der
squan-der-er
square
squared
squar-ing
square-ly
square-ness
square-dance
square-danced
square-danc-ing
squar-ish
squar-ish-ly
squash

squash-er
squash-es
squash-y
squash-i-er
squash-i-est
squat
squat-ted
squat-ting
squat-ly
squat-ter
squat-ty
squat-ti-er
squat-ti-est
squawk
squawk-er
squawk-y
squawk-i-er
squawk-i-est
squeak
squeal
squeal-er
squeam-ish
squeam-ish-ly
squeam-ish-ness
squee-gee
squeeze
squeez-ed
squeez-ing
squeez-er
squelch
squelch-er
squib
squid
squig-gle
squig-gled
squig-gling
squint--eyed
squire
squired
squir-ing
squirm
squirmy
squirm-i-er

squirm-i-est
squir-rel
squirt
squirt-er
stab
stabbed
stab-bing
stab-ber
sta-bil-i-ty
sta-bil-i-ties
sta-bi-lize
sta-bi-lized
sta-bi-liz-ing
sta-bi-li-za-tion
sta-bi-liz-er
sta-ble
sta-bled
sta-bling
stac-ca-to
stack-er
sta-di-um
staff-er
stag
stagged
stag-ging
stage-coach
stage-hand
stage--struck
stag-ger
stag-ger-er
stag-ger-ing
stag-nant
stag-nan-cy
stag-nate
stag-nat-ed
stag-nat-ing
stag-na-tion
stag-y
stag-i-er
stag-i-est
stag-i-ly
stag-i-ness
stain

stain-a-ble
stained
stain-er
stained glass
stain-less
stair-case
stair-way
stair-well
stake
staked
stak-ing
stake-hold-er
sta-lac-tite
sta-lag-mite
stalk
stalled
stal-lion
stal-wart
stal-wart-ness
sta-men
sta-mens
stam-i-na
stam-mer
stam-mer-ing-ly
stamp-er
stance
stand
stand-ing
stand-er
stand-ard
stand-ard-ize
stand-ard-ized
stand-ard-iz-ing
stand-ard-i-za-tion
stand-by
stnad-ee
stand--in
stand--off-ish
stand--off-ish-ness
stand-out
stand-pipe
stand-point
stand-still

sta-nine
stan-za
stan-za-ic
staph-y-lo-coc-cus
sta-ple
sta-pled
sta-pling
sta-pler
star
star-board
star-dom
stare
stared
star-ing
star-er
star-fish
star-gaze
star-gazed
star-gaz-ing
star-let
star-light
star-ling
star-ry
star-ri-er
star-ri-est
star-ri-ly
star-ry--eyed
star-span-gled
start-er
star-tle
star-tled
star-tling
star-tling-ly
star-va-tion
starve
starved
starv-ing
sta-sis
state
stat-ed
stat-ing
stat-a-ble
state-craft

state-hood
state-less
state-less-ness
state-ly
state-li-er
state-li-est
state-ment
state-room
state-side
states-man
states-men
states-man-like
states-man-ship
stat-ic
stat-ics
sta-tion
sta-tion-ar-y
ssta-tion-er
sta-tion-er-y
stat-ism
stat-ist
sta-tic-tic
sta-tis-ti-cal
sta-tis-ti-cal-ly
stat-is-ti-cian
sta-tis-tics
sta-tor
stat-u-ar-y
stat-u-ar-ies
stat-ue
stat-u-esque
stat-u-ette
stat-ure
sta-tus
stat-ute
staunch
stave
staved
stav-ing
stay
stay-ed
stay-ing
stay-er

stead-fast
stead-fast-ly
stead-y
steam-boat
steam-er
steam-fit-ter
steam-fit-ting
steam-roll-er
steam-ship
steam-y
steam-i-er
steam-i-est
steam-i-ly
ste-a-tite
sted-fast
steel-head
steel-works
steel-work-er
steel-y
steel-i-er
steel-yard
steep
steep-ly
steep-en
stee-ple
stee-ple-chase
stee-ple-chas-er
stee-ple-jack
steer
steer-a-ble
steer-er
steer-age
stein
stel-lar
stem
stemmed
stem-ware
stem-wind-er
stem-wind-ing
sten-cil
sten-ciled
sten-cil-ing
ste-nog-ra-pher

ste-nog-ra-phy
sten-o-graph-ic
sten-o-raph-i-cal-ly
sten-to-ri-an
step
stepped
step-ping
step-broth-er
step-child
step-child-ren
step-daugh-ter
step-fa-ther
step-lad-der
step-moth-er
step-par-ent
stepped-up
step-sis-ter
step-son
ster-e-o
ster-e-os
ster-e-o-phon-ic
-e-o-phon-i-cal-ly
ster-e-o-scope
ster-e-o-scop-ic
ster-e-o-type
ster-e-o-typed
ster-e-o-typ-ing
ster-ile
ste-ril-i-ty
ster-i-lize
ster-i-lized
ster-i-liz-ing
ster-i-li-za-tion
ster-i-li-zer
ster-ling
stern
stern-ly
stern-ness
ster-num
ster-na
ster-nums
stern-wheel-er
ster-oid

steth-o-scope
steth-o-scop-ic
ste-ve-dore
ste-ve-dored
ste-ve-dor-ing
ste-ward
stew-ard-ness
stick-er
stick-ing
stick-le-back
stick-ler
stick-pin
stick-up
stick-y
stick-i-er
stick-i-est
stiff
stiff-ly
stiff-ness
stiff-en
stiff-en-er
stiff--necked
sti-fle
sti-fled
sti-fling
sti-fler
sti-fling-ly
stig-ma
stig-mas
stig-ma-ta
stig-ma-tic
stig-mat-i-cal-ly
stig-ma-tize
stig-ma-tized
stig-ma-tiz-ing
stig-ma-ti-za-tion
sti-let-to
sti-let-tos
sti-let-toes
still-birth
still-born
still life
still-ness

stilt-ed
stilt-ed-ly
stim-u-lant
stim-u-late
stim-u-lat-ed
stim-u-lat-ing
stim-u-la-tion
stim-u-la-tive
stim-u-lus
stim-u-li
sting
sting-ing
sting-er
sting-ing-ly
stin-gy
stin-gi-er
stin-gi-est
stin-gi-ly
stin-gi-ness
stink
stink-ing
stink-er
stink-y
stink-i-er
stink-i-est
stint-er
sti-pend
stip-ple
stip-pled
stip-pling
stip-u-late
stip-u-lat-ed
stip-u-lat-ing
stip-u-la-tion
stip-u-la-to-ry
stir
stirred
stir-ring
stir-ring-ly
stir-rup
stitch
stitch-er
stock-ade

stock-ad-ed
stock-ad-ing
stock-brok-er
stock-hold-er
Stock-holm
stock-ing
stock-yard
stodg-y
stodg-i-er
stodg-i-est
stodg-i-ly
sto-ic
sto-i-cal
stoke
stoked
stok-ing
stok-er
stol-id
sto-lid-i-ty
stol-id-ly
sto-ma
sto-ma-ta
sto-mas
stom-ach
stom-ach-er
stone-ma-son
stone-ma-son-ry
stone-wall
ston-y
ston-i-er
ston-i-est
ston-i-ly
stop
stopped
stop-ping
stop-gap
stop-light
stop-o-ver
stop-page
stop-per
stop-watch
stor-age
store

stored
stor-ing
store-house
store-keep-er
store-room
sto-ried
storm-y
storm-i-er
storm-i-est
storm-i-ly
storm-i-ness
sto-ry
sto-ries
sto-ry-ing
sto-ry-book
sto-ry-tell-er
stor-y-tell-ing
stout
stout-ly
stout-ness
stout--heart-ed
stove
stoved
stov-ing
stove-pipe
stow-age
stow-a-way
stra-bis-mus
strad-dle
strad-dled
strad-dling
strad-dler
strafe
strafed
straf-ing
strag-gle
strag-gled
strag-gling
strag-gler
strag-gly
strag-gli-er
strag-gli-est
straight-en

straight-en-er
straight-for-ward
straight-for-ward-ly
straight-way
strain-er
strait-en
strait-jack-et
strait-laced
strange
strang-er
strang-est
strang-ly
strange-ness
stran-ger
stran-gu-la-tion
strn-gu-late
stran-gu-lat-ed
stran-gu-lat-ing
strap
srapped
strap-ping
strap-less
stra-te-gic
str-te-gi-cal-ly
strat-e-gy
strat-e-gies
strat-e-gist
strat-i-fi-ca-tion
strat-i-fy
strat-i-fied
strat-i-fy-ing
stra-to-cu-mu-lus
strat-o-sphere
strat-o-spher-ic
stra-tum
stra-ta
stra-tums
stra-tus
stra-ti
straw-ber-ry
straw-ber-ries
stream-er
stream-line

stream-lined
stream-lin-ing
street-car
street-walk-er
street-walk-ing
strength-en
strength-en-er
stren-u-ous
stren-u-os-i-ty
stren-u-ous-ly
strep-to-coc-cus
strep-to-coc-ci
strep-to-coc-cal
strep-to-coc-cic
strep-to-my-cin
stress
stress-ful
stress-ful-ly
stress-ful-ness
stretch
stretch-a-bil-i-ty
stretch-a-ble
stri-a
stri-ae
stri-ate
stri-at-ed
stri-at-ing
strick-en
strict
strict-ly
strict-ness
stric-ture
stride
strid-den
strid-ding
stri-dent
strid-u-la-tion
strife
strife-ful
strife-less
string
strung
string-ing

strin-gent
strin-gen-cy
strin-gent-ly
string-y
string-i-er
string-i-est
strip
stripped
strip-ping
stripe
striped
strip-ing
strip-ling
strip-per
strip-tease
strip-teas-er
stro-bo-scope
stro-bo-scop-ic
-bo-scop-i-cal-ly
stroke
stroked
strok-ing
stroll-er
strong
strong-ish
strong-ly
strong--arm
strong-box
strong-hold
strong-mind-ed
strong-mind-ed-ly
-mind-ed-ness
stron-ti-um
stron-tic
strop
stropped
strop-ping
struc-tur-al
struc-tur-al-ly
struc-ture
struc-tured
struc-tur-ing
struc-ture-less

strug-gle
  strug-gled
  strug-gling
  strug-gler
strum
  strum-mer
strum-pet
strut
  strut-ted
  strut-ting
strych-nine
  strych-nia
  strych-nic
stub-born
  stub-born-ly
  stub-born-ness
stuck--up
stud
  stud-ded
  stud-ding
stu-dent
stud-ied
  stud-ied-ly
  stud-ied-ness
stu-di-o
  stu-di-os
stu-di-ous
  stu-di-ous-ly
  stu-di-ous-ness
stud-y
  stud-ies
  stud-ied
  stud-y-ing
stuff-er
stuff-ing
stuff-y
stul-ti-fy
  stul-ti-fied
  stul-ti-fy-ing
  stul-ti-fi-ca-tion
  stul-ti-fi-er
stum-ble
stump

stump-er
stumpy
stun-ning
stunt
  stunt-ed
  stunt-ed-ness
stu-pe-fy
  stu-pe-fied
  stu-pe-fy-ing
stu-pen-dous
  stu-pen-dous-ly
stu-por
  stu-por-ous
stur-dy
  stur-di-er
  stur-di-est
  stur-geon
stut-ter
  stut-ter-er
  stut-ter-ing-ly
style
  styled
  styl-ing
  styl-er
styl-ish
  styl-ish-ly
  styl-ish-ness
sty-lus
  sty-lus-es
  sty-li
sty-mie
  sty-mies
  sty-mied
  sty-mie-ing
styp-tic
  styp-ti-cal
  styp-tic-i-ty
sub
  subbed
  sub-bing
sub-al-tern
sub-arc-tic
sub-as-sem-bly

sub-as-sem-blies
sub-as-sem-bler
sub-base-ment
sub-chas-er
sub-class
sub-com-mit-tee
sub-con-scious
  sub-con-scious-ly
sub-con-ti-nent
  sub-con-ti-nen-tal
sub-con-tract
  sub-con-trac-tor
sub-cul-ture
  sub-cul-tur-al
sub-cu-ta-ne-ous
  sub-cu-ta-ne-ous-ly
sub-deb-u-tante
sub-di-vide
  sub-di-vid-ed
  sub-di-vid-ing
  sub-di-vid-a-ble
  sub-di-vid-er
sub-di-vi-sion
  sub-di-vi-sion-al
sub-due
  sub-dued
sub-en-try
  sub-en-tries
sub-freez-ing
sub-group
sub-head
sub-hu-man
sub-ject
  sub-jec-tion
sub-jec-tive
  sub-jec-tive-ly
  sub-jec-tive-ness
  sub-jec-tiv-i-ty
sub-join
sub-ju-gate
  sub-ju-gat-ed
  sub-ju-gat-ing
  sub-ju-ga-tion

sub-ju-ga-tor
sub-junc-tive
sub-lease
sub-leased
sub-leas-ing
sub-let
sub-let-ting
sub-li-mate
sub-li-mat-ed
sub-li-mat-ing
sub-li-ma-tion
sub-lime
sub-lim-i-nal
sub-lim-i-nal-ly
sub-lim-i-ty
sub-lim-i-ties
sub-ma-chine gun
sub-mar-gin-al
sub-ma-rine
sub-merge
sub-merged
sub-mer-gi-ble
sub-merse
sub-mersed
sub-mer-sion
sub-mers-i-ble
sub-mi-cro-scop-ic
sub-mis-sion
sub-mis-sive
sub-mis-sive-ly
sub-mis-sive-ness
sub-mit
sub-mit-ted
sub-mit-ting
sub-nor-mal
sub-nor-mal-i-ty
sub-or-di-nate
sub-or-di-nat-ed
sub-or-di-na-tive
sub-orn
sub-or-na-tion
sub-orn-er
sub-poe-na

sub-poe-naed
sub-poe-na-ing
sub-scribe
sub-scribed
sub-scrib-ing
sub-scrib-er
sub-scrip-tion
sub-se-quent
sub-se-quence
sub-se-quent-ly
sub-ser-vi-ent
sub-ser-vi-ence
sub-ser-vi-en-cy
sub-side
sub-sid-ed
sub-sid-ing
sub-sid-ence
sub-sid-i-ar-y
sub-sid-i-ar-ies
sub-si-dize
sub-si-dized
sub-si-diz-ing
sub-si-dy
sub-si-dies
sub-sist
sub-sist-ence
sub-soil
sub-son-ic
sub-stance
sub-stand-ard
sub-stan-tial
sub-stan-ti-al-i-ty
sub-stan-tial-ly
sub-stan-tive
sub-stan-ti-val
sub-stan-ti-val-ly
sub-stan-tive-ly
sub-sti-tute
sub-sti-tut-ed
sub-sti-tut-ing
sub-sti-tu-tion
sub-stra-tum
sub-stra-ta

sub-stra-tums
sub-struc-ture
sub-teen
sub-tend
sub-ter-fuge
sub-ter-ra-ne-an
sub-ter-ra-ne-ous
sub-ter-ra-ne-an-ly
sub-ter-ra-ne-ous-ly
sub-ti-tle
sub-tle
sub-tle-ness
sub-tle-ty
sub-tle-ties
sub-tly
sub-tra-hend
sub-trop-i-cal
sub-trop-ic
sub-trop-ics
sub-ur-bia
sub-ver-sion
sub-ver-sion-ary
sub-ver-sive
sub-ver-sive-ly
sub-ver-sive-ness
sub-vert
sub-vert-er
sub-way
suc-ceed
suc-ceed-er
suc-ces-sion
suc-ces-sion-al
suc-ces-sion-al-ly
suc-ces-sive
suc-ces-sive-ly
suc-ces-sive-ness
suc-ces-sor
suc-cinct
suc-cinct-ly
suc-cinct-ness
suc-cor
suc-cor-er
suc-co-tash

suc-co-bus
suc-cu-bi
suc-cu-lent
suc-cu-lence
suc-cu-len-cy
suc-cu-lent-ly
suc-cumb
suck-er
suck-le
suck-led
suck-ling
su-crose
suc-tion
sud-den-ly
sud-den-less
suds-y
suds-i-er
suds-i-est
sue
sued
su-ing
su-er
suede
su-et
su-ety
suf-fer-ance
suf-fice
suf-ficed
suf-fic-ing
suf-fic-er
suf-fi-cien-cy
suf-fi-cien-cies
suf-fi-cient
suf-fi-cient-ly
suf-fix
suf-fo-cate
suf-fo-cat-ed
suf-fo-cat-ing
suf-frage
suf-fra-gette
suf-fuse
suf-fused
suf-fus-ing

sug-ar-coat
sug-gest
sug-gest-er
sug-gest-i-ble
sug-ges-tion
sug-ges-tive
sug-ges-tive-ly
sug-ges-tive-ness
su-i-cide
su-i-cid-ed
su-i-cid-ing
su-i-cid-al
suit-a-ble
suit-a-bil-i-ty
suit-case
suite
suit-ing
suit-or
sul-fa
sul-fa-nil-a-mide
sul-fate
sul-fide
sul-fur
sul-fu-ric
sul-fur-ous
sul-fur-ous-ly
sulk-y
sul-ly
sul-lied
sul-ly-ing
sul-tan
sul-tan-ic
sul-tan-a
sul-tan-ess
sul-tan-ate
sul-try
sul-tri-er
sul-tri-est
sum
su-mac
sum-ma-rize
sum-ma-rized
sum-ma-ry

sum-ma-ries
sum-mar-i-ly
sum-ma-tion
sum-ma-tion-al
sum-mer
sum-mery
sum-mer-house
sum-mit
sum-mon
sum-mon-er
sum-mons
sum-mons-es
sump-tu-ar-y
sump-tu-ous
sump-tu-ous-ly
sun
sunned
sun-ning
sun-bathe
sun-bon-net
sun-burn
sun-burned
sun-burnt
sun-dae
sun-der
sun-der-ance
sun-di-al
sun-dries
sun-dry
sunk-en
sun-light
sun-rise
sun-shine
sun-shiny
sun-spot
sun-stroke
sun-up
sup
supped
su-per
su-per-a-bun-dant
su-per-a-bun-dance
su-per-an-nu-ate

su-perb
su-perb-ly
su-per-car-go
su-per-car-goes
su-per-charge
su-per-charg-er
su-per-cil-i-ous
su-per-cil-i-ous-ly
su-per-e-go
su-per-e-rog-a-to-ry
su-per-fi-cial
su-per-fi-ci-al-i-ty
su-per-fi-ci-al-i-ties
su-per-high-way
su-per-hu-man
su-per-hu-man-i-ty
su-per-hu-man-ly
su-per-im-pose
su-per-im-posed
su-per-im-pos-ing
su-per-in-tend
-per-in-tend-en-cy
su-per-in-tend-ent
su-pe-ri-or
su-pe-ri-or-i-ty
su-pe-ri-or-ly
su-per-la-tive
su-per-la-tive-ly
su-per-man
su-per-mar-ket
su-per-nal
su-per-nal-ly
su-per-nat-u-ral
su-per-nu-mer-ar-y
-per-nu-mer-ar-ies
su-per-pow-er
su-per-scribe
su-per-scib-ing
su-per-scrip-tion
su-per-script
su-per-sede
su-per-sed-ed
su-per-sed-ing

su-per-son-ic
su-per-son-i-cal-ly
su-per-star
su-per-sti-tion
su-per-sti-tious
su-per-sti-tious-ly
su-per-struc-ture
su-per-vene
su-per-vened
su-per-ven-ing
su-per-ven-tion
su-per-vise
su-per-vised
su-per-vis-ing
su-per-vi-sion
su-pine
su-pine-ly
sup-per
sup-plant
sup-plan-ta-tion
sup-plant-er
sup-ple
sup-pler
sup-plest
sup-ple-ment
sup-ple-men-tal
sup-pli-ant
sup-pli-ant-ly
sup-pli-cant
sup-ply
sup-port
sup-port-a-ble
sup-port-er
sup-por-tive
sup-pose
sup-po-si-tion
sup-po-si-tion-al
sup-pos-i-to-ry
sup-press
sup-pres-sion
sup-pres-sor
su-pra-re-nal gland
su-prem-a-cy

su-prem-a-cies
su-prem-a-cist
su-preme
su-preme-ly
sur-cease
sur-charge
sur-charged
sur-charg-ing
sur-cin-gle
sure
sur-er
sur-est
sure-ly
sure--fire
sure--foot-ed
sure--foot-ed-ly
sure-ty
sure-ties
sure-ty-ship
surf
surfy
surf-i-er
sur-face
sur-faced
sur-fac-ing
surf-board
surf-board-er
sur-feit
sur-feit-er
sur-geon
sur-ger-y
sur-ger-ies
sur-gi-cal
sur-ly
sur-mise
sur-mised
sur-mis-ing
sur-mount
sur-mount-a-ble
sur-name
sur-pass
sur-pass-a-ble
sur-pass-ing

sur-plice
sur-plus
sur-plus-age
sur-prise
sur-prised
sur-pris-ing
sur-re-al-ism
sur-re-al-ist
sur-re-al-is-tic
sur-ren-der
sur-rep-ti-tious
sur-rep-ti-tious-ly
sur-rey
sur-reys
sur-ro-gate
sur-ro-gat-ed
sur-ro-gat-ing
sur-round
sur-round-er
sur-round-ing
sur-tax
sur-veil-lance
sur-veil-lant
sur-vey
sur-vey-ing
sur-vey-or
sur-viv-al
sur-vive
sur-vived
sur-viv-ing
sur-vi-vor
sus-cep-ti-ble
sus-cep-ti-bil-i-ty
sus-cep-ti-bly
sus-pect
sus-pend
sus-pend-er
sus-pense
sus-pense-ful
sus-pen-sion
sus-pi-cious
sus-pi-cious-ly
sus-tain

sus-tain-a-ble
sus-tain-er
sus-tain-ment
sus-te-nance
su-ture
su-ze-rain
su-ze-rain-ly
svelte
svelte-ly
swad-dle
swad-dled
swad-dling
swain
swain-ish
swal-low
swal-low-er
swal-low-tail
swa-mi
swa-mis
swamp
swampy
swank
swank-i-ly
swan's--down
swap
swapped
swap-ping
sward
swarth-y
swarth-i-er
swarth-i-est
swat
swathe
swathed
swath-ing
swat
sway-a-ble
sway-er
sway-back
sway-backed
swear-word
sweat
sweat-er

sweat-shop
sweep
swept
sweep-ing
sweep-er
sweep-stakes
sweet
sweet-ish
sweet-ly
sweet-heart
sweet-meat
sweet-talk
swell-head
swel-ter
swel-ter-ing
swerve
swerved
swerv-ing
swift
swift-ly
swim-ming
swim-ming-ly
swin-dle
swin-dled
swin-dling
swin-dler
swipe
swiped
swip-ing
swirl
swish
swish-er
switch
switch-er
switch-blade
switch-board
switch--hit-ter
swiv-el
swiv-eled
swiv-el-ing
swiz-zle
sword
sword-fish

sword-play
sword-play-er
swords-man
swords-man
swords-man-ship
syc-a-more
syc-o-phant
syc-o-phan-cy
syc-o-phan-tic
syl-lab-ic
syl-lab-i-cate
syl-lab-i-cat-ed
syl-lab-i-cat-ing
syl-lab-i-ca-tion
syl-la-bus
syl-la-bus-es
syl-la-bi
syl-lo-gism
sul-lo-gis-tic
sylph-like
syl-van
sym-bi-o-sis
sym-bi-ot-ic
sym-bi-ot-i-cal-ly
sym-bol
sym-bol-ic
sym-bol-i-cal
sym-bol-ism
sym-bol-ist
sym-me-try
sym-me-tries
sym-pa-thize
sym-pa-thized
sym-pa-thiz-ing
sym-pa-thiz-er
sym-pa-thy
sym-pa-thies
sym-pho-ny
sym-pho-nies
sym-phon-ic
sym-po-si-um
sym-po-sia
sym-po-si-ums

symp-tom
syn-a-gogue
syn-gog-al
syn-gog-i-cal
syn-apse
sync
synced
sync-ing
syn-chro-nism
syn-chro-nis-tic
syn-chro-nis-ti-cal
syn-chro-nize
syn-chro-nized
syn-chro-niz-ing
syn-chro-ni-za-tion
syn-chro-nous
syn-chro-nous-ly
syn-di-cate
syn-di-cat-ed
syn-di-cat-ing
syn-drome
syn-drom-ic
syn-od
syn-od-al
syn-o-nym
syn-no-nym-ic
syn-no-nym-i-cal
syn-no-nym-i-ty
syn-on-y-mous
syn-on-y-mous-ly
syn-on-y-my
syn-on-y-mies
syn-op-sis
syn-op-ses
syn-op-ti-cal
syn-tac-tic
syn-tac-ti-cal
syn-tac-ti-cal-ly
syn-tax
syn-the-sis
syn-the-ses
syn-the-sist
syn-the-size

syn-the-sized
syn-the-siz-ing
syn-the-ic
syn-thet-i-cal
syn-thet-i-cal-ly
syph-i-lis
syph-i-lit-ic
sy-ringe
sy-ringed
sy-ring-ing
syr-up
syr-upy
syr-up-i-er
syr-up-i-est
sys-tem
sys-tem-at-ic
sys-tem-at-i-cal
sys-tem-a-tize
sys-tem-a-tized
sys-tem-a-tiz-ing
sys-tem-a-ti-za-tion
sys-tem-a-tiz-er
sys-tem-ic
sys-tem-i-cal-ly
sys-to-le
sys-tol-ic

T

tab
tab-er-na-cle
ta-ble
ta-ble-spoon
tab-leau
tab-let
tab-loid
ta-boo
tab-u-lar
tab-u-lar-ly
tab-u-late
tab-u-la-ted
tab-u-la-ting
tab-u-la-tion

ta-chom-e-ter
tach-y car-dia
tac-it
 tac-it-ly
tac-i-turn
 tac-i-tur-ni-ty
tack
 tacked
 tack-er
tack claw
tack-i-ness
tack-le
tack-y
 tack-i-er
 tack-i-est
ta-co
tact
 tact-ful
 tact-ful-ly
 tact-ful-ness
tac-tic
 tac-tic-al
 tac-tic-ian
tac-tics
tac-tile
tact-less
tad
tad-pole
taf-fe-ta
 taf-fet-ized
taff-rail
taf-fy
tag
 tagged
 tag-ger
 tag-ging
tail
tail-gate
tail-ing
tai-lor
 tai-lored
 tai-lor-ing
taint

take
 took
 ta-ken
 ta-king
talc
tale
tal-ent
 tal-ent-ed
tal-ent scout
tal-is-man
talk
 talked
 talk-er
 talk-ing
talk-a-tive
tall
 tall-ish
tal-low
 tal-low
tal-ly
 tal-lied
 tal-lies
 tal-ly-ing
tal-on
ta-ma-le
tam-bou-rine
tame
 tamed
 tam-ing
 tame-ly
tam-per
 tam-pered
 tam-per-ing
tan
 tanned
 tan-ning
 tan-ner
 tan-ner-y
tan-dem
tang
tan-gent
 tan-gen-cy
 tan-gen-tial

tan-ger-ine
tan-gi-ble
 tan-gi-bil-ity
tan-gle
 tan-gled
 tan-gling
 tan-gly
tan-go
tang-y
 tang-i-er
 tang-i-est
tank
 tank-ful
tan-kard
tan-ta-lize
 tan-ta-liz-ed
 tan-ta-liz-ing
 tan-ta-liz-ingly
tan-ta-lum
tan-ta-mount
tan-trum
tap
 tapped
 tap-ping
 tap-per
tape
 taped
 tap-ing
ta-per
tap-es-try
 tap-es-tries
tap-i-o-ca
taps
tar
 tarred
 tar-ring
tar-dy
 tar-di-ness
tar-get
tar-iff
tar-nish
 tar-nish-able
tar-ot

tar-pau-lin
tar-ry
tart
  tart-ly
  tart-ness
tar-tan
tar-tar
  tar-tar-ic
task
tas-sel
taste
  taste-ful
  taste-less
tat-ter
tat-tle
  tat-tler
tattle-tale
tat-too
  tat-too
  tat-too-er
taught
taut
  taut-ly
  taut-ness
tau-tol-o-gy
tav-ern
  tav-ern-er
tax
  tax-able
  tax-a-tion
tax--ex-empt
tax shel-ter
tax-i
taxi-cab
tax-i-der-my
  tax-i-derm-ist
tea
teach
  teach-ing
  teach-able
teach-er
team
team-ster

tear
  teary
tease
  teaser
tech-ne-tium
tech-ni-cal
  tech-ni-cal-ly
tech-nique
tech-nol-o-gy
te-dious
  te-dious-ly
tee
teem
teens
teeth
tele-cast
tele-graph
  tele-graph-er
  tele-graph-ic
te-lep-a-thy
  te-lep-a-thic
  te-lep-a-thist
tele-phone
  tele-phoner
tele-pho-to
  tele-pho-to-graph
tele-scope
  tele-scopic
tele-thon
tele-vi-sion
tel-ex
tell
  tell-able
  tell-ing
  tell-er
tel-lu-ri-um
tem-per
  tem-per-able
tem-per-a-ment
  tem-per-a-ment-al
tem-per-ance
tem-per-ate
  tem-per-ate-ly

tem-per-a-ture
tem-pest
tem-ple
tem-po
tem-po-rary
tempt
  tempt-er
ten
te-na-cious
  te-na-cious-ly
ten-ant
tend
ten-den-cy
ten-der
  ten-der-ly
  ten-der-ness
ten-der-loin
ten-don
ten-dril
  ten-dril-ed
ten-nis
ten-or
tense
ten-sion
  ten-sion-al
tent
ten-ta-cle
ten-ta-tive
  ten-ta-tive-ly
ten-ure
te-pee
tep-id
  tep-id-ly
ter-bi-um
ter-cen-ten-a-ry
term
ter-mi-nal
ter-mi-nate
  ter-mi-nation
ter-mite
ter-race
ter-rain
ter-ra-pin

ter-res-tri-al
ter-ri-ble
 ter-ri-bly
ter-ri-er
ter-rif-ic
 ter-rif-ical-ly
ter-ri-fy
 ter-ri-fied
 ter-ri-fying
ter-ri-to-ry
 ter-ri-to-rial
 ter-ri-to-rial-ly
ter-ror
ter-ror-ism
terse
 terse-ly
test
 test-ed
 test-er
 test-ing
tes-ta-ment
 tes-ta-ment-ary
tes-tate
tes-ti-fy
 tes-ti-fier
tes-ti-mo-ni-al
tes-ti-mo-ny
tes-tis
test tube
test--tube baby
tet-a-nus
teth-er
text
text-book
tex-tile
tex-ture
 tex-tural
 tex-tural-ly
thal-li-um
than
thank
thank-ful
 thank-ful-ly

thank-ful-ness
thank-less
thanks
that
thatch
thaw
the
the-a-ter
the-at-ri-cal
 the-at-ri-cals
theft
their
the-ism
them
theme
 the-ma-tic
them-selves
then
thence
 thence-forth
 thence-for-ward
the-oc-ra-cy
 the-oc-rat
the-ol-o-gy
 the-ol-o-gian
the-o-rize
 the-o-re-ti-cian
 the-o-ri-za-tion
 the-o-rist
the-o-ry
 ther-a-peu-tics
 ther-a-peu-tist
ther-a-py
 ther-a-pist
there
 there-abouts
 there-after
 there-by
 there-fore
 there-from
 there-in
ther-mal
ther-mom-e-ter

ther-mom-e-tric
ther-mo-plas-tic
ther-mo-stat
 ther-mo-stat-ic
the-sau-rus
these
the-sis
they
they'd
they'll
they're
they've
thick
 thick-ly
 thick-ness
 thick-en
thief
thieve
thigh
thim-ble
 thim-ble-ful
thin
 thin-ly
 thin-ness
thing
think
 think-able
 think-er
third
thirst
 thirst-y
thir-teen
this
this-tle
thith-er
thong
tho-rax
 tho-racic
tho-ri-um
thorn
 thorn-y
thor-ough
 thor-ough-ness

thor-ough-ly
thor-ough-bred
thor-ough-fare
those
though
thought
thought-ful
thought-less
thou-sand
thrash
thrash-er
thread
thread-y
thread-bare
threat
threat-en
three
thresh
thresh-old
threw
thrice
thrift
thrift-i-ly
thrift-i-ness
thrift-y
thrill
thrill-ing
thrill-ing-ly
thrive
throat
throb
throm-bo-sis
throng
throt-tle
through
through-out
throw
thru
thrush
thrust
thru-way
thud
thug

thug-gish
thumb
thump
thun-der
thun-der-bolt
thun-der-cloud
thun-der-show-er
thus
thwack
thwart
thy
thyme
thy-roid
thy-rox-ine
ti-ara
tick
tick-et
tick-le
tick-ler
tidal wave
tid-bit
tide
tid-ings
ti-dy
ti-di-ly
ti-di-ness
tie
tier
tier-ed
ti-ger
tiger-eye
tight
tight-en
tight-en-er
tight-rope
tights
tile
till
till-er
tilt
tim-ber
time
time--shar-ing

time tri-al
tim-id
tinc-ture
tin-der
tin-der-box
tine
tinge
tin-gle
tin-gly
tink-er
tin-ny
tin-sel
tint
ti-ny
tip
tip-ple
tip-sy
tip-si-ness
ti-rade
tire
tire-less
tire-less-ly
tis-sue
ti-ta-ni-um
tithe
tither
tit-il-late
tit-il-lat-ing
ti-tle
toad
toad-stool
toast
toast-y
toast-er
to-bac-co
to-bog-gan
to-bog-gan-ist
to-day
tod-dle
tod-dler
tod-dy
toe
tof-fee

to-geth-er
  to-geth-er-ness
toil
  toil-some
toi-let
toi-lette
to-ken
tol-er-ate
  tol-er-a-tion
  tol-er-ance
  tol-er-ant
toll
tom-a-hawk
to-ma-to
tom-boy
  tom-boy-ish
tomb-stone
tom-cat
to-mor-row
ton
tone
tongs
tongue
ton-ic
ton-sil
ton-sil-lec-to-my
tool
tooth
  tooth-ed
  tooth-less
top
to-paz
top-coat
top-ic
top-most
to-pog-ra-phy
top-ple
top-sy--tur-vy
torch
tor-ment
  tor-ment-ing-ly
  tor-ment-or
tor-na-do

tor-pe-do
tor-pid
  tor-pid-ity
  tor-pid-ly
tor-rent
  tor-rent-ial
tor-rid
  tor-rid-ly
tor-sion
  tor-sion-al
tor-so
tort
tor-toise
tor-tu-ous
  tor-tu-ous-ness
to-tal
  to-tal-ly
to-tal-i-tar-i-an
  to-tal-i-tar-i-an
tote
to-tem
tot-ter
tou-can
touch
  touch-able
tough
  tough-ly
  tough-ness
tou-pee
tour
  tour-ism
  tour-ist
tour-na-ment
tour-ni-quet
tou-sle
tout
  tout-er
tow
to-ward
tow-el
tow-er
  tow-er-ing
town

town-ship
tox-e-mi-a
tox-ic
tox-in
toy
trace
  trace-able
  trace-ably
  trac-er
track
  track-able
  track-er
tract
trac-tion
trac-tor
trade
  trade-able
trade-mark
trade--off
tra-di-tion
  tra-di-tion-al
  tra-di-tion-al-ly
tra-duce
  tra-duce-ment
  tra-ducer
traf-fic
trag-e-dy
trail
trail-er
trait
trai-tor
tra-jec-to-ry
tram-mel
  tram-mel-er
tramp
tram-ple
  tram-pler
tram-po-line
  tram-po-lin-ist
trance
tran-quil
  tran-quil-lity
  tran-quil-ly

tran-quil-ize
trans-cend
  tran-scend-ent
  tran-scend-ence
trans-scribe
trans-script
tran-scrip-tion
trans-fer
  trans-fer-able
  trans-fer-ence
trans-fig-ure
  trans-fig-ura-tion
trans-fix
  trans-fix-ion
trans-form
  trans-for-mable
  trans-for-ma-tion
  trans-for-mer
trans-fuse
  trans-fus-ion
  trans-fus-er
trans-gress
  trans-gress-ion
  trans-gress-or
  trans-gres-sive
tran-sient
  tran-sient-ly
tran-sit
trans-late
  trans-la-tion
  trans-sla-tor
trans-lu-cent
trans-mis-sion
trans-mit
  trans-miss-ible,
  trans-mitt-able
  trans-mitt-er
trans-mute
  trans-mu-ta-tion
tran-som
trans-par-ent
  trans-par-ency
  trans-par-ent-ly

tran-spire
trans-plant
  trans-plant-able
trans-pose
trans-sex-u-al
trap
tra-peze
trap-shoot-ing
trau-ma
tra-vail
trav-el
  trav-el-er
tra-verse
  tra-vers-able
  tra-ver-sal
  tra-ver-ser
trawl
tray
treach-er-ous
  treach-er-ous-ly
  treach-ery
tread
trea-son
  trea-son-able
  trea-son-ous
treas-ure
  treas-ur-er
  treas-ur-y
treat
  treat-able
  treat-er
treat-ment
treb-le
tre-foil
trek
trel-lis
trem-ble
  trem-bler
  trem-bly
tre-men-dous
trem-or
trench
  trench-er

trend
  trend-set-ter
tres-pass
tri-al
tri-an-gle
  tri-an-gu-lar-i-ty
tribe
trib-u-la-tion
trib-un-al
trib-ute
tri-ceps
trick
  trick-y
trick-er-y
trick-le
tri-col-or
  tri-col-or-ed
tri-cy-cle
tri-dent
tried
tri-en-ni-al
  tri-en-ni-al-ly
trill
tril-lion
trim
tri-ni-tro-tol-u-ene
trin-ket
tri-o
tripe
trip-le
trip-let
trip-li-cate
tri-pod
trite
tri-umph
  tri-umph-ant
  tri-umph-ant-ly
triv-i-al
trol-ley
trom-bone
troop
  troop-er
tro-phy

trop-ic
trop-i-cal
  trop-i-cal-ly
tro-pism
tro-po-sphere
trot
troth
trou-ble
  trou-bler
  trou-bling-ly
trough
trounce
troupe
trout
trow-el
  trow-el-er
tru-ant
truce
truck
  truck-er
trudge
true
  true-ness
trump
trum-pet
trunk
truss
trust
  trust-er
  trust-less
truth
  truth-ful
  truth-ful-ly
  truth-ful-ness
try
  try-ing
tryst
tsu-na-mi
tub
tu-ba
tube
tu-ber
tu-ber-cu-lo-sis

tuck
tuft
tug
tu-i-tion
tu-lip
tum-ble
  tum-bler
tu-mult
tu-mul-tu-ous
tu-na
tun-dra
tune
tune-ful
tung-sten
tu-nic
tun-nel
tur-ban
tur-bine
tur-bu-lent
  tur-bu-lent-ly
tu-reen
turf
tur-key
tur-moil
tur-nip
turn-key
turn-off
turn-over
tur-pen-tine
tur-quoise
tur-ret
tur-tle
tur-tle-neck
tusk
tus-sle
tu-tor
tut-ti--frut-ti
tu-tu
tux-e-do
twain
tweed
twee-zers
twelve

twen-ty
twice
twid-dle
twig
twi-light
twill
twin
twine
twinge
  twing-ed
twin-kle
twirl
twist
  twist-er
twit
twitch
twit-ter
  twit-ter-y
two-fold
ty-coon
tyke
type
type-face
type-writ-er
ty-phoid
ty-phoon
typ-i-cal
  typ-i-cal-ly
typ-i-fy
  typ-i-fy-ing
typ-ist
ty-po
ty-ran-no-sau-rus
tyr-an-ny

U

ubiq-ui-tous
  ubiq-ui-tary
  ubiq-ui-tous-ly
  ubiq-ui-ty
ud-der
ug-ly

ug-li-er
ug-li-est
ukase
uku-le-le
ul-cer
ul-cer-ous
ul-cer-ate
ul-cer-at-ed
ul-na
ul-nae
ul-ster
ul-te-ri-or
ul-te-ri-or-ly
ul-ti-mate
ul-ti-mate-ly
ul-ti-ma-tum
ul-ti-ma-tums
ul-ti-ma-ta
ul-tra
ul-tra-con-serv-a-tive
ul-tra-high
ul-tra-ma-rine
ul-tra-son-ic
ul-tra-vi-o-let
ul-u-late
ul-u-lat-ed
ul-u-lat-ing
um-ber
um-bil-i-cal
um-bra
um-bras
um-brae
um-brage
um-bra-geous
um-brel-la
umi-ak
um-laut
um-pire
um-pired
um-pir-ing
ump-teen
ump-teenth

un-a-bashed
un-a-bash-ed-ly
un-a-ble
un-a-bridged
un-ac-cep-t-able
un-ac-cept-ed
un-ac-com-pa-nied
un-ac-count-able
un-ac-count-a-bly
un-ac-cus-tomed
un-ac-quaint-ed
un-a-dorned
un-a-dul-ter-at-ed
un-ad-vised
un-ad-vis-ed-ly
un-af-fect-ed
un-af-fect-ed-ly
un-a-fraid
un--Amer-i-can
unan-i-mous
una-nim-i-ty
unan-i-mous-ly
un-an-swer-able
un-an-swered
un-ap-pe-tiz-ing
un-ap-pre-ci-at-ed
un-ap-pre-ci-a-tive
un-armed
un-a-shamed
un-asked
un-a-spir-ing
un-as-sail-able
un-as-sail-ably
un-as-sailed
un-at-tached
un-at-tain-able
un-at-tained
un-at-tend-ed
un-au-thor-ized
un-a-vail-a-ble
un-a-vail-a-bil-i-ty
un-a-vail-a-bly
un-a-void-a-ble

un-a-void-a-bil-i-ty
un-a-void-ably
un-a-ware
un-backed
un-bal-anced
un-bar
un-barred
un-bar-ring
un-bear-able
un-bear-ably
un-beat-en
un-beat-able
un-be-com-ing
un-be-com-ing-ly
un-be-lief
un-be-liev-able
un-be-liev-ably
un-be-liev-er
un-be-liev-ing
un-be-liev-ing-ly
un-bend
un-bend-ing
un-bi-ased
un-bi-ased-ly
un-bid-den
un-bind
un-bound
un-bind-ing
un-blem-ished
un-bolt
un-bolt-ed
un-born
un-bos-om
un-bound
un-bound-ed-ly
un-bowed
un-bread-able
un-bri-dle
un-bri-dled
un-bri-dling
un-bro-ken
un-bro-ken-ly
un-buck-le

un-buck-led
un-bur-den
un-but-ton
un-but-toned
un--called--for
un-can-ny
un-can-ni-er
un-can-ni-est
un-can-ni-ly
un-cap
un-capped
un-cap-ping
un-ceas-ing
un-ceas-ing-ly
un-cer-e-mo-ni-ous
-cer-e-mo-ni-ous-ly
un-cer-tain
un-cer-tain-ly
un-cer-tain-ty
un-cer-tain-ties
un-chal-lenged
un-change-able
un-change-ably
un-changed
un-chang-ing
un-char-i-ta-ble
un-char-i-ta-bly
un-chart-ed
un-chris-tian
un-cir-cum-cised
un-civ-il
un-civ-il-ly
un-civ-i-lized
un-class-i-fi-able
un-clas-si-fied
un-cle
un-clean
un-clean-ly
un-clear
un-cloak
un-clut-tered
un-coil
un-com-fort-able

un-com-fort-ably
un-com-mit-ted
un-com-mon
un-com-mon-ly
un-com-mu-ni-ca-tive
un-com-pre-hend-ing
un-com-pro-mis-ing
un-com-pro-mised
un-con-cern
un-con-cerned
un-con-di-tion-al
un-con-di-tion-al-ly
un-con-firmed
un-con-nect-ed
un-con-nect-ed-ly
un-con-quer-a-ble
un-con-quered
un-con-scion-able
un-con-scion-ably
un-con-scious
un-con-scious-ly
un-con-scious-ness
un-con-sti-tui-tion-al
un-con-strained
un-con-test-ed
un-con-trol-la-ble
un-con-trol-la-bly
un-con-trolled
un-con-ven-tion-al
un-count-ed
un-cou-ple
un-cou-pled
un-cou-pling
un-couth
un-couth-ly
un-cov-er
un-cov-ered
unc-tion
unc-tu-ous
unc-tu-os-i-ty

unc-tu-ous-ly
un-curl
un-cut
un-daunt-ed
un-daunt-ed-ly
un-de-ceive
un-de-ceived
un-de-ceiv-ing
un-de-ceiv-a-ble
un-de-cid-ed
un-de-cid-ed-ly
un-de-cid-ed-ness
un-de-fined
un-de-fin-a-ble
un-de-mon-stra-tive
un-de-ni-a-ble
un-de-ni-a-bly
un-de-nied
un-de-pend-able
un-der
un-der-a-chiev-er
-der-a-chiev-ment
un-der-act
un-der-age
un-der-arm
un-der-bel-ly
un-der-car-riage
un-der-charge
un-der-charged
un-der-charg-ing
un-der-class-man
un-der-class-men
un-der-clothes
un-der-coast
un-der-cur-rent
un-der-cut
un-der-cut-ting
un-der-de-vel-oped
-der-de-vel-op-ing
un-der-dog
un-der-done
un-der-es-ti-mate
un-der-es-ti-mat-ed

un-der-es-ti-mat-ing
un-der-es-ti-ma-tion
un-der-foot
un-der-gar-ment
un-der-go
un-der-went
un-der-gone
un-der-grad-u-ate
un-der-ground
un-der-growth
un-der-lie
un-der-lay
un-der-lain
un-der-ly-ing
un-der-line
un-der-lined
un-der-lin-ing
un-der-ling
un-der-mine
un-der-mined
un-der-min-ing
un-der-min-er
un-der-most
un-der-neath
un-der-priv-i-leged
un-der-rate
un-der-rat-ed
un-der-rat-ing
un-der-score
un-der-scored
un-der-scor-ing
un-der-sea
un-der-sec-re-tary
un-der-sec-re-tar-ies
un-der-sell
un-der-sold
un-der-ell-ing
un-der-sell-er
un-der-shirt
un-der-shot
un-der-side
un-der-signed
un-der-stand

un-der-stood
un-der-stand-ing
un-der-stand-a-ble
un-der-stand-a-bly
un-der-state
un-der-stat-ed
un-der-stat-ing
un-der-state-ment
un-der-stood
un-der-study
un-der-stud-ied
un-der-stud-y-ing
un-der-stud-ies
un-der-take
un-der-took
un-der-tak-en
un-der-tak-ing
un-der-tak-er
un-der-the-coun-ter
un-der-tone
un-der-tow
un-der-wa-ter
un-der-weight
un-der-write
un-der-wrote
un-der-writ-ten
un-der-writ-er
un-de-sir-a-ble
un-de-sir-a-bil-i-ty
un-de-sir-a-bly
un-de-ter-mined
un-dies
un-dip-lo-mat-ic
-dip-lo-mat-i-cal-ly
un-dis-ci-plined
un-dis-closed
un-dis-posed
un-dis-tin-guished
un-di-vid-ed
un-doubt-ed
un-doubt-ed-ly
un-doubt-ing
un-due

un-du-lant
un-du-late
un-du-lat-ed
un-du-lat-ing
un-du-la-tion
un-du-ly
un-dy-ing
un-earth
un-earth-ly
un-easy
un-eas-i-er
un-eas-i-est
un-ease
un-eas-i-ly
un-eas-i-ness
un-em-ployed
un-em-ploy-ment
un-e-qual
un-e-qual-ly
un-e-qual-ed
un-e-quiv-o-cal
un-e-quiv-o-cal-ly
un-err-ing
un-err-ing-ly
un-eth-i-cal
un-eth-i-cal-ly
un-e-ven
un-e-ven-ly
un-e-ven-ness
un-ex-cep-tion-able
un-ex-pect-ed
un-ex-pect-ed-ly
un-fail-ing
un-fail-ing-ly
un-faith-ful
un-faith-ful-ly
un-faith-ful-ness
un-fa-mil-iar
un-fa-mil-i-ar-i-ty
un-fa-mil-iar-ly
un-fast-en
un-fas-ten-a-ble
un-fas-ten-er

un-fath-om-a-ble
un-fa-vor-a-ble
  un-fa-vor-a-bly
un-feel-ing
  un-feel-ing-ly
un-feigned
  un-feign-ed-ly
un-fet-ter
  un-fet-tered
un-fin-ished
un-fit
  un-fit-ly
  un-fit-ness
  un-fit-ting
un-flat-ter-ing
un-flinch-ing
  un-flinch-ing-ly
un-fold
un-for-get-ta-ble
  un-for-get-ta-bly
un-for-giv-a-ble
un-for-tu-nate
  un-for-tu-nate-ly
un-found-ed
  un-found-ed-ness
un-friend-ly
  un-friend-li-er
  un-friend-li-est
  un-friend-li-ness
un-frock
un-furl
un-gain-ly
  un-gain-li-ness
un-gird
  un-gird-ed
  un-gird-ing
un-glazed
un-god-ly
  un-god-li-er
  un-god-li-est
  un-god-li-ness
un-gov-ern-a-ble
  un-gov-ern-ably

un-gra-cious
  un-gra-cious-ly
  un-gra-cious-ness
un-gram-mat-i-cal
  -gram-mat-i-cal-ly
un-grate-ful
  un-grate-ful-ly
  un-grate-ful-ness
un-guard-ed
  un-guard-ed-ly
un-guent
un-gu-late
un-ham-pered
un-hand
un-handy
  un-hand-i-er
  un-hand-i-est
un-hap-py
  un-hap-pi-er
  un-hap-pi-est
  un-hap-pi-ly
  un-hap-pi-ness
un-harmed
un-healthy
  un-health-i-er
  un-health-i-ly
un-heard
un-heed-ed
  un-heed-ful
  un-heed-ing
un-hinge
  un-hinged
  un-hing-ing
un-hitch
un-ho-ly
  un-ho-li-er
  un-ho-li-est
  un-ho-li-ly
  un-ho-li-ness
un-hook
un-horse
  un-horsed
  un-hors-ing

un-hur-ried
un-hurt
uni-cam-er-al
  uni-cam-er-al-ly
uni-cel-lu-lar
uni-corn
uni-fi-ca-tion
uni-form
  uni-formed
  uni-form-i-ty
  uni-form-ly
uni-fy
  uni-fied
  uni-fy-ing
  uni-fi-er
uni-lat-er-al
  uni-lat-er-al-ism
  uni-lat-er-al-ly
un-imag-in-able
un-im-pair-ed
un-im-peach-able
  un-im-peach-a-bly
un-im-por-tance
  un-im-por-tant
un-im-proved
un-in-hib-it-ed
  un-in-hib-it-ed-ly
un-in-ter-est-ed
  un-in-ter-est-ing
un-ion
un-ion-ism
  un-ion-ist
un-ion-ize
  un-ion-ized
  un-ion-iz-ing
  un-ion-i-za-tion
unique
  unique-ly
  unique-ness
uni-son
unit
unite
  unit-ed

unit-ing
unit-er
uni-ty
uni-ties
uni-valve
uni-valved
uni-val-vu-lar
uni-ver-sal
uni-ver-sal-i-ty
uni-ver-sal-ly
uni-ver-sal-ness
uni-ver-sal-ize
uni-ver-sal-ized
uni-ver-sal-iz-ing
uni-verse
uni-ver-si-ty
uni-ver-si-ties
un-just
un-just-ly
un-kempt
un-kind
un-kind-ness
un-kind-ly
un-known
un-law-ful
un-law-ful-ly
un-law-ful-ness
un-learn
un-learned
un-learn-ing
un-learn-ed
un-learn-ed-ly
un-leash
un-less
un-let-ter-ed
un-like
un-like-ness
un-like-ly
un-like-li-er
un-like-li-est
un-like-li-ness
un-lim-ber
un-lim-it-ed

un-load
un-load-er
un-lock
un-looked--for
un-loose
un-loosed
un-loos-ing
un-loos-en
un-lucky
un-luck-i-er
un-luck-i-est
un-luck-i-ly
un-make
un-made
un-mak-ing
un-mak-er
un-man
un-manned
un-man-ning
un-mask
un-mean-ing
un-mean-ing-ly
un-men-tion-able
un-mer-ci-ful
un-mer-ci-ful-ly
un-mis-tak-able
un-mis-tak-a-bly
un-mit-i-gat-ed
un-mit-i-gat-ed-ly
un-nat-u-ral
un-nat-u-ral-ly
un-nat-u-ral-ness
un-nec-es-sary
un-nec-es-sar-i-ly
un-nerve
un-nerved
un-nerv-ing
un-num-bered
un-ob-jec-tion-able
un-or-gan-ized
un-pack
un-par-al-leled
un-par-don-able

un-pleas-ant
un-pleas-ant-ly
un-pleas-ant-ness
un-plumbed
un-pop-u-lar
un-pop-u-lar-i-ty
un-pop-u-lar-ly
un-prec-e-dent-ed
-prec-e-dent-ed-ly
un-prin-ci-pled
un-print-able
un-pro-fes-sion-al
-pro-fes-sion-al-ly
un-qual-i-fied
un-qual-i-fied-ly
un-ques-tion-able
un-ques-tion-ably
un-ques-tioned
un-quote
un-quot-ed
un-quot-ing
un-rav-el
un-rav-eled
un-rav-el-ing
un-rav-el-ment
un-read
un-re-al
un-rea-son-able
un-rea-son-ably
un-rea-son-ing
un-re-fined
un-re-gen-er-ate
un-re-lat-ed
un-re-lent-ing
un-re-lent-ing-ly
un-remit-ting
un-re-serve
un-re-served
un-re-serv-ed-ly
un-rest
un-ri-valed
un-roll
un-ruf-fled

un-ru-ly
  un-ruy-li-er
  un-ru-li-est
un-sad-dle
  un-sad-dled
  un-sad-dling
un-said
un-sa-vory
un-say
  un-say-ing
un-scathed
un-schooled
un-scram-ble
  un-scram-bled
  un-scram-bling
un-screw
un-scru-pu-lous
  un-scru-pu-lous-ly
un-seal
un-sea-son-able
  un-sea-son-ably
un-seat
un-seem-ly
un-set-tle
  un-set-tled
  un-set-tling
un-sheathe
  un-sheathed
  un-sheath-ing
un-shod
un-sight-ly
  un-sight-li-er
  un-sight-li-est
un-skilled
  un-skill-ful
  un-skill-ful-ly
un-snap
  un-snapped
  un-snap-ping
un-snarl
un-so-phis-ti-cat-ed
  -so-phis-ti-cat-ed-ly
  -so-phis-ti-ca-tion

un-sound
  un-sound-ly
un-spar-ing
  un-spar-ing-ly
un-speak-a-ble
  un-speak-a-bly
un-sta-ble
  un-sta-bly
un-steady
  un-stead-i-er
  un-stead-i-est
  un-stead-i-ly
un-stop
  un-stopped
  un-stop-ping
un-strung
un-stud-ied
un-sung
un-tan-gle
  un-tan-gled
  un-tan-gling
un-taught
un-think-able
  un-think-ing
  un-think-ing-ly
un-ti-dy
un-tie
  un-tied
  un-ty-ing
un-til
un-time-ly
  un-time-li-ness
un-to
un-told
  un-touch-a-ble
  un-touch-a-bly
un-to-ward
  un-to-ward-ly
un-truth
un-tu-tored
un-used
un-u-su-al
  un-u-su-al-ly

  un-u-su-al-ness
un-ut-ter-able
  un-ut-ter-ably
un-var-nished
un-veil
un-wary
  un-war-i-ly
un-well
un-whole-some
  un-whole-some-ly
un-wieldy
  un-wield-i-ness
un-will-ing
  un-will-ing-ly
  un-will-ing-ness
un-wind
  un-wound
  un-wind-ing
un-wise
  un-wise-ly
un-wit-ting
  un-wit-ting-ly
un-wont-ed
  un-wont-ed-ly
un-wor-thy
  un-wor-thi-ly
  un-wor-thi-ness
un-wrap
  un-wrapped
  un-wrap-ping
un-yield-ing
up-beat
up-braid
  up-braid-er
  up-braid-ing
up-com-ing
up-coun-try
up-date
  up-dat-ed
  up-dat-ing
up-end
up-grade
  up-grad-ed

up-grad-ing
up-heav-al
up-heave
up-heaved
up-heav-ing
up-hill
up-hold
up-held
up-hold-ing
up-hol-ster
up-hol-ster-er
up-hol-stery
up-keep
up-land
up-lift
up-most
up-on
up-per
up-per--class
up-per-cut
up-per-cut-ting
up-per-most
up-pish
up-pish-ly
up-pi-ty
up-raise
up-raised
up-rais-ing
up-rear
up-right
up-right-ly
up-right-ness
up-ris-ing
up-roar
up-roar-i-ous
up-set
up-set-ting
up-shot
up-side
up-stage
up-staged
up-stag-ing
up-stairs

up-stand-ing
up-start
up-take
up-to-date
up-town
up-trend
up-turn
up-ward
up-ward-ly
ura-ni-um
ur-ban
ur-bane
ur-bane-ly
ur-ban-i-ty
ur-ban-ize
ur-ban-ized
ur-ban-iz-ing
ur-ban-i-za-tion
ur-chin
urea
ure-al
ure-ter
ure-thra
ure-thrae
ure-thras
ure-thral
ur-gent
ur-gen-cy
ur-gen-cies
ur-gent-ly
uric
uri-nal
uri-nal-y-sis
uri-nal-y-ses
uri-nary
uri-nar-ies
uri-nate
urine
urol-o-gy
uro-log-ic
uro-log-i-cal
urol-o-gist
us-able

us-ably
us-abil-i-ty
us-age
use
use-ful
use-ful-ly
ush-er
usu-al
usu-al-ly
usurp
usurp-pa-tion
usurp-er
usu-ry
usu-ries
usu-ri-ous
uten-sil
uter-us
ut-eri
util-i-tar-ian
util-i-ty
util-i-ties
uti-lize
uti-lized
uti-liz-ing
uti-li-za-tion
ut-most
ut-ter
ut-ter-a-ble
ut-ter-er
ut-ter-ance
ut-ter-most
uvu-la
uvu-las
uvu-lae
ux-o-ri-ous
ux-o-ri-ous-ly

V

va-can-cy
va-can-cies
va-cant
va-cant-ly

va-cate
va-cat-ed
va-cat-ing
va-ca-tion
vac-ci-nate
vac-ci-nat-ed
vac-ci-nat-ing
vac-ci-na-tion
vac-cine
vac-il-late
vac-il-lat-ed
vac-il-lat-ing
vac-il-la-tion
vac-il-la-tor
va-cu-i-ty
va-cu-i-ties
vac-u-ous
vac-u-ous-ly
vac-u-um
vac-u-ums
vac-ua
vac-u-um--packed
va-gi-na
va-gi-nas
va-gi-nae
vag-i-nal
va-grant
va-gran-cy
va-gran-cies
va-grant-ly
vague
vague-ly
vain
vain-ly
vain-ness
vain-glo-ry
vain-glo-ries
vain-glo-ri-ous
val-ance
val-anced
val-e-dic-tion
val-e-dic-to-ri-an
val-e-dic-to-ry

val-e-dic-to-ries
va-lence
va-len-cy
val-en-tine
va-let
val-iant
val-iant-ly
val-id
val-id-ly
val-i-date
val-i-dat-ed
val-i-dat-ig
val-i-da-tion
va-lid-i-ty
va-lid-i-ties
va-lise
val-ley
val-leys
val-or
val-or-ous
val-or-ous-ly
val-u-able
val-u-ably
val-u-a-tion
val-u-a-tion-al
val-ue
val-ued
val-u-ing
val-ue-less
valve
valve-less
val-vu-lar
va-moose
vam-pire
vam-pir-ic
vam-pir-ism
va-na-di-um
van-dal
van-dal-ism
van-dal-ize
van-dal-ized
van-dal-iz-ing
vane

vaned
vane-less
van-guard
va-nil-la
van-ish
van-ish-er
van-i-ty
van-i-ties
van-quish
van-quish-a-ble
van-quish-er
van-tage
vap-id
va-pid-i-ty
vap-id-ly
va-por
va-por-er
va-por-ish
va-por-ize
va-por-ized
va-por-iz-ing
va-por-i-za-tion
va-por-iz-er
va-por-ous
va-por-opus-ly
va-que-ro
va-que-ros
var-i-able
var-i-abil-i-ty
var-i-ably
var-i-ance
var-i-ant
var-i-a-tion
var-i-a-tion-al
var-i-a-tion-al-ly
var-i-col-ored
var-i-cose
var-ied
var-ied-ness
var-ie-gate
var-ie-gat-ed
var-ie-gat-ing
var-ie-ga-tion

var-ie-ga-tor
va-ri-etal
var-i-etal-ly
va-ri-ety
va-ri-e-ties
var-i-ous
var-i-ous-ly
var-nish
var-nish-er
var-si-ty
var-si-ties
vary
var-ied
vary-ing
var-i-er
vary-ing-ly
vas-cu-lar
vas-cu-lar-i-ty
va-sec-to-my
va-sec-to-mies
vas-o-mo-tor
vas-sal
vas-sal-age
vast-ness
vat
vat-ted
vat-ting
vaude-ville
vault
vault-ed
vault-er
vault-ing
vaunt
vaunt-er
vaunt-ing-ly
vec-tor
vec-to-ri-al
veer-ing
veg-e-ta-ble
veg-e-tal
veg-e-tar-i-an
veg-e-tar-i-an-ism
veg-e-tate

veg-e-tat-ed
veg-e-tat-ing
veg-e-ta-tion
veg-e-ta-tion-al
veg-e-ta-tive
ve-he-ment
ve-he-mence
ve-he-men-cy
ve-hi-cle
ve-hic-u-lar
veil
veiled
veil-ing
vein
veiny
vein-i-er
vein-i-est
vein-ing
vel-lum
ve-loc-i-ty
ve-loc-i-ties
vel-our
vel-um
ve-la
vel-vet
vel-vet-ed
vel-ve-teen
vel-vety
vel-vet-i-er
vel-vet-i-est
ve-nal
ve-nal-i-ty
ve-nal-ly
ve-na-tion
ve-na-tion-al
vend-er
vend-or
ven-det-ta
vend-i-ble
vend-i-bil-i-ty
ve-neer
ve-neer-er
ve-neer-ig

ven-er-able
ven-er-abil-i-ty
ven-er-ably
ven-er-ate
ven-er-a-tion
ven-er-a-tor
ve-ne-re-al
venge-ance
venge-ful
venge-ful-ness
ve-ni-al
ve-ni-al-i-ty
ve-ni-al-ness
ve-ni-al-ly
ven-i-son
ven-om
ven-om-ous
ve-nous
ve-nous-ly
vent
vent-ed
vent-ing
ven-ti-late
ven-ti-lat-ed
ven-ti-lat-ing
ven-ti-la-tion
ven-ti-la-tor
ven-tral
ven-tral-ly
ven-tri-cle
ven-tril-o-quism
ven-tri-lo-qui-al
ven-tril-o-quist
ven-tril-o-quize
ven-tril-o-quized
ven-tril-o-quiz-ing
ven-ture
ven-ture-some
ven-tur-ous
ve-ra-cious
ve-rac-i-ty
ve-rac-i-ties
ve-ran-da

ver-bal
ver-bal-ly
ver-bal-ize
ver-bal-ized
ver-bal-iz-ing
ver-bal-i-za-tion
ver-bal-iz-er
ver-ba-tim
ver-bi-age
ver-bose
ver-bose-ness
ver-bos-i-ty
ver-bo-ten
ver-dant
ver-dan-cy
ver-dict
ver-di-gris
ver-dure
ver-dured
ver-dur-ous
verge
verged
verg-ing
ver-i-fi-ca-tion
ver-i-fy
ver-i-fied
ver-i-fy-ing
ver-i-fi-abil-i-ty
ver-i-fi-able
ver-i-fi-er
veri-si-mil-i-tude
veri-ta-ble
veri-ta-bly
ver-i-ty
ver-i-ties
ver-meil
ver-mic-u-lar
ver-mic-u-late
ver-mic-u-lat-ed
ver-mi-fuge
ver-mil-ion
ver-min
ver-min-ous

ver-mouth
ver-nac-u-lar
ver-nac-u-lar-ism
ver-nal
ver-nal-ly
ver-sa-tile
ver-sa-til-i-ty
versed
ver-si-fy
ver-si-fied
ver-si-fy-ing
ver-si-fi-er
ver-si-fi-ca-tion
ver-sion
ver-sion-al
ver-sus
ver-te-bra
ver-te-brae
ver-te-bral
ver-te-bral-ly
ver-te-brate
ver-tex
ver-tex-es
ver-ti-ces
ver-ti-cal
ver-ti-cal-i-ty
ver-ti-cal-ly
ver-ti-go
ver-ti-goes
ver-tig-i-nes
ves-i-cant
ves-i-ca-to-ry
ves-i-ca-to-ries
ves-i-cate
ves-i-cat-ed
ves-i-cat-ing
ves-i-ca-tion
ves-i-cle
ve-sic-u-lar
ves-pers
ves-sel
ves-tal
vest-ed

ves-ti-bule
ves-ti-buled
ves-ti-bul-ing
ves-tib-u-lar
ves-tige
ves-tig-i-al
ves-tig-i-al-ly
vest-ment
vest-pock-et
ves-try
ves-tries
vet
vet-ted
vet-ting
vet-er-an
vet-er-i-nar-i-an
vet-er-i-nary
ve-to
vex
vex-er
vex-ing-ly
vex-a-tion
vex-a-tious
vexed
via
vi-a-ble
vi-a-bil-i-ty
vi-a-bly
vi-a-duct
vi-al
vi-and
vi-brant
vi-bran-cy
vi-brate
vi-brat-ed
vi-brat-ing
vi-bra-tion
vi-bra-to
vi-bra-tos
vi-bra-tor
vi-bra-to-ry
vi-bur-num
vic-ar

vic-ar-ship
vic-ar-age
vi-car-i-ous
  vi-car-i-ous-ly
vice ad-mi-ral
vice--con-sul
vice--pres-i-dent
vice-roy
  vice-roy-al
vice ver-sa
vi-cin-i-ty
  vi-cin-i-ties
vi-cious
  vi-cious-ly
vi-cis-si-tude
vic-tim
  vic-tim-ize
  vic-tim-ized
  vic-tim-iz-ing
  vic-tim-iz-er
vic-tor
vic-to-ri-ous
  vic-to-ri-ous-ly
vic-to-ry
  vic-to-ries
vict-ual
vid-eo
view-er
  view-less
  view-point
vig-il
  vig-i-lance
  vig-i-lant
  vig-i-lan-te
vi-gnette
vig-or
  vig-or-ous
  vig-or-ous-ly
vi-king
vile
vil-i-fy
  vil-i-fied
  vil-i-fy-ing

vil-i-fi-ca-tion
vil-la
vil-lain
  vil-lain-ous
vil-lainy
  vil-lain-ies
vil-lein
vil-lous
vil-lus
  vil-li
vin-ci-ble
  vin-ci-bil-i-ty
vin-di-cate
  vin-di-cat-ed
  vin-di-cat-ing
vin-dic-tive
  vin-dic-tive-ly
  vin-dic-tive-ness
vin-e-gar
vin-e-gary
vine-yard
vi-nous
vin-tage
vint-ner
vi-nyl
vi-ol
vi-o-la
  vi-o-list
vi-o-la-ble
  vi-o-la-bil-i-ty
vi-o-late
  vi-o-lat-ed
vi-o-la-tion
vi-o-lence
vi-o-lent
vi-o-let
vi-o-lin
  vi-o-lin-ist
vi-o-lon-cel-lo
  vi-o-lon-cel-list
vi-per
vi-ra-go
vi-ral

vir-eo
  vir-e-os
vir-gin
  vir-gin-al
vir-gin-i-ty
vir-gule
vir-ile
  vi-ril-i-ty
vi-rol-o-gy
  vi-rol-o-gist
  vir-tu-al
vir-tue
vir-tu-os-i-ty
  vir-tu-os-i-ties
vir-tu-o-so
vir-tu-ous
  vir-tu-ous-ly
vir-u-lence
  vir-u-len-cy
vir-u-lent
vi-rus
  vi-rus-es
vi-sa
vis-age
vis-cera
  vis-cer-al
vis-cid
  vis-cid-ly
vis-cos-i-ty
  vis-cos-i-ties
vis-count
  vis-count-cy
  vis-count-ship
vis-count-ess
vis-cous
vis-i-bil-i-ty
  vis-i-bil-i-ties
  vis-i-ble
vi-sion
  vi-sion-ary
  vi-sion-ar-ies
vis-it
vis-i-tant

vis-it-a-tion
vis-it-ing
vis-i-tor
vi-sor
vis-ta
vi-tal
  vi-tal-i-ty
  vi-tal-i-ties
vi-tal-ize
  vi-tal-ized
  vi-tal-iz-ing
  vi-tal-i-za-tion
vi-tals
vi-ta-min
vi-ti-ate
vit-re-ous
  vit-re-os-i-ty
vit-ri-fy
  vit-ri-fied
  vit-ri-fy-ing
  vit-ri-fi-a-ble
  vit-ri-fi-ca-tion
vit-ri-ol
  vit-ri-ol-ic
vi-tu-per-ate
  vi-tu-per-at-ed
  vi-tu-per-at-ing
vi-tu-per-a-tion
vi-va
vi-va-cious
vi-vac-i-ty
  vi-vac-i-ties
viv-id
viv-i-fy
  viv-i-fied
  viv-i-fy-ing
vi-vip-ar-ous
vivi-sec-tion
vix-en
vi-zier
vi-zor
vo-cab-u-lar-y
  vo-cab-u-lar-ies

vo-cal
vo-ca-tion
  vo-ca-tion-al
vo-cif-er-ous
vod-ka
voice-print
void-able
vol-a-tile
  vol-a-til-i-ty
vol-can-ic
  vol-can-i-cal-ly
vol-ca-no
  vol-ca-noes
  vol-ca-nos
vo-li-tion
vol-ley
  vol-leys
vol-ley-ball
volt-age
vol-ta-ic
volt-me-ter
vol-u-ble
  vol-u-bly
  vol-u-bil-i-ty
vol-ume
vo-lu-mi-nous
  vo-lu-mi-nous-ly
vol-un-tary
  vol-un-tar-i-ly
vol-un-teer
vo-lup-tu-ary
  vo-lup-tu-ar-ies
vo-lup-tu-ous
vom-it
voo-doo
vo-ra-cious
vo-rac-i-ty
vor-tex
  vor-tex-es
  vor-ti-ces
vo-ta-ry
  vor-ta-ries
vot-er

vo-tive
vouch-er
vouch-safe
  vouch-safed
  vouch-saf-ing
vow-el
voy-age
  voy-aged
  voy-ag-ing
  voy-ag-er
vo-ya-geur
vo-yeur
  vo-yeur-ism
  voy-eur-is-tic
vul-can-ite
vul-gar
  vul-gar-ism
vul-gar-i-ty
  vul-gar-i-ties
vul-gar-ize
  vul-gar-ized
  vul-gar-iz-ing
vul-gate
vul-ner-a-ble
  vul-ner-a-bly
vul-pine
vul-ture
vul-va
  vul-vae
  vul-vas

W

wab-ble
  wab-bled
  wab-bling
wacky
  wack-i-er
  wack-i-est
  wack-i-ly
wad
  wad-ded
  wad-ding

wade
wad-ed
wad-ing
wad-er
waf-er
waf-fle
wag
wagged
wag-ging
wag-ger
wag-gish
wage
waged
wag-ing
wa-ger
wag-gery
wag-ger-ies
wag-gle
wag-gled
wag-gling
wag-on
wag-on-er
wain-scot
wain-scot-ing
wain-wright
waist-band
waist-coat
waist-line
wait-er
wait-ing
wait-ress
waive
waived
waiv-ing
waiv-er
wake
waked
wok-en
wak-ing
wake-ful
wake-ful-ly
wak-en
wale

waled
wal-ing
walk-a-way
walk-er
walk-ie-talk-ie
walk-out
walk-o-ver
walk-up
walk-way
wal-al-by
wal-la-bies
wall-board
wal-let
wall-eye
wall-eyed
wall-flow-er
wal-lop
wall-to-wall
wal-nut
wal-rus
wal-rus-es
wam-pum
wan
wan-ner
wan-nest
wan-ness
wan-der
wan-der-lust
wane
waned
wan-ing
wan-gle
wan-gled
wan-gling
wan-gler
want-ing
wan-ton
wa-pi-ti
wa-pi-ties
war
warred
war-ring
war-ble

war-bled
war-bling
war-bler
war-den
war-den-ship
ward-er
ward-robe
ware-house
war-fare
war-head
war-horse
war-like
war-lock
warm
warm-er
warm-est
warm--blood-ed
warm-heart-ed
war-mon-ger
warmth
warn-ing
war-path
war-rant
war-ran-ty
war-ran-ties
war-ren
war-ri-or
war-ship
war-time
wary
war-i-er
war-i-est
war-i-ly
wash-able
wash-ba-sin
wash-board
wash-bowl
wash-cloth
wash-er
wash-ing
wash-out
wash-room
wash-stand

wash-tub
wasn't
wasp
  wasp-ish
  wasp-ish-ly
was-sail
wast-age
waste
  wast-ed
  wast-ing
  waste-ful
  waste-ful-ly
  waste-ful-ness
waste-bas-ket
waste-land
waste-pa-per
wast-er
wast-rel
watch-dog
watch-ful
watch-man
  watch-men
watch-tow-er
watch-word
wa-ter
wat-er-buck
wa-ter-col-or
wa-ter-course
wa-ter-cress
wa-ter-fall
wa-ter-foul
wa-ter-front
wa-ter-less
wa-ter lev-el
wa-ter lily
  wa-ter lil-ies
wa-ter line
wa-ter-llogged
Wa-ter-loo
wa-ter main
wa-ter-man
  wa-ter-men
wa-ter-mark

wa-ter-mel-on
wa-ter moc-ca-sin
wa-ter-proof
wa-ter-re-pel-lent
wa-ter-shed
wa-ter-side
wa-ter ski
  wa-ter-skied
  wa-ter-ski-ing
wa-ter-spout
wa-ter-tight
wa-ter-way
wa-ter-works
  wa-tery
watt-age
watt-hour
wat-tle
  wat-tled
  wat-tling
wave
  waved
  wav-ing
wave-length
wave-let
wa-ver
wav-y
  wav-i-er
  wav-i-est
  wav-i-ly
wax
  waxed
  wax-ing
wax-en
wax-wing
wax-work
waxy
  wax-i-er
  wax-i-est
way-far-er
  way-far-ing
way-lay
  way-laid
  way-lay-ing

way-side
way-ward
weak-en
weak-kneed
weak-ling
weak-ly
  weak-li-er
  weak-li-est
weak-mind-ed
weak-ness
wealthy
  wealth-i-er
  wealth-i-est
  wealth-i-ly
wean
weap-on
  weap-on-ry
wear
  wear-ing
wea-ri-some
wea-ry
  wea-ri-er
  wea-ri-est
  wea-ried
  wea-ry-ing
  wea-ri-ly
wea-sel
weath-er
weath-er--beat-en
weath-er-cock
weath-er-glass
weath-er-ing
weath-er-man
  weath-er-men
weath-er-proof
weather vane
weave
  weaved
  wov-en
  weav-ing
  weav-er
web
  webbed

web-bing
web-foot
web-foot-ed
wed-ding
wedge
wedged
wedg-ing
wed-lock
weedy
weed-i-er
weed-i-est
week-day
week-end
week-ly
weep-ing
wee-vil
weigh
weight
weighty
weight-i-er
weight-i-est
weight-i-ly
weird
weird-er
weird-est
wel-come
wel-comed
wel-com-ing
wel-fare
well--be-ing
well-born
well--bred
well--dis-posed
well--done
well--found-ed
well--groomed
well--ground-ed
well--known
well--mean-ing
well--nigh
well--off
well--read
well--spo-ken

well-spring
well--thought--of
well--timed
well--to--do
well--wish-er
well--worn
wel-ter
wel-ter-weight
were-wolf
were-wolves
west-bound
west-er-ly
west-ern
west-ern-er
west-ern-ize
west-ern-ized
west-ern-iz-ing
west-ern-i-za-tion
west-ern-most
west-ward
wet
wet-ter
wet-test
wet-back
whale
whaled
whal-ing
whale-boat
whale-bone
whal-er
wharf
wharves
what-ev-er
what-not
what-so-ev-er
wheat
wheat-en
whee-dle
whee-dled
whee-dling
whee-dler
wheel and ax-le
wheel-bar-row

wheel-chair
wheeled
wheel-house
wheel-wright
wheeze
wheezed
wheez-ing
wheezy
wheez-i-er
wheez-i-est
wheez-i-ly
whelm
whelp
whence-so-ev-er
where-abouts
where-as
where-by
where-fore
where-in
where-on
where-so-ev-er
where-to
where-up-on
wher-ev-er
where-with
where-with-al
wher-ry
wher-ries
whet
whet-ted
whet-ting
wheth-er
whet-stone
whch-ev-er
whim-per
whim-si-cal
whim-sy
whim-sies
whine
whined
whin-ing
whin-ny
whin-nied

whin-nying
whin-nies
whip
whipped
whip-ping
whip-lash
whip-per-snap-per
whip-pet
whip-poor-will
whir
whirred
whir-ring
whirl-i-gig
whirl-pool
whirl-wind
whisk-er
whis-key
whis-ky
whis-keys
whis-kies
whis-per
whist
whis-tle
whis-tled
whis-tling
whis-tler
white
whit-er
whit-est
whit-ish
white--col-lar
white-fish
whit-en
white-wash
white water
whith-er
whit-ing
whit-tle
whit-tled
whit-tling
whit-tler
whiz
whizzed

whiz-zing
whiz-zes
whoa
who-ev-er
whole-heart-ed
whole-sale
whole-saled
whole-sal-ing
whole-sal-er
whole-some
whole-wheat
whol-ly
whom-ev-er
whom-so-ev-er
whoop-ing
whop-per
whop-ping
whorled
whose-so-ev-er
who-so-ev-er
wick-ed
wick-er
wick-er-work
wick-et
wide
wid-er
wid-est
wide--awake
wide--eyed
wid-en
wide-spread
wid-geon
wid-ow
wid-ow-er
wid-ow-hood
width
wield-er
wieldy
wie-ner
wig-gle
wig-gled
wig-gling
wig-gly

wig-gli-er
wig-gler
wig-wag
wig-wagged
wig-wag-ging
wig-wam
wild-cat
wild-cat-ted
wild-cat-ting
wild-cat strike
wil-der-ness
wild-fire
wild-fowl
wild--goose chase
wild-life
wild-wood
wile
wiled
wil-ing
wil-i-ly
wil-i-ness
willed
will-ful
wil-lies
will-ing
will--o'--the--wisp
wil-low
wil-lowy
wil-ly--nil-ly
wim-ble
wim-ple
win
win-ning
wince
winced
winc-ing
wind
wound
wind-ing
wind-bag
wind-break
wind-ed
wind-fall

wind-flow-er
win-dow
wind-row
wind-shield
wind-storm
wind-up
wind-ward
windy
  wind-i-er
  wind-i-est
wine
  wined
  win-ing
win-ery
  win-er-ies
wine-skin
winged
win-ner
win-ning
win-some
win-ter
win-ter-gree
win-ter-ize
  win-ter-ized
  win-ter-iz-ing
  win-ter-i-za-tion
win-try
wipe
  wiped
  wip-ing
wire-haired
wire-les
wire-tap
wiry
  wir-i-er
  wir-i-est
wis-dom
wise
  wis-er
  wis-est
wise-acre
wise-crack
wish-bone

wish-ful
wishy-washy
wisp
  wispy
wis-ter-ia
wist-ful
witch-craft
witch-ery
  witch-er-ies
witch-ing
with-draw
with-er
  with-ered
  with-er-ing
with-hold
  with-held
  with-hold-ing
with-in
with-out
with-stand
  with-stood
  with-stand-ing
wit-less
wit-ness
wit-ted
wit-ti-cism
wit-ting
  wit-ting-ly
wiz-ard
  wi-zard-ly
  wi-zard-ry
wiz-en
  wiz-ened
wob-ble
woe-be-gone
woe-ful
wolf-hound
wolf-ram
wol-ver-ine
wom-an
  wom-en
  wom-an-ly
  wom-an-hood

womb
wom-bat
wom-en-folk
won-der
won-der-ful
won-der-land
won-der-ment
won-drous
wont-ed
wood-bine
wood-cut-ter
wood-ed
wood-en
wood-land
wood-man
  wood-men
wood-peck-er
wood-shed
woods-man
  woods-men
wood-wind
wood-work
woody
  wood-i-er
  wood-i-est
woof-er
wool-en
wool-gath-er-ing
wool-ly
  wool-li-er
  wool-li-est
wool-ly-head-ed
woozy
  wooz-i-er
  wooz-i-est
word-book
word-ing
word-less
  word-less-ly
work-a-ble
  work-a-bil-i-ty
  work-a-day
work-bench

work-book
work-day
worked-up
work-er
work-horse
work-house
work-ing
work-ing-man
  work-ing-men
work-man
  work-men
work-man-like
work-man-ship
work-ta-ble
world-ly
  world-li-er
  world-li-est
world-ly--wise
world-wide
worm--eat-en
worm-wood
wormy
  worm-i-er
  worm-i-est
worn--out
wor-ri-some
wor-ry
  wor-ried
  wor-ry-ing
  wor-ries
wor-ry-wart
wors-en
wor-ship
  wor-ship-ful
wor-sted
worth-less
worth-while
wor-thy
  wor-thi-er
  wor-thi-est
  wor-thi-ness
would--be
wouldn't

wound-ed
wraith
wran-gle
  wran-gled
  wran-gling
  wran-gler
wrath-ful
wreak
wreath
wreathe
  wreathed
  wreath-ing
wreck-age
wreck-er
wrench
wres-tle
  wres-tled
  wres-tling
wretch-ed
wrig-gle
  wrig-gled
wrin-kle
  wrin-kled
  wrin-kling
wrist-band
write
  wrote
  writ-ten
  writ-ing
write-in
writ-er
writhe
  writhed
  writh-ing
wrong-do-er
  wrong-do-ing
wronged
wrong-ful
wrong-head-ed
wrought
wry
  wri-er
  wri-est

wry-ly

X

X chro-mo-some
xe-bec
xe-non
xen-o-pho-bia
X-ray
x-sec-tion
xy-lem
xy-lo-phone
xy-lose

Y

yacht
  yacht-ing
  yachts-man
  yachts-men
yak
yam
yank
Yan-kee
yap
  yapped
  yap-ping
yard-age
yard-arm
yard-mas-ter
yard-stick
yarn
yar-row
yawn
year
year-book
year-ling
year-long
year-ly
yearn
  yearn-ing
year--round
yeast

yeasty
  yeast-i-er
  yeast-i-est
yel-low
  yel-low-ish
yel-low-bird
yel-low fe-ver
yel-low-ham-mer
yel-low jack-et
yelp
yen
  yenned
  yen-ning
yeo-man
  yeo-men
ye-shi-va
  ye-shi-vas
yes-ter-day
yes-ter-year
ye-ti
yew
yield
yield-ing
yip
  yipped
  yip-ping
yo-del
  yo-deled
  yo-del-ing
  yo-del-er
yo-ga
  yo-gic
yo-gi
  yo-gis
yo-gurt
yoke
  yoked
  yok-ing
yo-kel
yolk
yon-der
yore
young

young-ling
young-ster
your-self
  your-selves
youth-ful
yowl
yt-ter-bi-um
yt-tri-um
yuc-ca
yule-tide
yum-my
  yum-mi-er
  yum-mi-est

Z

za-ny
  za-nies
  za-ni-er
  za-n-est
  za-ni-ly
  za-ni-ness
zeal
zeal-ot
zeal-ous
ze-bra
  ze-bras
ze-bu
ze-nith
zeph-yr
zep-pe-lin
ze-ro
  ze-ros
  ze-roes
zest
  zesty
  zest-i-er
  zest-i-est
  zest-ful
  zest-ful-ly
zig-zag
  zig-zagged
  zig-zag-ging

zinc
zing
zin-nia
zip
  zipped
zip-per
zip-py
  zip-pi-er
  zip-pi-est
zir-con
zir-con-ni-um
zith-er
zo-di-ac
  zo-di-a-cal
zom-bie
  zom-bi
zon-al
zone
  zoned
  zon-ing
zoo
  zoos
zoo-ge-og-ra-phy
zo-ol-o-gy
  zo-o-log-i-cal
  zo-o-log-i-cal-ly
  zo-ol-o-gist
zuc-chet-to
zuc-chi-ni
zwie-back
zy-gote

Most Often Misspelled Words

absence
  absense
abundant
  abundent
accept
  except
accommodate
  accomodate

achieve
acheive
acquaintance
acquaintence
advice
advise
affect
effect
all right
alright
alter
altar
angle
angel
appearance
appearence
argument
arguement
article
articel
ascent
assent
athletic
atheletic
attendance
attendence
bathe
bath
battery
batery
beautiful
beautyful
belief
beleaf
believe
beleave
benefit
benifit
boundary
boundry
breathe
breath
bureaucracy

burocrasy
business
busness
calendar
calender
career
carear
cemetery
cemetary
certain
certan
choose
chose
commence
comense
committee
comittee
competitive
competative
complement
compliment
compliment
complement
conscience
conschense
convenient
convenyent
courtesy
curtesy
criticize
critisize
dairy
diary
definite
definit
delight
delite
democracy
democrasy
dependence
dependance
description
discripsion

diary
dairy
disappear
disapear
discussion
diskusion
disease
decease
distant
distint
economy
econamy
effect
affect
efficiency
efficiensy
embarrass
embarass
employee
employe
enough
enuf
envelope
envelop
equipped
equipt
error
erer
especially
expecially
exaggerate
exagerate
excel
excell
excellent
exselent
except
accept
exhibit
exibit
explain
explane
explanation

explanashan
extinction
extinktion
fail
fale
fallacy
falacy
familiar
familier
fascinate
fasinate
fasten
fasen
favorite
faverite
February
Febuary
finally
finely
finance
finanse
foreign
foren
forward
foreward
foreward
forward
foul
fowl
fraud
frawd
friend
frend
frighten
friten
gale
gail
galaxy
galaksy
gallon
galon
girl
gerl

govern
guvern
government
goverment
governor
governer
gruesome
grusome
guarantee
guarante
guess
gess
gym
gim
handle
handel
hangar
hanger
headache
headake
height
heighth
history
histrey
hospitable
hospitible
humorous
humerus
hygiene
higene
idea
idia
island
iland
illegible
iledgible
illusion
elusion
impatient
impatiant
imply
implie
independent

independant
industrious
industrus
influence
influense
intelligence
inteligense
interest
intrest
icicle
isicle
jewelry
juwlry
juice
juce
knowledge
knowlege
llabel
lable
laboratory
labratory
leisure
leisier
length
lenth
license
licence
literature
litrachur
major
majer
maneuver
manuever
mechanical
mekanical
middle
midel
mountain
mounten
mystery
mistry
narrative
narative

naval
navel
necessary
neccesary
neither
niether
need
nead
nickel
nickel
noticeable
noticable
occasion
ocasion
occurrence
ocurence
often
offten
official
oficial
opportunity
opertunity
ordinary
ordnary
parallel
paralel
parliament
parlement
partial
parshal
particle
particel
particularly
particlerly
pastime
pastime
permanent
permnent
picnic
picnik
picnicking
picnicing
pleasant

pleasent
poem
pome
politician
politishan
possible
posible
potatoes
potatos
practically
practickly
precede
preceed
precedent
presedent
prescription
perscription
privilege
privledge
probably
probly
proceed
procede
professor
perfessor
pronunciation
pronounciation
psychiatry
sikiatry
psychology
sikology
pursue
persue
qualify
qualifi
question
quesion
radio
radeo
rain
rane
race
rase

recede
resede
receipt
receit
receive
recieve
recommend
recomend
reflex
reflecks
register
rejister
rehearse
reherse
relieve
releve
remove
remoove
reply
replie
requirement
requierment
residential
residensial
resign
resine
restaurant
restarant
revenue
revenew
rewrite
rerite
ridiculous
ridiculos
road
rode
rough
ruff
routine
rutine
ruin
rooin
sacrifice

sacrifise
safety
safty
salary
celery
sanitation
sanatation
sandal
sandle
sandwich
sandwitch
sardine
sardeen
satellite
satilite
satisfactory
satisfactry
Saturday
Saterday
savage
savige
scarcity
scarsity
scene
sene
scissors
sissers
schedule
skedule
secretary
secretry
seize
sieze
separate
seperate
several
sevarel
shaddow
shadow
should
shood
sign
sine

sincerely
sinserely
sink
zink
sneaker
sneeker
solution
solushun
someone
sumone
souvenir
soovenir
speak
speek
special
spesial
squad
squod
stable
stabul
standard
standerd
static
stattic
stencil
stensil
stereo
sterio
strategy
stratagy
strength
strenth
studied
studyed
suburb
suburb
succeed
sucsede
successful
sucsesful
surgeon
surgen
syllable

sylable
symmetry
simmetry
tangent
tanjent
teach
teech
technical
tecnical
technique
tecneek
temperature
temprature
thorough
thureh
through
thru
Thursday
thersday
twelfth
twelth
unanimous
usanimus
until
untill
usually
usualy
vague
vage
value
valu
vowel
vowl
Wednesday
Wensday
weird
wierd
yield
yeild
your
yore
zoology
zoologey